D0393815

Peter Scott

PAINTER AND NATURALIST

Peter Scott
Painter and Naturalist

ELSPETH HUXLEY

Introduction by
Sir David Attenborough

FULCRUM PUBLISHING
Golden, Colorado

First published in 1993
by Faber and Faber Limited
3 Queen Square London WCIN 3AU
Copyright © 1993 Elspeth Huxley

Copyright © 1995 Fulcrum Publishing
Library of Congress Cataloging-in-Publication Data

Huxley, Elspeth Joscelin Grant, 1907–
    Peter Scott, painter and naturalist / Elspeth Huxley ;
introduction by Sir David Attenborough.
        p.   cm.
    "First published in 1993 by Faber and Faber Limited ... London"–
–T.p. verso.
    Includes bibliographical references (p.) and index.
    ISBN 1-55591-204-4 (hardcover)
    1. –Scott, Peter Markham, Sir, 1909– . 2. Naturalists—England—Biography.
3. Conservationists—England—Biography. 4. Artists—England—Biography.
5. Wildlife conservation—History. I. Title.
QH31.S36H88   1995
333.7'2'092—dc20
[B]   95-35181
                                                                                    CIP

Cover design by Heidi Herndon

Printed in the United States of America

0 9 8 7 6 5 4 3 2 1

Fulcrum Publishing
350 Indiana Street, Suite 350
Golden, Colorado 80401-5093
800/992-2908

Contents

Sir David Attenborough

National heroes are somewhat out of fashion these days. Not so long ago, they were the personification of the qualities a nation most admired in itself—valor, self-sacrifice, patriotism. Their spoken words were recorded and revered. Their diaries were published. Their images were put on pedestals, both literally and metaphorically. Peter Scott had the mixed blessing of being the son of one. His father had caught the public's attention by his bold explorations in the Antarctic and when he died there, on his journey back from the South Pole, some of his fame and a great deal of expectation fell upon the three-year-old Peter. It must have been a considerable burden to bear as he grew up. He also had another. His mother, a fashionable portrait sculptor, was both doting and possessive and she took great pride in ensuring that her son became known to the most famous and influential figures of the day. Armchair psychologists among us might predict that such a gilded childhood would produce a spoiled and self-indulgent man.

Nothing could be farther from the truth. Peter had, without any question, inherited much of the physical bravery and steely determination that had brought his father fame. He deployed these qualities in sport and, as a result of them, became a champion skater, a world-class competitive glider pilot, and an Olympic yachtsman. His professional career, on the other hand, was determined not so much by his father's characteristics as by his mother's. Like her, he became an artist. He trained as a painter and for his subjects he chose birds, for he had been fascinated by the natural world since childhood. And he was as successful in art as he was in sport. Prints of his pictures of wildfowl flighting over marshes eventually hung in thousands of homes. His very name came to define a style.

But it was neither sport nor art that brought him his greatest celebrity. That came from his expertise as a naturalist. Forty years ago, his insights and obsessions with wildfowl led him to recognize that ecological disaster threatened the world. Having perceived it, he did something about it. He became one of the moving spirits in the foundation of the first worldwide conservation charity. He traveled, lectured, broadcast, and wrote, indefatigably preaching the cause. He cajoled, argued, and persuaded politicians and businessmen, millionaires and royalty, to give their patronage—and great sums of money. In the end, the mission took over his life, dominating all his activities and waking hours.

Once again, he was extraordinarily successful. Because of him, more than any other single person, animals that forty years ago seemed doomed to extinction still exist. Because of him, people of every race and every faith on every continent are dedicated conservationists, believing as he did, that humanity has a moral responsibility toward the other forms of life on this planet. How he achieved all this, Elspeth Huxley relates in the following pages. That he did so made him a different kind of hero from his father. Not national but international; not a distant figure on a pedestal but known directly through his broadcasts and writings and his visits to important conservation sites throughout the world. But a hero, nonetheless, in the eyes of millions. Including mine.

Acknowledgments

There are advantages and disadvantages in tackling a biography of an individual whose family and friends are for the most part still alive. On the one hand you can tap living people's memories; on the other, you risk bruising the feelings of well-disposed people. It is well known that families can be a hazard—Kipling's daughter and Rupert Brooke's mother are cases in point—but I have met with nothing but help and cooperation from Peter Scott's widow Philippa; from his three children; and from his brother Wayland, Lord Kennet of the Dene, and his wife Elizabeth. Since most of the research has been carried out in Lady Scott's house, her help extended to giving me the run of her home, as well as answering endless questions, for about three years: a potentially abrasive situation which passed off with patience on her part and pleasure on mine. And without June White's uncomplaining and unfaltering guidance through a plethora of papers—Peter Scott seldom, if ever, threw anything away—I should have been hopelessly at sea. I have been fortunate also in having the help of John Lee as a research assistant; in addition to his Shakespearean studies at the University of Bristol for a Ph.D. he has delved with diligence, skill and unfailing good humor into boxes and files at Slimbridge, undertaken away-from-base assignments, and word-processed everything (often several times).

Almost all the material I have drawn on is in private hands, and in the memories of living people. The principal exception is the set of diaries kept by Peter Scott's mother Kathleen and lodged in the Cambridge University library, and I am grateful to Lord Kennet for permission to quote from them. Another major source has been Peter Scott's own diaries, all seventy-four volumes, at present in Lady Scott's private possession. (A selection has been published in three volumes by Collins.) Since neither these nor other sources such as letters, interviews, tape recordings and the papers at Slimbridge are available to the public, it would, I think, be pointless to add a numbered list of sources at the end of each chapter, or at the end of the book, as is the usual custom with biographies. If and when a Peter Scott archive is gathered together, perhaps at a university library, everything will no doubt be catalogued and made available for public scrutiny.

I have mentioned tape recordings: the tedious task of transcribing them has been shared between two generous volunteers, Peter's daughter Mrs. Nicola Starks and Mrs. Terry Saltmarsh, and I would like to thank them both most sincerely.

I am especially indebted to Elizabeth Jane Howard for allowing me to make use of Peter's letters written to her during and before their marriage; and to John Winter for permission to quote from letters written to him during Peter's service at sea during the Second World War. Major John Berkeley has lent me correspondence with his father relating to the start of what is now the Wildfowl & Wetlands Trust; Mrs. Aline Dalgety has given me access to her late husband Christopher's correspondence and diaries; Mrs. Cecily Thorpe has done the same with regard to her late husband Kenzie, Peter's factotum when he lived in a lighthouse on the Wash—a lighthouse now restored to its pristine condition by Commander David Joel, RN (Rtd.), whose help I also gratefully acknowledge.

For family history, Mrs. Janie Hampton and Mrs. Verily Paget have been my mentors, and for Peter's childhood Mr. Ivor Graham, grandson of Lord Knutsford, who was Peter's guardian when his father went to the South Pole; Mr. J. F. Cornes, former headmaster of the West Downs preparatory school; Dr. Tim Maurice of Marlborough; and Mrs. Patricia Baker, who lent me Peter's letters to Winkie. For his schooldays at Oundle, I have to thank Lady Talbot, sister of the former headmaster Kenneth Fisher; the late Mrs. Margery (Angus) Fisher, widow of James, Peter's friend and fellow naturalist and son of the headmaster; and their son Mr. Edmund Fisher, for helpful information; also Mr. Michael Mills of the Old Oundelian club.

Despite his many preoccupations, Sir Andrew Huxley, OM, FRS, then Master of Trinity College, Cambridge, found time to unravel the complicated story of Peter Scott's academic career. Two fellow students at the Royal Academy Schools, the Very Reverend Dean Tony Bridge and Mrs. Eileen MacKenzie, supplied lively appreciations of his studies, and diversions, there. Charles Currey and, again, John Winter, recalled his adventures as a racing dinghy sailor, Mr. Tony Boyden and Mr. Paul Anderson those when he skippered the British challenger for the America's Cup, and Mr. Tom Hodgson contributed a view from an unusual angle.

The chapters covering Peter's wartime service in the Royal Navy owe much to Commander Christopher Dreyer, RN, DSO, DSC, with sidelights from fellow RNVR officers James Grout and H. G. Bown, from Petty Officer J. W. H. Stevens (DSM and bar), from former Leading Seaman George Jennings, from former WRNS Mrs. Fanny Hughill, and from Mrs. Gillian Warr (nee Dearmer).

This is perhaps an appropriate place to record my thanks to Prince Philip for giving me an audience, when he recalled some recollections of a fellow sailor he had known for over forty years.

The start of the present Wildfowl and Wetlands Trust was fresh in the memories of Tommy and Diana Johnstone, Keith Shackleton, Dr. Hugh Boyd, Eunice Overend, and Mrs. Penty Fraser, among others. Mike Garside, Peter's secretary for twenty-five years, gave me invaluable help; others to whom I am indebted include Jane Fenton, for some years Peter's wildlife assistant; Dr. John Berry, formerly director of Nature Conservancy in Scotland; and Keith and Irina Bromley. Many of those who have served the Trust, or are still doing so, came up with helpful memories, including Mr. Peter Gladstone, Dr. Geoffrey MaKhews, Dr. Janet Kear, Brigadier Steven Goodall, Messrs Tony Cook, Don Revett, Tony Richardson, Mike Ounsted, Doug Hulyer, Geoff Proffitt, and the present director-general Dr. Myrfyn Owen.

Incidents in Peter's broadcasting career, detailed in the BBC's archives at Caversham, were remembered by Sir David Attenborough, by Desmond Hawkins, by Christopher Parsons, and by Charles Lagus, who traveled round the world with the Scotts gathering material for *Faraway Look*. Fellow pilots have told me of Peter's gliding exploits: these informants include David and Barbara Carrow, Robin and Jane Cole, Rear-Admiral Nicholas Goodhart, CB, RN, Mr. Derek Piggott, Mr. Frank Irving, Mr. Lorne Welsh, Mrs. Liz Douglas, and several hospitable individuals at the Bristol gliding club at Nympsfield which was Peter's gliding base.

For recollections of the birth and development of the World Wildlife Fund, now the World Wide Fund for Nature, I am indebted to Max Nicholson, late of the Nature Conservancy Council; to Ian MacPhail, its first campaign manager; to Richard and Maisie Fitter; and to the present director-general, Mr. Charles de Haes. I would also like to thank Mrs. Cassandra Phillips of WWF International for her help, especially about whaling and Antarctica, and Mr. Tony Mence for his, in regard to the International Union for the Conservation of Nature.

For light on a diversion, the tale of the Loch Ness Monster, I am indebted to, among others, Dr. Robert Rines of the Academy of Applied Sciences in Boston, Massachusetts; to the Hon. Mrs. James of Mull, widow of David James, MP, and to Nicholas Witchell. Sir Max Williams, Lord Buxton of Anglia Television, and Mr. Mervyn Cowie have told me of incidents during the Scotts' wide-ranging travels; Lord Hunter, former Vice-Chancellor of Birmingham

University, of Peter's stint as Chancellor; and Dr. E. J. Powell of Aberdeen University of his election as Rector. Mr. Robert Gotten of Worldwide Butterflies has spoken of his interest in the *lepidoptera*; Sir James Craig, GCMG, offered guidance through the Middle Eastern labyrinth; Nancy Nash of Hong Kong and Dr. Schaller of the New York Zoological Society have described incidents during Peter's six visits to the People's Republic of China. Dr. Roger Tory Peterson has done the same in regard to shared voyages as lecturers on the *Lindblad Explorer*.

Between 1933 and 1978 Peter held sixteen one-man exhibitions of his paintings at Ackermann's gallery, now defunct, in New Bond Street, and I am grateful to Mr. S. C. Myall for looking up the catalogs and prices, and to Mrs. Jill Ford for other information.

Among the many others to whom my thanks are due are Peter Scott's daughter, Dr. Dafila Clutton-Brock, and his son Falcon; Mrs. Jane Dawson, widow of Peter's friend Rodney; Mr. Jocelin Winthrop Young, a cousin, and Mrs. Marr-Johnson, for personal recollections; to Mrs. Joy Dawes, formerly the wife of Michael Bratby; to Mrs. Meath-Baker of the Medici Gallery; to Mr. Dennis Bird of the National Skating Association; to Douglas Botting, biographer of Gavin Maxwell; to Nigel Sitwell, who compiled an anthology of Peter's writings; and to Dr. Gerald Durrell, who told in his racy manner of the Scotts' interest in the torrent duck of Chile and Bolivia; and to many others. Needless to say, my interpretation of all they told me, in writing or on tape, is entirely my own, and if I have got it wrong the fault is mine alone.

Chronology

1909   September 14: Peter Markham Scott born at 174 Buckingham Palace Road, London, the son of Captain Robert Falcon Scott, Antarctic explorer, and of Kathleen Scott (nee Bruce; afterward Lady Kennet), sculptor.

1911   Spring: his father leaves for the Antarctic and dies there about March 29, 1912, on the return from the South Pole.

1918   (to 1923) At West Downs preparatory school, in Winchester.

1922   March: his mother marries Edward Hilton Young, later Lord Kennet of the Dene.

1923   August 2: his half-brother, Wayland, is born.
(to 1927) At Oundle School, near Peterborough.

1926   Illustrates *Adventures Among Birds* by Three Schoolboys, privately printed. Family moves to 100 Bayswater Road, "Leinster Corner."

1927   (to 1930) At Trinity College, Cambridge to read natural science. Switches to the history of art and architecture in his final year.

1931   At Munich State Academy, in the animal painting class of Professor Angelo Jank.
       (to 1933) Enrolled at Royal Academy Schools, London.

1932   Christmas: makes his first attempts to catch geese with nets.

1933   Summer: leases and moves into East Lighthouse, where the river Nene enters the Wash.
       First Exhibition at Ackermann's Galleries, 3 Old Bond Street, London (an annual event up to and including 1940).

1935   Autumn: *Morning Flight* published.

1936   Illustrates *A Bird in the Bush* by Lord Kennet.
       August: wins a bronze medal for single-handed sailing at the Olympic Games in Kiel.
       August 21: broadcasts a fifteen-minute talk on dinghy racing for the BBC.

1937   Wins the Prince of Wales' Cup (an international 14-foot dinghy competition) in *Thunder*, with Charles Currey as his crew.

1938   *Wild Chorus* published.
       Wins the Prince of Wales' Cup for a second time in *Thunder and Lightning*, with John Winter.
       November: exhibition in Arthur Harlow's gallery in New York.

1939   January: visits Northern Ireland to substantiate the existence of another race of whitefronted geese.

1940   February: Joins HMS *Broke* as sub-lieutenant in the Royal Naval Volunteer Reserve. Appointed First Lieutenant in August.
       (to 1942) Servicing HMS *Broke* in Battle of the Atlantic.
       Invented camouflage scheme which was adopted by the Admiralty.

1941   April 6: mentioned in dispatches for his role in the rescue of the crew of the burning HMS *Comorin*.
       August: flies with RAF on two bombing raids over Germany.

1942   Receives MBE in Birthday Honors list.
April 28: marries Jane Howard.
Summer: takes command of Steam Gunboat 9, later HMS *Grey Goose*.
Takes part in Dieppe Raid and is mentioned in dispatches.
November: appointed Lieutenant Commander.
December: Peter and Jane move into 105 Clifton Hill in St. John's Wood, London.

1943   February 2: a daughter, Nicola, born.
March: appointed Senior Officer in charge of Steam Gunboat Flotilla.
Subsequently involved in several notable actions, for which he receives a DSC and bar and a third mention in dispatches.

1944   March: joins planning staff of the Captain Coastal Forces (Channel) to prepare for D-Day.

1945   After victory in Europe he is appointed to command a new frigate being built, HMS *Cardigan Bay*.
Battle of the Narrow Seas published.
Spring: Peter and Jane move into 8 Edwardes Square, London.
July: resigns from the Navy to stand as Conservative candidate for Wembley North in the General Election. Loses by 432 votes.
November: his first postwar exhibition at Ackermann's.

1946   Illustrates *The Snow Goose* by Paul Gallico.
(to 1966) Becomes a joint presenter of *Nature Parliament*, a BBC radio *Children's Hour* program, and a contributor to *The Naturalist* and *Birds in Britain*.
June: wins the Prince of Wales' Cup in *Thunder and Lightning*, his third win.
November 10: the Severn Wildfowl Trust inaugurated.

1947   Summer: Jane, his wife, leaves.
July 24: his mother dies of leukemia, aged sixty-eight.
November: employs Philippa Talbot-Ponsonby as his secretary.
November 20: as one of the BBC's commentators on the royal wedding, broadcasts to an audience of 250 million.

1948   As Chairman of Olympic Yachting Committee, he is involved in orga-
        nizing the Olympic yachting events at Torquay; continues to be so in-
        volved up to the Tokyo Olympics in 1964.
        February: the testing of rocket netting on the New Grounds results in
        the first large scale capture of live geese.
        Sells 8 Edwardes Square and moves to Slimbridge early in 1949.

1949   *Portrait Drawings* published.
        Key to the Wildfowl of the World published.
        June: explores the Perry River region of Arctic Canada to study the breed-
        ing grounds of Ross's goose.

1950   May: two Hawaiian geese (ne-nes) are brought to Slimbridge for cap-
        tive breeding.

1951   *Wild Geese* and *Eskimos* published.
        June: leads expedition to the breeding grounds of the pinkfooted goose
        in central highlands of Iceland.
        August 7: marries Philippa Talbot-Ponsonby in Reykjavik.

1952   February: first Hawaiian goose bred at Slimbridge.
        June: his second daughter, Dafila, born.

1953   *A Thousand Geese*, with James Fisher, published.
        Awarded CBE for his role as Honorary Director of The Wildfowl Trust.
        Becomes vicepresident of International Union for the Conservation of
        Nature.

1954   June: his son, Falcon, born.

1955   The Severn Wildfowl Trust becomes The Wildfowl Trust. Principal pre-
        senter of television program *Look* (renamed *Faraway Look* in 1957) on
        natural history subjects, which ran until 1970.

1956   *Wildfowl of the British Isles*, written with Hugh Boyd, published.
        April: takes up gliding.
        December: snorkeling on the Great Barrier Reef introduces him to the
        world of coral fish and to the science of ichthyology.

1957   *Wildfowl of the British Isles*, with Hugh Boyd, published.
        Coloured Key to the Wildfowl of the World published.
        April: Wildfowl Trust Centre, Peakirk, Cambridgeshire, opened to the
        public.

1959   January: visits Galápagos Islands to make a film for the BBC and helps to found the Charles Darwin Foundation.

1960   *Faraway Look I* and *Faraway Look II*, with Philippa Scott, published. (to 1963) Rector of Aberdeen University.

1961   His autobiography, *The Eye of the Wind*, published.
October 10: World Wildlife Fund founded, with Peter as its first chairman. From 1962 to 1982 he was vicepresident of the WWF's British national appeal, and Honorary Chairman of the WWF's Council.
December: with three colleagues, sets up the Loch Ness Investigation Bureau to study reports of sightings of the Loch Ness Monster.

1962   Originated the Red Data Books identifying endangered species. These books become an essential tool of conservation.
(to 1981) Chairman of Survival Service Commission of the IUCN (thereafter Chairman Emeritus).

1963   May: wins National Open Gliding Championship (League I).

1964   September: at the helm of *Sovereign* in an unsuccessful challenge for the America's Cup.

1966   January: visits the Antarctic to make a film for BBC. Subsequently returns four times.

1968   As guest lecturer goes on the first of twenty-six cruises organized by Eric Lindblad.

1969   First of four visits to the Danube delta in Romania to study redbreasted geese.

1970   *The Wild Swans at Slimbridge*, with Philippa Scott, published.
Welney Wildfowl Trust Centre, Cambridgeshire, opened.

1971   Caerlaverock Wildfowl Trust Centre, near Dumfries, opened.
Appointed director of Survival Anglia and starts presenting commentaries for Anglia Television's *Survival* series.

1973   Created Knight Bachelor, the first person to be knighted for services to conservation and the environment.

1974   (to 1983) Chancellor of the University of Birmingham.

1975   Martin Mere Wildfowl Trust Centre, Lancashire, and Washington Wild-
        fowl Trust Centre, Co. Durham, opened.
        June: underwater photographs taken in Loch Ness suggest the presence
        of an unidentified object and a symposium is arranged to study them.
        December: the scientific establishment is unconvinced and the Loch
        Ness Investigation Bureau is closed down.

1976   Arundel Wildfowl Trust Center, Sussex, opened.

1977   Receives, with Jacques Cousteau, the United Nations International
        Pahlavi Environment Prize, his share being $25,000.

1978   July: travels to Siberia to search for the breeding grounds of Bewick's
        swans.

1979   January 16: while in the Falkland Islands, co-founds the Falkland Islands
        Foundation.

1980   *Observations of Wildlife* published.

1981   Awarded IUCN John Phillips Medal, and WWF Twentieth Anniversary
        Special Award.

1982   Annual meeting of International Whaling Commission agrees to phase
        in a moratorium on whaling.

1983   *Travel Diaries of a Naturalist* (vol. I) published.
        The Swans Fly In, with Philippa Scott, published.

1984   May: suffers a mild coronary attack at home.

1985   *Travel Diaries of a Naturalist* (vol. 2) published.

1986   September: recieves J. P. Getty Prize of $50,000 and a fortnight later is
        awarded the WWF Gold Medal at that organization's twenty-fifth anni-
        versary celebration.
        November: the fortieth birthday of the Wildfowl Trust: the six centers
        now have an annual budget of £3,500,000 and five hundred thousand
        visitors a year.

1987   *Travel Diaries of a Naturalist* (vol. 3) published.
June: appointed a Companion of Honour for services to conservation.
Elected a Fellow of The Royal Society.

1988   A coral fish, *cirrilabrus scottorum*, named after Peter and his wife.

1989   His sixteenth one-man show at Ackermann's is opened by Prince Philip,
and all but four paintings are sold on the first day.
The Wildfowl Trust changes its name to The Wildfowl & Wetlands Trust.
August 29: dies in a Bristol hospital, two weeks short of his eightieth
birthday.

CHAPTER ONE

Son of a Legend

"Oh Peter dear," wrote a friend of his youth, reclining in her hammock during the hot June of 1933, "have you ever realized how much you walk in the sun?" Peter Scott was then twenty-three years old, strong and healthy, already a successful painter, with Cambridge University, Munich State Academy and the Royal Academy Schools in London behind him. He was a skillful sailor of racing dinghies, an experienced wildfowler, an elegant dancer, and a skater in the championship class. He enjoyed the comradeship of a close circle of fellow sailors and wildfowlers as well as the company of a number of attractive young women, several of whom hoped to marry him. The only son of a national hero and an accomplished and devoted mother, doors had opened for him from infancy to manhood as smoothly as those electronically controlled portals which part before customers of supermarkets. He did, indeed, walk in the sun.

It was his mother who pressed the buttons that opened the doors to a recognition which less fortunate painters may take many years, even a lifetime, to gain. Kathleen Scott, nee Bruce, was a woman of forceful personality, unconventional opinions, and ready wit, and with a considerable talent as a sculptor. Her forte was sculpting the busts of men prominent in public life. Two Kings and four Prime Ministers were among her subjects. Perhaps her best known work is the statue of her first husband, Captain Robert Falcon Scott, which stands in Waterloo Place in London, with a replica in Christchurch, New Zealand. Her subjects were almost always men.

Whether Peter inherited a gene, if such a one exists, that carries an artistic bent must be a matter for speculation; it is certain that Kathleen Scott encouraged in her son a latent creativity that burgeoned in his infancy. He couldn't recall a time, he wrote, when he hadn't a pencil in his hand. While Kathleen toiled at her sculpting, he lay beside her on the floor drawing boats, dogs, houses, butterflies—anything that came to mind. What came to mind most often were caterpillars, birds, moths, beetles. So, from infancy, the two main passions of his life, for nature and for painting, were fused.

Kathleen was the youngest of eleven children born to Janie, wife of the Reverend Lloyd Stewart Bruce, rector of a small parish in Wiltshire at the time of their marriage and later to become a Canon of York. "Dull, shabbily dressed and too old" was how Janie's elder sister Zoe described him, though she could not fault him in respect of ancestry. He was a younger brother of Sir Hervey Bruce, third Baronet, former High Sheriff of Londonderry, MP for Coleraine and, inevitably, a descendant of Robert the Bruce. The family seat, Downhill in County Antrim, whose halls of marble had been brought from Italy, was the creation of the fourth Earl Bishop of Bristol and Derry, a celebrated eccentric who left a trail of inns named after him over much of Europe and was anything but dull.

Janie Skene was twenty-seven when she married the Rev. Lloyd Bruce. She produced her family, including two sets of twins, within the next thirteen years. Then she died at the age of forty-two, worn out, and with failing eyesight and Bright's kidney disease.

Her mother was a Greek named Rhalou Rizo-Rangabé, who came of a community formerly living in Constantinople and known as the Phanariots. In the seventeenth century the Turks had handed over the administration of their provinces of Moldavia and Wallachia, in what was to become Romania, to this branch of the Greek Orthodox church, taking the view that its members were best equipped to govern the Ottoman empire's Christian subjects, and because of their expertise in finance and administration.

Naturally they used these skills to enrich themselves, but they belonged to families of culture and sophistication; they encouraged the arts, built splendid palaces to live in, endowed monasteries, and kept the flag of civilization flying as best they could amid the turmoils and cutthroat intrigues of these provinces in eastern Europe. Amongst themselves they spoke and wrote in French. But compliance with the maxim that all power corrupts did not escape them. They became tyrannical as well as rich, and in the revolution of 1821 which swept through Bucharest and its surrounding regions they took the wrong side. Most of them retreated to Greece, taking with them as much of their wealth as they could salvage.

During their regime the Pharaniots had married into the ruling families of their principalities, and claimed as an ancestor that Rangabé who, in around 800 A.D., became Michael I, Emperor of Byzantium. Another school of genealogists prefers a line leading back to Bogdan I, prince of Moldavia from 1363 to 1367. His descent proceeded through such reigns as that of Bogdan the One-Eyed and John the Terrible (bypassing a cousin, Vlad the Impaler, the model for Dracula) to reach eventually Jacob Rizo-Rangabé (1779 to 1855), grandfather of Janie Skene who married the Rev. Lloyd Bruce, and great-grandfather of Kathleen Scott.

How did a girl descended from Byzantine emperors and Moldavian princes come to marry a colorless, if concupiscent, English country parson? The story is a romantic one. Jacob Rizo-Rangabé had a lovely daughter Rhalou who, at the age of sixteen, when walking along a street in Athens, was frightened by a dog, fled into the nearest house and leapt upon a table; the dog's owner lifted her down and fell in love on the spot. He was a young Scot named James Skene, a grandson of Sir William Forbes of Monymusk, fifth Baronet. Thus the aristocracy of Scotland was linked with that of Moldavia.

Kathleen Bruce, born in 1879, was three years old when her mother Janie died. Within nine months of Janie's death the Rev. Lloyd Bruce married a well-to-do widow. As a stepmother she was not a success. The care of eleven high-spirited children between the ages of three and sixteen cannot have been an easy assignment. Less than four years later, in 1886, their father followed Janie to the grave. The orphans were dispersed among their relatives, most of them, including Kathleen, finding their way to the home in Edinburgh of their great-uncle William Skene, a bachelor, a lawyer, an archaeologist, and the Historiographer Royal for Scotland—"a gentleman of the old school, courtly and somewhat stately in manner." He had come to the financial rescue of Lloyd and Janie Bruce on many occasions. Now his aid became even more generous: he invited most of the Bruce children to share his home.

In Kathleen's own account of her childhood she stresses the austere, not to say gloomy, aspects of her great-uncle's household in Edinburgh. At mealtimes the children were seen and not heard until after the meat course, and then obliged to speak only in French, German, or Greek; on Sundays the blinds were kept drawn until after church and no books allowed except the Bible. But it was not all goodness and gravity. William Skene loved children so long as they were well behaved. He arranged for them to learn to play the piano and to sing, and had a bagpiper in to march round his long library skirling away while the floorboards shook to the pounding of young feet dancing reels. Then Uncle William died and the family was faced with another diaspora. Kathleen was plunged into the even more austere surroundings of a high Anglican convent in Scarborough, where the girls were obliged to take their baths in chemises lest they set eyes on their own bodies. They had to attend chapel three times a day on weekdays and five times on Sundays. It was little wonder that Kathleen grew up to become an agnostic, and brought up her son in the same absence of religious faith. On the other hand, two of her brothers took Holy Orders and one of them, Rosslyn, became her closest friend and confidant.

Rosslyn Bruce was a most unusual parson. His love for animals of every kind equaled, and perhaps even exceeded, that of his nephew Peter. His first sermon after his installation as senior curate in the parish of St. Anne's, Soho (there were seven curates), was entitled "Do animals live after death?" He affirmed that they did, and if they didn't he, Rosslyn, would be no candidate for heaven. Love for an animal immortalized it. Children of this tough, unruly, and cosmopolitan part of London, full of prostitutes and cutthroats, found the gentleman who might at any moment produce a mouse or a squirrel from his pocket an irresistible attraction, and before long he had them organized into Sunday school classes and parties to feed the ducks in St. James's Park. A white dove called Purity, released from the sleeve of his surplice, enlivened his sermons, and he was soon preaching to packed congregations.

It was as a breeder of fox terriers that he won international fame. He provided bitches, it was said, for all the crowned heads of Europe. After he had sold a puppy to the Queen of Greece, Queen Victoria expressed a wish to have its litter sister, and Rosslyn was commanded to take it to Windsor Castle. On the appointed day, much to his chagrin, it came in heat. Rosslyn took the sire in its place, intending to explain to Her Majesty that father and daughter were very much alike. At the last moment he was instructed that on no account must he address the Sovereign until she had first spoken to him. She came out on to the terrace, smiled and nodded, but spoke no word directly to him. Rosslyn unleashed the dog, who trotted off to sniff the flower pots that flanked the terrace. Only one outcome seemed possible. Prospects of utter disgrace loomed before the young clergyman: lèse-majesteé charges of deception, ridicule. A near-miracle occurred: Lennie (for such was his name) trotted back to his master without lifting his leg. In due course Lennie's daughter was delivered to the Queen, who was later to be painted by William Nicholson with the bitch at her side.

Rosslyn scored his greatest breeding triumph with mice. Following Mendelian theory, his aim was to produce strains of different colors. Red, blue and lavender mice occupied his cages, then came strawberry and champagne colored ones, followed by an apricot vole. His crowning achievement was a strain of green mice, produced after fifty generations. The first were grass green; they gave birth to bottle green offspring and further crosses were needed to stabilize the strain. "I am still hopeful of producing something approaching perfection in green mice," he told a reporter. "The secret of breeding a champion," he wrote, "is that the dam's dam's dam is the chief factor in a pedigree, over and above the sire's sire's sire." Applied to his nephew's pedigree, this would give precedence to Rhalou the Greek over the naval purser who was his sire's sire's sire.

Kathleen, whom her brother called Kiddie, left her convent as an attractive, bright, and self-assured young lady with a mass of curly brown hair. Her eldest brother, who was more or less in charge of the brood, wanted her to train as a teacher, but in the autumn of 1900 she secured a place at the Slade School of Fine Art in London, and began her career as a sculptor.

Hers was an unusual lifestyle for someone of her class at the turn of the century. In an age when no unmarried girl might venture forth without a chaperon, she enjoyed a freedom not generally to be experienced by young women until fifty years and two world wars had gone by. There was no one to chaperon her, and the nearest she had to a family home was a small house belonging to her elder sister Podge in Scarborough. Sir Hervey Bruce, her uncle, invited her to share his establishment in County Antrim where she could pour the tea, mend the china and keep out of mischief; a prospect not alluring to an independent-minded girl of nineteen.

Glimpses of her somewhat checkered career are to be caught in the pages of her brother Rosslyn's biography, written by his daughter Verily. In his Soho parish there were 8 theaters, 122 pubs, and the Empire music hall; many theatrical folk were therefore in his cure of souls. He soon became involved in the theatrical world and prevailed upon several managers to allow him to address their audiences for four minutes, after which the curtain came down: a valuable lesson for a parson, he said. In January 1902 he took Kathleen to supper with the cast of a play running at the Garrick theater in which the young actor Nigel Playfair had a part.

In the following April the actor and the curate took their bicycles to France to visit Kathleen in Paris, where she was working in the studio of the sculptor Caloressi, living on the Left Bank, and consorting in considerable poverty with students from all parts of the world. She had, she said, only one mug in her one room, so the two young men bought her another mug on the way. In Paris, Rosslyn sold a fox terrier to Pablo Picasso, one of her friends. Rosslyn and Nigel Playfair joined a picnic to celebrate the birthday of Auguste Rodin, who put Kathleen's hand into that of the American dancer Isadora Duncan, and told them that they must help each other. They did indeed: Kathleen brought Isadora to stay in Soho Square, and assisted at the birth of Isadora's first illegitimate baby. (She had two: both were drowned when the car in which they were traveling fell into the Seine. Their mother also met a tragic end when her scarf got caught up in a wheel of her car and she was strangled.) Gertrude Stein, in her Autobiography of Alice B. Toklas, wrote that Kathleen was a "very beautiful and very athletic English girl, a kind of Sculptress," who, although penniless herself, brought half her dinner every evening to Isadora's brother's pregnant wife, who was even hungrier. Rosslyn, asked how he had enjoyed his holiday in Paris, evasively replied: "I learnt how to eat for 95 centimes a day, including tips."

Since by all accounts Kathleen was good to look at and fun to be with, she had many admirers among the cosmopolitan students in the art center of Europe. She cherished an unusual *idée fixe*: she would choose for her mate only a man worthy to be the father of her son. By what criterion she judged his fitness for this role was not divulged, but during her five years in Paris none of her fellow students, however talented, attractive, or ardent, measured up to her standard. Aspiring boyfriends were repulsed. That, at least, is what readers of her diaries are led to infer.

Despite her repeated avowals that she had no time for women and only liked men, she did in fact have a number of women friends. Isadora Duncan was one, Mabel Beardsley another, the latter a sister of the homosexual artist Aubrey Beardsley, who had breathed an air of *fin-de-siècle* decadence over London's literary scene. (What Kathleen really meant was that dull women bored her, and she found most women dull.) It was at Mabel Beardsley's luncheon table in December 1906 that she first met Robert Falcon Scott. Nothing came of it at the time. Kathleen merely took note of a naval officer, neither young nor particularly handsome, but "healthy and alert"; however, she "glowed rather suddenly" when she saw him ask a neighbor who she was. About ten months later (October 1907) Mabel Beardsley invited them both to tea. The fuse was lit. Scott fell headlong in love, and to Kathleen it appeared that here at last was a worthy father for her son.

Captain Scott, RN, was at this time on half-pay pending his appointment to command the battleship HMS *Essex*. Three years earlier, in September 1904, he had returned in triumph as leader of the British Antarctic expedition on the ship *Discovery*. He and two of his companions, Edward Wilson and Ernest Shackleton, had not reached the South Pole, or even got close to it; 480 miles separated them from that geographical abstraction when they turned back on the last day of 1902. But they had advanced over 300 miles farther south into the Antarctic than had any other mortals, into a waste of snow and ice, blizzard and crevasse, with temperatures reaching to 70°F of frost. They and their fellows in *Discovery* had survived two winters in the Antarctic and had returned intact with a mass of scientific data. So Captain Scott had come back to a hero's welcome, and few doubted that he would lead another expedition to finish the work so bravely begun, and claim for Britain a "first" at the South Pole. Meanwhile, until money could be raised and the enterprise set in motion, Captain Scott had returned to his naval duties and, in his periods of leave, to enjoy—if he did enjoy it—being feted by the hostesses of London. He was thirty-nine and unmarried.

Despite the glamour surrounding his fame as an explorer, in the marriage market he was not much of a catch. Naval pay was meager, and Scott had to share it with his widowed mother, to whom he allowed one-quarter of his £800 a year. He had no private income, no property, and no prospects beyond that of making his way by slow degrees along the clogged channels of promotion in a peacetime navy. He was not exaggerating when he wrote to Kathleen: "I review a past—a real fight from an almost desperate position to the bare right to live as my fellows."

That poverty equals insecurity is an absolute equation in the context of an affluent society. It is no wonder, then, that Con Scott's courtship was beset by doubts: he was too old and too dull for Kathleen, their temperaments were too discordant; he would come between her and her creative talent, clog her spirit; in short he had no gifts to lay at her feet. Agonized letters sped between them. "What I know and you do not is our Service with its machinelike accuracy and limitations. It offers place and power but never a money prize, so it must be poverty always." Poverty not only in terms of money but of spirit also. Like many—most?—people whose backgrounds are humdrum and whose feet are set on conventional paths, he felt ill at ease among Kathleen's artistic and sometimes rather peculiar friends; while they flashed like fireflies, he felt himself to be a clumsy grub. Kathleen's talent as a sculptor and her carefree spirit over-awed him. "I love your splendid independence and the unswerving directness and candor of you. I love the unblinking courage that admits no difficulty yet shirks no responsibility." Beside all this, would he be fitted only for "the outer courtyards of your heart?" Had he a soul that "such a sweet free-thinking creature as you could ever find companionable?"

At first Kathleen was puzzled by these soul-searching doubts. To her it all seemed quite straightforward: they were in love, they would marry, they would manage; money, or rather the lack of it, had never worried her. "We are both perfect dears and together we shall be *splendid*," she wrote. But then doubts assailed her too. She was house-hunting, and could find nothing they could afford. Former suitors came to disturb her, especially Gilbert Cannan, a young barrister with "corn-colored hair and a crooked smile" and literary ambitions, who had been taken under the wing of the playwright James Barrie and his wife Mary. Barrie was a friend of Scott's, whom he had met after the latter's return from the Antarctic in 1904: "an entrancing man," Barrie wrote—so entrancing that, after a dinner party, they had walked to and fro between each other's lodgings so much absorbed in their conversation that they did not part company until the early hours of the morning. Five years later, Barrie was to become Peter's godfather. Kathleen found her Con's mother and his two prim sisters offputting.

> Kiddie is a quaint child [Rosslyn wrote]. For instance no power on earth will make her wear jewellry, not on any principle but because she thinks it unsuitable for her, so she has absolutely refused to have the conventional ring and has offered to give me a pearl necklace Nellie sent her. Isn't she mad? But she looks so much more beautiful than she ever did before, with a wonderful breadth of earnestness in her skyie sort of eyes. She is frighteningly in love I should think, but she tells me she never writes to him without saying let's put it all off and forget and forgive! What odd things girls really are!

At last these doubt were overcome, or pushed into the background, and on September 2 1908 the marriage took place in considerable style in the Chapel Royal at Hampton Court, where Kathleen's aunt Zoe Thomson, widow of a former Archbishop of York, had an apartment. Kathleen was contemptuous of fashion; she thought money spent on smart clothes, which didn't suit her anyway, was wasted. "I can't bear myself dressed up," she wrote. But Scott was tactfully firm about the wedding; it wouldn't do, he said, if he looked well-groomed in naval uniform and her dress showed "a saving spirit." For once she must give in to convention and for once she did, and wore a proper wedding dress of white satin trimmed with lace, a veil, and a wreath of myrtle. After a brief honeymoon in France, Scott went back to his job as captain of the flagship HMS Bulwark, a prestigious appointment but one which separated him from his bride for all but brief and infrequent periods of leave, and brought on fresh attacks of doubt and self-abasement. Matters improved when he was offered a temporary post at the Admiralty and was able to move into a terraced house at 174 Buckingham Palace Road (since demolished to make way for the Victoria coach station) whose twenty-seven-year lease they had bought for £50 a year.

By then the die was cast for Captain Scott, and Ernest Shackleton's was the hand that cast it. Of the three-man team that had reached "farthest south" at the end of 1902, this young Irish merchant navy officer from the Union Castle line, appointed to the post of third officer in *Discovery*, had suffered most. On the return journey symptoms of scurvy had developed, he had coughed and spat blood and, despite a dogged determination literally to pull his weight, he had to give in and walk beside the sled. When the exhausted party reached their ship they found that a relief vessel, *Morning*, had arrived in McMurdo Sound. Her captain carried instructions to Scott to extricate *Discovery* from her moorings and return home. But *Discovery* was frozen in, and it had to be accepted that she was stuck there for another winter.

Scott told his crew that anyone who wanted to go home in *Morning* was free to do so, and eight men volunteered. A ninth was sent against his will. This was Shackleton. There were two doctors in *Discovery*, and Scott consulted them both. Wilson said plainly that it would be wiser for Shackleton to go home. The other doctor, Reginald Koettlitz, at first expressed the view that Shackleton's attack of scurvy had done no permanent damage; pressed on the point, he observed: "I cannot say that he would be fit to undergo hardships and exposure in this climate." Scott gave the order. The young Irishman was in tears as the relief ship sailed away. Shackleton never forgave Scott for this insult which, as he regarded it, reflected on his manliness and courage. He resolved to raise his own expedition, return to the Antarctic, reach the South Pole and prove himself a better man than his former leader.

For a penniless young man of twenty-nine, now jobless, with no friends in high places and a record, deserved or no, of failure due to physical frailty, this was a fantastic ambition. Yet in a little less than four years he had achieved it. Thanks mainly to the generosity of a Clydebank shipowner, William Beardmore, and an advance from Heinemann for an unwritten book, he bought a small, run-down sealing vessel, *Nimrod*, recruited a team of fellow optimists, laid in two years' supplies and, after a strained correspondence with Scott about the propriety of establishing his base in McMurdo Sound, sailed from the East India dock on July 30, 1907.

Six months before, Scott had written to the secretary of the Royal Geographical Society to say: "It will soon be on record that I want to go and only need funds." Like it or not, both men were now rivals for the frozen prize. For Scott, everything depended on whether Shackleton succeeded; if he did, there would be no need for another Antarctic expedition, but if he failed, Scott would be irrevocably committed. He would not know for two years.

He knew in March 1909. Shackleton had turned back 113 miles short of the Pole. He had crossed the Ross ice barrier, climbed the dreadful glacier which he named after his patron William Beardmore, and altogether made a heroic journey. On June 14, 1909 he returned to London and a welcome considerably more enthusiastic than that which had been accorded to Scott: cheering crowds, gold medals, a dinner for eight thousand people including the Prince of Wales, and finally a knighthood, which had been denied to his former leader. Shackleton had not achieved his aim—"I thought you would rather have a live donkey than a dead lion," he said to his wife—but he had achieved fame. The prize had yet to be won.

By this time Kathleen's long wished for son was well on the way. Her approach to pregnancy was as unconventional as the rest of her behavior. Sustained by a diet mainly of nuts, wild raspberries, and mushrooms, she slept on a beach in Devon wrapped in a blanket and swam by moonlight far out to sea. "My son will love the nights, and he will love the sea," she wrote prophetically. And a son he turned out to be. He was born at 174 Buckingham Palace Road at 9 a.m. on September 14, 1909. "And then a strange thing happened to me," wrote his mother. "I fell for the first time gloriously, passionately, wildly in love with my husband. I did not know I had not been so before, but I knew now." He had fulfilled the purpose for which he had been chosen, and she "worshipped the two of them as one, father and son, and gave myself up in the happy abandonment to that worship."

His parents named their son after Peter Pan, James Barrie's seemingly immortal creation. The germ of the story lay in a novel, *The Little White Bird*, which Barrie had written in his house in the Bayswater Road which his wife had called Leinster Corner: a spacious Regency house overlooking Kensington Gardens with its own garden, large by London standards, and a coach house whose loft had been turned into a study. Some twenty years later, Leinster Corner was to become Peter's home.

On the day before Peter's birth his father launched an appeal for £40,000 to mount the expedition. Soon afterward he was on the road addressing ill-attended meetings in industrial towns in an endeavor to stir up interest in a project that aroused little enthusiasm among the public at large. In January 1910 the Government came up with £20,000 and, although the fund was still short of its target, Scott was able to buy *Terra Nova* for £5,000. The expedition was then all set to go ahead.

"Write and tell me that you *shall go* to the Pole," Kathleen had written to him shortly before their marriage. "Oh dear what's the use of having energy and enterprise if a little thing like *that* can't be done. It's got to be done, so hurry up and don't leave a stone unturned." If this remark might seem, with hindsight, to be somewhat heartless, at that stage there was no reason to anticipate disaster; explorers might fail to reach the Pole but they were expected to get safely back. Hardships and dangers there would be, but Scott had faced these before and would do so again. And Kathleen knew that he was committed—and could not honorably turn back.

On June 1, 1910 *Terra Nova* sailed for New Zealand with her crew of scientists and sailors, their transport in the shape of Siberian dogs and ponies plus two embryonic motor sleds, and supplies of every kind needed to sustain the explorers for two years. "Looking back on my life," Kathleen wrote, "I can think of nothing that hurt more hideously than unlocking the sturdy fingers that clung round mine as I left the laughing, tawny-headed baby Hercules for four months." The baby Hercules had been consigned to the care of Sydney Holland, second Viscount Knutsford, whose seat at Kneesworth Hall near Royston in Hertfordshire offered a congenial country home for Peter and his nanny. Kathleen's brother Rosslyn and his wife, whose son Merlin was almost exactly Peter's age (he was not called after the wizard but after "a splendid dashing brave bird who fears nothing except disgrace and defeat"), had offered to look after him, and other siblings had pressed their claims to act as guardians. It was to avoid family arguments that Kathleen's choice fell upon an outsider.

Lord Knutsford was a genial, friendly man who had worked indefatigably for many years to raise money for the London Hospital and other charitable causes. Kneesworth Hall was a comfortable and commodious red brick mansion built in 1903, set in a park which contained a lake adorned with ornamental ducks. No doubt the infant Peter's eyes took note of them as he was wheeled by in his pram. Lord Knutsford had stocked his lake with trout and trained his Labradors to land them. Also he kept tame bullfinches, played the clarinet, and had two daughters, the younger of whom, the Hon. Rachael Holland, then aged eighteen, became at first Peter's surrogate mother and subsequently his lifelong friend.

After Kathleen returned from New Zealand early in 1911 she started a diary for her husband to read when he got home. "I began this book as a most matter of fact record of my doings, but gradually it has changed its character and I have found that snapping Peter for you became such fun that it has become a sort of Peter scrap-book." She resumed her sculpting, thinking herself lucky to sell an occasional statuette or terracotta for a few badly needed guineas. Her unconventional ideas extended to her son's clothing. While children of the time were kept well wrapped up from head to foot against the elements, Kathleen's rule was to expose him to them to the maximum extent. A legend has grown up, still current today, that he went about more or less naked. This is untrue, although the germ of truth is there in that he wore fewer clothes, and different clothes, from those worn by other boys of his age: he wore shorts instead of breeches and gaiters, a sweater rather than a jacket, no cap, and as a rule no shoes. At one stage in his childhood he wore plain, short-sleeved tunics designed by Isadora Duncan's brother, which caused raised eyebrows among nannies in the park and their employers. However, they caused envy among some of his contemporaries. Tired of mufflers, heavy overcoats, and woolen gloves, Anita Leslie, the future writer, implored her mother to let her dress in the same sort of way. Certainly not, said her mother; do you want to be covered with long golden hairs like Peter Scott? Just look at his arms and legs. That was exactly what Anita did want, but she failed to get her way.

Peter's earliest memories were of railway engines rather than of wild-fowl, for the windows of 174 Buckingham Palace Road looked over the shunting yards of Victoria station, where the green locomotives of the London, Brighton and South Coast Railway could be seen maneuvering on to turntables and filling their water tanks through long hosepipes. Horse-drawn buses and hansom cabs were still about, although giving way to lumbering motor buses and lofty taxis. From this urban scene Kathleen and her son would now and then escape to a small coastguard's cottage near Sandwich, carrying their supplies for a mile along a sandy track, and sleeping out among the dunes. It was here that Peter made his first acquaintance with marine creatures such as sand-pipers, shrimps, crabs, and the occupants of seashells, heard the mew of the seagull and, when he was older, discovered in cracks in a wall a viviparous lizard—"the first of a long line of lizards," he was to write, "which I have counted among my friends."

The eventful peace of this existence was shattered when, on March 7, 1912, news came through that the Norwegian Raold Amundsen, with his superbly trained dogs and efficient organization, had reached the South Pole and returned safely to his base in the Bay of Whales. There was no news of Scott. This came as a shock to the public, and to Kathleen as a very bitter blow. "I am not going to recount what I feel," she wrote, "it would not be pleasant reading." But, following the advice of the Chinese sage Lin Yutang, she put out more flags and gave a party to which 120 people came. There was no suggestion that Scott and his men were in trouble; presumably they were making their way back from the Pole and were expected at Cape Evans toward the end of March 1912. Yet Kathleen was uneasy. On February 18 she wrote in her diary: "I was very taken up with you all evening. I wonder if anything special is happening to you. Something odd happened to the clocks and watches between nine and ten P.M." Shortly after the news had come of Amundsen's triumph, Peter had said: "Amundsen and Daddy both got to the Pole. Daddy isn't working now." "I'm lonely," Kathleen wrote. "There's absolutely nobody to talk to about it all. The young people don't care and the old people don't feel."

The plan was for *Terra Nova* to pick up the members of the expedition at Cape Evans and proceed to New Zealand, where their families and friends would welcome them back. Early in 1913 Kathleen set out for the rendezvous, and was in mid-Pacific when a wireless message reached her liner with the news that her husband and his three companions—Wilson, Bowers and Oates—had perished of starvation, exhaustion and frostbite when only eleven miles from a depot of supplies that would have enabled them to survive. Kathleen reacted as strong-minded people often do to tragedy, shielding her feelings from the rest of the world and going about her business—a Spanish lesson, table tennis, talk of American politics as if nothing had happened. The Captain told a young officer to keep an eye on her lest she throw herself overboard. She might have done so, she wrote, had she believed in an after-life. "But I am afraid my Con has gone altogether, except in the great stirring influence he must have left on everyone who had knowledge of him."

Of the dozen letters found beside Scott's body in the blizzard-bound tent, possibly the one most often quoted was that written to his wife about the upbringing of their son. "Make the boy interested in natural history if you can. It is better than games. They encourage it in some schools. I know you will keep him in the open air. Try to make him believe in a God, it is comforting ... and guard him against indolence. Make him a strenuous man."

If, as a young man, Peter walked in the sun, he also walked in the shadow of his father. To break free of that shadow was the mainspring of the determination to excel which drove him to the forefront of whatever activity he undertook. His father's fame was a double-edged legacy. On the one hand it smoothed his path, on the other it set him standards hard to live up to and disastrous to betray. He was almost placed in the situation of a minor royalty, with the spotlight of the media on him, as always readier to concentrate on failure than on success. Peter's reaction was born of a naturally optimistic nature. Brought up to respect and revere his father, he would not follow in his father's footsteps but strike out a line—or several lines—of his own, and pursue them with the same dedication that his father had manifested in the wastes of the Antarctic, where a national legend had been born.

CHAPTER TWO

"Here Am I, Send Me"

"For God's sake look after our people" were Captain Scott's last written words. He had cause for concern. Contributions from the public towards the cost of the expedition had been niggardly. Cash was so short that for their second year in the Antarctic the expedition's members had agreed to serve without pay, such as it was—£5 a week for the navigator, £2 for the surgeons and 13s 6d for leading seamen. Scott got £20 in theory, little in practice. *Terra Nova* returned to Britain nearly £30,000 in debt. Only the death of the leader and his companions saved the enterprise from financial disaster. Generosity denied to the living was extended to the dead, and the Scott Memorial Fund, headed by the King and Queen with £100 each, raised a total of £75,509. This settled debts, provided modest grants to the dependents and left a residue of £8,500 to go toward the founding of the Scott Polar Research Institute in Cambridge. Kathleen got £8,500 in trust for her son after her death, and Peter another £3,500, also in trust, to provide for his education.

So Kathleen was poor but not poverty-stricken. She was used to making do and getting what she needed. As a sculptor she was becoming better known. "Asquith waiting for me at home," runs a note in her diary in December 1913. "He really is the most erudite and entertaining man I know." The bust she sculpted of him, considered to be one of her best achievements, is now in the Tate Gallery in London. Peter would watch her as she modeled, lying on the floor beside her, pencil in hand, drawing whatever came into his head: at first taxicabs and air balloons as seen through the windows, later on animals of every kind inspired by visits to the zoo. He was left-handed. According to Kathleen, quoted in his autobiography, this came about because Lord Baden-Powell, the Chief Scout, when sitting next to her one evening at dinner, spoke so convincingly of the advantages of being ambidextrous that thenceforward she took the pencil from her son's right hand and put it into his left whenever he was drawing. She must have done so many times to change an inborn characteristic, and Peter added that he doubted her story, and thought he was probably left-handed anyway. He always wrote and painted with his left hand.

When the prime minister looked in at Kathleen's studio, Peter was allowed to call him Squiff. Even at this early stage of his life he was on easy terms with the eminent, and indeed with royalty. His mother took him to a garden party given by Queen Alexandra, and Peter, then going on four and barefoot, seized the back of Her Majesty's skirt and propelled her forward, saying, "Chuff, chuff, chuff, let's be a train." Kathleen was by then Lady Scott, the King having conferred on her the rank she would have held had her husband lived to become a Knight Commander of the Order of the Bath.

The declaration of war on August 4, 1914 found Peter and his mother in her rented cottage, Shingle End, on the sea near Sandwich. It lay under the flight path of German bombers, clumsy forerunners of Dorniers and the like, on their way to bomb London and the coastal towns. One of these airplanes was brought down in flames near Ramsgate while Peter, much against his will, was taking cover in a cupboard under the stairs shared with the ballet-dancer Mme Marie Rambert, a friend of Kathleen's and her guest at the time. Mme Rambert knelt in prayer for deliverance, which was granted; both bombs and bomber fell some distance away. On a more relaxed occasion Mme Rambert taught the six-year-old boy to turn cartwheels, at which he became proficient and proud of his skill.

Kathleen had firm ideas about her son's upbringing. It was to be spartan, and he was to grow up strong, fit, and healthy. She took him several times a week to the public baths, then generally regarded by the nanny-employing classes as full of germs, and haunts of the *hoi polloi*. The *Daily Mirror* reported that Peter started his day, winter and summer, with a cold bath, that he was a vegetarian, was enjoying a book on anatomy, and that his favorite treat was a visit to the Natural History Museum. His mother's wide and catholic circle of friends and acquaintances included the distinguished zoologist Sir Ray Lankaster, a former director of that museum, and she enlisted him as an unpaid tutor, a situation both man and boy enjoyed. On October 25, 1916 she wrote in her diary:

> I took Peter to lunch with Ray Lankaster and them two scientific gents argued and agreed and gloated together till four. It was very delicious to see the big old man entering absolutely into the mind of the little boy, each finding the other good company. There was a sharp discussion about the fin of a bass. Pete said it was sharp enough to cut wire even, and Sir Ray wouldn't believe

it. Pete drew his bass, and Sir Ray said the fin was in the wrong place. They discussed salamanders and skeletons.

These meetings continued, sometimes at weekly intervals. On November 1, 1916:

> Pete and I called for Sir Ray and went to the South Kensington Museum [of Natural History] and home with him to tea. They were engrossed with each other, and in snail's eggs, octopus suckers, eel spawn, tsetse fly bacillus, pearls, puffins, peacocks, fox-cubs, and badgers, and crystals, and flint implements, sea-urchins, radium, and a flint which when it came to rest after spinning one way began to spin another, all a feast for Pete. They were lovely together, and how much better a game for him than soldiers or trains.

To interest this evidently inspired teacher in interesting the boy in natural history was a brilliant ploy. The young Peter was hooked. It is not every seven-year-old boy who has one-to-one instruction from a Fellow of the Royal Society.

Another lifelong interest had its roots in the house in Buckingham Palace Road. In the drawingroom was a piano and attached to it a pianola. These mechanical player pianos have vanished with the hansom cab, the lamp-lighter, and the muffin-man, but their rolls of parchment perforated with holes may have been, however tinny, a better introduction to the world of music than today's transistor radio or compact disc, because their player took an active part in the creation of sound. He worked the bellows with his feet and manipulated levers to regulate speed and volume, thus to a limited extent controlling the performance according to his whim. Through the pianola, at which he was an enthusiastic performer, Peter became acquainted with the great musical classics which were to give him so much pleasure in later years.

Then there were visits to Sir James Barrie's rooms in Adelphi Terrace House, full of tobacco smoke and books, where the diminutive playwright (5 feet 2 inches tall) sometimes fell into long moody silences and sometimes entertained his godson with whimsical rhymes, or read aloud stories of his own making. His christening present to his godson had been a life membership of the Zoological Society of London, which carried with it free entry into London's zoo. (Peter's other godfather, Sir Clements Markham, president of the Royal Geographical Society, died in January 1916 after setting fire to his bedclothes while reading by candlelight in bed.)

Peter's godfathers were well known; did he have a godmother as well? The only hint of such a person's existence is to be found in a letter written in 1931, when he was twenty-two, referring to Lady Baxter, who had sent to America for a pamphlet on the blue goose. "I wonder how many godmothers who had never seen their godson would go to so much trouble?" he asked. Never to have seen one's godson does indeed seem odd, and no recollection of Lady Baxter has survived in the memories of Peter's family. On the other hand his honorary godmother, as she might be described, kept in close touch with him from his infancy until her death. Lord Knutsford's younger daughter Rachael sent him these memories of his childhood when he was half a century old:

> I saw a very great deal of you together [with Kathleen] at Sandwich in the coast guard's cottage, and when she brought you to Kneesworth and to stay in Scotland with us. I remember meeting her and you at some highland station early in the morning. You had traveled up in a 3rd class ordinary carriage and I can see you now, climbing down from the luggage rack in a blue cotton bathing suit like you always wore—no sleeves or legs to it—in the very sharp air of Scotland in any February. As we drove through the village she got out at the general store and bought some red flannel—the only woollen stuff to be got I expect—and at once she cut out a perfect pair of shorts on her bed, which were on you—and on the pony's back—before luncheon! Of course her wonderful eye and brain had no difficulty of the sort most people would have, but I wonder if she ever sewed—I doubt it—I expect my mother's "ladies' maid" did that part of it. I hardly remember her saying "don't" ever and she was so heavenly, childishly happy with you and me.

Rachael Holland believed that it was her father's collection of ornamental ducks at Kneesworth, which "Uncle Sydney" and the small boy fed together on the lake, that triggered Peter's interest in waterfowl. At the Sandwich cottage, she added:

> We used to sit looking out of the window at a long table and I can still picture your mother, you and I just chewing an apple or drinking milk with a huge bit of bread and jam—as we liked—you will remember the delightful free happy way you lived … I can only repeat and accentuate that she [Kathleen] did not seem to correct you—just "don't be a stupid ass Pete." You always had a book, a pencil and paper … I never saw her angry with you and never remember your being cross or rude or even tiresome. You were expected to be sensible and being with her so much alone made you her perfect companion as she was to you … I shall never see a son like you were to your mother, nor a mother like

she was to you. Everyone knew it, and saw it, and went on influenced by what they saw.

A word must be said about Winkie, one of the eleven children of an impoverished parson in Dorset. She joined the Buckingham Palace Road household when Peter was four and she twenty-one: small, lively, cheerful, well educated, and freckled, she took charge of the three R's side of Peter's education, leaving the scientific side to "scientific gents." Most of Peter's surviving letters to her, decorated with drawings like all his childhood letters, ended "I do adore you so." When he left home for his preparatory school she moved to Norfolk to instruct the grandchildren of Beerbohm Tree, and at the age of twenty-nine married a former captain of the *Cutty Sark*, Richard Woodget, who was more than thirty years her senior. Eight years later he died, leaving her the wherewithal to travel in India and Africa. She never remarried.

During the war years and after, the tally of callers at 174 Buckingham Palace Road reads like a dip into the pages of the *Dictionary of National Biography*. Cabinet ministers, admirals and generals, bishops and diplomats, writers and playwrights, actors and musicians—Franklin D. Roosevelt on one occasion—all came to be sculpted or entertained, or Kathleen met them at the dining tables of her friends. "I was drying my son's hair in front of the fire when the prime minister arrived," she wrote of Asquith in January 1915. Prime ministers continued to arrive, one after the other—Asquith, Lloyd George, Baldwin, Chamberlain—and to pour out their troubles, triumphs, and perplexities; the veil of the temple of discretion was rent asunder when they passed through her door. Baldwin—"an odd, simple little fellow"—got so excited that he jumped over a low stool in the studio as he paced to and fro. Because her son was so often present, probably lying on the floor and drawing pictures, neither awe of the eminent nor envy of the privileged entered into his soul. The great and famous were just part of the landscape. Bernard Shaw "sat holding forth on life, politics and the drama, with our babe tucked comfortably on his arm." Rudyard Kipling lit a match and taught the babe how to put it out by saying "boiled pork."

Herbert Asquith, prime minister from 1908 to 1916, was a frequent and regular visitor, coming to her, he said, "for wisdom and sympathy. I told him I could find the second but not the first." How far did her sympathy go? Today no one would be troubled by doubts, especially in view of Asquith's reputation as a womanizer. But that leaves out of account Kathleen's attitude toward amorous adventures. No one savored more keenly than she did the satisfaction of seeing would-be lovers taking the bait, but she liked to play her fish rather than to land him. Perhaps she summed it up in an entry in her diary after Asquith's death in 1928. "Probably it was more the excitement of discretion that was so thrilling—more than his actual love. It was a marvelous acrobatic stunt knowing everything that the PM knew during the war and yet not only not telling, but not letting anyone know I knew ... even Violet [Bonham Carter] whom I saw constantly, I know she had no notion that I was seeing him almost daily for several years."

That Kathleen had a masculine mind, whatever that may mean, was remarked upon by several of her friends. Barrie told her that she was half man and half woman, but the female half was twice as feminine as that of most women. Bernard Shaw said to her one day at luncheon: "My affection for you is the nearest I ever came to homosexuality." She remarked many times on the abundance of her lovers, but may have used the word in a romantic sense. It was babies that she really adored. "How absurd that I, able bodied and self support-ing, and having proved my capacity, am debarred from producing babies with-out binding myself to some man I don't want."

After a stint in a munitions factory, Kathleen transferred to the unlikely job of secretary to the permanent secretary to the Minister of Pensions, Sir Matthew Nathan. The hours were 9.30 A.M. to 8 P.M. and she hated it. In 1918 she was sent to Paris to sort out a muddle that had arisen about the payment of pensions and allowances to British subjects living in France. Peter went too. They lived in a grand hotel on the Champs Elysees and Peter went to school; even in Paris he found a bird's nest, as he reported to Winkie, adding "we are being bombarded dayly." The bombardment was the work of Big Bertha, the giant German gun that fired giant shells every half hour into the heart of Paris from the front only 4 miles away. Kathleen was ordered home until the danger should be over; in London she modeled the mutilated faces of wounded men in order to help plastic surgeons plan the reconstructed ones. "I worked on a man with a wonderful face and no nose. These men with no noses are beautiful, like antique marble." Earlier in the year she had written: "I, so to speak, state my war aims. What am I up to, being alive? Fame?—no, certainly not. To rear good specimens for a future generation? To be happy and make happiness? Is it health and beauty, I think?—to make health, happiness and beauty, and to enable other people to make it and feel it." This was the philosophy she hoped to instill into her son.

The time had come for him to go to boarding school. It can be imagined how much Kathleen disliked this English educational tradition, regarded in many other nations as a proof of the brutality inherent in the English people. But education of upper- and middle-class males was so closely geared to the board-ing school system that she felt obliged to conform. Her choice fell upon West Downs in Winchester, a preparatory school of high academic standards and good repute that had been started in 1897 by Lionel Helbert, a Winchester scholar and former clerk to the House of Commons. Helbert belonged to a breed of schoolmasters all but extinct today, dedicated wholly to the task of modeling the recalcitrant clay of boyhood into the image of the English gentleman. He was a kindly, humorous, patient man and a devout Christian, possessing a sympathetic understanding of boys combined with adherence to a moral code which he strove to pass on to his pupils. He never married, and by the autumn term of 1918 was an ailing man.

"Pete has developed a cold," Kathleen wrote a few days before the parting came. "Damn! I suppose it is due to putting on clothes." She had asked the headmaster to exempt Peter from the usual rules about school uniform. Helbert met her more than half way.

> Aertex shirts by all means. And why a waistcoat for Sunday suit? Quite unnecessary if you think he has enough without it. Do you really think it safe to get him a trouser suit at all for Sundays? Why not a dark sweater instead of a white one, so that he may not be over conspicuous in Chapel or at meals—but still shorts? (Dark blue.) I don't mind two straws if you don't, and I can't believe that a trouser suit on Sunday, and next to nothing on Monday, can land him anywhere but in disaster on Tuesday!

Kathleen proposed to visit West Downs soon after term began. "It really does go to my heart to write it," Helbert advised,

> but if you can possibly hang on till Sunday week, it would be a most tremendous kindness to the other little new boys. Once or twice one mummy has come and the others kept away, and neurasthenia is not the word to describe the state of the ones who are looking on: all the mummy-memories come back with a rush … It's just a question of degree: if you feel you can't bear it any longer, the others must just have to do without … So I will leave it to you: the heavens shall not fall if you turn up, I promise you.

Kathleen held on for two weeks, sustained by two progress reports from the headmaster. Peter had "quite distinguished himself by being extraordinarily nice to another new boy who arrived today, and was unhappy when his mother went away. Peter regularly comforted him and said 'it would be all right tomorrow.' One up to Peter? Blackberry picking was the afternoon job." However, all was not sweetness and light. The following week Helbert reported:

> a continuous feud between him [Peter] and a boy called Tennant, two months younger and two years younger in ways: he has never seen boys, and very few English people at all, having been born and bred in the depths of Wales. He has a portentous voice and a face that apparently invites criticism from Peter: anyhow he is

the boy that Peter would have knocked down the other day "if he had time." ... He sings away all over the house and has a very jolly little voice.

Kathleen arrived at the school to find her son sitting on the floor, dressed in shorts and an aertex shirt with rolled-up sleeves, while all the others were in dark trousers. "There is no mistake, he is certainly a very happy little boy ... well liked by both bigger and smaller boys. There is no possibility of my being sorry for him. But he is getting rougher." He enjoyed Rugby football but was apt to turn cartwheels instead of joining in the scrum.

Peter's first term was also Helbert's last as headmaster, and early in 1919 he handed over to his senior master. Before doing so, he wrote a perceptive report on his new pupil.

> He is intensely proud, ambitious, and sensitive, and for some time seemed inclined to say or do anything rather than that his pride should suffer and his prestige be lowered. This may quite well be only shallow criticism, but such weakness as he has certainly appeared to be due to his intense desire to stand well with his school fellows.
>
> He is a clever and very able boy: his chief job this term was to get his bearings: in actual bookwork he did not achieve very much and was not expected to. Much the nicest thing about him was the way in which he tried to help a very lame dog (Tennant) over his stiles telling him to "come on" and "buck up" just when a word was wanted. His big heart, common sense and uncommon physical strength ought to ensure him success: and he shows all the signs of turning into a leader of men.

Helbert's successor, Kenneth Tindall, while regarding Peter as a "very charming individualist," regretted that he did not take a more active interest in the corporate affairs of the school. He went his own way, and his way led him into the already familiar world of birds, bugs, and beetles. West Downs, later to be embedded in the city of Winchester, still had open country on its doorstep, and the boys were allowed to go birds nesting and bug-hunting in spring and summer, mushroom-gathering and blackberry-picking in autumn. The problem faced by most boarding school children, finding something to say in letters home on Sundays, never troubled him. "I have some nests to show you, 2 thrushes and 2 blackbirds and I want a bicycle so you must come down." (May 1919) A week later he had found the nests of four linnets, four robins, three wrens, and one golden wren, and started a club whose members were honor bound not to touch or tell of the nests. He also got his bicycle: a first-class machine with pump and tool kit cost £5 9s 9d at Gamages. His letters home were illustrated with detailed drawings of the various stages of moth and butterfly development, and included instructions about the care of a menagerie he had left behind in Buckingham Palace Road. "You must feed all the animals including the little snake he is in the back dining room under the glass funnel are the geckos all right." "Remember to lift the belljar a little once a day, preferably in the evening. Feed the terrapins once in 4 days." History does not relate what the prime minister, let us say, thought of a snake in Kathleen's dining room, or what she thought of terrapins in the bathroom and, in the course of time, "a number of scorpions" in the drawing room or hall.

Hawk moths, especially, had a powerful attraction, and Peter's near obsession with them had a curious result. Traveling by train with his mother toward Sandwich, a door between the second- and third-class carriages slammed on his thumb, leaving its top hanging by a shred of flesh—like half a plum without the stone, as he was later to describe it. At Tunbridge Wells they found a doctor who dressed the painful wound. "Think of the nicest thing you can think of," Kathleen advised. The nicest thing he could think of was the caterpillar of a privet hawk moth, velvety green with white and purple stripes. He fixed his mind on this and the pain disappeared. He had discovered, as he wrote in his autobiography, "a sort of safety curtain which I could lower between my imagination and reality. It has been a useful standby many times since then."

Early in 1920 Peter missed a term at school to enjoy an unusual holiday. Kathleen had decided to take her son to Syracuse for the Christmas of 1919. In the train en route they shared a carriage with an old man wrapped in a rug, who wore dark steel-rimmed spectacles and had a sinister air. This was Axel Munthe, who invited them to stay with him on the island of Capri. Here Peter was enthralled by several shrunken human heads kept in a biscuit tin, and by a beautiful green wall lizard in the garden. On the way home, Syracuse forgotten, they fell in with an American colonel and two sergeants traveling round Italy on a "reparations mission" in a handsome Cadillac. On impulse the colonel invited Kathleen and her son to go with them, and on impulse she agreed. They did the rounds— Naples, Bologna, Padua, Verona, Ravenna, Venice. In Naples Kathleen took Peter to the aquarium, where he identified by their scientific names many of the fish and sent a list to Rachael Graham *Astropecten auranliocus* (starfish) in one tank, *Cynthia papilosa* (coral) in another, and so on. A seed of the passionate love for coral fish that was to overwhelm him in later life may have been sown in this aquarium in Naples, when he was only ten years old.

In Venice matters took an unexpected turn. The colonel declared that he could go no further without making love to Kathleen, and to end the torment he would go home the following day.

This neither he nor I nor Pete wanted. Between them they nearly broke my heart. Pete lay on his bed and sobbed, for the alternative is to go back to Rome, up the Adriatic with him, on to Milan and Paris via the Riviera. Great tussle with myself. Finally decided to go home, and an hour later Colonel K said he would do exactly what I wanted and be as good as gold. So agreed to go on.

They proceeded, uneasily, to Florence, the colonel "dreadfully affectionate all the way" and Peter carsick. The Cadillac had several flat tires, giving Peter the opportunity to stalk sun-basking lizards in wayside walls. Next morning Florence was so beautiful and the day so sunny that her confidence returned. They sketched together in the Uffizi. "The child has a very great gift—too many gifts. We were so happy together all day ... I think I care for nothing on earth save Peter. Sculpture, music, men, I'd miss them all but Pete is the only thing I really love with a hungry love ... I want nobody but my adorable son."

After such dramas, the regimented life of even the most lenient school must have seemed an anticlimax; but, for Peter, the emergence of a hawk moth was a great deal more important than the amorous torments of a colonel or his mother's perplexity. And he was learning new skills. He was a keen Boy Scout, and faced a test to win his entertainment badge. For this, he had to select his own subject and deliver a lecture to the assembled school, together with the masters and any parents who wished to attend. Peter chose "Prehistoric Animals" for his subject and delivered his lecture in the spring of 1921 when he was not yet twelve years old. "Don't worry," his mother said to him before the lecture. "We all wish you well." "Worry?" Peter was heard to reply. "I know my subject." Self-assurance rather than conceit? "He was the only one to get it [the Scout badge]. He spoke for forty minutes with complete command of his subject and unhesitating flow of language ... He compared the skeleton of the pterodactyl with that of the bat ... Showed the evolution of the elephant ... The most amazing thing I ever heard." In fact, Peter was not the only boy to win the badge; the son of the headmaster of Harrow delivered a witty speech which had the audience laughing but was short on facts; Peter's lecture, he was told, was well researched and meaty but short on humor. He took this lesson to heart, and when he became an accomplished public speaker always spiced the meat with a number of jokes.

Changes, meanwhile, were pending at home. In 1921 Kathleen was forty-two years old. Her "hungry love" of babies and her regret, mingled with resentment, that her tally was limited to one was a constant theme in her diaries. There was still time to add to it, but not much. A number of suitors came to call: Stephen Gwynne, the writer; the poet Geoffrey Dearmer; and the Bishop of St. Albans, who told her that he had a "flutter" every time he saw her, and insisted on stroking her hair. But none of these struck the match to light the blaze to make a bonfire of her independence. "I think the reason I don't marry," she wrote, "is because I don't want anyone to know how selfish I am."

In August 1920 she met Edward Hilton Young, a man of many talents and achievements which foreshadowed greater ones to come. He was the youngest of three sons of Sir George Young, third baronet; an Etonian; a former president of the Cambridge Union with a first class honors degree in the natural sciences, and a classical scholar as well. Turning to journalism, he became financial editor of the *Morning Post* at the age of thirty-one. In 1914 he joined the Royal Naval Volunteer Reserve, won a DSC at the siege of Nieuport-les-Bains and, in 1918, took part in the raid on Zeebrugge led by Admiral Sir Roger Keyes. While commanding a gun turret in HMS *Vindictive*—and smoking a cigar, it was said—his right arm was shot away. He was rewarded by a bar to his DSC and the prospect of intermittent pain for the rest of his life. During the war he had been elected in his absence Member of Parliament for Norwich in the Liberal cause, as a supporter of Lloyd George. At the time of his meeting with Kathleen he was forty-one, a year younger than she, and unmarried— although he had proposed to a childhood friend, Virginia Stephen, who became Virginia Woolf. Others of the Bloomsbury circle were among his friends, such as E. M. Forster, and Lytton Strachey, who wrote *Eminent Victorians* while living at the Hilton Youngs' country cottage during the First World War. The eminent historian George Trevelyan was perhaps his closest companion. He had taught himself to write with his left hand in a dear upright script; published a book of poems; and was at once president of the Poetry Society and of the Society of Actuaries. He had an air of distinction, courteous manners constrained by shyness, and was not an easily approachable man. Kathleen's first impressions were unfavorable. "He's not really good company, very self-conscious, reticent, and terrified. There is too often more jeering than wit in his criticisms. He often contradicts himself in argument. And yet—well, there it is."

Meanwhile a distraction had appeared on the scene. Fresh from his triumphs in Arabia, an aura of legend already encircling his head, Colonel T. E. Lawrence had come to Kathleen's studio to sit for a marble statuette. Unlike Hilton Young, he made an instant impression. "Great fun is this lad. He has an entrancing humour, subtle as the devil," she wrote, and later: "One whole lovely day of Lawrence. He came at eleven and left at seven or so. Worked and talked and had fun. 'Every man's own louse is a gazelle.' He showed me in the atlas his many journeys ... He's an entrancing child."

Rightly or wrongly Kathleen, whose own louse was sometimes a gazelle, cast Lawrence in the role of a suitor, and sat long and long over the fire comparing the merits of the two.

Hilton Young—Lawrence—hours pass most unprofitably ... I at last extinguish one—for the moment. Till I've finished my statuette I can't extinguish Lawrence so I'd best extinguish H Y. Difficult, he obsesses. Peter, H Y, Peter. If I travel I forget them. When I'm social I forget them. If I work they clamour.

At this juncture Major Vickery, a gunner who hated Lawrence, intervened. "Hair-raising stories" were told of Lawrence's conduct in Arabia where he was known, according to Vickery, as the "royal mistress," and in Egypt where (said Vickery) he pimped for the Emir Feisal. These tales, together with a "foolish letter" from Lawrence, ended a passing fancy. Kathleen rang up Hilton Young and suggested a visit to Kew to see the crocuses. This was in February 1921. By the following July she had surrendered to her own feelings but, even so, not yet to her suitor.

I'm now experiencing what I've let hundreds of men experience about me. I am mad crazy in love. It's without sense or reason. I know he's no better than plenty of men who have been equally mad and crazy in love with me. I know his brains are no better than any of my intimates and his body worse, for all that when he is here or near I cannot give the most sidelong attention to anyone else. I stay awake all night after I see him, and this night I wept. It's the most fantastic affair.

Hilton Young was conducting, as it were, a double courtship; to win the mother and disarm the son. For eleven years Peter had been the sole focus of his mother's love. Now there was another claimant; a reaction was inevitable. On the way to Norwich they paused in a beech wood to eat sandwiches and the Member of Parliament stood on his head to pick up his pipe, keeping up "a flow of fun for Pete." More than this display of acrobatics was needed to dispel the boy's unease and apprehension. Back in London, he walked in his sleep and was "terribly maudlin in his devotion to me ... he is convinced that something is going to happen to separate us. Almost daily he weeps about this unforeseen and much feared tragedy."

For the summer of 1921 Kathleen took a villa set in pine woods on the island of Noirmoutier at the mouth of the Loire, which she shared with the Austen Chamberlains, two of whose three children were about Peter's age. Hilton Young was to follow a week or two later. With its sand dunes and pine woods, fish in the river and lizards in the walls, it was a paradise for any young naturalist. Peter wrote to his prospective stepfather:

Oh how lovely, we will kill the fatted lobster for you and pick the fatted figs. I caught a lovely snake yesterday and the peasants thought I had charmed it. All the lizards have on their best bibs and tuckers like this one. [Drawing.] Most of the lizards are scheduled to change their skins on September 1st, best hurry up and catch them in full bloom. Good-bye oh most pleasant of men. Your Pete. If you fail me I shall drown myself in moonlight.

So all seemed to be well. But a few days later Peter made a "horrifying hysterical scene about lizards" which put his mother to shame. Hilton Young took charge and restored order.

Another holiday was planned, this time in Tunisia. The trio arrived at Gabes on Christmas Day 1921 and joined a cavalcade of camels to ride into the desert, camping beside oases at night. Peter mastered the art of camel riding sufficiently to go off on his own to look for creatures of the desert, and was rewarded with a terrapin, which he carried back in triumph on his mount. Things did not go so well for his elders. "The perfect man does not exist—he doesn't so there it is," Kathleen wrote after three days. On the last day of the year they were back in Gabes and on unhappy terms. After shouting to Hilton Young that she never wanted to see him again, she went to the shipping office and booked her passage home. Meeting him and Peter in the street, they went together to the museum, "a hard spiked wall between us," followed by "an awful lunch at the hotel."

Afterward, in the hotel lounge, the dam burst and the waters of understanding flowed sweetly again. All three went off to the railway station behaving in what must have seemed to any Tunisians looking on to be a very strange fashion, the middle-aged couple capering gaily on the platform and the boy turning cartwheels. On the boat homeward bound from Marseilles even seasickness did not quench Kathleen's lightness of heart. Hilton Young returned with a clutch of mantis eggs in his buttonhole. Back in London, their engagement was announced. Peter wrote from West Downs, "When and where do we go for our honeymoon?"

It might have been expected that so close an involvement in this tumult of adult emotion, combined with his displacement from the center of his mother's universe, would have sown in the boy's mind seeds of a whole crop of psychological disorders and hang-ups, with disastrous consequences in adult life. No such disasters occurred. A mental toughness to match his physical strength had evidently been forged, and in this his mother's influence can again be seen. He had never been excluded from the adult world, or treated as a different kind of creature called a child, unlike many children at the time; and so, treated as an adult, he behaved like one, and coped with emotional strains instead of burying them. Perhaps, too, the curtain between imagination and reality that he had discovered in the train to Tunbridge Wells came down; perhaps he fixed his mind on an especially attractive lizard or a scorpion of particular charm. And herein may have lain, in part at least, the origin of that singleness of purpose that was to be the taproot of his character in later life. In their early stages he learned to set aside painful and puzzling distractions, the better to concentrate on matters he could understand and value. The gain was a basic stability, the price a curtain of reserve which could be lowered to shield him from the finer points of other people's sensibility.

Edward Hilton Young, Financial Secretary to the Treasury, and Kathleen Scott were united in the crypt of the House of Commons on March 3, 1922 by the Bishop of St. Albans, who later told Kathleen how painful an experience this had been for him, since he had so much wanted to marry her himself. She was given away by Austen Chamberlain. Peter stood beside her during the ceremony and took her arm to face the cameras, dressed in shorts and an open-necked white sweater, but in deference to the occasion he did wear shoes and socks. Kathleen had reluctantly bought a smart, expensive dress. "I felt awful spending in five minutes what I used to live on for six months, and what other folk are still living on."

Until 1911 Members of Parliament were unpaid, and after that allowed £400 a year. Hilton Young—called Bill thereafter, at Peter's suggestion, by family and friends—was not a rich man, or even well-to-do. As he had no house or flat in London, he moved into 174 Buckingham Palace Road. He did, however, possess a small thatched cottage called the Lacket, bought before the First World War for £250, on the edge of a village in a fold of the Marlborough downs. The date 1701 is carved on one of the dark oak beams. The cottage lies behind a thick box hedge, a number of gray sarsen stones are scattered over the field in which it stands, and an ancient wood, home to a variety of birds, is close at hand. The cottage was then rather cramped, and devoid of electricity or heating other than log fires. There were trout in the river Kennet, nightingales in the dene, scudding clouds and skylarks above the windswept downs. Here the honeymoon was spent; it rained every day but Kathleen wrote: "God may I never wake up."

Back at West Downs, Peter resumed the breeding of *Lepidoptera*, reporting such stirring events as the emergence from its chrysalid of a Kentish Glory. His marks in class were good but not outstanding, though at swimming and drawing he excelled. He enjoyed singing in concerts and in chapel. There was a lot of chapel—too much in Kathleen's opinion. "I'm awfully afraid that Pete is taking it seriously," she wrote. His zest for life was infectious. One of his school letters ended: "Oh how good it is to be alive!"

The holidays were never uneventful. Kathleen either took her son abroad or to country houses owned by her many friends. There was Kneesworth Hall, and Lord Knutsford's place in Scotland with its fishing and shooting; Lord

Montagu's Beaulieu Abbey on the Solent in Hampshire; Menabilly in Cornwall, model for the "Manderley" of Daphne du Maurier's novel *Rebecca*. And best of all, perhaps, was the Lacket. Bill was an experienced and patient bird-watcher, and took pleasure in passing on his knowledge and enthusiasm to his observant stepson. The foundations of Peter's expertise in ornithology were laid during these walks in the West Woods, a surviving pocket of England's ancient forests, and on the Marlborough downs. Poplars were planted in these woods for hawk moths to breed in.

There was also fishing in the river Kennet. Peter and Tim Maurice, son of the local doctor—there have been Dr. Maurices in Marlborough for seven generations—shared a punt, and developed an unorthodox form of fishing. Peter became adept at striking grayling while they swam under water, a feat demanding close coordination of hand and eye and lightning execution. He also designed a kind of box kite, which the two boys built together. Taking it to a crest of the downs, they attached their bicycles to it, took off into the wind and hoped that it would make them airborne. It very nearly did, but not quite.

As Bill rose on the political ladder, he was sent on missions to advise developing countries, as we now call them, on their finances, and his stepson sent him progress reports on home affairs. "I have caught four lovely scorpions," he wrote from the south of France, "one of which ate an earwig before my eyes. The caterpillars are all progressing eternally along the ceiling in mother's room and drop most inopportunely on and around her bed." There may have been moments when Kathleen wished that her son had not been *quite* so interested in natural history.

Besotted as she confessed herself to be with other women's babies, the time came for her to have another of her own. She was forty-four. A difficult birth was predicted and so it proved to be. She and Bill were having lunch when metallic noises were heard from the hall. An operating table was being wheeled in, and a message left to expect two surgeons at four o'clock. A cesarean had been advised, but Kathleen was set upon a natural birth. In the early hours of August 2, 1923 a prodigious thunderstorm heralded the arrival of Wayland; the nurse wanted to draw the curtains but Kathleen delighted in the lightning flashes sundering the sky. At 6:30 in the morning her second son was born.

In almost every market town and city in the British Isles, in the early 1920s, memorials were unveiled to the dead of the First World War. Every boys' school had its roll of honor, among them West Downs, whose governors commissioned Kathleen to design a suitable monument. On March 31, 1920 she recorded in her diary: "Began life-size statue of a four-foot boy for West Downs with model." And on the next day: "Worked like a demon for three hours. How happy I am when I work!" She was sculpting a slender, well-proportioned naked boy with one arm uplifted, which was to bear the inscription "Here am I, send me" from the book of Isaiah (chapter 6, verse 4). In due course the statue, cast in bronze, was erected in a little garden specially made for it at West Downs. Later, a second cast of the same statue was installed at Oundle school.

Everyone at both schools, boys and visitors alike, believed that Peter had been the model. The likeness was close, the age right, the sculptor known to be his mother. But they were wrong. A statue of himself in the nude standing in a prominent position at his school would embarrass any boy and there is no reason to suppose that Peter was an exception, but he showed no outward sign of this emotion. It might also be supposed that the statue would be the butt of schoolboy humor, and certainly in later years it suffered indignities such as being daubed with paint and dressed in peculiar garments. But this was not the case, so contemporaries have asserted, in Peter's schooldays; in fact they were the ones who sometimes felt embarrassed on his behalf. "Oundle," one of them remarked, "was a civilized school."

Who, then, was the model? Kathleen told Peter that it was the son of an Italian called Fiorini who cast all her bronzes in Italy. Many years later Peter and his wife met this individual, by then a man in his sixties, in San Francisco. So the matter seems to be clinched, but a riddle remains: what was the son, approximately ten years old, of an Italian bronze caster doing in London in March 1920; and, if he was there on a visit with his parents, why did Kathleen not mention the fact in her diaries?

Whatever the answer, it is clear that Peter was not the model for the statue "Here am I, send me." The statue at Oundle has been moved to a less prominent position; while that at West Downs, the school having been closed and the site put up for sale to make way for development, stands now in a grove of trees at Slimbridge, one arm uplifted toward the companies of geese, swans, and ducks that pass overhead.

CHAPTER THREE

Owls and Oundle

Oundle had not been Kathleen's first choice for Peter's public school. She had thought first of Eton. Although his name had not been put down in infancy, one of the housemasters had agreed to take him, so in March 1920 she went to Eton to see Mr. Raynor Wood. "He was very nice, and thought Eton education *exceedingly* bad, that they learned nothing whatever of any use to them." Not surprisingly, she had second thoughts and turned to Oundle, which had been strongly recommended to her by her friend H. G. Wells.

Oundle was an old foundation that had undergone a revolutionary change. Its birth could claim to antedate Eton's by some seven centuries if its origins in a monastery founded by St. Wilfrid, who died in A.D. 708, be accepted. Out of the monastery's song-school grew a grammar school, flourishing at the end of the fifteenth century when a boy called William Laxton went to London, was apprenticed to a grocer, and rose to become Master of the Grocers' Company and Lord Mayor of London. On his deathbed in 1556 he endowed his old school with a substantial legacy to be administered by his livery company. Thenceforward, Oundle remained under the wing of the Grocers' Company.

After Laxton's endowment the school passed through many ups and downs, including some appalling downs when it fell into the state described of English public schools in general as one of "birch, boorishness, buggery, and the bottle." The student body dwindled to a dozen or less. After sinking to its nadir, the school recovered slowly and unsurely, and at the end of the nineteenth century the number of pupils was only ninety-two.

Then came a dramatic change. In 1892 the Grocers' Company, at last taking the bit between its teeth, appointed by a single vote a headmaster of an entirely different stamp from the general run of such dignitaries. He was not a clergyman; he was not a scholar; he was not a cricketer; he was not a gentleman; he was not even a graybeard, being only thirty-five; and his line was "stinks," as chemistry was known. He was Frederick William Sanderson, described by H. G. Wells, who sent both his sons to Oundle, as "one of the greatest headmasters the world has ever seen."

Sanderson's origins could scarcely have been more humble. He was the son of a laborer on an estate in County Durham who learned his letters at a village school. The vicar and the lord of the manor, spotting his talent, encouraged him to try for a scholarship at Durham University and paid his expenses when he won it. He gained a first in mathematics and divinity, and at the age of twenty-eight became senior physics master at Dulwich College.

Sanderson was a practical idealist. His purpose was to move the compass of education's aims from turning out a ruling class of officers and gentlemen to that of inspiring young men to transform the dark satanic mills of the industrial revolution into temples of light, culture, and humanity. If that seems far-fetched and high falutin, so did it seem to most of Sanderson's colleagues and contemporaries. Revolutions are seldom welcomed by the middle classes, and it was from those middle classes that his pupils came. In practical terms, he introduced science and engineering into the curriculum, built new laboratories, a machinery hall, a foundry, a smithy, woodwork and metalwork shops, and started a farm where scientific experiments were carried out, all on the principle that "boys come not to learn but to create." Creation was born of the union of hand and intellect. Practical innovations were balanced by the formation of a choral society and an orchestra, by regular Shakespearean performances, by the start of a debating society, and by other means. He was too down-to-earth and humorous a man really to believe that Utopia could arise on the banks of the Nene, but he meant to have a very good try.

At first both masters and boys opposed and derided his ideas with equal determination, and it took him seven unhappy and frustrating years to get his way. His personality and determination won over his enemies. He was a kindly, generous, humorous, and occasionally explosive individual whom Wells described as a "stout, ruddy man, speaking in a rich, jolly voice through a thick, reddish moustache, his eyes twinkling behind his glasses as he flashed some quick allusion from platform to audience." Kathleen, when she went to Oundle to inspect the school, found the dormitories and bathrooms squalid but the intellectual stimulus miles ahead of Eton's, and the headmaster "a *delightful* man."

Sanderson exercised no direct influence on Peter because, in June 1922, after delivering a lecture at London University, he collapsed on the platform and died of a heart attack. A new headmaster was in charge when Peter went to Oundle in the following autumn, but it was to Sanderson's Oundle that he went.

Sanderson's reforms had not extended to the school uniform, and Kathleen, who had had her way with Helbert and Tindall, suffered defeat at the hands of the new headmaster, Kenneth Fisher. "Pete in trousers for the first time, he looks *awful,"* she noted. Peter himself may not have agreed. He had been placed in the headmaster's School House, which was full, and pending a vacancy was consigned to The Firs, a somewhat dingy establishment presided over by a Mr. and Mrs. Bray. "Ma Bray told me to tell you [Kathleen] that I look very nice in Eton collars," he wrote, adding: "You cannot imagine what fun it all is … The fellers in The Firs are all very genial and exceedingly witty. Dilke is very kind and helps me a lot. Then Ryder has brought some stick beetles (alive) and is very keen on bugs, so we shall have some times together. The other boys are awfully kind to me. Some of them helped me carry my trunk from the cloisters … There is very good coarse fishing here and we propose to fish."

Peter's recollections of his schooldays were concerned more with the fish he caught in the river Nene, the animals he kept in his study or in odd corners of the buildings or even in his desk—if you opened its top, a contemporary recalled, instead a pile of books you were liable to see a row of owls—than with his lessons or with games and school events. Games were compulsory but he would break the rules to go off with his fishing rod or binoculars instead of pounding about the football field. In order to avoid cricket he took to rowing on the river Nene. He was too much of a loner to be popular with his peers, but he wasn't unpopular either: rather, he was accepted as an individual who went his own way. He could also be a source of entertainment. A classmate remembered a bat that Peter handed round to his companions during choir practice; another, an occasion when Peter got up very early, bicycled to a winter haunt of birds, and arrived back to breakfast with a heron's egg he had got by swimming to an island in an icy lake.

Kenneth Fisher gave his pupil a long rope. As Sanderson's successor, he had faced a difficult task. He was the son of a Lancashire cotton merchant, and had been senior science master at Eton at the time of his appointment to Oundle. His task was to consolidate what had been so well begun, but not without leaving a good many loose ends. "Sanderson built in a hurry," it was said, "and Fisher put in the drains." Like his predecessor, he was a jovial and approachable man with a pronounced sense of humor, known to his pupils as Bud, after Bud Fisher the cartoonist on the *Daily Mirror* who created the characters Mutt and Jeff. Under Fisher, the boys were kept so well occupied that "sensual lusts were effectively thwarted," in the words of Oundle's chronicler; there was simply no time for buggery and the bottle, though the birch was still at hand. No school was better able to fulfill Captain Scott's last wish that his son would grow into a strenuous man. Moreover, Fisher was a keen and well-informed ornithologist; the river Nene and its surroundings were rich in bird life, and Fisher would take a few enthusiasts, Peter to the fore, on bird-watching expeditions in the woods and water-meadows, and sometimes turn a blind eye when they went off on their own. But there were limits. On one occasion Fisher came upon Peter fishing when he should have been on the playing fields. They had an amicable conversation about fishing and nothing more was said. Next day a half-holiday, for some reason, was asked for by the head prefect, and granted. "The whole school will have a half-holiday," Fisher announced, adding after a pause: "except for Scott, who had his yesterday."

The abolition of corporal punishment, still almost universally practiced in Britain from the smallest village to the greatest public school, had not been among Sanderson's reforms. No longer were boys flogged mercilessly, but birch, cane, and lash were still in the armory not only of masters but, in the public schools, of prefects who had power to use the cane for minor offenses. During his first term Mr. Bray caught Peter and two other boys engaging in horseplay in the changing room and subsequently leaving their clothes about all over the place. Mr. Bray, an elderly and irascible man, lost his temper and gave the offenders the traditional six of the best. Peter reported this with some glee to his mother, and, no doubt anticipating her reaction, added:

> Do not be alarmed about my being flogged because it was only because he was in a bad temper at the moment. This place surpasses (is that the right word?) any dreams I ever had. The Firs is not so *very* bad after all. Dilke is awfully nice. We go and fish together almost every day and we listen to birds. He knows all bird songs and I am learning them. Did you ever hear a partridge's evening call; I never had till yesterday, it is a very weird noise. I feel as though I had lived here all my life now and everyone is nice. You can talk to school prefects as if they were chums of yours. We do have fun.

These soothing words did not soothe Kathleen, and she motored to Oundle to find her son "with a rotten little man in a rotten little house, but he adores his work and the music ... I went to talk to Fisher and found he was not agin' caning. I am awfully sorry. I gave him Joe Chamberlain's letter when Austen was going to be caned."

Joseph Chamberlain's letter, dated April 17, 1879, expressed forthright views much in advance of their time. That this "brutal punishment," he wrote, having almost disappeared from the army and navy, should be awarded for trivial matters like "a thoughtless boy's lark" filled him with disgust and indignation. If his son were to be beaten, the boy would immediately be removed from the school. Kathleen sought the advice of Lord Knutsford, who replied:

If a son of mine were caned for such a trivial act of forgetfulness or untidiness I should take him away from the school. It is monstrous and gives rise to a distrust and hatred of masters ... Corporal punishment should be reserved for gross offences only—stealing, immorality, lying, perpetual and constant breach of important rules. I remember a dear master, a gentleman, sending two boys to get a cane—we always had to get them at Wellington—to be caned for making a row in class. When they came back he said "hold out your hands" and then he hurled the cane into a corner and said: "Ugh! I can't treat you as if you were dogs!" Do not you know that both these boys worshipped him forever. I have remembered it for fifty-one years! I wish Pete had refused to be caned and been expelled.

Kathleen and her friends took the matter more seriously than her son. There was a scale of punishment for boys who had infringed minor rules, such as skipping games; for the first offense four strokes of the cane from the house prefect; for the second, six from the housemaster; and finally six from the headmaster. Peter told of an occasion when he was having tea with a friend who had just been made a house prefect. A message came that Peter had failed to watch the afternoon's football match. "I've got to give you four," the house prefect said. "Shall we get it over with or wait till we've finished tea?" Such punishments were futile, Peter believed, because they carried no stigma. "I was probably beaten more often than any other boy in my house. Perhaps I was not proud of the fact, but it certainly brought me no shame." A certain element of pride did, in fact, enter into the matter. Such beatings were not severe, but to endure them stoically was counted a virtue and brought a corresponding glow of self-esteem.

In later years Peter's indifference to money was often stressed, but at Oundle he was not averse, like other schoolboys, to supplementing his income by means of individual enterprise. Rabbits would fetch 1s 3d at the poultryman's besides being fun to catch. He acquired a ferret called Rebecca, who was at home in a poacher's pocket he made in his jacket. She enjoyed turning over the pages of books with her nose, and "when she came to a colored illustration her surprise was immense." Rebecca was boarded out, against the rules, with one of the school servants, and had a litter of five, but then disaster struck. She got tangled up in tree roots and stones, and by the time Peter had dug her out she was dead. He conducted a mournful funeral service and put up a tombstone inscribed with the words:

> Here lies Rebecca. No Jewess was she
> But a little white ferret most useful to me.

His closest friend at Oundle was Michael Dilke, a great-grandson of Sir Charles Dilke who fell from grace because of a scandal in his private life which cost him his parliamentary seat, and possibly the office of prime minister as well. Young Dilke was a keen ornithologist; he put together a collection of his observations, Peter illustrated them, and a third boy, John Brereton, helped to arrange for its publication. A limited edition of 525 copies was privately printed under the title *Adventures Among Birds* with Peter's drawings in the margins, a technique he was to use in many books to come. The trio also made a collection of mammal skins, starting with a badger run over by a train, proceeding to a fox and an otter, and on to moles, weasels, shrews, rats, and anything else they could find, or sometimes trap. The skins became extremely smelly, and did not increase their owners' popularity with other boys.

Sanderson had introduced a system by which every boy spent one week in every term in one or other of the workshops, to learn a practical skill. This custom was continued by Fisher, and Peter especially enjoyed the forge. "I am rather good at shoeing horses," he told his mother, "and the only person who does any work out of six. I have taken the old shoes off twenty-seven hooves this week. Nobody else had done any. This is how it is done." There followed a series of drawings to illustrate the shoeing of a horse, done in such detail as to give Kathleen a thorough grounding in the farrier's art.

In view of all these activities it is not surprising that such comments as "too easily distracted to make full use of his undoubted ability" frequently occurred in his school reports. In the spring of 1925, when he was fifteen, he was afflicted by mumps, which kept him in the infirmary playing German whist, eating fruit sent by his mother, and watching birds on a table rigged up beside the window. While his mother was worried about his diet, his stepfather was concerned about the diet of the mind, which he tried, with tact, to enrich. What was Peter reading during this enforced idleness? He had enjoyed Walpole's *Mr. Perrin and Mr. Traill*, but reserved his enthusiasm for Buchan's *John MacNab*.

In the following summer term he sat for School Certificate, the precursor first of "O" levels and then of the General Certificate of Education. Those whose marks were high enough were exempted from Littego, the qualifying examination that would-be undergraduates at Cambridge University had to pass. Peter had hoped for this exemption but failed to reach the required standard in Latin, always a weak point, but he came out top in science, and gained his School Certificate. Drawing and music were other subjects in which he consistently did well. Among Sanderson's legacies was an annual performance of one of the great oratorios, in which every boy, musical or not, took part. During the first year at Oundle Peter sang treble in Bach's B minor mass, in his second year alto in Bach's Christmas oratorio, in his third year tenor in Handel's Messiah, and finally bass in a repetition of Bach's B minor. Oundle stimulated his already well-developed appreciation of music, but he never played an instrument himself.

Another of Sanderson's innovations was a *conversazione*, modeled on those held by the Royal Society, which took place at the end of each school year. Boys were divided into groups, each of which chose a theme and staged an exhibition to interpret it. These exhibitions had to be ingenious and well devised. One such, for example, repeated Faraday's experiment that led to the harnessing of electricity; another displayed archaeological finds made at the ruins of Fotheringay Castle where Mary Queen of Scots had met her end. When it came to Peter's turn, he chose as his subject Birds of Prey, and exhibited a number of birds he had reared himself, and a selection of his drawings. It was well received.

Many holidays were spent abroad, occasionally encumbered by Peter's acquisitions. Someone brought him a linnet with a damaged wing, which he kept in his room while it recovered. "We have to keep him till the autumn moult—he's very sweet, he's got a bright red chest and poll," Peter told his mother. The summer holidays intervened. A trip to Sweden had been arranged, and the whole family set out in a cheerful frame of mind "even the wounded linnet in a tiny cage seemed in good form," Kathleen wrote.

The winter holidays of 1925 were spent in the Pyrenees, where Peter "displaced vast masses of Spain in his effort to find creatures that live under boulders," according to his mother. He contracted a throat infection that took a dangerous turn. The local doctor diagnosed diphtheria and proposed to operate. Peter's distraught mother doubted the diagnosis, feared the worst should such an operation take place, and refused to allow it—taking, as she recognized, a dreadful risk. The crisis passed, and she took the patient home to spend his convalescence at her cottage near Sandwich. Spotting from the window a sea bird covered in oil and unable to fly, Peter plunged into icy waves—this was in January—and rescued the bird, returning soaked to the skin. Both recovered. Kathleen's devotion to her son was sorely tested but seemed to know no bounds. A pond was being built at the Lacket, to Peter's own design, to accommodate his collection of fish, newts, and other freshwater fauna. After collecting him from school at the end of an Easter term, they drove to Wiltshire "with a tarpaulin across our knees containing sixteen live fish, some three pounds," for the tank.

At the end of 1925 Bill's job at the Treasury took him to India on a financial mission, and Kathleen went too. India, so far as Peter was concerned, meant snakes and lizards, and he charged her to bring back some specimens. In Calcutta she bought two enormous lizards, which were secured in a box and left outside the Viceroy's private secretary's bedroom for the night. At about three A.M. blood-curdling screams woke guests and staff of the Viceregal lodge; the lizards had been stolen and the thief, opening the box to ascertain its contents, had been confronted by what he thought were crocodiles. The reptiles were recaptured, and Kathleen duly delivered to Oundle a pair of three foot-long lizards, four smaller ones and quantities of moths and caterpillars. "They gained a great reception," but she did not add how and where they were kept. Oundle was undoubtedly a tolerant school. She stayed on to watch her son etching, to hear him sing "Hail bright abode" from *Tannhäuser*, and to speak against flogging in a debate. "He spoke with such subtlety and confidence. He is a member of the debating society—thirty members out of six hundred boys."

Skating was another art he mastered with remarkable speed. He first took to the ice at a hotel in the Pyrenees in 1925, and according to his mother, herself an experienced skater, was a better performer than she was within three days, executing difficult figures "like a young god—or rather porpoise." Yet his figure did not suggest elegance and balance. He had grown into a stocky lad of medium height, rather unkindly described by a contemporary as possessed of a large mouth, a double chin, and a retroussé nose, redeemed by a wide forehead, expressive eyes, and a very charming smile. Nevertheless the natural balance was there. "He has always been a beautiful mover," Kathleen wrote. "He used as a small thing to walk about on the piano among china and so on, so sure-footed and graceful." Skating almost became an obsession during the next few years. His letters to his mother took on a tutorial note. He sent her instructions to be pinned on her sleeve, when she skated with a professional, to show her the correct poise, and urged her to practice and practice again—anyone could become a gold medalist if they would only practice enough.

Then there was sailing and shooting. His introduction to the world of small boats took place on the Norfolk Broads under the tutelage of his stepfather. With his one arm, Bill had become a proficient sailor, and could even tie knots with one hand. Peter's former guardian, Lord Knutsford, invited his ward to spend the winter holidays of 1926 at his deer forest near Inverewe, and Peter shot his first stag on the slopes of Aridchar. "I was an uninhibited hunter answering quite simply the urge to kill," he wrote. Crawling about in the heather in pursuit of red deer was balanced by gentler social adventures, such as weekends at Cliveden Place as the guest, together with his parents, of Waldorf Astor and his wife Nancy, Britain's first woman Member of Parliament.

Cliveden, like its owners' parties, was enormous, having been rebuilt in the nineteenth century in the Italianate style by Sir Charles Barry. Guests were welcomed by the butler or by a liveried footman, of whom there were five, conducted to their rooms, and then left to their own devices to mingle with their fellow guests, known to them or not; quite often not, as it was said that Nancy Astor liked to mix her guests as she mixed her flowers. The house was full of beautiful and expensive furniture, but hot water was carried to basins in the bedrooms and coal to open fires. Distinction in some field or other was the hallmark of the guests. In April 1927 the Hilton Youngs and Peter shared the

Astors' hospitality with seventeen others, including Bob Boothby, then a rising politician, Robin Barrington-Ward, editor of the *Times*, and Lionel Curtis, together with their wives. "Fishing and canoeing" runs a note in Kathleen's diary.

Kathleen was an outspoken opponent of women's suffrage, Nancy Astor an ardent supporter; Kathleen an agnostic and Nancy a devout Christian Scientist; both were fervent teetotalers and both delighted in argument. Nancy Astor never forgot her youthful poverty in Virginia, Kathleen her hungry days in Paris; like Kathleen, Nancy had a seaside cottage in which to enjoy the simple life, but hers had fifteen bedrooms and an ample staff. At the end of 1928 the Hilton Youngs and Peter were again at Cliveden and a fellow guest was Bernard Shaw, who read aloud the play he was currently writing—*The Apple Cart*—irritating some of his audience by laughing loudly at his own jokes.

Peter was by then an undergraduate, his school days behind him. In October 1927 he had gone up to Trinity College, Cambridge, his stepfather's former college, to study natural science.

CHAPTER FOUR

Cambridge and the Fens

Humphrey Trevelyan, a son of the eminent historian and future Master of Trinity College, G. M. Trevelyan, was a long-suffering young man. In Trinity's Great Court he shared rooms with Peter, and not only with Peter but with a variety of birds and beasts, including a flying phalanger (a long-tailed furry marsupial which flew, or glided, all over the place) as well. It came as no surprise to him to find a squirrel curled up among his socks. The rooms were on the top floor with a low balustrade outside the window; within a few days of his arrival, Peter made an aviary incorporating half his own bedroom, a narrow balcony, and the window of the shared study; and a crested cardinal, some budgerigars and a rook had moved in. "I watch the birds in the morning before I get up," he wrote to his mother. "It doesn't matter about the carpet; the rug you gave me covers all that is left of the bedroom part."

Peter started at Cambridge as he meant to go on. Within the first fortnight he enjoyed four days' beagling, and on his first day out the master of the pack presented him with the hare's pad. A week or so later he reported a 2 1/2 mile point at the end of which he was the only person up with the hounds and had to hunt them himself—"I must say I didn't know I was such a good runner." He had made a new aviary for two partridges, and sent for his father's gun. "I really have got properly settled down at last." Remembering, perhaps, that he was writing to his mother he added: "I am truly working quite hard."

He was truly working hard at his painting. At Oundle he had painted regularly, but with the greater freedom of the university came a burgeoning of his talent, stimulated by the discovery that he could sell his pictures for hard cash. The subject was, as ever, wildfowl; and wildfowl it was to remain. He also developed an ability to make portrait sketches in pencil or crayon which showed a pleasing delicacy of touch, and which he executed with remarkable speed; it took him twenty-five minutes to make a good one, and he had drawn ten of his friends. Of the paintings he wrote, "I sold a picture for two guineas yesterday so I'm rather pleased ... My fame as a duck painter is spreading because I have cunningly given pictures to people who entertain ornithologists and they are all clamouring for pictures! The next big picture I sell will be four guineas."

Then came a breakthrough: a print shop, Bowes and Bowes, gave him a whole window for a display. It was a success. "There seems to be a tremendous demand for my pictures in the university, so perhaps Bowes and Bowes' [display] may give me a chance to sell outside the circle of my personal friends." He had painted what he considered to be "the best ever" for a new friend, Christopher Dalgety, and received four offers for it before it left his rooms. In a single term he made £37 8s 6d, a tidy sum in those days. All these paintings were done with his left hand. Although left-handedness was, in those days, regarded as a handicap, none of his mentors had attempted to change his habit.

He had been up at Trinity little more than a month before he discovered the attractions of the Fens. It started with a snipe. An acquaintance told him of an area north of Cambridge, beside the river Ouse near Earith, called the Washes (not to be confused with the Wash) where good shooting could be had. In November 1927, he and his companions were squelching their way across a semi-flooded field when a snipe got up at his feet. Beginner's luck was with him and the snipe fell dead. This was, as he wrote himself, a monumental fluke, and it was some time before he shot another bird; but on that November day, when he was eighteen years of age, the lines of his destiny were drawn. He was to be a wildfowler, first their killer and then their preserver, for the rest of his days.

"Very flat, Norfolk," says a character in Noel Coward's *Private Lives*, and the same applies to most of Cambridgeshire and other Fenland counties. Flat equals dull to those addicted to mountains, but to Fen-lovers these level treeless landscapes, intersected by watercourses, patterned by dikes, and swept by chilly winds, conceal an ancient magic. Their great open skies and uncluttered horizons, their burning sunsets and mist shrouded dawns, their lonely winter snowscapes and radiant summer flowers, stir emotions such as those fleetingly captured in a verse by John Freeman about the river Alde, sister to the Ouse, Nene, and Welland of the Fens.

> Seamews circle over.
> The winter wildfowl wings,
> Long and green the grasses wave
> Between the river and the sea.

> The sea's cry, wild or grave
> From bank to low bank of the river rings;
> But the uncertain river though it crave
> The sea, knows not the sea.

"My son will love the night, and he will love the sea," Kathleen had foretold. He loved both, and loved too the marshes and inlets and tidal reaches of this land of the ancient Iceni and the marauding Danes.

Through his friend Christopher Dalgety, a year ahead of him at Trinity, Peter was introduced to the art of wildfowling on the estuaries and marshes of the Norfolk coast. Dalgety, already an experienced fowler—fair-haired, slight of build, and quick of temper—was a born naturalist who, from his school days, had preferred to search for birds' nests and to trap weasels on his father's Hampshire estate, and in the nearby New Forest, to paraphrasing Latin texts. Good friends as they became, there were moments of tension. Dalgety had a spaniel called Pansy to whom he was devoted. Peter had no dog, and sometimes enlisted Pansy to retrieve his birds, a practice to which Pansy's master took strong exception. Peter, for his part, thought that Pansy preferred working for him because she did not get shouted at so much. "I have never been nearer shooting anyone," Dalgety wrote after one such disagreement with Peter. Reasoning that Dalgety, from his base at Lockersley Hall, was likely to number among his acquaintances people whose stately homes had plenty of wall space, Peter wrote to ask whether he had any friends who wanted to buy a picture. "If so, send me their addresses, and I'll send them a selection to choose from. I haven't enough money to pay for the punt."

The punt in question, which he shared with Dalgety, was a small, low, battle-scarred, comfortless vessel on which was mounted a wide-bored, antiquated gun with an immensely long barrel. The punt had a very shallow draft, and was propelled by a man lying on his stomach and wielding a short pole or paddle. The gun was a muzzle-loader; you rammed powder and shot down its barrel, as soldiers did two centuries ago, primed it and pulled the string. The recoil, if you were not careful, would blow you half out of the punt. The range was no more than 60 or 70 yards, so you had to creep up close to your quarry, noiselessly and flattened, for your one and only shot. Generally this took place at dawn or dusk, perhaps with an ebb tide running that might, if you were unwary, carry you out to sea where the punt with its shallow draft might be swamped and its occupants drowned. A number of punt gunners lost their lives in this way. The antiquated gun was another menace.[1] Your quarry, a bunch of ducks or geese, was perpetually alert and ready to take off at the least murmur or fleeting glimpse of danger. There was little, if any, cover. The hunters—one to paddle, one to fire the gun—could not stand upright or bend double, let alone talk or even sneeze. Few sports called for greater skill, endurance, and self-discipline. Christopher Dalgety was a dedicated punt-gunner. In his and Peter's sorties together, he was the one who saw that the gear was properly stowed, that the gun was fired only when the quarry was well within reach, and who remembered to take the sandwiches; Peter, in his apprentice days, was the impetuous one inclined to take risks, fire hasty shots, and forget the sandwiches.

Their first jointly owned punt was a small sea going one bought second-hand and named *Penelope,* the scientific name of the wigeon. It soon proved inadequate and a new one was commissioned from a boatbuilder in Cambridge who completed it in ten days for a cost of just over £10. Many of the wildfowlers' punts were old, and had been kept water-worthy by the constant application of pitch and tar; consequently they were black. Black shows up conspicuously on water, and many wildfowlers painted their punts in lighter colors. The new one, christened *Grey Goose,* was painted white and off-white to disguise it. The punt was 19 feet long, 3 feet 8 inches wide, had a freeboard of only 3 inches, and was fitted with an old and unreliable gun, which blew up the first time it was fired.

Shooting wildfowl from a punt was, of course, only one way of killing them: the more usual method was to take up a position well before dawn in a ditch or behind a sea wall on a freezing winter's night, and wait for the birds to fly over on their way to inland feeding grounds. Sometimes they did so, more often they took a different route. At times of full moon the wildfowlers, in order to take the morning flight when the geese returned to the salt marshes from feeding inland, would sometimes stay out all night. They would eat a hot curry from a thermos flask and would warm themselves by sitting on the radiator of the car. Often it was too cold to sleep and they ran about to keep warm. Peter's delight in this bone-chilling occupation satisfied at once his craving for adventure and his love of nature's wilder places, moods, and creatures, an aesthetic satisfaction no less than a physical one. In his autobiography he attempted to put these feelings into words.

> While the moon was still low and red, the first geese, often a family party of six or seven, would cross the bank and sweep silently round the chosen fields. Sometimes they murmured to each other as they flew, but more often they came in with no sound at all but the "frp-frp-frp" of vibrating pinions as they settled. Often we ran feverishly to try to get under the line, or to intercept a bunch we could hear approaching; and almost as often they went straight over the place where we had been ... But however it went the nights were permeated by one sound—the wild call of the geese.

Winters, it is often thought, were colder then than they have since become, and the winter of 1928–9 was particularly bitter. Inlets and estuaries froze over and blocks of ice lay strewn about the shore as if the Arctic had advanced to embrace East Anglia. The landscape was blanketed in snow. The Cambridge wildfowlers pulled white pajamas over their clothing—surplices were also used—to lie in wait for the geese. It was no wonder that Peter had written, when he was still a beginner, "One failure after another, I suppose my one and only goose has really made up for all the hellish discomfort of this bloody game." That first goose was recorded in a game book bound in red leather and stamped in gold letters: "Red Letter Days."

> He turned out to be a Bean Goose—a considerable rarity. But at the time he was to me a plain wild goose, and that was all that mattered.
>
> Success was rare in those early days and when it came my enjoyment was very great—the primitive enjoyment of the hunter. If anyone asked me, and they frequently did, how I could equate the killing with my evident love of the living birds, my answer was given without hesitation. They were man's traditional quarry and it was part of man's instinct to hunt: it was part of the birds' instinct to be hunted. My delight and admiration for wild geese was based as much upon their supreme capacity to remain watchful and to look after themselves as it was upon their beauty and grace. There was nothing sentimental about my regard for them. Our relations were simple and straightforward, to be carried to the logical conclusion to the death; and there, when I was eighteen, the argument ended.

In order to reach their chosen shooting grounds, the hunters left Cambridge in Dalgety's snub-nosed Morris in the small hours of the morning. Since gates were locked and egress forbidden, they had to climb out of college. Most undergraduates needed to climb in rather than out, and a venerable tradition had been built up over the centuries as to the best routes and methods. In fact there was a textbook on the subject, *The Roof-Climber's Guide to Trinity*, and Peter drew the illustrations for a new edition. He was one of a party which made the first complete circuit of the Great Court, and, with a colleague—Jack Longland—did the library chimney climb in bright moonlight. "It was fun. We had a rope of course. We took the Guide and read it by moonlight at the bottom of the chimney." Longland was so proficient a climber that he could get round Neville's Court pillar using only one hand.

The punt *Grey Goose* was fine for use on inland floodwaters, less so for venturing out to sea in the Wash, so a new and bigger punt, built to the design of Major C. W. W. Hulse, an expert wildfowler encountered in Scotland, was commissioned; it was launched in December 1929 below Magdalene bridge, and sailed to an anchorage on Terrington marsh, west of King's Lynn. Two weeks later, Dalgety and Peter decided to sail *Kazarka* (as she was called) from the marsh along the coast to the mouth of the river Nene, a distance of about 12 miles by sea, with a strong south-southeasterly gale blowing. In a punt with only a few inches of freeboard and a heavy gun on board, this was a very foolish undertaking, especially as they did not set out until the December evening was approaching. Night overtook them, they stuck on a sandbank, waves flooded the punt; despite non-stop baling they got chilled to the marrow, and were utterly exhausted when, more by good luck than good management, they just made it to the shelter of the river banks below Sutton Bridge. Never before had he been so frightened for so long, Peter confessed. "The whole thing was madness but a very good experience." It was one they did not repeat.

In the letters he wrote from Cambridge there was scarcely a hint that he was in fact at a university, supposedly studying for a degree. One of his contemporaries recalled that, when he did attend a lecture, he drew ducks all the time instead of attending to the lecturer. Sooner or later this situation was bound to come to the notice of his family. Bill wrote a pained rather than an angry protest. Peter apologized, but came to his own defense.

> Somehow or other being out in the wilds seems much more necessary to me than learning the fossils of the Devonian period ... It's such a rare thing to be able to enjoy and understand a wild place: that sounds stupid I know, but it's what I feel. Anyone can learn the names of fossils and the classification of animals but I don't want to do the things that anyone can do. Anyone can't paint—and I suppose that's why I like it, and anyone can't "understand" (I use the word for lack of a better one) and get the best out of the elements and the wastes—the places where "anyone" wouldn't even want to go.

Sailing was the main pursuit in summer. Peter joined the Cambridge University Cruising Club and was introduced to dinghy racing on the river Ouse at Ely. As the river was in places no more than fifteen yards wide and the dinghies rather primitive and clumsy, dexterous sailing skills were called for, and these he soon acquired. Through weekend regattas at Ely he made two new friends. One was Stewart Morris, destined to become Britain's outstanding small boat sailor and Olympic gold medalist, and, in Peter's own words, the spur to his subsequent career in dinghy racing. The other was John Winter, a son of the Rear-Commodore of the University Cruising Club, who had been brought up in Grantchester and been a small boat sailor almost from birth: tall, dark, and good-natured, according to Peter, with a friendly smile.

Peter and his mother spent the Christmas vacation of 1927–8 at St. Moritz where they skated by day and danced by night gracefully together, although she did draw up a timetable which included a few hours of study. Their hotel was built round a courtyard where the washing was often done, and in the morning, before the sun was fully up, a film of ice covered the surface. An impression of two figures, Peter and a slim blonde girl—probably Vivi-Anne Hulten, the women's skating champion of Sweden—skating round the yard with flying scarves and lighthearted abandon lingered in the memory of a fellow guest. In England he took lessons from professionals in "free skating," a combination of jumps, spins, spirals, spread-eagles, and other complicated steps, in fact a ballet on ice—"fast and glossy as silk" as he described it. In the hard winter of 1928–9 the Cam froze over and people skated up to Grantchester. He became so proficient that passersby stopped to watch his solos. "A friend counted two hundred and fifty people watching my patch ... The spin is coming on and I can get six or seven turns most times now, and I did get nine." But he was still having trouble with his loops.

What with skating, roof-climbing, wildfowling, painting, sailing, and other pursuits one might have thought his leisure time was amply filled, but in October 1929 he took a week off to go to sea in a fishing trawler. It was "great fun but rather smelly—we measured 24,000 haddocks in a week, me personally 14,000." Haddocks, he discovered, were the vilest smelling fish except hake.

So much for his leisure pursuits. Falling in love, probably for the first and certainly not for the last time, was another. At St. Moritz he met Elizabeth, a small, dark, vivacious Canadian, who came to visit him in Cambridge and then stayed at the Lacket, where she poured out her heart to Kathleen while walking on the downs. Kathleen approved. "Pete is in love with this lass and I think it's a very good thing for him to be. He needed something to pull him up ... I love love." But Peter was off to sail on the Broads and Elizabeth returned to Canada.

With Angela, he became more deeply involved. Her mother wrote to Kathleen to say that her daughter was "very seriously in love" with Peter, whom she supposed "would not be in a position to marry for some time." Kathleen replied: "Leave them alone and they will come home bringing their tails behind them." She showed the letter to her son. "Poor wee Angela, she is having a rotten time. Pete is just—well like Byron, 'his heart always alights on the nearest perch.'" Angela's letters were distraught and passionate to the point of desperation, one of them ending "Yours utterly, to the depths of hell," and implying more than a casual flirtation. But she was only eighteen and he not yet twenty-one. There was also Vivi-Anne, slender, graceful, and attractive, who wrote from Stockholm that she longed to convey to him in better English the depths of her feeling. Alice, an American, thanked him for giving her "one of the most blessed weeks I've ever had" and despaired at the prospect of parting. All these letters he kept—fair, forgotten scalps, taken when all the world was young and every lass a queen, and the prettiest girl in the room asked to meet him because he "danced with his eyebrows."

In the fifty-six pages of his autobiography allocated to his three years and one term at Cambridge, Peter devoted fifty-five to his leisure pursuits and roughly two paragraphs to his studies. Given that descriptions of punt-gunning in dangerous waters held the attention better than accounts of the dissection of frogs in a laboratory, this proportion probably reflected not inaccurately the balance of his interests. But a day of reckoning comes to all. For Peter it cannot have been altogether unexpected, but it was nevertheless unpleasant, and for Kathleen and Bill it was a body blow. Success was the norm in their circle, and failure, unless due to acts of God or natural disasters, simply did not happen. It was true that he scraped through to the lowest form of degree, but by the standards of his family and friends he had failed. (Bill, it will be remembered, had achieved a first, besides becoming president of the Cambridge Union.)

Peter had entered Trinity to study for the natural science tripos, an Honors degree. At the end of his first year he failed in his preliminary examinations, and switched to working for an Ordinary degree. He had become disenchanted with the natural sciences as taught at Cambridge in his day. There was too much dissection, anatomical detail and emphasis on the dead animal or plant rather than on the live one. The science of ethology—the study of animal behavior in the natural environment—had not yet emerged, while that of ecology was in its infancy. Had these modern sciences existed then, and been well taught at Cambridge, his interest would no doubt have been held; as it was, his teachers failed to make the dry bones live. Moreover he had become increasingly enthralled by painting, and convinced that it was in this direction, rather than in that of the sciences, that his future lay.

This conviction awoke him to a realization of his own ignorance. What did he know of art, architecture and the humanities in general—literature, history, drama, the march of mankind? Practically nothing. Music and painting he appreciated, but on a fairly superficial level. He saw himself as an uneducated goof, or at best a semi-educated one, groping about in a sort of cultural twilight. He decided to switch in his third and final year to the history of art and architecture, a decision he never regretted and which, he wrote, changed his life.

This change of direction brought him into contact with people of a different type from those he had mixed with hitherto—aesthetes rather than hearties, in the parlance of the day. Trinity, together with King's College, was the base of the Apostles, that semi-secret society devoted to the pursuit of culture in its more esoteric forms that was reluctantly dragged into the limelight when the so-called Cambridge spy ring of the 1930s, most of whom were Apostles, was unmasked. Peter's path would almost certainly have crossed that of Anthony Blunt, who was one year his senior at Trinity and a brilliant student of architecture and art, as well as a spy for communist Russia. That Peter was not invited to join the Apostles can be safely assumed, nor would he have been at home if he had. He joined the University Pitt club, a highly respectable institution modeled on London West End clubs where, he was told, it was correct to wear a hat when coming and going.

In his final examinations in December 1930, delayed for a term because of his change of horses in mid-stream, Peter passed two out of the three "principal subjects" required for a degree, the history of art and architecture (class II) and botany (class III). He had already achieved a pass in zoology (class II), and so qualified for an Ordinary degree. "I suppose this amounts to the most undistinguished way in which it has been possible to obtain a Cambridge degree, at least during the current century," was the verdict of a subsequent Master of his College, Sir Andrew Huxley.

It was not in Peter's nature to brood over setbacks. After all, he did get a degree. His sharpest critic was a contemporary who was suffering from hemorrhages of the lung—possibly lung cancer—from which he did not expect to recover. He did not mince his words.

> It would have been a gross injustice if you had got more than a bad third ... We have both been spoilt in our youth. At least we have been strong minded enough to spoil ourselves. It is absolutely impossible to write without reading and liking reading as a habit. I don't think you are likely to take that view. The prerequisites of a writer are honest intellectual processes. These you have not got. Most of your character, even to me, is a fabrication, and if I may say so, deliberately so. This is not subtlety but lack of literary intelligence. You may see what I mean if you read Aldous Huxley's *Brief Candles*, particularly the first and third stories.

After this harsh broadside, the writer relented a little.

> Don't give up painting. Your chief assets are boundless mental and physical energy and great superficial charm. These can secure you all this world can grant of a temporary nature and what more could you want. All the same I expect you do. I don't know what the answer is. You might explore, but the world is tamer than it was twenty years ago and there would be a limit to following rather feebly in your father's footsteps.

Following in his father's footsteps was the one thing Peter was most determined not to do. Kathleen's disappointment with her son's academic failure was considerable but she had seen it coming, and blamed herself.

> I spoilt him really. I let him take the Buick back to Cambridge and went about myself by bus or walking. He grows selfish— bother—I am fussed about Pete—I went to see the phalanger he was supposed to return to the zoo and found he had not done so … He doesn't work and seems indifferent—what a bother. I suppose I sent him to Cambridge too young—oh curse!

His behavior became a bone of contention between Kathleen and her husband, who thought that "it is bad for Pete to have everything he wants and never have to hope or struggle." Kathleen lamented in her diary:

> I too desperately want him not to become engrossed in sport so that he takes longer to get to grips with work and realities. Bill thinks he never will I believe—I know he will, only I'd sooner he hurried a bit … He neglects himself terribly. He is always wet— he lives in wet clothes—he eats irregularly and often nothing all day … I created and nurtured such a glorious piece of humanity … His carelessness is doing irreparable harm.

It fell to Kathleen to administer a reprimand for his poor performance. This she did with tact and humor, but there was a sting in the tail.

> Pete my darling, I don't like to hit a fellow when he's down and you must remember that I'm trying to review the situation quite boldly as some indifferent or critical acquaintance might do. I imagine this situation:
> a. Do you know Peter Scott?
> b. Yes, rather a slovenly, ill-dressed fellow with dirty hands.
> a. Yes, but he's so clever.
> b. Is he? He couldn't get a degree.
> a. Well, a degree isn't everything. Have you seen his drawings?
> b. Yes, not at all bad, but not up to exhibition form.
> a. Well he's young. Have you seen him skate?
> b. Yes, quite strong but he's given a lot of time to it and he wasn't up to silver medal standard.
> a. Well, anyway, have you seen him wildfowling?
> b. No I haven't, but no doubt he does it very well.
> 　　You know, you said the other day, can't I have one week's

holiday. The truth is that you've had three years' holiday. We've
got to face up to it. It isn't very enjoyable to write letters like this.

Although it seemed to be so at the time, Peter's days at Cambridge were not
wasted. He may have learned little about the anatomy of the dogfish but he
learned a great deal about the habits of the *Anatidae* (ducks, geese and swans),
about the ecology of estuaries and floodlands, about the ways of nature, and the
beauties of his native land. He learned to submit his body to his will, to venture
and to endure, and to delight in "the wind on the heath, the sun and the stars
and all sweet things." He was a practical ecologist before the word came into
general use. What he taught himself at Cambridge was the foundation on which
he was to build his chief achievements in years to come. Had he spent more
time in the laboratory and less out in the Fens he might have been a poorer
man, and the cause of conservation might have been promoted in less effective
and understanding ways.

ENDNOTES

[1] An accident which took place in December 1932 illustrates this danger. Two young
officers in the Argyle and Sutherland Highlanders were punt-gunning on the river
Alde when the charge was detonated before the breech was properly closed. One
man's right hand and most of one thigh were blown off, the other man's left leg was
shattered. An RAF officer wildfowling nearby heard the shot, suspected something
was amiss, and towed the injured men's punt to the garden of a house situated near
the river where, by an extraordinary fluke, a trained nurse happened to be staying.
After emergency first aid, an Ipswich surgeon saved their lives, though one man lost
his leg and the other his hand.

CHAPTER FIVE

Apprentice Painter

When Peter Scott left Cambridge at the end of 1930 the Great Depression which was to engulf the world for most of the decade was well under way. Luckily for him, he had no need to job-hunt in conditions of rising unemployment and economic gloom; he was to become a self-employed painter. After some deliberation, the decision was reached to enroll him at the State Academy of Arts in Munich. As a bonus, he could learn German at the same time as studying art.

Before leaving for Germany he gave a skating exhibition at the Queen's Road rink in London dressed in black tights. "Good—encore magnificent" was his mother's verdict. A celebrated skating instructor, Wilhelm Boekl—four times men's world champion and Olympic silver medalist—said to her: "Give me that boy for a month and I'll make him champion of England. Give him to me for three months and I'll make him champion of the world." Kathleen was dubious. "The thing is would Pete put his back into it or would he laze as he has so far lazed over everything. Oh damn him I wish he'd wake up. I know he's going to wake up but he does take a devilish long time about it."

He and his mother went to Munich to inspect his lodgings with the family of Herr Professor Angelo Jank, the Academy's senior instructor who specialized in drawing horses. The Jank family inhabited a large house in the Karl Theodore Strasse and took in a number of foreign students of both sexes. A son, Ruli, was about the same age as Peter, and a daughter, Anna-Louise or Mouse, a year or two younger. Frau Jank was a stout and kindly lady, the atmosphere friendly, and Peter soon felt at home.

Safely passed into the Academy [he wrote soon after arrival], so
now I am drawing horses in the morning and cows in the afternoon ... The animals are awful fun and terribly hard because of
the colour ... When the horse gets restless he has to be exercised and we ride him bareback round the Academy gardens.
This morning I had a splendid gallop with him. He's a cart-horse
with a back like this [drawing] but nevertheless great fun.

Munich introduced him to what soon became another dominant interest. An American fellow lodger asked him one day whether he cared for opera.
"Not much," he replied, adding that he only liked the human voice when it sang
in chorus. "Then try *Die Meistersinger*," advised the American. This was the first
opera Peter had heard live, and he fell headlong at the feet of Wagner, and then
of other great composers. His student's card entitled him to tickets at half price,
and for fifty pfennigs, equivalent to sixpence (2 1/2 p) he could hear all the
great operas under such conductors as Bruno Walter and Hans Knappertsbusch,
sung by such virtuosos as Lotte Lehmann and Julius Patzak, whom Peter particularly admired. "Of course I know all the songs practically by heart, and it
was so thrilling to hear the orchestration for the first time. I never before really
realized the merits of the old pianola!" Before he left Munich he had sat through
forty-one performances, and heard many operas for the second or third time.

In leaving England, Peter was escaping from complications brought about
by his romantic entanglements. Angela's mother was on the warpath on behalf
of her besotted daughter, and other young ladies were writing him loving but
reproachful letters. Munich was a case of fresh woods and pastures new. In May
1931 Kathleen paid her son a visit. She watched students drawing the cart-
horse, went to the zoo where Peter "knew every animal's Christian name," danced
with him at the smartest hotel, sampled the opera and next morning was "caught
in bed" by a worried Frau Jank who reported that Naomi, one of the English
lodgers, had fallen in love with Peter and been seen going into his room. He
was sharing a room with Ruli, Frau Jank thought, in order to use her son as a
human shield. "I didn't disillusion her," was Kathleen's comment. Peter was "quite
petulant" about Naomi, but charmed his mother by reading her a short story he
had written. He had also composed "an enchanting minuet after Mozart."

Weekends were spent exploring the Bavarian countryside with his fellow students, in particular the valley of the river Loisach near Oberau, where he
went to fish and to marvel at the meadows' carpet of gentians, purple orchids,
and rose-pink campions. While Peter and a companion were walking one evening
through the village a strange, high-pitched, continuous buzzing puzzled their
ears. When they reached a bridge over the river the sound became a reverberat-
ing roar, and he identified the source: the throats of millions, even billions, of
frogs, croaking in unison in a marsh. He returned often to this village, and on

one occasion, with a party of fellow students, took a train to the next station above Oberau and climbed to the saddle of a pass.

> We found three Alpine Salamanders just walking about after the rain. We saw black redstarts and buzzards and talked to the most lovely Bavarian cows, with bells. They are a lovely smooth fawn colour and very tame—want to be patted on the nose and they chase away any other cow that wants also to be patted. And so we climbed up the pass until it began to get dark. There was a most wonderful effect of clouds against the mountain and yet bright orange, lit by the setting sun.

They came to a little village with a large *schloss* and a tiny pub, and at supper one peasant played traditional tunes on an instrument with thirty strings, and another a guitar which he combined with a mouth organ. "And two peasant men did a marvelous dance." Bavaria—at least its countryside—was enjoying the tailend of an Arcadian era. The Brownshirts were drilling in Munich, and by the first six months of 1932 over half the working population of Germany was unemployed. By the end of that year the Weimar Republic had collapsed and Adolf Hitler had become Chancellor.

One winter evening, as Peter was walking with an unattractive girl—plain and podgy—whom he scarcely knew, a roe-deer buck bounded across the lane and stood for an instant poised upon a bank, dark against a sprinkle of snow, his horns like twin thorns. It seemed to him that in the roe-deer was the spirit of the god Pan, abroad to work his pagan magic on the innocent. Back in the girl's home, he sat at tea beside an open fire, lamps not yet lit, women's conversation flowing like a murmuring river, the girl in shadow, firelight glinting on her hair. Suddenly there was a transformation: in the girl's face he saw an image of perfection, the nonpareil of beauty such as men have sought through the ages and never found save in the mind's eye. Then the hostess rang the bell, lamps were brought in, the image vanished. Pan was busy elsewhere. Peter turned this experience into a short story and his mother sent it, with another called "Mr. Spriggs and the Crane," to Desmond Macarthy, editor of *Life and Letters*. Macarthy saw a "lively promise" in the stories and advised their author to persevere. "What I thought promising about it ["The Roebuck"] was that he was working out an idea that was *his own* and not following some other writer who had impressed him. The first qualification for writing is to be interested in *your own* ideas, even though they may seem slight compared with the ideas of others."

Thus encouraged, Peter tried his hand at several more short stories and, more profitably, wrote a number of pieces for *Country Life*, illustrated with his drawings, so continuing a long association with that magazine which had begun at Cambridge. (His first contribution, illustrated by five of his paintings, described his adventures stalking wildfowl during the harsh winter of 1929–30, and was published during his final year at Cambridge.) He also embarked upon a play which he never finished, about Charles Darwin, and looked through his diaries in search of "little incidents and events" on which to base a collection of essays. He assembled fifty-four such subjects and reckoned they would make a book of eighty six thousand words. For a while it appeared that writing rather than painting was to be his métier. The truth probably was that he was bored with the horse, which at intervals would empty its bladder and engulf the students in the stench of urine. As a sideline, he took to musical composition.

> I who can't play a note on the piano, and who don't know one key from another, have written three songs. Two are rather serious ones, quite good, and the third a jazz foxtrot [called "The Elephant's Cakewalk"]. I have a friend who runs the band at one of the hotels here [the Vierjahreszeiten]. It is to my mind the best band in Munich. They play my foxtrot every afternoon and once every evening. They think it's quite good. It somehow tickles my fancy to sit at a table and watch a dozen couples dancing to my tune, and people sitting round beating time with their feet etc. Of course it's stupid and can only make me conceited.

In 1931 the world skating championship was held in Berlin and nothing would have kept Peter away, especially as Vivi-Anne Hulten, whom he called "my Scandinavian love," was competing. At the Sportpalast he saw Sonja Henie of Norway, not Vivi-Anne, win the women's championship, but remained convinced that, though the Norwegian's jumps might be higher, in grace and artistry Vivi's performance outdid them all. And the same offer that had been made to him in London the previous December by Boekl was repeated, with stiffer conditions, by the skating instructor Bernard Adams. "Loops or no loops, if you will give me your uninterrupted time for the next two years I will make you world champion." Peter was tempted, but after his return to Munich decided that he would stick to painting after all.

On one of his visits to London Prince Rupprecht, the man born to be king of Bavaria, had met the Hilton Youngs, and subsequently invited Peter to lunch at the palace on the outskirts of Munich where he still resided, despite the overthrow of the Wittelsbach dynasty in the revolution of 1918. (Prince Rupprecht was the eldest son of the last king, Ludwig III, who was dethroned in 1918 and died in 1921.)[1] Advancing on the palace in an old raincoat, hatless and with ruffled hair, Peter was relieved to find the atmosphere pleasantly informal. The butler was "much more royal than anyone else in the room. He had a large beard, a large tummy, and a red nose, and shoes that squeaked," and in the middle of luncheon one of the royal couple's small children, a boy of six or seven, upset his plate of duck and green peas into his lap. "We talked of everything under the sun—including wild geese and skating," as well as Darwin, slavery, Rasputin, and the upstart from Munich, Adolf Hitler. "I asked him [the Prince] whether the man had a real brain for good or evil and he said, 'He has more tongue than brain—he is the finest orator in Bavaria, probably in all Germany.'"

> When I departed I bowed so low and so did the king that we nearly bumped heads! Altogether I enjoyed myself exceedingly. But I do feel such a snob. I should have liked, when I got into my train to go home, to have told the conductor all about it, in the hearing of all the passengers!

Royalty, whether native or foreign, always had this rather naive effect on Peter; at least he recognized it as a foible, and could smile at his own response.

To hear the finest orator in Bavaria, he and Ruli went to a Brownshirt meeting in the in the center of the city. Peter was duly impressed by the oratory but Ruli, who had a gift for caricature, was not, and next day filled several pages of his notebook with derisive drawings. (Ruli was to be killed in action on the Russian front in the Second World War.) In Munich in 1931 it was still possible to say: "How can a man with a Charlie Chaplin moustache expect to be taken seriously?" But suddenly the University was closed. Peter reported the ostensible reason in some bewilderment to his mother. A Jewish professor, whose daughter was in Peter's class at the Academy, had delivered a lecture in which he made some comparison between the Treaty of Versailles and a treaty made by Bismarck. The authorities construed this to mean that because Bismarck's treaty had been good for Germany, the Treaty of Versailles was good for Germany too. "Of course it was all planned beforehand and had nothing to do with the poor little man's lecture. It had to coincide with the closing of the University in Berlin. It's all rather comic."

But the comedy wore thin when the Jank family was rocked by a piece of news that shocked them to the core. The son of a close friend had married a Jewess. They discussed little else for several days in terms of amazement and dismay: that a well-brought-up young man should bring such shame on his family, that a family should be so polluted. Peter had never come across anti-Semitism before, and it shocked him almost as much as the Jank family were shocked by the misalliance. The Janks were a kindly, *gemutlich* family, fond of practical jokes, music, food, and laughter; Ruli was his friend and he himself quite seriously in love with Mouse, the brown-eyed daughter; yet here in their midst was this baffling aberration. He remained on good, indeed affectionate, terms with the family, but the incident left a question mark.

In the summer of 1931, Peter's sojourn in Bavaria came to an end. Nearly forty years later he wrote that he could still see in his mind's eye the flower-spangled valley of the river Loisach, smell the new-mown hay, taste the wild strawberries, see a fat trout leap below an overhanging willow, hear Wagner's surging music and the arias of *Don Giovanni*, recall how he caught a badger cub in an umbrella, and recall, too, the face of Kathi whom he painted against a deep blue sky, and the dark brown eyes of Mouse—"I loved her very much," he wrote.

On July 7, 1931 Kathleen noted in her diary that Walter Russell, Keeper of the Royal Academy, had lunched at Leinster Corner, seen some of Peter's drawings and observed: "There is very great talent there." To gain admission to the Royal Academy Schools, students had to submit a number of drawings to a committee; the Keeper's opinion no doubt helped them to reach a satisfactory decision. Peter was accepted as a student, starting in the autumn of 1931. The full course lasted for five years.

On the last day of July the senior tutor of Sydney Sussex College in Cambridge telephoned to say that Peter was seriously ill with appendicitis and was to be operated on in three days' time (he had been taken ill while visiting one of his undergraduate friends, Michael Bratby, in that College). Kathleen drove at once to Cambridge to find that her son had been out duck-shooting from two A.M. and, though he was now free from pain, the operation was to go ahead as planned. A prospect of the surgeon's knife acted on Kathleen as red rags are said to act on bulls. She located a consultant who found no trace of an inflamed appendix, but who nevertheless considered it safer to operate in case the trouble recurred. At six o'clock Peter departed with several friends to see the evening flight of wild geese, promising to be back by midnight at her hotel. Next morning, half distraught with anxiety and some irritation, she insisted on taking him to London to see another doctor, "who found nought and said it would be madness to operate." So Peter temporarily escaped the knife, and departed first to shoot more wildfowl in Cambridgeshire and then to catch fish and stalk deer in Scotland. Early in October he began his studies at the Royal Academy Schools. "I wonder how long he will do that for?" Kathleen commented. A few weeks later he was lunching with his mother when a telephone call came to offer Bill the Ministry of Health in Ramsay MacDonald's National Government. Bill was on a train to Sheffield, which was stopped at Nottingham and he accepted. He had reached the peak of his political career.

During his apprenticeship at the Royal Academy, Peter lived with his mother and stepfather at Leinster Corner where, despite the Depression, entertaining proceeded briskly. Bill as an up-and-coming Cabinet Minister, Kathleen as a fashionable sculptor were, if not actually rich, relieved of financial worries and so gave parties that were large, smart, and diverting. There were feasts at Claridge's, seats at the opera, dinner with the Prince of Wales—"just like any other nice little dinner party"—and a grand occasion at Buckingham Palace when they dined off gold plate. Kathleen sat next to Lloyd George, and talked to the Duke of Norfolk who "knew all about Pete's wildfowling adventures— just when and where and with whom he's shot seventy-two geese in one night." He was becoming famous for his enormous bags of dead birds.

Peter drove daily to Burlington House in Piccadilly in an Austin Seven which continued on its way along a passage that ended in a stairway to the basement, where the school had its being. On entry he received his "bone," an ivory disc engraved with his name which entitled him to free entry to the exhibitions held above. A long, dark corridor ran the length of the building and linked the studios opening off it; several smaller studios, lined with blackened casts, led off the corridor's other side. "In the breaks," a fellow student recalled, "we sat about in the corridor around the plaster casts, or on one long bench outside the porter's room, where one could talk to visitors if summoned, discreetly, by the porter from the life classes. He never came inside the room when a model was posing." The whole of the first year was devoted to drawing from life under the instruction of Royal and Associate Academicians. Walter Russell was the chief of these—aloof and much respected. Tom Monnington and Ernest Jackson were his assistants. For the life classes the students sat on circular benches in two tiers round the model's "throne," or on "donkeys" lower down in front. The Keeper, Walter Russell, a former student remembered, "would sometimes appear silently and enigmatically, walk round and sit down beside one or other of us and demonstrate his ideas of form and line and balance and structure by drawing on the side of our work. He never altered our drawings. The emphasis was on a thorough academic approach to drawing."

Drawing nudes never appealed to Peter, so the life classes bored him, but landscapes he enjoyed. From time to time the students were given a subject to test their skills in composition. The baptism of Christ by John the Baptist in the river Jordan was one such set piece. In Peter's rendering, two small matchstick figures could be seen in the distance, while in the foreground was a splendid array of ducks and geese feeding in the reeds of the river.

Peter's two years at the Royal Academy Schools had little apparent influence on the development of his art. He improved his technique, but resisted his teachers' attempts to broaden its subject matter. "We were not great admirers of his work," Eileen MacKenzie, a fellow student, recalled nearly sixty years later. "Though his paintings were very skillful, in our youthful superior way we were critical. He worked hard and was exhibiting at Ackermann's gallery already. We used to go and look at his paintings when they were hung. On one occasion he had to paint in the feet of a flight of geese which he had forgotten to add. *Pinkfeet Dropping In* would have been severely handicapped."

"We all liked him," Eileen added: "He was fun and interesting to be with, also very debonair—youthful, blond, blue-eyed—full of enthusiasms—always thinking up some new project." He was better off than many of the students and used to stand them waffles and maple syrup at a cafe in the Burlington Arcade. His Austin Seven was also an attraction—"part of his bouncy energetic character. He was of small build, stocky, roundish, with hair that bounced, we thought, like one of his tufted ducks. One of the most pleasurable things was to walk in St. James's Park in the lunch hour, studying the myriad of ducks and learning their names in the sun. We were very attached but at eighteen I was too young for serious decisions."

Kathleen welcomed these young friends to Leinster Corner. Eileen found her impressive and friendly; on one occasion she slipped a £5 note into Eileen's rather shabby bag. Bill was more reserved and somewhat intimidating:

> impatient perhaps. There were lovely evening parties with inter-
> esting people and Lady Young was always surrounded. Marie
> Rambert was a friend and on one occasion some of the Rambert
> ballet danced in the garden. It was a very beautiful summer
> evening, relaxed and informal. People played and sang amusing
> songs and Peter sang sad railroad songs very appealingly ... Some-
> times we went skating, probably to Richmond. Peter would float
> off elegantly partnering some star, on one occasion Sonja Henie
> ... So many girlfriends! I know he was serious but also cautious. I
> think he was brought up to be wary of committing himself—
> which was just as well.

At this remove a glow of innocence seems to suffuse such recollections, as if the forest of Arden had reappeared across the way in Hyde Park. "Few of us could afford to get tight more than very occasionally," Tony Bridge, another former student, recalled:

> I suppose a few people went to bed together, but I remember
> one twenty-year-old girl asking another, a friend of mine, whether
> she would become pregnant if she let anyone kiss her. Mervyn
> Peake was an exception—highly attractive and perpetually randy,
> but loving and gentle with it ... I don't think he [Peter] had any
> religious belief—nor did I. It wasn't fashionable at that time. A
> kind of left-wing humanism plus optimistic hedonism was al-
> most inherited with the colour of one's hair or shape of one's
> nose—agnosticism came with one's genetic make-up in the twen-
> ties and thirties.

To what extent, Tony Bridge wondered, was Peter putting on an act when he sang so fetchingly his railroad songs at the Hilton Youngs' evening parties? How much had the unrelenting pressure of his fame as his father's son forced him to create a facade between his true self and an inquisitive public? "I think he suffered from being not so much a chap called Peter Scott as the great explorer's son. How much did the *real* Peter hide behind the public Peter?" He had need of some such hiding place. With the unfailing regularity of a cuckoo clock, every reference to him in the press—and there were quite a lot—tagged on to his name the words "son of the famous Antarctic explorer." He developed an immunity to the irritation this must have caused: an immunity which perhaps hardened his nature against too much intrusion by outsiders and led to a recoil from intimacy. Nevertheless, "he was a dear," in Tony Bridge's words, "friendly, unsnobbish, generous, highly talented as a draftsman and painter of his own subject and completely dedicated to it."

In January 1933 Kathleen recorded that "Pete has become impatient with the Academy and simply does not work there. He avows he wants to get away and paint birds or do a hard job of work in the cinema … So I consented to his going up to the Decoy [in Lincolnshire] and painting his birds for a week or two, the pact being that he brings back eight canvasses." Peter might be twenty-two but he still needed his mother's permission—or so, at any rate, she believed—to do as he wanted. A fortnight later he returned "all gay and fresh and merry, having painted quantities of pictures and being very happy and amusing." This was in mid-term: it is hardly surprising that his attendances at the Academy were very poor—in 1932 less than half the possible number (118 out of 258) and in 1933 about one third (87 out of 258). Nevertheless he had two pictures hung that year in the Royal Academy's summer exhibition, *Grey Geese* and *Pink-footed Geese*—complete with feet—his first to be accepted.

Several successful exhibitions of Kathleen's sculptures had been staged at Ackermann's galleries in New Bond Street. The joint managing director, Albert Haschke, agreed to consider holding a one-man show of Peter's paintings in the summer of 1933. By way of advance publicity Kathleen gave a large party in March at Leinster Corner to display a selection of his paintings. The house was "thick with Ministers, Ambassadors, Cabinet and wives, but what I liked best was a goodly crowd of painters and sculptors," who duly admired Peter's paintings and Kathleen's bronzes. Next day Ackermann's clinched their agreement to hold a one-man show. Peter had gone off to Scotland, and his mother rang him up to tell him the news. "How many days have I got?" he asked. About sixty, she replied. "I should be able to do something in sixty days." Three weeks later he returned with a dozen or so fresh paintings.

Kathleen threw herself into a round of chasing framemakers and "introducing Pete to every sort of person who could help him," including Gerald Kelly, president of the Royal Academy. Then Peter was back in Lincolnshire painting feverishly, sixteen pictures in as many days. "It really is magical how prolific he is … Very big pictures now … He has made a marvelous picture of a fork of lightning and three ducks going back on their haunches in the air in surprise—a lovely motive." But Walter Russell, vexed at Peter's decision to quit the school after only two years, dismissed his work as no better than what one might expect to see in shop windows. "Pete duly dejected," Kathleen noted.

When his first one-man show opened at Ackermann's in June, forty-six oil paintings were displayed. Except for three which he had brought back from Bavaria, all depicted wildfowl of various kinds against a background of marsh, field, and estuary. In price they ranged, according to size, from twelve or fourteen guineas to sixty-eight guineas for *Whitefronted Geese in a Snowstorm*. Each of his exhibitions was opened by a well-known public figure, on the first occasion by a Conservative politician, then Secretary of State for India, Sir Samuel Hoare. The opening was a fashionable social event. Only about half a dozen paintings remained unsold.

This exhibition established Peter, at the age of twenty-three, as a painter with his own individual style and vision. He remained uninfluenced by experiments in abstract painting that were breaking new ground all over Europe. What concerned him was the subject matter: technique was a means to the end, not a part of the end in itself. The subject was wildfowl: not just birds as objects, with details of their plumage and posture, but birds in their appropriate landscape, and the interaction of the birds with their habitat; the clouds and mud flats, sunsets and moonscapes, the power of their flight, the sweep of their wings, the way they took off and swooped in to land, their awareness, their social groupings, their strength, and their mystery. All these things he had seen for himself and responded to, as he responded to music. The sound that thrilled him above all others was the cry of wild geese as they swept overhead in their V-shaped formations, a cry haunting and plangent, the voice of the wilderness as it seemed to him. To translate the essence of their cry into paint on canvas lay at the core of his endeavor. To this end he worked hard at the technique. He had to get the bird just right—the angle of the wings, the leg's anatomy, the neck's outstretched length, the bending of the reeds. In all this, he was a perfectionist.

"I wanted things to *happen*," he wrote of himself in his youth. So it was with wildfowl. In his paintings something had to happen, the birds must take off or come in to land, preen or feed or display, encounter snowstorms and gales, or fly across furious sunsets. In short, he was a romantic painter. Large sections of the British public have always favored the romantic in works of art; so although his paintings tended to be ignored or patronized by avant-garde critics, they sold well and continued to do so for many years to come, affording pleasure to his patrons and a comfortable income to himself.

ENDNOTES

[1] It would have been Prince Rupprecht's second wife, Antonia of Luxembourg, who was Peter's hostess. The Prince had four children by his first wife and three by his second. At the outbreak of the Second World War he took refuge in Italy and, after it was over, returned to Bavaria, where he died in 1955. The House of Wittelsbach had reigned for eight hundred years.

CHAPTER SIX

Duck Decoys and Racing Dinghies

During his punt-gunning excursions on and around the Wash, Peter and his companions had observed a change of habit by the pinkfooted geese. Whereas they had formerly fed close to the sea-wall, they had taken to flying further inland in search of food. In the course of following the geese inland by car to locate their feeding grounds, the punt-gunners made the acquaintance of a number of Lincolnshire farmers. Among them was William Tinsley, a bachelor who lived with his sister at a farm called The Poplars on Holbeach marsh.

He was an unusual farmer in that he was much more interested in the habits of wildfowl than in growing potatoes. In a pond in his garden he kept most of the common species of duck which he had pinioned, and in his orchard grazed a number of geese which had been shot and wounded, but had recovered and grown tame. He and Peter had recognized each other as kindred spirits, and became lifelong friends.

It was to The Poplars that Peter had gone to paint his pictures in a hurry for his first one-man show at Ackermann's. In the winter of 1933 he introduced his mother to the world of rustic Lincolnshire and its inhabitants, possibly more alien to her than Tunisian camel-drivers or Italian peasants.

Attended a dinner party! of a dozen farmers and their wives, they all dressed in velvet and fine linen, Pete and I in jerseys. Nice worthy folk with limited outlook. Everyone calls Pete by his Christian name and he them. They are on the most affectionate terms. Pete is gay, energetic, at his best—a queer taste but for the moment a definite one.

It was Will Tinsley who, in March 1932, introduced Peter to the Borough Fen decoy at Peakirk, near Peterborough in Cambridgeshire. This was one of the few survivors of a network of wild duck decoys that had been operated since the early seventeenth century throughout the Fen country and in other parts of wetland Britain. The sale of ducks to London and other cities became a profitable enterprise, and the operation of decoys a convenient way of stocking the larders of the great landowners, whose pigeon lofts, fish ponds, and rabbit warrens served the same purpose. King Charles II had a decoy in St. James's Park, and the Royal Decoyman who looked after it gave his name to Storey's Gate.

The drainage of the Fens put nearly all the duck decoys out of business. When Peter first saw the one near Peakirk, only four survived in England and one in Wales, which had become a ringing station used for research on bird migration. To bring about the same change of use for Borough Fen—to ring the ducks' legs instead of wringing their necks—became his intention. The Borough Fen decoy had been operated since around 1670 by the Williams family, father to son, for seven generations, and the current decoyman, Billy Williams, showed Peter how the system worked.

In the middle of these flat arable lands was, and is, a 17-acre wood with a pond in the middle. From this pond radiate eight "pipes"; curved and tapering channels, each one spanned by hoops made of saplings and covered with nets. Each "pipe" is screened by overlapping reed panels. Seen from above, the decoy looks like a starfish with eight tentacles. Ducks always take off into the wind, so they are enticed into the entrance of whichever of the pipes faces in the appropriate direction.

The method by which wild ducks are caught has changed little, if at all, for over three centuries. It is best described in *British Duck Decoys* by J. Whittaker, published in 1918:

> After a moonlit night, having fed well, they [the ducks] soon settle down, so the decoyman tries them at 11 A.M.. and again at about 2 P.M. If there are many fowl about in the pipe that the wind favours, he gives a gentle whistle, which at once attracts the tame ducks for it is a call always used at feeding time and they come at once and swim to the pipe.
>
> He then throws corn, crushed oats, barley or hemp seed which floats on top [of the water] and they immediately start feeding. The wild ducks generally are attracted and swim to participate in the good things. He moves further up and throws more. They go deeper into the pipe.

At this stage the dog comes into play. Just as small birds will mob an owl or other predator, ducks will mob foxes and weasels to drive them away. So the decoyman's dog has to be reddish in color like a fox, with a bushy tail, and is called Piper. (In the wood enclosing the decoy there are twenty-five small tombstones commemorating twenty-five bygone Pipers.) The dog jumps over a low screen between two reed panels to be seen by the ducks, who rush toward it; back jumps the dog to repeat the maneuver, luring the birds farther and farther up the "pipe."

> The ducks get more confused, lashing against the side and top, but on they go. The pipe grows smaller and smaller, and they get more mixed up and confused, and at last into the tunnel net they crowd. The decoyman gets quickly to it and unties it, and placing the end between his knees, takes duck after duck out, and with a short twist breaks their necks—a painless death ... Old George Kelton, famous designer of decoys, took 2,400 ducks in seven days in 1819, [and] from the same place was sent to London a ton of ducks twice a week, bringing the decoyman £1000 in a season.

Ducks were killed before they started on their last journey but geese, domestic ones that is, had to walk. Droves of several thousand birds were driven to London, grazing stubbles as they went, from as far afield as Norfolk and Gwynedd. To protect their feet they were sometimes shod by driving them through pans of Stockholm tar and then through sand. Wearily, no doubt, they would enter the city through Aldersgate, pausing to drink at the "goose well" which gave its name to Goswell Road, thence to waiting buyers in the street called Poultry adjacent to Scalding Alley and St. Nicholas Shambles, where they were slaughtered, plucked, and dressed. The last flocks of geese walked to London in 1838.

In May 1933 Peter's appendix again threatened trouble and, at his own insistence, was removed. (He kept it in alcohol in a jam jar on his bedroom mantelpiece for some time.) According to his mother he was so tough and muscular that four times as much anesthetic as a normal patient needed had to be used to put him out. Not surprisingly, he was very ill and took a fortnight in a nursing home to recover. During this interlude he read the two standard works on duck decoys, and returned to Borough Fen for his convalescence, which he spent hacking his way through blackthorn thickets with Billy Williams and building a reed thatched hut from which he could watch and draw the ducks and observe the working of the decoy.

Up at 5.30 every morning and down to feed the pipes and watch the dawn and the flight. Back for breakfast and paint. 11.30 down to the decoy to watch ducks till lunch time, drawing the while in the hut. After lunch paint till 4 and then down to the 'coy to catch ducks, then tea and monochrome drawings till bed.

It was at Borough Fen that he made his first experiments in filming. He acquired a sixteen millimeter ciné camera and filmed ducks on the decoy. While crude by later standards, the film proved useful in illustrating the talks that he soon began to give to local audiences, such as the Spalding Gentleman's Society, founded in 1710. When the lamp blew a fuse, or other technical hitches occurred, he kept his audience happy by drawing ducks and geese on a blackboard while repairs were carried out. This proved a useful dodge which he was to employ on many future occasions to introduce his lectures, to get his audience into an amused and appreciative frame of mind.

The time had come for him to fly the nest, downy as it was, and to make a home of his own. For some time he had had his eye on twin lighthouses standing on each bank of the river Nene where it enters the Wash. They had been designed by John Pennie, architect of Waterloo bridge, and built between 1829 and 1834 to commemorate the draining of the Great Fens, but the lamps had never been lit to warn ships at sea. A customs officer from Sutton Bridge, three miles upstream, arrived twice a day half an hour before high tide to hail through a megaphone any ship that might be entering or leaving the river, and left half an hour after the turn of the tide. One of these lighthouses, on the eastern bank, was unoccupied and in reasonably good repair. In the summer of 1933 Peter secured a lease from the Nene Catchment Board for a rent of £5 a year. He arranged for a few repairs and moved in. An old man known as Samphire Charlie was living in the basement with his dog in some squalor, collecting cockles and mussels off the shore which he sold for salads. (It could also be cooked lightly and eaten with melted butter, often as an accompaniment to crabs.) For some time he stayed on to give a hand about the place, but he was a boozer, and had to go.

The East Lighthouse was to be Peter's base for the next six years, his home only intermittently. Painting, sailing, shooting, stalking, skating, writing, traveling, wildfowl collecting, making friends, going to parties, to cinemas, to plays, falling in love and out again—Kipling's unforgiving minute was abundantly filled. He was loosening the ties with his mother, but they were still strong. She was worried about his cavalier attitude toward his painting. Sometimes he worked frenetically and would complete two pictures in as many days, sometimes he painted nothing for weeks or even months on end. "It is so hard to make him work," she complained. "He is so lazy born." When she scolded him for lying in bed in the mornings, "as always when reprimanded he lost his temper, everything was my fault and so on." But he repented, got up earlier and had a bath, a custom for which he displayed little enthusiasm.

Late nights were perhaps a cause of morning sleepiness, and the by-product of an infatuation with the Austrian actress Elizabeth Bergner, who was bewitching London in Margaret Kennedy's play *Escape Me Never*. Peter saw the play four times before he met her, and another thirteen times afterward. He was painting a portrait of his godfather James Barrie, who sat by an open fire in the top flat of Adelphi House Terrace enveloped in tobacco smoke, brooding over the past—he was seventy-four—and talking about village cricket, his five adopted Davies boys, the theater of his maturity and many other things. It was three years since he had been to a theater, and Peter determined to take him to *Escape Me Never*. Overruling Barrie's objections, his godson carried him off to the theater and backstage to meet the star. It was an emotional encounter, which ended in Barrie inviting Elizabeth Bergner to tea; Peter seized his opportunity and took her in his car. So an acquaintance was struck up that ripened swiftly through the spring days. Kathleen approved of her. "She was quite intensely captivating … She threw her arms round my neck and kissed me and then carried on the most arrant milk-maidish flirtation with Pete—Pete replying in character—absurd and charming. She drove me home in her smart blue car and bade Pete go to see her in the evening which he did."

He was also painting her portrait, escorting her in his dilapidated open Morris to tea with Barrie, and taking her home afterward. There is no evidence to suggest that he stayed on and they became lovers, but it seems more than likely. She was very beautiful, he was young and ardent, and spring was in the air. She captivated Barrie as well; he decided to break his silence and write a play in which she would play the lead. Two years later, *The Boy David* proved a tragic flop, casting a pall of failure over the last few months of Barrie's life. Peter's portrait was rejected by the Royal Academy, much to his mother's indignation. It was bought by Elizabeth Bergner.

When Peter took over his new home the sea surrounded it on three sides at high tide, flooding the salt marshes that lay between the lighthouse and the Wash. On the fourth side was the wide, slow-flowing river Nene. The seawall that protected reclaimed farm land ran within 20 yards of the conical brick building. Today, more land has been reclaimed, and beyond the seawall stretch arable fields; the sea is out of sight and the lighthouse has been painted white. But there is still a sea-tang in the air, gales blow fiercely from the east, and little checks their force between the Ural mountains and the Norfolk coast.

The lighthouse had, and has, four stories, the bottom one 16 feet in diameter, the top one only just big enough to hold a divan bed. A steep curved staircase connects the ground floor with the room above, which was fitted with beds that could be hauled up to the ceiling to allow the floor space to be used to sit in. Above that, Peter's bedroom was reached by a ladder, its pale green walls decorated by a frieze of white ducks. Above that was an eyrie with an eagle's view over the watery landscape. Peter loved his lighthouse dearly.

On a cold November weekend he took his mother to inspect his new domain.

> We slept the night in the pub at Sutton Bridge. Pete woke me at 4:30 A.M. bringing me thigh rubber boots and 3 pairs of socks. Then we tip-toed down to a meal laid for us the night before. Bread, butter, ham (not for me) and ginger beer, said to be warming. Then we started forth in the dark and rain, first ten miles by car, then in pitchiness along a grass bank, then for a mile or two over the saltings, stumbling about and falling into kind of crevasses.
>
> Pete was tenderly mindful of me—at last we got to a creek full of water—along this we waded—me in imminent danger of sticking in the mud, Pete's boots being so big and heavy ... Presently just before dawn groups of five or six geese began to fly over us and then suddenly with a grand flurry and honking over they all flew, about 1500 of them. As grand a sight as I could hope to see. Then we went down on the beach just as day was breaking—tide far out, lovely—arm in arm and happy. Then back inland to see the Pinkfeet again, now settled quietly feeding in the potato fields—Pete knows exactly where to find them—then home to a very welcome breakfast and then off to see his lighthouse.

Next morning they repeated the performance. Kathleen enjoyed herself but with reservations.

> It was fun being out with him those mornings. He calls all the birds and they fly over him—countless curlews, greenshanks etc. He is so completely in his element there. A grand fellow. It must be right not to interfere too much with what *appears* to be a waste of time. It isn't work it's true, it does no good to anybody, it makes no money but—at any rate it does no harm to anybody and I think some good to yourself. Anyway I felt those nights I would not have him any other sort of boy at all! So there.

Kathleen's life was full of contrasts. A few days later she was at an evening party at Buckingham Palace "stiff with royalty," and two days after that at the Duke of Kent's wedding. The Queen had agreed to unveil her bust of King George V— "so it had better be good."

By now Peter's Cambridge contemporaries had gone their separate ways, but several of those who shared his interests formed a circle of close friends. John Winter was in Stafford, working for a company called Universal Grinding Wheels. Michael Bratby—his correct first name was Malpas—was the joker, with a sense of the ridiculous, and a gift for finance that lured him into stockbroking in Manchester. It was he who had taught Peter the American railroad ballads whose recital became a useful parlor trick, such as "The Wreck of the Ninety-Seven," "The Jealous Lover of Lone Green Valley" and "The Ballad of Casey Jones." He was a fluent talker, with a line in fantasy that could have won him a reputation in radio in a class with that of masters of the genre such as Gill Potter. His radio performances were in fact devoted to talks to children about birds, talks in which he involved Peter—they were sometimes joint affairs. In these lay the seeds of Peter's postwar participation in programs such as *Nature Parliament.*

Slight of build, boyish looking, and wearing glasses, Michael Bratby was an enthusiastic wildfowler who, while still an undergraduate, had rented a shoot near Cambridge and, later, Brogden marsh in Westmorland, now part of Cumbria, to which Peter, John Winter, Christopher Dalgety, Menyn Ingram, and other shooting friends often went, using as their headquarters the Ship Inn near Sandside. Here they gathered for convivial evenings after the day's sport and before starting well before dawn to stalk their quarry. They treated the Ship Inn as a second home—Peter sat out an attack of chicken-pox there—and thought highly of its hospitality, but more critical visitors found it less than ideal. The first of the group to get engaged to be married was Christopher Dalgety, whose fiancée joined a weekend shooting party there. Aline had been brought up in Galway in Ireland, so shooting and fishing were second nature to her; she was no stickler for creature comforts, but was a little taken aback to see bugs emerging from her bedroom walls.

Menyn Ingram was another wildfowling crony, who completed his finals on the same day as Peter—December 17, 1930—and went snipe shooting with him that same afternoon. After he had come down from Trinity, he embarked on the hard slog of being a medical student at one of the London hospitals. Nearly all these young men wrote long and detailed letters to each other about their wildfowling adventures, with tallies of their bags. In years to come Peter disliked composing letters and was so slow a writer, and a slow reader too, that some people thought he was dyslexic. Nevertheless throughout his life he penned a prodigious number of words—diaries, letters, scientific papers, articles, books—in a beautiful hand. He sent Menyn Ingram long descriptions of his exploits. To one of these Ingram replied: "Stop sending me those bloody long lists of birds you've killed while I have to bugger about in a hospital." Another of his wildfowling companions, David Haig Thomas, Peter described as "uncomplicated, unpredictable, unafraid and completely friendly," as well as being "tough, ruthless, irresistibly charming, cheerfully good-looking and fundamentally kind," a description that might have fitted Peter himself.

Wildfowling was a winter pursuit: from February or March onward to September migrants vanished, and resident birds were given a respite to rear their young. For Peter, summer was for sailing. He was already proficient in handling small boats when he joined the Cambridge University Cruising Club and was introduced to the highly competitive world of racing 14-foot dinghies, in which the ultimate accolade was to win the Prince of Wales' Cup.

Racing dinghies were comparative newcomers to the yachting world—the first race for the Prince of Wales' Cup was held in 1927—and their design was constantly being improved. The builder who had emerged as the champion was Uffa Fox, whose yard was at Cowes. He was revolutionizing the design of these 14-foot dinghies, and to own one of his boats was every dinghy racer's ambition. "I set out," he wrote, "to design boats that would lift out of the water when sailed hard off the wind." This was called planing, and meant that in the right conditions the boat could skim over and above the waves, thus not only making it go a lot faster but providing a most exhilarating sensation for its sailors. Of these there were two: the helmsman, who was the skipper and often the owner, and his crew, who looked after the sails and the general trim of the boat.

In 1928 *Avenger*, built by Uffa Fox to this new design and sailed by him, swept all before it and carried off the coveted cup. Stewart Morris then commissioned a leading naval architect, Frank Morgan Giles, to build him an even better boat in which to challenge *Avenger*. The result was *Clover*. Morris's name already stood high in the dinghy racing world when he invited Peter to be his crew for the 1930 season, including the big race which was to be held at Lowestoft. (The venue varied from year to year.) For a young man still at Cambridge this was a great opportunity, and Peter's hopes were bright.

The morning of the race dawned clear and windless. After several delays and a false start, the race had to be postponed until the next day. Once again the wind was fickle, and the fifty or so competitors had to drop anchor and wait for the breeze to freshen and the tide to turn. With Morris's permission, Peter decided to have a swim to cool off and enjoy himself. By the time he noticed that anchors were being hauled up and sails were filling, and had hurried back to *Clover* and climbed on board, about twenty boats were under way. Half an hour later, the wind failed altogether and the race was again postponed. His luck was still holding.

The third and final day again dawned calm and windless, just like the previous two. Peter was staying at Horsey Hall, about twenty miles from Lowestoft, which his family had taken for the summer holidays. He reckoned that the start of the race was sure to be postponed again, so he set off in a leisurely fashion after breakfast in the family's Austin Seven, thinking he had

plenty of time. When he reached a view of Lowestoft harbor, not a racing dinghy was in sight. Speeding to the clubhouse and leaping into a motorboat moored
beside it, he dashed out to the harbor mouth where the dinghies were maneuvering for position ready for the start. A replacement crew climbed out of *Clover*
as Peter climbed in to the accompaniment of the five minute gun and, one may
assume, caustic and even ruder remarks by the skipper. *Clover* made a poor start
and finished eleventh. Morris did not invite Peter to crew for him in the following season, when he won the race. "I was simply not to be depended upon,"
Peter ruefully admitted. He did not repeat his mistake.

A second chance came three years later. Alan Colman, whose father was
Russell Colman of mustard fame, owned a 14-footer *Telemark*, built by Uffa Fox,
and invited Peter to crew for him in the big race in 1933, to be held again at
Lowestoft. Although on this occasion Peter's punctuality was impeccable,
Colman's boat was unplaced and once again Stewart Morris was the winner.
(He won the cup twelve times in all, a record.) Alan Colman nevertheless invited Peter to join a team which was to take three 14-footers to the United
States. So a dozen enthusiasts sailed with their dinghies in the liner *Olympic* to
race them in Oyster Bay, Long Island, as guests of millionaires more accustomed to yachts of America's Cup dimensions than to little dinghies. On Long
Island Peter stayed with the Philip Roosevelts, dined with Theodore Roosevelt,
and drove himself about in a twelve-cylinder Packard. The races, he wrote,
were "not even successful."

Included in the team was a tall, white-haired, and strenuous lady from
County Fermanagh, the wife of Colonel Henry Richardson, who had taken part
with near-success, crewed by her husband, in almost even race for the Prince of
Wales' Cup but never actually won it. She was a friendly if, on occasion, impe-
rious lady. Once, when she arrived at Belfast station to catch the Dublin express, the guard had already blown his whistle and the train was moving away.
"I am Mrs. Henry Richardson!" she shouted. "Stop the train!" The guard did so.
Phyllis Richardson was more at home in Long Island than Uffa Fox, who joined
the team in New York. Fox liked nothing better than to *épater les bourgeois*—or, in
this case, *les millionaires*. His only footwear was a pair of gym shoes, and he spiced
his full-throated conversation with four-letter words before they became acceptable in polite society. "He had a rugged commonsense philosophy, he sang
sea shanties, he liked beer and was basically kind," Peter wrote. Kathleen was less
charitable. At this period of Peter's life he was apt to turn up at one of the houses
she and Bill had taken for the summer with a gaggle of young and not always
polished friends. When Uffa Fox came to luncheon, the only contribution he made
to the conversation, she wrote, was: "Ah! I've swallowed a plum stone."

During the races off Long Island Peter looked after Alan Colman's boat, and by
the end of the visit he reckoned that he knew enough about handling and main-

taining racing dinghies to own one of his own. It goes without saying that Uffa Fox was commissioned to build it. Such boats, made from the best materials and beautifully hand crafted, were far from cheap. But so long as his pictures continued to sell and he found time to paint them, he could pay for his boat; by the spring of 1934 she was ready, and he named her *Eastlight* after his lighthouse.

"Sailing a fourteen-foot dinghy—my very own fourteen-foot dinghy was utterly satisfying," he wrote. *Eastlight* was a success. In her Peter won twenty-three firsts, twelve seconds and fourteen thirds in a single season in various regattas. In July 1934 he took her to Canada in the *Empress of Britain* with a team picked to take part in a three-cornered contest between Britain, Canada, and the United States. Stewart Morris was the captain, Uffa Fox the manager, and the races took place on Lake Ontario, where the sudden, unpredictable, and savage storms for which the Great Lakes are famous put on a formidable display. *Eastlight*, after being half swamped by enormous waves and running through an icy fog which reduced visibility almost to nil, won a critical race by twelve seconds, and the British team comfortably won the series.

Back in England, there remained the crucial contest, the Prince of Wales' Cup. The race was held off Falmouth. The wind was light and fickle, and neither Peter's skill nor his luck prevailed. *Eastlight* finished sixteenth. Although Peter admitted that his own inexperience was largely to blame, his failure wiped some of the luster from his cherished dinghy. He set his sights on *Whisper*, which, sailed by Mrs. Henry Richardson, had won third place. She was so beautiful, her purplish mahogany color (*Eastlight* was yellower) and the grain of her timber so fetching, her responses to light breezes so sensitive, that he decided to buy her, and did so for £130. In 1935 he sailed her in the big race in Osborne Bay; but luck, like nature's sea breezes, was once again not on his side. The wind was strong and on the first time round the course—there were five circuits—*Whisper* was in the lead. Then her mast began to bend at an alarming angle and, as she breasted an extra big wave, it snapped, and she was out of the race. Morris won it again, with John Winter second.

So yet another boat had to be built, by Uffa Fox again but this time incorporating Peter's own ideas. She was called *Daybreak*. "Most designers and builders resented a customer or owner inventing and proposing new ideas," wrote Fox, "but I invited and encouraged it." He was building about thirty new boats every year and reckoned that he had "thirty new men every year thinking independently and inventing new ideas for me to perfect." Peter's new idea was a radical one. The centerboards of these dinghies were made of phosphor-bronze and weighed 120 pounds. Why not make them of wood, which would weigh 10 pounds? This would be a gamble, because what the boat would gain in speed she would lose in stability; but the gain in speed would be so great that Peter decided to take the gamble. *Daybreak* was fitted with a wooden centerboard, which was kept a close secret. The board was painted bronze, and when they lifted it Peter and his crew—a stalwart young American, Beecher Moore—put on an act of staggering along bearing the weight of a heavy metal centerboard. No one saw through the trick which was, of course, perfectly legal. The race that year, 1936, was held on the Clyde, and a gale which blew for three days forced its postponement until the last possible moment, one o'clock on the third day. After a spectacular race, *Daybreak* came in third, with Morris the winner and Winter in second place. Nothing but a win would satisfy Peter but he had climbed to within reach of the top.

Meanwhile he entered his name in the single-handed sailing class in the Olympic Games, to be held that August at Kiel. Stewart Morris agreed to go as his spare man. The boats were Olympia Jolle-monotypes, which were 16 feet long, had a mainsail only, and were heavy to handle; neither Morris nor Peter liked them much. Twenty-six nations took part, and the series of races extended over seven days. By the seventh day a Dutchman, Daniel Kagghelland, was so far ahead in points that he was certain of the Gold. Peter and a German, Werner Krogmann, were running neck and neck for second place, and the last race of the series would decide the issue. While they were sailing side by side the wind veered slightly and, in putting about to escape the German's wind shadow, Peter's boat nicked the stern of Krogmann's very slightly, a mere tap. Nevertheless this rated as a collision and Peter withdrew from the race. So he missed the Silver, but won the Bronze.

To dinghy enthusiasts the Prince of Wales' cup was a much more important trophy than an Olympic medal for single-handed sailing. For Peter's fourth attempt, another boat was designed and built by Uffa Fox, with, as before, a wooden centerboard. This time—1937—Lowestoft was the venue, *Thunder* the name of the boat, and his crew was Charles Currey, a tall, fair-haired, and enthusiastic son of a naval commander. Once again Peter had a trick up his sleeve. A careful study of wind and tide the day before the contest convinced him and Currey that the best way to gain an edge over their competitors would be to sail as close inshore as possible on one leg of the race. But a number of jetties jutted out from the shore, and between them was a line of posts connected by submerged boards which prevented this maneuver. However, some of these boards had rotted or been washed away, leaving gaps through which a skillfully handled dinghy might sail. The question was, how to identify these gaps. The answer was ingenious. Peter and Currey bought a box of intakes, fished empty cigarette packets from little bins, and tacked them on to the posts on each side of the gaps to act as markers. Charles Currey completed the story:

> Then came the race. As we came onto the last beat—the 5th beat—we were lying second to John Winter in *Lightning*. We'd previously done well by going between our markers but the tide had now slackened so that it was no longer necessary to go close

inshore. After two long tacks only about half a mile to windward, we had closed right up on John. Then a few hundred yards
from the finishing line we crossed just in front of him on the
port tack and were able to keep him carefully covered to the
finish and so win the Prince of Wales' Cup at last.

Thunder won the race by sixteen seconds, with John Winter second in
Lightning and Stewart Morris third in *Alarm.* The stratagem that may have been
decisive in winning the race was "just an example," in Currey's words, "of the
detailed thought Peter put into everything he did. It was carefully discussed and
carefully dealt with, with naval precision."

For the summer of 1938 Peter commissioned yet another dinghy from Uffa Fox.
This time she was to be sailed according to a plan quite new in dinghy racing.
Normally the helmsman was the boss who sailed the boat and determined the
tactics, while the crew controlled the sails. Peter and John Winter decided to
merge the two roles. They would change places halfway, and the crew, not the
helmsman, would decide when to tack. Not only were they to work closely as a
team but they were to be the new boat's joint owners. Peter's winning boat in
1937 had been *Thunder,* John Winter's in 1934 had been *Lightning.* The new joint
boat was christened *Thunder and Lightning,* which her owners thought an irresistible combination.

The race for the cup was held in Falmouth Bay with a record number of
entries, fifty-two. Once again, Peter had a secret weapon. To keep the boat
from keeling over in a strong wind, normally both crew and helmsman sat on
the gunwale with their feet under a strap, and leaned out backward as far as they
could go. This practice was as old as sailing; Polynesians had followed it two
thousand years ago when they had clung to creepers tied to the masts of their
catamarans while they leaned back over the sea. Peter's idea was to fit the crew
with a simple harness which, clipped to the mast, would enable him to lean
much farther backward and to stay in that position for an indefinite time. He
tried out the device first at Wroxham Broad at dawn, in a flat calm and heavy
rain, with his fourteen-year-old brother, Wayland, as the crew, strapped into a
kind of straitjacket; modifications were needed and further trials carried out
with Charles Currey in a boat called *Storm Cock* belonging to Currey's father.
"We kept these experiments extremely secret," Currey said, "and we had the
harness underneath our zippers so nobody could see it. We actually painted the
wire blue and grey, Peter's camouflage colors, so it wasn't noticeable." They
called this invention the trapeze. In order to avoid charges of deception, on the
evening before the race Peter and Winter showed it in a pub where many of the
competitors had gathered. It was greeted with derision—a hare-brained idea—
and no one lodged an objection.

Peter was helmsman for the first half of the race, and made a poor start. Robert Hitchens in his homemade *Venture II* was slightly ahead when Winter brought the trapeze into action. The sight of Peter's crew apparently throwing himself backward overboard was so startling that the attention of other competitors was momentarily diverted. "For a critical ten seconds," Peter wrote, "Robert sailed his boat 'off the wind,' which allowed us to luff across his wake and get our wind clear." *Thunder and Lightning* surged ahead, and won the race by four minutes. Cries of "Not fair, not fair" went up after the race, but no one could point to a rule that disqualified the trapeze, and the fact that no objections had been raised beforehand clinched the matter. Nevertheless the dinghy committee of the Yacht Racing Association banned the device in all future races. The ban lasted for seventeen years and was then rescinded, and the trapeze is now in general use; while *Thunder and Lightning*, with the original trapeze belt, is now in the National Maritime Museum at Greenwich.

So, in the technique of dinghy racing, Peter made two major improvements that came to stay, the wooden centerboard and the trapeze. As in other matters, he was not an inventor who discovered revolutionary new skills, he was an innovator who improved existing ones. He would not have discovered the wheel, but he might have fitted it with stronger spokes. He was essentially a practical man.

CHAPTER SEVEN

Morning Flight

In five years Peter had bought four top-class international dinghies from the best small-boat builder in the country, possibly in the world. They were expensive. In addition he had his lighthouse and its growing collection of birds to maintain, his wildfowling and sailing forays to pay for, and the general expenses to meet of a young man who at no time displayed a parsimonious spirit. It was to the sale of his paintings that he looked to settle most of these commitments.

After his first one-man show in 1933, exhibitions at Ackermann's gallery became annual events up to and including 1940. They were orchestrated by his mother. Tirelessly, she led her horse to water but the problem was to make him drink. His quicksilver lifestyle left all too little time for serious painting, but when he did get down to business she was amazed. "No critic must know this and I scarcely ought to write it," she recorded in her diary on June 1936, "but the whole show of forty-eight pictures has been painted since April 18th when not a thing was begun." He had painted five pictures in four days, and the whole forty-eight had been completed in less than six weeks. And they caught the public fancy. "Eight pictures were sold while we were hanging them."

It was the sense of drama inherent in his paintings, the life he had instilled into his birds, that pleased many of his critics. "The roar of mighty flocks of wild geese rising upon thousands of wings, the swish of ducks descending into quiet pools, salt breezes and the chill of the air at dawn come to you when you look at these pictures," wrote Frances Pitt in *The Field*. "It is their great charm that they seem filled with understanding of the birds. From these canvases look out real beings, not mere patterns of paint; sagacious and wary geese ready to sense danger while it is yet afar, and the more happy-go-lucky ducks taking things as they come." The renowned ornithologist Lord William Percy made the same point. Of the painting *Pinkfeet Stubbling* he wrote: "These six geese seem to have pitched but a moment before. Their whole attitude speaks of a guilty conscience and lack of a sense of security that every self-respecting wild goose must be supposed to feel and certainly displays when he is tempted by man's grain from his rightful surroundings to the enclosed stubbles."

Another critic, writing anonymously in *Country Life*, detected an oriental influence. "The theme rather than the treatment brings to mind the great painters of the Far East." With oils, the painter could not attain the full flexibility of brushwork possible with watercolors, but Peter was "approaching the effect of tempera or watercolor by laying on his paint very thin. Indeed, one painting, an upright of a shoveller with beautiful green reflections in the water below, is Oriental even in shape and seems too delicate for its heavy wooden frame ... The painting of geese flying in a mist, and of ducks swimming with their black and white bodies reflected in the yellow water, also approaches the decorative conventions of the East." Probably this oriental influence came to Peter indirectly through the Swedish landscape and wildlife painter Bruno Liljefors (1860–1939), whose works he much admired. Liljefors had traveled in the East, and Japanese art in particular had inspired him.

In a fragment of autobiography written in 1945 and discovered only after his death, Peter wrote of his years at the Royal Academy Schools: "I was a bad painter with a certain facility for drawing. I was still deeply bitten with the pursuit of wildfowl and my paintings of them were regarded [by critics] with deep suspicion. I showed my work to the Fine Art Galleries but they saw no promise in it. Ackermann's Galleries however showed more perspicacity—I say that advisedly because though you may not like my pictures, or think they are any good as pictures, there is no denying that they were a goldmine."

His sharpest critic was not a professional but a lad eight or ten years his junior, an aspiring young painter and wildfowler who would now and then turn up at the lighthouse with a rucksack and nothing else. He was a nephew of Mrs. Henry Richardson, of County Fermanagh, called Brian D'Arcy Irvine, and described by Kathleen as "vague, absent, imprecise—a waif." There was nothing waiflike, however, about his opinion of Peter's paintings:

> I can't think why you waste your time covering large expanses of blue canvas and then put in little white birds with yellow wings on it, a thing I did last year I'd have you know. An eight-foot picture in the Akademy [sic] of course demands attention but it also in my opinion enlarges the sin. To go on year after year painting for the Akademy like Mr. Russel Flint is your only future ... Really Peter I am disgusted or at least I am rather fright-

ened that you are really beginning to come into the everlasting
rut from whence it is damn difficult to escape.

Peter did not take offense. If he was already in a rut it was a rut of his own
choosing, and greater painters than he had chosen to follow the same course.
Birds in their landscapes were what he loved and understood and was best at
painting, so he stuck to his last as, on a loftier plane, Stubbs had stuck to his
horses, and Dutch flower painters of the seventeenth and eighteenth centuries
to their flowers.

Another younger friend and fellow painter was to come to his defense.
"If you look not perhaps at his published work but at his unpublished things,"
Keith Shackleton was to write:

> you'll see that he loved ideas and experimenting with ideas, and
> he played games like any artist will with abstract painting. And
> he did some gorgeous portraits. I always had the concept that if
> you were drawing a head—a portrait—you roughed in the whole
> framework and then began on the detailed structure of the head.
> But Peter had such an incredible sense of proportion that he
> would start just somewhere—an eye, perhaps, then almost fin-
> ish that eye, then work across and do the bridge of the nose,
> then follow that down and perhaps do the other eye; he could
> preserve the scale from one to the other in a way I couldn't
> begin to do.

After his first exhibition had been a virtual sellout, Peter's prices were
substantially raised. The lowest price of any oil painting in 1933 was twelve
guineas for *A Pair of Mallards*. In the following year the lowest price was twenty-
eight guineas for *Suspicious Wigeon*, and in 1939 it was forty guineas each for
individual paintings of a whitefronted, greylag, and a brent goose. At the other
end of the scale his prices rose every year to reach a maximum of 220 guineas
for *Barnacle Geese* in 1939. During all this period there was no inflation; on the
contrary, prices fell. The total of the asking prices for the sale in 1939 would
have been, in modern values, about £60,000, of which the gallery would have
taken one-third. (In the words of one of its directors, "If Lady Kennet had anything to do with the arrangements, it could well have been as low as twenty-five
percent.") Kathleen noted that in 1939 he was making about £4,000 a year from
his paintings and prints, in those days a very handsome sum.

Private commissions helped to swell the bank account. Sir John Beale—
Peter had crewed for his son in the races in Toronto—commissioned a very
large painting to hang in his hall. It was the biggest canvas Peter had ever attempted to fill, and he put off the task until four days before his patron was due

to collect it. Using his largest brushes, he started on the sky, roughed in the birds and water, and at the end of the third day was left with a foreground of tall reeds still to be done. He had to admit defeat; the reeds could not be painted, single-handed, in a day. In this predicament, he followed the example of the Old Masters in whose studios assistants and students were kept busy painting details of the background and of the sitters' elaborate robes. He called in an assistant in the shape of his mother. Kathleen went to work on the reeds on the one side of the canvas, Peter on the other, and the finished product was drying on its easel when Sir John Beale arrived.

In financial terms, this turned out to be the most rewarding picture Peter ever painted. The rights of reproduction were bought by the Medici Society, which in 1930 had launched a "modern artists" series: Peter's contribution, called originally *Norfolk Spring-Shovellers and a Pair of Garganey* but renamed *Taking to Wing*, became the sixtieth print in the series. This print enjoyed a runaway success. The startling total of 355,423 copies sold by 1959 has been given, but they were not all true prints; greetings cards, Christmas cards, even table mats were included. Nevertheless, sales of prints as such were impressive: about ten thousand large sized prints and twenty-eight thousand smaller ones were sold after *Taking to Wing* was marketed in 1934.

From 1936 onward Ackermann's gallery published a regular output of prints after his work in limited and signed editions, selling first for three guineas each, then four guineas, and then for £4 14s 6d, a price that remained stable for thirteen years. In 1970 the edition was raised to 850 and the price to £160 a print, reflecting runaway inflation. Altogether, Ackermann's made prints of twenty-nine of Peter's paintings between 1936 and 1982, and sold very nearly all. And there were sidelines. The firm of Player's paid £1,000 for a set of twenty-five small paintings to be reproduced as cigarette cards, and Wedgwood's commissioned paintings of a dozen individual birds to decorate a set of plates. His portraits were in demand among his friends, and singled out for approval in his exhibitions. If perhaps not quite a gold mine—Peter never grew rich, because he spent so freely—painting was to remain the mainstay of his fluctuating income for the rest of his life.

Writing was another source of income. His first book was published by *Country Life* in a limited and signed edition, illustrated by several of his paintings reproduced in color, in the autumn of 1935. Despite a price of three guineas, at a time when novels were selling for seven and six (about thirty-seven pence), *Morning Flight* was an immediate success. The limited edition was followed in the spring of 1936 by an ordinary edition, the first of many which kept it in print until 1947, when the ninth edition appeared.

It was a very personal book. He told of his adventures in the estuaries and mud flats of East Anglia and the Fens, his enjoyment of its beauties, his discomforts and disappointments in simple and informal words, with no at-tempt at fine writing, philosophical reflection, or self-analysis. It was as if, com-ing in cold and wet to hot tea and bacon and eggs, he had poured out the tale of his experiences with all the spontaneity and freshness of the first-hand reporter, and often with a vivid turn of phrase. His aim, as with his paintings, was to communicate something of what he called his understanding of wild places, his personal response to the call of the wild geese. "I think there is a wild corner in the human spirit," he wrote elsewhere, "that answers the call of the wild geese."

What Peter had done was to discover a new country, the Empty Quarter of his native land, and to bring back travelers' tales of its remoteness and beauty: a country that few of his readers had heard of, fewer still had seen for them-selves, and which was dismissed by most of those who had as a lot of dreary mud and boring flatness. Its fauna was stranger to the average reader than In-dian tigers or African lions, and while stirring episodes concerned with hunting lions and tigers were the stuff of many books and movies, tales of stalking ducks and geese in punts were not. While this latter pursuit might not appear to be as dangerous, risks from angry seas and fickle tides were at least as great as risks from charging lions with a white hunter standing at the sportsman's elbow. "You don't need to go to Timbuktu," Peter remarked, "to lead an adventurous life."

However, it was not so much adventure that he wrote of as sensation: the feelings stirred in him by the lonely, wild and empty nature of the terrain and the mystery of the migrant wildfowl:

> Suddenly a goose called ... All that day they arrived in skeins of thirty and forty and fifty, and all next day too, until there were five thousand geese on the high sand. They have come south again to exist against incredible odds in a land of human beings, until the season of midnight sun thaws out their northern breed-ing places. When the moon is full they will pass unseen in the steel-grey sky to their feeding grounds, but their cry will echo across the flat fields. Like a symphony of Beethoven, the call of the geese is everlasting, and those who have once known and loved it can never tire of hearing it.

Morning Flight ends on the same note, celebrating that sound which, heard at dusk or dawn or by moonlight over the saltings, was for him the true call of the wild.

> And I hear the geese calling—a music of indescribable beauty and wildness, and fitness for the flat marsh which is their home. The moon has just risen, very large and orange over the sea, and the tide is high, half covering the salting, and filling the creeks right up to the sea wall. There are a few wigeon calling as they

fly along the shore, and away to the west a big pack of knots and dunlins twitter incessantly. Just an occasional note reminds one that the geese are there, waiting for enough light to come in and feed on the potato fields over the bank. Suddenly there is a little burst of calling—the first ones are up—they are coming.

While Peter loved his birds with passion he continued to kill them with relish. Part of the explanation of this paradox lay in the fact that wildfowling was a sport at which he excelled, and very few people willingly give up a skill they are very good at and therefore enjoy. Nor had the anti-blood sports movement taken its hold on public opinion; hunt saboteurs and animal-rights activists lay in the future. Nevertheless, qualms had begun to emerge in Peter's mind as long ago as the winter of 1931–2, when, while shooting one day with Haig Thomas, twenty-three greylag geese fell to their guns. Would it not have been better, they speculated, to have brought them back alive, tamed them, and bred from them perhaps? "So we set out to devise a method of catching them." This was the origin of the improved contraption for netting wildfowl which he and two or three of his companions were to perfect.

Meanwhile he went on killing wildfowl, but with gathering doubts as to the propriety of killing in such numbers. Very often, probably more often than not, a long and gruelling punt-hunt yielded nothing, or perhaps a single bird, but on a good day, or night, the slaughter was great. On a December night in 1932 he and a companion shot eighty pinkfooted geese—the seventy-two that had so impressed the Duke of Norfolk, and a further eight picked up later. It was too much. "A great bag of pinkfeet should only be dreamed about," he wrote in *Morning Flight*. "The species can ill afford to lose so many individuals." A typically British compromise was agreed among these wildfowling friends; in future, bags of geese were to be limited to a dozen. Twelve of those eighty geese were only wounded and were taken home alive. Three died, but the remaining nine recovered and were cared for either by Will Tinsley or by others among Peter's friends.

He himself had started a small collection. Soon after he had moved into the lighthouse, he had fenced in a small pond and installed twelve pinkfooted geese bought from flight-netters at Terrington marsh. In the following February (1934) his makeshift pen was wrecked by gales and a mighty spring tide, and all the pinioned geese swam away. Peter gave them up for lost, but next morning one of the party was waiting for his breakfast where the pen had been. He had walked back. The rest were brought in by friendly wildfowlers, except for three that had been sold, and one shot. Those eight birds were the founders of a wildfowl collection that was to become the largest and most complete in the world.

There were several ways in which a collector could acquire his birds. He could bring home wounded ones and, instead of finishing them off, nurse them back to health. Those merely wing-tipped would generally be as good as new in a couple of days, and even the more severely wounded ones would often heal themselves. Another method, more expensive of course, was to buy from dealers. These specialists found a profitable market among landowners who enjoyed the sight of ornamental ducks and geese on lakes set in landscapes designed by Capability Brown or his disciples. The brothers Noel and Ronald Stevens of Walcot Hall near Lydbury in Shropshire supplied the bulk of Peter's needs. In 1933 their prices for ducks ranged from £2 a pair to £20—scaups— and for geese from £3 to £45—emperors. The equivalent in modern terms of about £500 a pair was quite a lot to pay.

Another method was to catch the birds by trickery. Either they could be lured into traps such as the Borough Fen decoy, or on to ponds and lakes by means of decoy ducks which deceived wild ones into supposing that they had found a safe haven, a technique devised by North American Indians at least a thousand years ago. Or decoy ducks could be used to entice wild birds to land on places where a net had been spread to entrap them. This was the technique used by plover-netters who were still in business in the 1930s on the East Anglian marshes. They belonged to a dying race: the race of Fenmen who got their living from that flat, dyke-patterned landscape which flooded in winter, and in summer became the resort of nesting birds, abundant wildflowers, and grazing cattle. Their small, dun-colored houses in isolated villages seemed to hunch their backs against a biting, unimpeded wind. In summer the Fenmen cut canes from ozier beds, stripped and treated them, and wove baskets which they sunk in rivers to catch eels. In winter they stalked wild ducks in punts with their long, lethal cannon; they caught moles whose skins they made into waistcoats; they were expert skaters, swam since infancy, loved their booze, and were tough as the eelskins their women made into garters.

The plover-netter spread his net on water just deep enough to conceal it, and beneath the flightpaths of flocks of plovers coming in at dawn to wash themselves after feeding in muddy potato fields. Tempted by the decoys, they alighted on the water, and when twenty or thirty of them were in the right position, the man would jerk the rope which released the springs that con-trolled the poles, and the net rose and folded over the birds like the page of a book. The netter quickly killed the birds, extracted them from the net, flung them into a sack and set the trap ready for the next lot. Plovers were there in tens of thousands in those days. One of the last surviving Fenmen, Ernie James, recalled his record morning's catch of 240 birds. As a boy, he cycled six miles to the railway station with a sack of plovers over each handle-bar, each sack con-taining up to a hundred birds, to catch the London train. Back came substantial payments from Leadenhall market dealers, who had no trouble selling plovers to restaurants whose customers accounted them a delicacy. In 1947 plovers were declared a protected species, and plover netting on the marshes came to an end.

It was one thing to catch smallish birds like plovers, quite another to net geese which were much more intelligent and perhaps ten times as heavy. This Peter set out to do with the help of several friends. In August 1932 an old plover-netter, Barney Shawl, gave him and Will Tinsley a demonstration. Peter adopted Shawl's procedure as his model and had two similar nets made, of different meshes, and delivered to The Poplars. The prize, he wrote, would be "a bag of fine live geese instead of bloody corpses."

During much of that autumn and winter, when he should have been painting in the basement of Burlington House, Peter was squelching over the sodden fields of Lincolnshire or crouching in ditches, while geese settled every-where except on the patch on which his net was so placed as to catch them. He had fitted torsion springs instead of ropes to propel the poles, and made other improvements. Before dawn on a December day he, Haig Thomas, and Dalgety took the net to a field near Holbeach and put it in place, setting some decoy ducks to windward. Soon parties of geese were flying in until about a thousand had settled, a few within range. Peter pulled the rope; the trap sprang; one of the poles snapped; the geese took off; the experiment ended in disaster. Dalgety was scathing, Haig Thomas rather more consoling. Three weeks later, a new trap was ready, the poles made of tubular steel instead of wood. Peter spent Christmas Day 1932 sitting by the net waiting for the geese. They never came. Two days later he was again on Holbeach marsh, when four birds pitched within range. The net swung over, three birds escaped, but one was entangled. It was a job to release it, but soon "my very first netted goose" was, literally, in the bag.

Two days later he netted another singleton, and on the second day of 1933 on "one of the nastiest mornings I ever ventured forth in" with a gale blowing and pelting rain, a third bird, "a very nice female in beautiful condi-tion," brought his tally to three pinkfeet. They were pinioned, and fetched up at the lighthouse to join the growing collection. (To pinion a bird, you clip its wingtips to prevent the feathers growing again, so making it flightless.) Three geese may seem a poor reward for months of cogitation, cold, discomfort, and frustration, but Peter did not think so. He had discovered a new sport. "Not only is the catching of wild geese alive far more diffficult than shooting them, but also far more exciting." He had lain in wait for four hours to catch a single goose, but it "was alive and well and worth a dozen strung up by their necks."

Nevertheless he went on killing geese. An offer from The Field of a week's free shooting, all expenses paid, on the plains of Hungary, in return for a couple of articles, proved irresistible. In March 1936 he and a cousin, Eric Bruce, ar-rived at a small village called Hortobagy on the great Hungarian plain. The migration of whitefronted geese bound for their breeding grounds in Siberia was in full spate, and geese in transit were settling on the plain in almost un-imaginable, and certainly uncountable, numbers. "If there were not more than one hundred thousand geese, there were certainly not less," Peter reported.

The short-grassed plains surrounding Hortobagy were dotted with shallow pools, perfect staging posts for migrating birds. Comfortable quarters for humans were provided at a *csarda*, whose chimney offered a nesting site for storks. Before dawn each morning Peter, Bruce, and their guide climbed into a cart which took them to the shooting grounds where pits had been dug, each pit 5 feet deep and with a seat on one side, to conceal the shooters. With the chilly dawn came vast flocks of geese that landed with a noise like the roar of an express train. Shooting them, Peter admitted, was too easy. To Michael Bratby he reported a bag of about 350 to his own gun during the week, including 103 in one morning. He had planned from the start to take back lightly wounded birds for his collection. He and Bruce gave them first aid at the cs*arda* before crating them for transport to England.

It was the redbreasted goose (*Brantis ruficollis*), a small, neat bird with a beautifully patterned plumage in red, white, and black, that Peter particularly wanted to capture. On two successive mornings he saw from his pit two small flights go over among the whitefronts, and this was the highlight of the trip so far as he was concerned. But none was killed or wounded.

"Peter returned characteristically by air with fifteen live geese in crates," his mother noted on March 24, 1936. "I met him at Croydon first as he was having trouble with the Customs over his strange cargo." Trouble with the customs at Croydon, then the terminus of Imperial Airways, became endemic as Peter's collection grew. He was not always there to sort it out.

For some time Bill and Kathleen had been looking for a permanent home in the country where they could spend their holidays, instead of taking a different place each year. In February 1936 they moved into Fritton Hithe, a sprawling thatched house near Great Yarmouth in Norfolk equipped with two grand pianos and with a garden running down to a lake where they and their guests—there were nearly always guests—could fish, swim, and sail in small boats. There were also greenhouses with grapes and peaches, and a superb herbaceous border. (Palgrave had put his *Golden Treasury* of verse together here.) On a day in September 1936, having deposited their son Wayland at Stowe school in Buckinghamshire, Kathleen arrived at Fritton Hithe "very tired, and got a telephone from Imperial Airways that a crate of live wild geese had arrived at Croydon, would we fetch them with £6 15 2d to pay. After much cajoling they consented to send them and also to take a check. After endless enquiries found Pete on the telephone in Westmorland ... Finally went to bed and was very sick. The geese plonked into the water every few minutes under my window all night—and yet I am *still* fond of my sons!"

In the following November (1936), Peter was lured back to Hungary by his growing passion for redbreasted geese. He had stayed at Woburn, and the Duchess of Bedford had given him a pair. Now he wanted to see redbreasts in the wild and to capture several if he could. His departure for foreign parts was seldom uneventful. "He was to start next morn leaving at six," wrote his mother. "He set his alarm clock for five, at five-thirty as I heard nothing I went to see. He was sound asleep and the clock had failed. In four minutes he was out of the house not shaved or washed and I had a hectic four minutes trying to ring a taxi. Nothing answered. However he caught one and set off in an awful state. A telegram at seven thirty said safe so far at Vienna. Darling Pete, I wish I didn't adore him so, it isn't good for either of us."

It was mid-November when he left England, and in Hungary winter had come, with blizzards and snowstorms. Nevertheless he pushed on across Romania to the Black Sea and the Danube's delta, which he explored in a sleigh, to be rewarded by the sight of fourteen redbreasted geese in amongst a large flock of whitefronts. All he could do was to look at them through a mist of powdery snow, but he had seen enough to know that he must return at a better time of year. Back at Hortobagy he found that the csarda's owner, Nemeth Ur, had saved for him sixteen geese lightly wounded during the autumn season.

Everyone at the csarda welcomed him as a long-lost friend, gypsies serenaded him with his favorite songs, and even composed a new one to celebrate his hunt for redbreasted geese. After setting out for home from Budapest by air with three crates of protesting birds, his airplane ran into trouble and out of fuel, made a forced landing just in time. Fog enveloped England, and at Cologne he and the geese caught a train for the Hook of Holland, by the skin of his teeth and by the barbs of their feathers. In due course all arrived safely at the lighthouse.

The question of who was to look after Peter's birds during his frequent absences had naturally arisen. When out on Terrington marsh one day in 1928 with David Haig Thomas, while both were still undergraduates at Cambridge, they had had an altercation with a notorious poacher, who had claimed a goose shot by Haig Thomas. Fortunately the dispute ended peaceably, for the poacher was also middle-weight boxing champion of Lincolnshire and had won fifty-seven fights. His name was Kenzie Thorpe. His father was a gypsy who had married a local girl and raised a large family at Sutton Bridge. (His grandmother was named Leviathon, he had an uncle called Emperor, and his full name was Mackenzie.) From the age of twelve he had virtually lived out on the marshes poaching everything poachable with snare, catapult, twenty-two rifle, and antiquated shotgun. He knew inside out the ways of local wildlife and read the signals of the weather; he was tough as beef jerky and resourceful as a monkey. Kenzie was one year older than Peter by the calendar and many years older in experience, and when the young man lately from Cambridge had settled into his lighthouse, the young poacher began to take an interest in the former's experiments in keeping wild birds in captivity.

Before long Kenzie had more or less attached himself to the lighthouse, and been entrusted with the care of the collection during its owner's absences. No one could have called Kenzie reliable but he was an engaging rascal, and Peter took a chance, hoping that his birds would not end up in a poulterer's shop, by taking him on as a part-time curator. By then (April 1936) the collection had grown to thirty-two ducks—mallard, pintail, wigeon, and shelduck—and twenty geese—pinkfeet, brent, greylag, and one bean goose bought for £1 from Kenzie, who had caught it.

Intrigued by his boss's painting, Kenzie decided to have a go himself, using that boss's brushes, paints, and canvas during his absence. Kenzie revealed an unexpected talent. As Peter's fame grew, visitors would turn up at the lighthouse to be shown round by Kenzie, and sometimes to buy one of Kenzie's "genuine Peter Scotts." Another source of income lay in taking out parties of wildfowlers in Peter's punt. They paid £1 per man per flight, a modest charge considering his experience and skill. His biographer, Colin Willock, reckoned that in 1951 he shot one-and-a-half percent of the whole world population of pinkfeet, and that by 1962 he had killed in all some 3,700 geese, as well as 250 mute swans.

Peter continued to employ him until the outbreak of war, when Kenzie was rejected by the navy because of a crippled finger broken by a saucepan hurled by his mother. The introduction of rationing led to a bonanza. Pheasants fetched ten shillings each instead of a shilling, geese twelve and sixpence, even green plovers one and sixpence. Before long Kenzie was making an average of nine pounds a week, over twenty-five pounds on one or two occasions, for him a fortune. He built a houseboat, towed it to a mooring near Shep Whites, and used it as a base for his wildfowling excursions. He married, fathered six children, and settled down in Sutton Bridge. After his death in 1976 his houseboat was burned with his personal possessions inside it, in true Romany style.

By the later 1930s Peter's crowded life had achieved a pattern. Sailing in summer, travel in autumn, wildfowling in winter, and in the spring he would settle down to serious painting in the lighthouse in order to prepare for his summer exhibition. Each year his mother recruited a different celebrity to open it; after Sir Samuel Hoare in 1933 came John Buchan in 1934, Hugh Walpole in 1935, and in 1936 the Astronomer Royal, Sir James Jeans. The Royal Academy continued to be standoffish. For four years running, from 1934 to 1937, they hung only a single picture and skied it, which, he admitted, was appropriate in the case of birds. After 1937 there was a gap of over twenty years before a picture was accepted.

As a sideline, he illustrated a number of books, including a collection of essays by his stepfather called *A Bird in the Bush*. The somewhat prudish disdain of anthropomorphizing animals had not yet taken hold, and Bill indulged freely in this now unfashionable approach. He told of a pair of mallards who visited the pond at Leinster Corner, "an elderly pair much attached to each other but realistic in their approach to parenthood," since the female, Florence, "a student of the works of Malthus," regularly broke each egg as she laid it.

Beneath his celebration of the pleasure he derived from the company of birds, in A *Bird in the Bush* Bill anticipated in remarkably exact terms the warnings his stepson was to deliver many years later:

> The shape and nature [of our species] have arrived at their present forms as a result of long ages during which they have been moulded by their surroundings, and particularly their living surroundings ... Man, trees, birds and butterflies all owe their present nature to each other. If that be so, it is something of an experiment for man to take himself out of the company of trees, grass, butterflies and birds, as he has increasingly taken himself in the life of the great cities for the last thousand years or so. It is as if an animal were to make up its mind that it could get along without an alimentary system ... Our experiment is nothing less than an effort to isolate ourselves from all other forms of life, and it has for its logical consequence that we should destroy all other forms, and leave *homo sapiens* the only living species.

It is reasonable to suppose that during Bill's walks with his stepson on the Marlborough downs these matters would have been touched upon, to be stored away in Peter's mind.

By the time A *Bird in the Bush* appeared in print in 1936, Bill had received his peerage and retired from politics. He had been "kicked upstairs" for refusing to allow compensation to be paid to slum landlords, and had joined an informal team, recruited by Sir Archibald Jamieson and named "the Lifeboat," which rescued troubled businesses from bankruptcy. But his heart was at the Lacket, and in the service of his wife. On a day in 1935 her failure to coax him out of a fit of depression had reduced her to tears. "*How* could she not know," he penciled into her diary after her death, "that by now I only lived in her." Probably she did know. "I don't think," she wrote, "that Bill likes anything whole-heartedly except Wayland and me and Spinoza." When motoring between Fritton Hithe and London, she recorded, "he said Gray's Elegy to me on the way up. Last time he said the whole of the Ancient Mariner, 11 Penseroso, Lycidas. This time he said some Shelley and Kubla Khan. Not only does he say them without hitch or hesitation, but so very beautifully. I have a glorious possession. What an amazing mind it is!"

At the Lacket Bill would often read to his son and stepson: Plato, Herodotus, Shakespeare's sonnets, Dante, and Dickens are among the classics named. His learning and enthusiasm must have left a mark on Peter's mind, perhaps at an unconscious level. But it was his bird lore rather than his love of Herodotus and Spinoza that really sank in.

CHAPTER EIGHT

Searching for Redbreasted Geese

"Pete's train left for Persia at 11 A.M. At 10:05 he was painting a picture in his pajamas in his bedroom." Kathleen added: "Oh dear he looked so like Con sitting at his desk making a list of his requirements. I almost expected him to look up and say 'Now girl, how many pounds of pepper will sixty men use in three years?'" Thus Peter set out in December 1937 in a renewed search for the redbreasted goose, hoping to solve the puzzle surrounding its migrations. He intended to recoup some, at least, of the expedition's costs by writing articles for *Country Life* and other journals, and possibly a book. His baggage included a pair of guns, a flight-net for catching geese and a tailcoat for evening wear. In Baghdad he stayed with the Ambassador, Sir Archibald Clark-Kerr, glad to have brought his tails but in trouble about a permit for his guns. After waiting vainly for a week for the permit, he set off without it in a hired car along the Golden Road to Samarkand, crossing the Persian frontier at Khosrovi. In Tehran he found comfortable quarters in the compound of the British Consul, Christopher Summerhayes, who helped to plan the rest of his expedition.

Peter's hopes of finding his quarry in large numbers along the shores of the Caspian sea were based on a monograph by a Russian ornithologist called Alpheraky, *The Geese of Europe and Asia*, and on observations by subsequent travelers. In 1886 a Dr. Walter had "met this beautiful *Kazarka* [its Russian name] in colossal flocks" in the region, and a few years later a M. Zhitnikov had found "the whole eastern shore of the lake thickly covered with a black mass of them which flew off to feed on the steppe." So it seemed reasonably certain that the geese flew south from their breeding grounds in northern Siberia to winter in the region of the Caspian sea, which lay mostly in the USSR, forbidden territory to travelers. But the southern portion lay in Persia, as Iran had been called until 1935. So it was to Iran that Peter went. After much consultation with the works of Alpheraky and Walter, he identified two areas where the goose seemed most likely to be found. One was in marshes round the mouth of the river Atrek, which formed, for part of its course, the boundary between Iran and Russian Turkestan. The other was in the region of a lagoon near Pahlavi on the Caspian's southwestern corner, and it was there that Peter decided first to search.

Setting out from Tehran in a taxi whose driver weighed 280 pounds and whistled like a wigeon, they crossed the Elburz mountains by the Chalus pass at over 18,000 feet. Down on the fertile plain bordering the Caspian, an extraordinary sight met his eye: concourse after concourse of ducks, looking solid as sandbanks in the water, mostly pochards, tufted ducks, and mallards. He reckoned he had seen up to two hundred thousand birds along a forty-mile stretch of coast. Then came an even more fantastic sight: a solitary and enormous hotel. "It was vast and completely surrounded by the most elaborate gardens and parterres. There were banana palms about and bronze tigers and eagles. There were fountains and gravel paths and geometric shapes and concrete roads with promenades, and at the top a hotel with, I should say, a thousand bedrooms." It was completely deserted: a monument to the ambition of the current Shah, Reza Shah Pahlavi, to create on the Caspian sea a leisure resort that would rival France's Cote d'Azur. Ramsar was its name: a name that was to become familiar to him, and to the world of conservation, forty years later. His journey ended at Rascht.

A garbled story was current in Tehran about a peculiar way of catching ducks, done in boats equipped with a strong light, a loud gong, and a large butterfly net. Peter decided to investigate. After making contact with some local fishermen, he was taken to a reed-thatched hut on an island in a lagoon near Pahlavi, where after dark the party transhipped into two very small puntlike boats. One had a hood made of reeds, rather like a cobra's hood, in the bows, protecting a small mud platform to take the flare; the other had a large brass gong in the stern.

> As soon as we started, the man in the stern began to beat the gong with a rapid stroke and he did not stop until we returned ... The purpose of this is obviously to drown the sound of the approaching boats We set off with a lump of bulrush fluff dipped in paraffin flaming away merrily under the hood, a very uneven light flickering a good deal and having to be re-fueled by putting on a handful more every two minutes or so.

Amidships stood a man with a net on a long pole. The ducks, confused by gong and flare, tried to hide in rushes or swam about hoping not to be seen, but a high-pitched squeak from one of the men persuaded them to take off, and then:

there was a swish and he [a duck] was in the net, which was then held upright so that he came tumbling down into the loose part of the net which hung in a sort of bag. From this he was taken out and had his wings locked. They always keep their birds alive because they have to kill them with a knife which they can do more easily when they get back.

The bag on the first time round was three mallards and one teal. Peter was reproached for wringing the birds' necks, which he did because he thought they were uncomfortable with locked wings. In his companions' estimation the birds' discomfort did not weigh against the Prophet's injunction in the Koran to cut the throat of every animal intended for human consumption while it was still alive.

After a break for tea and a chicken pilaf in the hut, the party started out again and this time Peter wielded the net. He had not yet learned the art of "scooping," and when he clapped the net over a mallard on the water it dived and swam away. "I went to my camp bed in the hut with a very high opinion of duck netters, about six of whom slept in the hut all round me." Next evening, after a lesson in "scooping," he was back in the boat and scooped a teal, leaned out to catch a mallard in his hand, and netted another teal in the air. He found it intensely exciting. But where were the *kazarkas*? He saw pelicans, greylags, whooper swans and ducks of many kinds in plenty, but not a feather of a redbreasted goose.

Retracing his steps to try the Caspian's eastern shore, he spent a night in the palatial Ramsar Hotel where he and Prince Peter of Greece, unexpectedly encountered, were the only guests. He was carrying a meticulously drawn picture of the quarry which he showed to everyone of whom he made inquiries; one and all they nodded and said yes, there were plenty of those, the *Ghazal Gohz*, plenty of all kinds of birds in Iran. At Bandar-i-Gaz on the Caspian's southeastern shore he found a guide who was quite positive that the bird was to be seen at a spot not far away. Peter was elated. "The Great Search may be at an end." He and the consul Christopher Summerhayes, come from Tehran to join him, hired a ramshackle boat which quickly filled with Peter's driver, the guide, a cook, Ismail his German-speaking interpreter, two policemen, three net catchers, and six opium-smoking boatmen. Feeling like characters in *The Hunting of the Snark* they set sail to discover the *kazarka*, no less elusive than the snark. The guide pointed proudly to "a great bright pink line of birds" on the water—the *Ghazal Ghoz*. They were flamingos.

Although the *kazarka* had eluded him, Peter was not downhearted. He decided to return to the *murdab* (meaning marsh, lagoon, dead water) near Pahlavi, in order to master the art of flare-and-gong netting and, if possible, to capture some live birds to add to his collection. His toughness was extraordinary. He did not merely tolerate discomfort, he invited it. As well as catching ducks from boats, the local wildfowlers trapped them in nets spread on the ground, or rather mud. Peter spread a net himself and built a hide beside it in which he lay, immobile on his stomach, for nine hours each day and for four days on end. In this position he scribbled, and scribbled legibly, copious notes on all that was going on amongst the birds. It was January, and bitterly cold. At night he shared a tiny hut, only 4 feet high, with six other netters, and in the middle was a fire which filled the hut with smoke. The fug was stifling, and when he emerged at four-thirty A.M., he felt sick and dizzy. His clothes were seldom dry.

Iran was uneasily digesting changes brought about by the determination of the Shah to break free of Islamic tradition and to Westernize his country. Hats were a symbol of this transformation. Islamic headgear was out; for men, either the homburg or trilby or the Pahlavi hat, a soft cap such as that worn in the West by chauffeurs, was compulsory. "It is an Alice in Wonderland country," Peter wrote to his mother. "There is a station in Tehran as big as Waterloo but only two trains a week, one in and one out. There is no water supply or drainage but they are seriously preparing a system of pipes which will be the water supply by day and the sewer by night. There are enormous roundabouts in villages making four cross roads, but two of the four lead straight into walls—they have such things in the West so why should a little matter like there being only one road through a town prevent it from having a crossroads and a roundabout." But the landscape was marvelous, the country "alive with friendly people," and alive with wildfowl too.

There were, however, difficulties. A permit was needed to take photographs, and Peter's restricted him to photographing wild birds. He had been seen to train his camera on other objects, and on two occasions the police had politely but firmly requested him to surrender his films. On the first occasion he had managed to substitute a roll of unexposed film. On the second, he had no unexposed film to surrender. Explaining that he needed darkness to extract the film from his camera, he had made a tent of his overcoat and slipped a small tube of ointment into the film's container. So he was not surprised when the day of reckoning dawned on Tehran's railway station. The timely arrival of the British Consul, an apologetic explanation—all a mistake—Peter's charm and, no doubt, the fact that he was staying at the Embassy, combined to get him off the hook. After some shopping he set out for Baghdad in the courier's car bearing the diplomatic bag.

In mid-February his mother met him at Croydon. "There was my preposterous Pete dressed in a Persian yellow sheepskin coat, he had come in the oilman Reckitt's private plane. It was a joy and rapturous relief to have the creature home from a really high adventure. He has been gone two and a half months." A lecture to members of the Royal Geographical Society followed. "He spoke very clearly, his language was simple and straightforward, he carried you along with him and I dare swear no one was bored."

He had cast the day-by-day story of his adventures into the form of letters to Michael Bratby, which he intended to work up into a book. A contract with a publisher was actually signed, but he never completed the revision. He was too busy. The idleness of which his mother had complained had been honed away; he had become the strenuous man his father had hoped for; but strenuous for what? Merely, it seemed at times, for indulgence in any pursuit that pleased him. By the time he had, in snatches, kneaded his manuscript into a more or less acceptable shape, Hitler's intention to conquer the rest of Europe could no longer be ignored; gas masks had been issued and trenches dug in Hyde Park; although Hitler's false promises made to Neville Chamberlain in Munich secured a year's postponement, a young man's adventures in the region of the Caspian sea were no longer deemed likely to interest the British public. The book never appeared.

Ironically, the geese that had eluded him in Iran proved simple to obtain at home. About a year after his return, he heard of twenty-five pairs of wild-caught red-breasts on offer by a Belgian dealer for £50 a pair. The dealer accepted £350 for the lot. Peter sold seven pairs for the full price, and thus got eighteen pairs for nothing. His bird collection was growing apace. He—or more likely Bill—had discovered that the Inland Revenue would accept the cost of buying and keeping "bird models" as a legitimate expense to be set against income derived from painting them. He enclosed seven acres of saltmarsh and seawall in a dog- and fox-proof fence, and many species bred there. His first collection was in being.[1]

Permanent residents were pinioned, and were joined by wild birds who came to visit and enjoy free meals. One such was Anabel. She was a young Pinkfooted goose who flew in to join her co-specifics in September 1936, having evidently lost contact with her family. She spent the winter at the lighthouse, and stayed on after the normal time for setting off on the northbound migration had come and gone. But on a night in May 1937 she departed, and Peter did not expect to see her again. On October 9, 1937 he heard a cry from a speck in the sky, and down she came without hesitation to settle a dozen yards away from Peter and his bucket of corn—a "plump little round person ... I was overwhelmed," he wrote, "with joy and relief and wonder." She wintered there, but in May 1938 instinct summoned her, alone at first, to join the northward migration. He looked out for her in the following October, but in vain. Four out of five pinkfooted geese that wintered in the British Isles were believed to fall victim to wildfowlers' guns.

The spring and early summer of 1938 saw another successful exhibition at Ackermann's galleries, and his second win in the Prince of Wales' cup—the year of the trapeze. Then he set out for Canada, again in the *Empress of Britain*, to race against the Toronto yacht club with John Winter in their jointly owned dinghy *Thunder and Lightning*. The Canadians won by three matches to one.

For some time plans had been brewing to stage a one-man show of Peter's paintings in New York, and arrangements were finalized to hold an exhibition at Arthur Harlow's gallery on Fifty-seventh Street in November 1938. Before it opened, he decided to travel about North America to study the great variety of its wildfowl, in order to equip himself to write a monumental work he was planning on the wild geese of the world. He was especially interested in the greater snow goose, a handsome white bird with black wingtips which bred in the north of Greenland and in several Arctic islands, and wintered mainly in marshes bordering the St. Lawrence river in Quebec. By mid-October most of the birds had arrived and Peter was taken by Colonel Eric Mackenzie to a duck shooting clubhouse on the edge of the marsh where, from a glass-enclosed veranda, the geese could be seen at closer quarters than Peter had ever seen living wild geese (except for Anabel) before. "So ended an hour and a half of thrills piled upon thrills and a never-to-be forgotten day," he wrote to Winter. From the glass-enclosed veranda he had watched snow geese, with some blue geese amongst them, advance upon the clubhouse literally in thousands, until a great mob of them was cropping grass, preening and flapping, quarreling and taking flight, right up to the walls of the house. Years later, when he built his studio at Slimbridge, he took this extralarge window for his model, set his easel beside it, and through it watched the wildfowl that gathered on the lake outside to within 3 or 4 feet of the studio's wall.

Dr. Frank Chapman, director of the bird division of the American Museum of Natural History, put him in touch with leading ornithologists across the United States, and his friends the Paul Hammonds lent him a cottage on their Long Island estate to use as a base. The Hammonds had a sculptor stepdaughter. "I'm a little bit in love with this sculptor girl who is a funny plain girl with a turned-up nose and the most enormously long eyelashes you have ever seen," he told John Winter. As a distraction, he experimented with the Iranian method of catching ducks on a lake in Connecticut as the guest of Dillon Ripley, "a most charming young man of twenty-five who has lately been round the world as an ornithologist;" this was a profession in which Ripley was to win international renown. Peter, Dillon Ripley and another young man, Hugh Birkhead, borrowed a cymbal from a band to understudy for the gong and a lamp left overnight by a road-repairing gang to act as the flare; then they embarked in a canoe, Peter wielding a net made to the Iranian design. American mallards behaved exactly like Iranian ones, trying to hide in reeds and scurrying on shore. The hunters had some near misses, but caught none.

Peter had left behind unfinished business and was still working on his second book. Following the success of *Morning Flight*, *Country Life* had commissioned another on the same lines, to be called *Wild Chorus*, scheduled for publication in the autumn of 1939 and illustrated, as before, by his paintings. The paintings but not the text were done when Peter took off for North America. He wrote the last chapter in a schooner cruising on Lake Ontario while its owner's wife knitted him a pair of spotted socks. The manuscript was sent to his mother and to Bill, who had undertaken to correct it and deliver it to the publishers in a hurry. Bill was candid. "I'm afraid I do not think that some of the letter press is as good as you can do. Where you have taken pains it is good,

where you have not taken pains I don't think it is good enough. It seems to me
that the places where you have not taken pains are those where you have just
stuck in letters and other second-hand material to make up the book.'

Peter wrote respectfully while in an aeroplane flying to Los Angeles to
thank Bill for his trouble. 'You have no idea how nice it feels to know … Personally I like reading letters, but then I'm so nearly illiterate anyway that this
in itself is probably a good reason against it.' The publishers were both patient
and quick. *Wild Chorus* apeared in late November 1938 and was sold out before
publication, a limited edition of 1,250 copies having been subscribed at the
handsome sum of five guineas a copy. The author's royalty was one guinea a
copy. The book was immediately reprinted, and an ordinary edition followed
in September 1939. 'He is making a great deal of money,' his mother wrote,
'but also spending a great deal. His Persian expedition cost a great deal, and he
has built himself a lovely studio at the lighthouse. These are both legitimate
expenses, but the money he is spending on buying birds amazes me. He is one
of, if not the, finest collector of wildfowl in England, but he ought not to buy
birds to my way of thinking. He is an artist, not a dealer.'

Like its predecssor, *Wild Chorus* was a mixture of evocative passes expressing
his delight in the wildness and romance of 'mysterious birds coming from faraway
northern lands impelled by an unknown force and kept infallible on their course
by an unknown sense', and factual accounts of his wildfowling experiences. He
wrote with gusto of a 'great occasion' when, with John Winter and Stewart Morris,
they had shot between them twenty ducks at Leighton Moss, driven furiously to
the Lake District where they shot two stags, then back to the marsh for more duck
shooting and to bed at the Ship inn at eleven o'clock. Their day's bag was one
hundred and twenty-nine ducks and geese, plus the two stags. Peter was still killing
the thing he loved without managing to resolve the paradox. He thought *Wild
Chorus* a better book than *Morning Flight*. The critics liked it, and its sales fulfilled the
hopes of its publishers and reduced Peter's overdraft.

The same could not be said of the exhibition of his paintings that duly
opened in New York. 'The show has not been going with a swing so far as sales are
concerned,' he wrote to this mother. 'Enormous numbers of very smart people are
there all the time. So far i have sold only four, and vefy tiresoely they are all new
ones painted here. The prices were too high—30 x 20 at $750 was too much—I
sold one at that, £160. So now we have printed the catalogue again and reduced
them a little to see if that makes any difference." The groundwork Kathleen had
put in before each show had played a more important part in the success of his
exhibitions than he had realized. "I haven't educated them over here to my high
prices, like I have done for the last six years in England," he wrote to Winter. After
about a week, during which he gave several lectures, he escaped from the hectic
social life and demanding engagements of New York, heading first for California.

There was a great deal to be learned about the management of wildfowl from authorities in the United States. Many "refuges" were well established, some under federal and some under state control, to provide safe havens for migrants bound to and from Alaska and northern Canada. The low limits set on individual bags—ten ducks, two pheasants a day for example—were counterbalanced by the enormous number of shooters, so that the slaughter was still great, but so regulated that no wildfowl species was under threat of extinction. Peter found the numbers of migrants astonishing, greater even than the legions he had seen on the Hungarian plains. At the Gridley State Refuge in California, covering about 50,000 acres of marshland, he reckoned that fifty thousand snow geese and whitefronts settled at dawn, after feeding in the rice fields, on a part of the refuge no larger than Brogden marsh's 500 acres. The warden of the even larger federal refuge at Willows told him that in the previous winter three hundred thousand geese had roosted on a lake at a density of about one thousand geese to the acre. Ducks were there in comparable numbers. His brief Californian experience left him with material for his monograph and ideas about wildfowl sanctuaries which he was to put to good use. He headed east again to meet a new friend, the wildfowler, angler, and writer Van Campen Heilner, who was to conduct him to the Gulf of Mexico.

After surviving a forced landing in a tobacco field in North Carolina, they arrived at a spot called Belle Isle deep in the marshes of the Mississippi delta, which stretched in all directions to a flat horizon. Occasional huts of muskrat trappers were the only signs of human life. Thousands of skins were shipped out every year from these marshlands, which were also the haunt of blue geese in prodigious numbers. Transport was by means of a "marsh buggy" which had slatted drums for wheels, each slat fitted with a blade that dug into the mud. Once the geese were spotted, Peter and Van Heilner disembarked and crawled on hands and knees through the lush vegetation until they were in amongst the birds, which took off in waves—some fifty thousand of them, they reckoned, snow and blue geese together. "We left the marsh," Van Heilner wrote, "with the cries of the geese ringing in our ears and the great long line of them streaming across the horizon to infinity."

Their final port of call was Avery Island, where E. A. McIllhenny ruled over a fiefdom encompassing the Tabasco Sauce factory which underpinned his prosperity, a salt mine, a "Bird City" where snowy egrets came in thousands to rear their young, a nutria farm, an alligator hatchery, and a statue of the Buddha enthroned in a pagoda set among magnificent camellias and clumps of bamboo. Numerous ponds were the home of black bass, terrapins, and ducks of many species. Mr. McIllhenny gave Peter ten geese, thirty-two ducks, and four baby alligators. In New York these joined forces with thirty geese sent from California, and Peter embarked in SS *Bremen* with his sizeable menagerie to reach home for Christmas 1938.

It was high time. He had been away for over four months and in his absence matters needing his attention had pestered his mother like a swarm of bees. A new note of exasperation sounded in letters reaching him in New York:

"Today alone I've had hours of work releasing your snow geese from Liverpool because they hadn't got a certificate, pacifying the income tax, hearing Grimwood's groans, writing to Kenzie, answering a letter from a magazine … This sort of thing happens often. I *think you should come home.*" Peter's overdraft was another worry. Just when checks from Ackermann's or royalty payments seemed to be winning, another withdrawal kept it in the red. "Was that £200 just for expenses?" Kathleen inquired, "or are you—oh! I do hope you aren't! buying birds again?" Bill weighed in with some Polonaiselike advice. "Please cut down your expenditure until you've got a working balance at your bank and keep it so. It is the only path to wisdom and happiness."

There were also problems about girlfriends, especially Dinah. Her parents, who were friends of the Kennets, believed that there had been an "understanding" between Peter and their daughter, and wrote to Kathleen to ask, in effect, what was he going to do about it. But Peter had gone off to Canada. "Now, lambkin," his mother wrote, "you went off so quickly you didn't tell me whether you were really contemplating Dinah for keeps. It seems she rather thinks you are and I am wondering whether she is right or whether a lighthearted phrase like 'don't you go getting engaged while I'm away' was misleading her." Dinah wrote sadly to Peter: "What I want is for us just to be friends and not even that if you don't want it, but I have always put you on a pedestal and I don't mind your knowing it." She turned to a more constant swain; Kathleen saw him dancing with her at the Grosvenor Hotel and commented: "He sticks out his behind and has a heavy black moustache but Dinah seemed to like him." Kathleen supposed that Dinah would marry him on the rebound; rebound or not, marry him she did.

A more serious entanglement was that with Brenda, the daughter of neighbors in Suffolk, whom Peter had met at a regatta and invited to stay. She was young and very beautiful; "she loved sailing, she loved dancing—and danced superbly," Peter wrote in his autobiography. "She loved me and I loved her." They seemed to be well suited and were certainly in love. What went wrong?

Time and reticence have blurred the answer. Perhaps it lay partly in Kathleen's doubts about Brenda's suitability, despite the lack of obvious drawbacks, as a daughter-in-law. The fact that Bill had taken a dislike to her father could hardly have been an adequate reason for discouraging the match. Few young women would be seen by Kathleen as worthy of so enviable a prize as her son: perhaps she looked for an intellectual, sophisticated background not to be expected in the ranks of East Anglian neighbors. Her own feelings were ambivalent; some of her letters to her son read almost like love letters; yet she wanted him to marry, but to marry someone of her own choice. Nor had Peter himself made up his mind, although he wrote that he hoped to marry Brenda (whom he disguised as Dierdre in his autobiography). On a spring day in 1938 he and his mother went punting on the lake at Fritton Hithe. "All a hot afternoon he talked very frankly and thoroughly," she wrote. "He is expecting a war, thinking of being killed, wondering whether it would not be wise to perpetuate his name if that were so. Said he'd told one lass who loves him that he is not going to marry her because he is too unstable."

No doubt the lass was Brenda. The reason he gave for his reluctance to marry sounds like an excuse, and the few letters that survive suggest a reluctance either to commit himself wholeheartedly or to break off the affair. So Brenda was left in a twilight world of uncertainty and unhappiness. "Once I asked you if you wanted to finish things," she wrote. "Please be kind and let me know what has happened. Do tell me if I've done something, because if so I didn't mean it, and this suspense is unbearable." Brenda's mother wrote him a gentle letter, not a rebuke. "I'm quite sure she feels life would have been poorer had you not known each other, in spite of the unhappy times she's had. The happy times have been worth storing up in her memory." A store of memories was all she was left with. Rumors of war and war itself disrupted private lives, the affair fizzled out, but Brenda did not forget him.

After the Munich crisis of September 1938, war with Hitler's Germany seemed as certain as it was unwelcome to the British people. The navy was the obvious niche for Peter, and soon after his return from North America he enrolled in the Royal Naval Volunteer Supplementary Reserve. Meanwhile his life proceeded in its comfortable groove. A farm worker's wife, Mrs. Wayman, came to the lighthouse every morning to cook breakfast, do the cleaning, and leave a cold lunch on a tray, and returned to prepare his evening meal. Mr. Grimwood, sexton of the church at Sutton Bridge, spent two hours every morning dealing with correspondence, while Kenzie fed the birds and did odd jobs about the place. These included painting the posts of the birds' pen a particular shade of green which Peter favored: Kenzie enjoyed mixing the colors, and also decorating a hen kept to brood ducks' eggs; he painted one leg yellow, one blue, and her comb green. Peter reprimanded him for this because he thought it unkind to the hen. The two men had occasional disagreements, but Kenzie told Colin Willock that Peter was "a good boss and a good man. I've never had a better boss, though I reckon he underpaid me for that bean goose I got him."

In January 1939 Peter left the lighthouse with John Winter for a brief wildfowling sortie into Northern Ireland, with a scientific objective as well as a sporting one. For some time, a question about the color of the bill of the whitefronted goose had been niggling at his mind. The bills of all the whitefronted geese he had shot or seen in East Anglia had been pale pink. In 1935 he had seen on a lake at Millechope Park in Shropshire a pair of whitefronted geese with yellowy-orange bills, which had surprised him. These birds had been brought from Greenland by David Haig Thomas, and Peter had put down the aberrant color to the fact that they had been shipped over as goslings, and fed on an unnatural diet en route. Then, in 1937, Haig Thomas had made a second expedition to Greenland and brought back four whitefronted geese for Peter's collection. Their bills were yellowy-orange, and they had come as adults, so the dietary explanation was ruled out. It could only be that there were two races of whitefronted geese, one with yellowy bills breeding in Greenland, the other with pink bills breeding mainly in Siberia. To the layman it may seem of minimal importance if a goose's bill is pink or yellow, but it was upon such small and seemingly insignificant variations, resulting from the isolation of each species on the various islands in the Galapagos group, that Darwin's theory of evolution by natural selection had been based.

The next stage was to find out where these yellow-billed Greenland geese spent the winter. It came to Peter's mind that the chief pundit of the shooting world, Sir Ralph Payne Gallwey, in a book published in 1896, had described the bills of his whitefronted victims as yellowy-orange. So he must have been shooting Greenland birds. Peter further recollected that Payne Gallwey had done most of his wildfowling in Ireland, so Ireland was the place to look for wintering geese that bred in Greenland.

Peter and Winter took their punt with its gun to Lough Foyle and drew blank for a bitterly cold week. On their last night, when it was freezing hard, they heard the whitefronts call and then a skein came over. Three birds fell, two dead and one wing-tipped. They caught it, wrapped it in a mackintosh, and waited in the punt until daylight to check the color of the birds' bills. They were yellowy-orange. Both men were elated. The wing-tipped goose was taken to the light-house, and the author of *The Handbook of British Birds*, H. F. Witherby, came there to see birds of the two races feeding side by side. He confirmed the difference, and Peter was able to claim an ornithological discovery, a minor one perhaps but nevertheless satisfactory, which was to form the subject of a paper he and Christopher Dalgety were to read jointly to the British Ornithological Club in 1948.

In June 1939, the seventh Peter Scott exhibition at Ackermann's gallery was opened by the Canadian High Commissioner, Vincent Massey. As well as thirty-nine oil paintings, it included ink drawings done to illustrate his own *Wild Chorus* and Michael Bratby's book *Grey Goose*, and pencil drawings of several friends. As usual it was a success; £1,000 worth of paintings were sold in the first few days and scarcely any were left without a buyer.

Later the same month, Kathleen took her son to stay with the pianist Prince George Chavchavadze in Venice. The Prince lived with his American wife in a beautiful palazzo and had a private gondola with his own gondoliers Emilio and Julio, a butler called Pepino, a pretty maid Rosinance, and a little white lapdog with blue ribbons in its hair and a bell round its neck which he led about on a chain. He and his guests enjoyed delicious luncheons on the Lido, they bathed and sunbathed, and in the evenings they floated in the gondola with lights flickering on the water. For Peter the churches and palaces, the works of Titian and Giorgione, Veronese and Tiepolo, were a feast for the senses. The Prince (known for short to Anglo-saxons as "George Shove-shout") gave a dinner party for two Russians, two Italians, two Germans, two French, one Greek, and his two English guests. "If ever I said anything about war," Kathleen wrote, "the attitude was war? what war? Oh yes of course you're English, the English are always bothering about war."

It was true that Peter was bothering about war, and especially about what was to become of his birds. They could not be left indefinitely to Kenzie's care, nor could their food supply be assured. Ration books were already being printed. Will Tinsley agreed to look after some of them, and David and Nancy Haig Thomas, who had bought a farm on Horsey Island on the coast of Essex, were to take the rest. As it turned out, these birds had to be redistributed because Haig Thomas was unable to obtain enough food. One of Peter's admirers, whose peculiar nickname was Longbung, volunteered to look after the birds while they were on the island, and added to the complications by falling in love with Peter "wildly and deliriously," according to Kathleen. Longbung sent Peter distracted missives, and Haig Thomas wrote to his friend: "You have made poor Longbung just about as lovesick as it is possible to be. There were floods of tears when you left … Nancy and I want to make it quite clear that we don't want you to come back here unless you are really genuinely thinking of marrying her." Probably Peter was too taken up with searching for a home for his birds to do much sporting with Longbung in the shade.

As the summer wore on he became increasingly restless. He took part successfully in the annual "Sea Week" at Lowestoft but "it no longer seemed important to win a 14-foot dinghy race." He did not compete in the Prince of Wales' cup. Soon after the Lowestoft regatta he went to Stafford to stay with John Winter, and filled in the time by designing a system of camouflage for the factory which manufactured Universal Grinding Wheels. Perhaps coincidentally, perhaps not, this factory was never bombed, although several others in the town were hit. He was still in Stafford, impatiently awaiting his call-up, when on September 3 Neville Chamberlain gloomily announced that Britain was at war with Germany, and London's air raid sirens sounded for the first time.

Another seven weeks passed before his call-up came. "Pete has gone," wrote his mother. "He looks more like Con than ever." Echoing the thoughts of many mothers of many nations in every age, she continued: "He's a creature that for a decade was the one light on earth that concerned me, and even for the subsequent twenty years has loomed so very largely in the forefront of my mind. Planning, plotting, praying (if I pray!) for his success, for his decency, for his happiness. *Shoved* my vitality into him, fed him physically, mentally and worldly, with every nourishing diet I know. Egged him, spurred him, sheltered him, and now maybe it will all end. But there! Maybe it won't." Fortunately, it did not.

ENDNOTES

[1] By October 1938 there were over 250 birds of thirty-two different species in the collection. His tally of geese included three Lesser Whitefronts, two Beans, six Greylags, two Barnacles, five Brents, one Blue Snow, two Ross's, two Chinese, four Emperors and two Redbreasteds. This was before he bought the eighteen pairs of the latter species.

CHAPTER NINE

HMS Broke

HMS *King Alfred* was a huge underground garage cum swimming pool in Hove, East Sussex, where a concentrated course converted an assortment of professional men, many of them amateur yachtsmen, into Probationary Temporary Sub-Lieutenants of the Royal Naval Volunteer Reserve—the Wavy Navy, so called because the gold braid bands on the sleeves of officers' uniforms were serpentine instead of straight. Somehow Peter found time to devise a light-hearted revue with songs and dances, and put it on at the end of a packed ten days. Although the atmosphere of 1939 was very different from that of 1914, a sense of national unity pushed like tender seedlings through the crust of disillusionment born of the First World War. There was even the same fear of missing the bus. "I'd be angry," Peter wrote, "if the war stopped before I got to sea." He was earmarked for destroyers, "*the* thing that every Wavy Navy man dreams of getting into," and was on top of the world.

Not only was he to be sent to a destroyer, he was to join an "A" class, modern one, HMS *Acasta*, whose first lieutenant was an old sailing friend. He had contacted the Captain and officers at Devonport and looked forward to joining them in a week's time. Four days later, he came down with a sore throat and high temperature and missed his chance of joining *Acasta*. Instead he proceeded to an anti-submarine course in the land-based HMS *Osprey*, followed by another in HMS *Defiance* at Devonport, where he dived twice in a submarine, brought it back himself alongside the depot ship, and seriously considered becoming a submariner. "My conclusions about the navy so far are these," he wrote to his stepfather. "That you will get nowhere unless you ask for it. That you will get almost anything you ask for. That I shall not have much trouble finding something of interest to do—by interesting I mean exciting." Family connections might be able to help. He dined with the Commander-in-Chief Western Approaches, Admiral Sir Martin Dunbar Nasmith, VC, and his wife, friends of Bill and Kathleen's, "who could not have been nicer."

In February 1940 he joined HMS *Broke*, an older and much less well found ship than *Acasta*. But his guardian angel had not slept. On June 8, 1940 *Acasta*, with her sister ship *Ardent*, was escorting the aircraft carrier *Glorious* during the evacuation of British troops from Nanik in Norway, when the German battlecruisers *Scharnhorst* and *Gneisenau* attacked and sank all three. Only one man from *Acasta* survived. Leading Seaman Carter described the last moments after the order "abandon ship" had been given. "When I was in the water I saw the Captain [Commander C. E. Glasfurd] leaning over the bridge, take a cigarette from his case and light it. We shouted to him to come on our raft, he waved 'Goodbye and good luck'—the end of a gallant man." "Thus perished 1,474 officers and men," Churchill wrote in *The Second World War* (Vol. I). "Despite prolonged search, only thirty-nine [from all three ships] were rescued and brought in later by a Norwegian ship."

Before joining HMS *Broke* Peter went on leave, looking, his mother wrote, "absurdly like Con in his naval uniform. Full face he is not so *very* like him because Con's eyes were purple and Pete's are greenish blue, but in profile he is exactly the same." Christmas was spent in Essex where the war was still a world away. Their hosts, Lord and Lady Rayleigh, ordered the slaughter of two bullocks and distributed beef and beer to between 100 and 150 tenants and their families. "We sit fifteen to a meal," Kathleen reported, "footmen and butler as usual. They are making no changes." Five months later, the Rayleighs' son, serving in the RAF, was reported missing.

HMS *Broke* was an elderly, cramped, and uncomfortable vessel, in rough weather permeated with the smell of fuel oil which seeped up from the tanks to mingle with smells of cooking. In Peter's eyes her shortcomings were redeemed by his pride in her performance—a poor thing, but mine own—and by the personality of her Captain. To say that he hero-worshipped Captain Brian Scurfield would perhaps be an exaggeration, but few men of his acquaintance won more of his respect, admiration, and eventually affection. Peter described him as tall and friendly, with bright blue eyes and an easy manner, and as a man of immense courage and noble character.

What Peter had not reckoned on was seasickness. It had never troubled him in small boats, but in rough Atlantic storms the destroyer pitched and rolled so savagely that he soon succumbed. The Captain ordered a bucket to be lashed to the gun director on the bridge and Peter made frequent use of it, but got no better. The fact that Nelson had suffered in the same way brought no consolation. Finally he became so ill that he was forced to lie for ten days in the sickbay living on orange juice and continually vomiting, and the possibility arose that he might be rejected by the navy as unfit for active service. He had developed jaundice, and was given a month's sick leave. Subsequently he overcame his seasickness, but always felt queasy for the first thirty-six hours at sea.

His half-brother Wayland, in his last year at Stowe school, was at Fritton Hithe for the Easter holidays, and Kathleen had invited two children of an old friend to keep him company. The elder of the two was just seventeen. Her name was Elizabeth Jane Howard.

Yellow with jaundice, debilitated and depressed, Peter cannot have been a lively addition to the party. Nevertheless Kathleen enjoyed "a heavenly week, Wayland composing a lovely sonata, Pete painting lovely pictures, Bill as consanguineous and sweet as could possibly be." A week later she was less euphoric. "I got rather cross with Pete because he would sleep on indoors lying on the floor drawing geese when the doctor wanted him to take exercise." During his month's sick leave he painted sixteen pictures. When it ended he was sent to Scapa Flow, but a change of plan directed *Broke* back to Plymouth and on the way she ran aground. She was docked for examination and Peter, now fully recovered, found himself back at Fritton. Jane Howard was still there.

"I wish he'd find a binding person," Kathleen had written. "Oh how I wish it." Exactly what she meant by a binding person she did not divulge, but it certainly was not a seventeen-year-old girl whom she considered to be a bit of a flibbertigibbet, while conceding that she was "rather pretty, rather sweet, and might possibly develop into something." She added: "The weather is sensational after the long winter, and Pete thinks he will be killed in the war, the combination has sent him off the deep end. It would be brutal and cynical to tell him so, one must just watch the fever taking its course." Peter was thirteen years Jane's senior, held the King's commission, was endowed with charm, and experienced in affairs of the heart. Spring flowers were out in the garden, mallards nesting on the lake, and across the water Hitler's armies were gathering for the kill. Small wonder that, in this charged atmosphere, Jane was bowled over. They were still at Fritton when, on May 10, Hitler's Panzer divisions swept into the Low Countries and on into France. By the time Peter rejoined his ship both were, in their different fashions, falling in love.

"An avalanche of fire and steel," in Churchill's words, "rolled across the frontiers." It rolled with such speed that within three weeks French resistance had crumbled and the British Expeditionary Force had been cut off by a lightning German thrust to the sea. On May 26 the evacuation of British forces from Dunkirk began. By June 4, almost by a miracle it seemed, an armada of vessels, from Royal Navy destroyers, minesweepers and corvettes to cross-channel ferries and the "little ships" of amateur sailors, the yachts and cabin cruisers, barges and rowboats, had rescued some 338,000 men.

To Peter's intense frustration, *Broke* was still in dock while this great drama was going on. He was detached to serve as First Lieutenant in HMS *Venetia*, a destroyer which had struggled back to Dover after a pounding from enemy aircraft and shore batteries while she was attempting to enter Boulogne harbor. The Captain had been severely wounded, one officer and nine others killed and twenty wounded, and the ship looked like a colander. This was Peter's first taste of battle, though as yet at second-hand. Back in *Broke* there was "a desperate air of hurry"— yet he found time to write an article on the greater snow goose for *Country Life*.

The drama of Dunkirk by no means completed the evacuation of British and Allied troops from France. Many more, trapped by the German advance, were making their way in dispersed units toward the coast between Boulogne and Brest, hoping to be picked up by Allied ships. On June 9 *Broke*, back at sea after her repairs, together with two Canadian destroyers, approached Le Havre through a pall of smoke and narrowly escaped destruction when straddled by bombs which fell 5 feet from her sides. That evening, she intercepted a signal from the naval liaison officer of the 51st (Highland) division asking for a ship to approach St. Valery-en-Caux, some 30 miles northeast of Le Havre, at midnight, to evacuate about forty stretcher cases and forty walking wounded. St. Valery was behind enemy lines and might fall at any minute, if it had not already done so before the ship could arrive. *Broke* responded to the signal and Peter was put in charge of the shore operation. This was an adventure indeed. He described it in a long letter to his mother.

> I was to land from a motor-boat after a pre-arranged signal and ascertain whether the British or the Germans held the village with its tiny harbor. We entered armed to the teeth (pistols) and crept up the harbor, the ship being some two miles off-shore, with the motor going as slow as possible and as silently as we could make it. The time was 2:15 A.M. and there was no sign of life in the village at all. It was extremely ghostly and we crept in giving orders in whispers. We penetrated deep into the harbor when suddenly we heard motor cycles—"enemy mechanised troops" we said "for sure." We came alongside [the pier] and I climbed gingerly ashore saying I'd be back in five minutes. The boat's crew said they hoped I would but good-bye in case.
>
> I crept into the village brandishing my pistol without much conviction and all ready to say "Wer ist da!" if I saw a German helmet. Suddenly at a corner I saw the legs and tunic of a solider sitting, but his face was hidden. So I popped round on him with my pistol and said "Hands up!", he jumped up and said "Yes, sir,

certainly, sir" and I said "Thank God I thought you were a Jerry, where's the C.O.?" Then followed ages of hunting for the folk I was to get away [the wounded], but at last we found them. Time was all important as we had to be well away to avoid being sunk by bombs at daylight. So it was a race against time to get these wounded—half of them stretcher cases—into boats, some of which we took from the quayside. So I was the first person to land and become embarkation officer of a place that may become as well known as Dunkirk.

As Peter was seeing the last of the stretcher cases into the boats a Major appeared who told him that eight thousand men, including the 51st (Highland) division, assembled near the village, hoped to be evacuated from St. Valery that night. The Major then fetched the Chief of Staff of the 51st division who said there would be a lot more than eight thousand men to embark. Peter asked whether they could hold on till nightfall; if not, he would signal his Captain "and we would begin the evacuation at once. In a very tired voice he said 'No, I think we can hold on till midnight—but no longer.' He added 'If we don't, there won't be anyone to evacuate—we're the last remnants of the B.E.F.' The Chief of Staff went away in his car. I wished him luck and promised that we would be there at dusk."

HMS *Broke* returned to Portsmouth, disembarked the wounded, and Peter and Captain Scurfield reported immediately to the office of the Commander-in-Chief. They received a shock. In the face of enemy air superiority, no more destroyers were to be risked in operations along the French coast. "The group of senior officers round the blue baize-covered table did not seem to grasp the situation at all," Peter wrote. His Captain argued in vain. "Here they were visibly making up their minds, as we thought wrongly. 'I'm sorry, Scurfield,' said the Chief of Staff, 'but I'm afraid your sailing signal [to return to Plymouth] will have to stand.'" A further signal came that night from France to say that this was the last chance to evacuate fifty-four thousand troops, half of them French. The last chance was not taken.

Peter was angry and bitter, and blamed himself. He wrote to his mother:

So now we are haunted by the thought that we should not have waited till nightfall but have gone to it right through the day, and a signal from me would have set all that in motion. I really failed pretty badly there, and yet I had to take the Chief of Staff's word for it that he could hold out till dark. It would have been quite outside my orders, but I should have gone outside them. The ship would probably have been sunk but the risk should have been taken. The Captain would, of course, have backed me to the full, had I decided the other way, in spite of it being against orders.

That was on June 11. On the following morning German troops commanded the beaches at St. Valery-en-Caux. At eight A.M. the French IXth Corps surrendered and at ten-thirty the 51st division did the same. "The question is," Peter wrote, "which was right—which was more valuable, two or three ships or all those men. For a brief moment the decision was mine." It was stated officially that on the night of June 11–12 St. Valery had been shrouded in fog, making the evacuation of the troops impossible. The fog did not seem to have affected other parts of the Le Havre peninsula. "I missed a tremendous chance there of doing great service by being too ordinary," Peter's letter went on. "With real initiative I could have saved six thousand British troops ... If I had done what I should have had to do I should have been court-martialled. But what is a court-martial when an Expeditionary Force is at stake?"

Had the navy attempted to rescue the 51st (Highland) division and the IXth (French) Army Corps it would have done so without air cover; the Luftwaffe was already flying from French airfields and would have attacked in force. Six days later, one of the grimmest episodes of the war was to underline the dangers faced by ships at sea unprotected from attack by air. On June 17 the 20,000-ton *Lancastria*, after embarking troops from St Nazaire, had five thousand men on board. As she was leaving the harbor she was bombed and set on fire, and the sea around her became a sheet of burning oil. Nearly three thousand men perished in a scene that surpassed any medieval painter's rendering of the torments of Hell. News of this disaster so shocked Churchill that he forbade its publication, one of the few occasions on which he shrank from revealing a military disaster. Had Peter sent the signal he believed he should have sent, and had his Captain endorsed it, men of the 51st (Highland) division and of the IXth (French) Army Corps might have ended up not in prisoner-of-war camps, but at the bottom of the sea.

Two days after the surrender at St. Valery, the Germans entered Paris; the French government had withdrawn to Tours; capitulation was inevitable. "What had formerly been the finest army in Europe was now, for all practical purposes," wrote Arthur Bryant in *The Turn of the Tide*, "a herd of sheep being hounded by wolves." About 140,000 British troops were still in France, and retreated along roads choked with refugees to the ports of Cherbourg, St Malo, Brest, and St. Nazaire. On June 17 Petain's government capitulated, and on the next day the last ship carrying the last Allied troops left Cherbourg, with the Germans three miles from the port.

HMS *Broke* played her part in these events, which provided Lieutenant Peter Scott with more exciting adventures. The destroyer was ordered to Brest, with instructions to embark any troops that could be found and to demolish port installations before leaving. *Broke* entered the harbour to find that no one knew what was happening or about to happen, the enemy was at the gate, and

.there was no one in overall command. In another letter to his mother he described his small part in the great drama of the fall of France:

> Back safe again from another tremendous adventure. This time we have done a real service in the war effort, having saved and brought back with us some very valuable units of the French fleet as well as about 250 odd refugees, B.E.F., Poles etc: mixed. I had the most terrific time—made five separate landings on my own—acted as embarkation officer at the port—we were bombed four times, once heavily. I had an interview with the French General who was holding on to the last. The French have been much maligned. This garrison were displaying great bravery. They were disorganized but they refused to quit French soil although a very small band. I'm afraid they must mostly have been killed by now.
>
> Chief adventures were driving wildly through streets of the town in lorries we found lying about and subsequently destroyed—collecting and saving all equipment in the form of guns and small arms ammunition—blocking roads and quays with useless lorries. Setting fire to oil tanks and blowing up cranes, power-houses etc. This was mostly done by special demolition parties but I was sent to destroy a 150 ton crane. We went in a motorboat notoriously difficult to start when warm. We lit the fuses (at pistol point from French sentries who queried our orders) and had kept the motor running. We had ten minutes to get half a mile away for the biggest explosion of the evening. It was about 11 p.m. and the Germans were supposed to have entered the town at 7 P.M., actually they hadn't but were just outside. We jumped into the motorboat and put the clutch in and the motor stalled and there we were, within 30 yards of an explosion that we knew would wreck everything within a quarter of a mile. About a minute of sweating anxiety and then she started and we got away. We made a splendid noise and down came the crane, 200 feet high.

There was poignancy as well as excitement. French ships in the harbor were embarking soldiers, sailors, and civilians of military age while their wives, mothers, and sweethearts remained behind to fall into enemy hands. A French couple implored Peter to take their two sons. "They will fight. They have money with them." British ships were not supposed to take French subjects. Peter asked the Captain, who said, "All right, bring them on board and anyone else you think we really ought to take." Two hundred Polish soldiers were collected, including the Colonel's wife. "A very charming French lady" brought her English governess. At midnight *Broke* moved out of the harbor and anchored in the bay to embark the last of the demolition parties. A light was seen flashing from the cliffs and Peter was sent ashore for the sixth time, accompanied by a signalman, to investigate. He continued his letter to his mother:

> It was dawn—I had been at full bore for twenty-seven hours so was pretty tired, but we stepped out along the cliffs as if we were setting off on a walking tour. Gorse and broom—hayfields—maize—a Dartford warbler flitted across the path. Dawn broke. Enormous clouds of oil-smoke from the fires we had started streamed out to sea and filled the southern sky. From time to time we would stop and get directions flashed to us. Over a crest we came on a cove and could just see about 400 men climbing down a steep path to the beach. They couldn't be Germans from their behaviour, clearly French evacuating. I signalled to the ship for instructions and was told to abandon the search and return.

Kathleen's response to this missive was ecstatic. "My sweet, what an adventure—it's breath-taking—I rush round with you, I demolish, I ignite, I embark, I signal, and most of all I stride out, dead tired along the gorse covered cliff. What a life, what marvellous service, how grateful we are to you ... Your letter has gone to be copied."

Copied it was, and circulated to everyone she could think of in positions of influence, and she could think of a good many. Her friends were suitably impressed. "What a wonderful description of a gallant and splendid episode," wrote one. "It really is an epic of the sea." While Peter was enjoying his active life immensely, his mother was less content. She was not impressed by Churchill's famous speech about fighting on the beaches. "He as good as told us we'd all be in our graves tomorrow but there wouldn't be time to put us there, but we should all be very pleased and proud about it." She had done her duty by taking in eight evacuee children from London's East End, but some of them had trickled back because, in their opinion, "German bombs only fall here and there, but in the country there's a cow whichever way you look." Then she was kept busy organizing another exhibition of Peter's paintings at Ackermann's gallery. With seventeen new pictures "the show looks as good as ever," she observed, and the paintings sold well. A year later, Ackermann's was to be demolished by a German bomb.

"The worst of things has happened," she wrote on June 26, 1940. "They are going to put guns in Pete's lighthouse, they are going to blow the top off and put on a concrete roof. I cried for the first time since the war." Going into action with a dispatch worthy of her son, she rang up Lord Sysonby who "says he has got the idea squashed—a very great relief. The lighthouse kept its top, but Lord Sysonby was unable to prevent considerable damage to its interior by troops billeted there under his command."

The long, hot, cloudless summer continued through August and September when the Battle of Britain was fought and narrowly won. Among the first of the casualties was one of Peter's close wildfowling friends, Brian D'Arcy Irvine. Although Kathleen had described him as vague, absent, and imprecise, he had become, to the surprise of many, an efficient, professional, and brave fighter pilot. A letter from a fellow pilot told all that was known of his end:

> Brian failed to return after a terrific air battle five or six miles south-west of the Isle of Wight on August 8th. None of us saw what happened. We were attacking a number of bombers which were bombing a convoy, and were ourselves attacked by a crowd of enemy fighters. In the melee of 100 or 150 planes, you will realise that it is each man for himself. Brian was leading a section of three [Hurricane] machines. Just before we broke formation, he warned his No. 2 over the radio that he had an enemy on his tail, by which action he saved this boy's life ... The squadron has suffered a terrible loss. He was a brilliant pilot. On leaving Cranwell he was classified as "exceptional" and was soon given command of a section. The airmen loved him, so it is small wonder that his machine was always the most efficient and best cared for.

The writer added that Brian had idolized his older friend, and "was forever grateful for the help Peter had given him in his painting, and for the thrills and sense of companionship they had together in punting."

Following his camouflage designs for John Winter's factory in Stafford, Peter had turned his attention to the camouflaging of ships. This technique had been used extensively in the First World War when "dazzle painting" had been developed by Norman Wilkinson, like Peter a painter by profession and an RNVR officer. There was no attempt to hide the ship; on the contrary, it was painted in bold contrasting colours intended to confuse: in which direction was the ship going, at what speed, and how far away was it? While the U-boat commander was making up his mind, quite often wrongly, the ship increased its distance from its predator and, with luck, escaped a torpedo.

This worked well for large ships in daylight, but not for smaller destroyers and torpedoboats at night, when most of the hunting and being hunted took place. Peter's punt-gunning ventures had taught him that "to make a ship less visible at night it must be painted almost white, that is to say in a very pale tone." Concealment, not confusion, was to be the aim. He showed his designs to Captain Scurfield who, with Admiral Nasmith's approval, decided to try them out on *Broke*. In July 1940 she was painted in fetching shades of pale blue, green, pink, and tan, and opinions were invited from officers of the watch in various vessels. *Broke* did, indeed, become less visible at night—sometimes embarrassingly so, since the effective camouflage was to be the cause of a good many collisions. The experiment with *Broke* was so successful that eventually Peter's designs spread throughout the navy. Two years later, in the Birthday Honours, he was to receive an MBE. No specific reasons are given for these awards, but he thought it might be for his camouflage, possibly his greatest personal contribution to the winning of the war.

After the summer of 1940 the danger of invasion receded and German strategy shifted to a relentless attempt to knock Britain out by starvation, both of food for her people and supplies for industries faced with the task of re-equipping virtually weaponless armies. (It was even proposed to arm the Home Guard with pikes.) The toll of merchant vessels, Allied and neutral alike, sunk by U-boats and enemy aircraft mounted month by month. Convoys guarded by warships were the only answer, imperfect as that answer was. HMS *Broke* was transferred to Londonderry, her base for convoy duty, which was to be her job for the next two years. Peter was by then her First Lieutenant. The speed of his rise in the Service could be described as supersonic. He had joined *Broke* as a temporary sub-lieutenant in February and was appointed First Lieutenant in August; his predecessor had waited fourteen years for this promotion. Although the navy's mushroom growth was mainly responsible, the backing of his Captain was a crucial factor, plus, of course, his own abilities and favorable reports. He believed that he was the first RNVR officer to become Number One of a destroyer. Even at this early stage he had his own command in his sights.

Meanwhile two years lay ahead of hard, comfortless, and dangerous work in the North Atlantic in the face of bitter winter gales, packs of submarines, and enemy bombers whose range exceeded that of the outnumbered defending aircraft. Whoever wrote that war consists of weeks of boredom punctuated by moments of intense fear might have had the Battle of the Atlantic in mind. Before winter gales set in, life on board was tolerable and Peter was able to write in September 1940 to John Winter:

> Dear me, how much I like my job. It's fascinating because so full of variety. I was always one for liking people and most of my job has to do with people. It is nearly all delegating and de-centralising. Telling people to do things and seeing that they have. In the course of it I have become quite attached to them all. They're a fine lot of chaps. I find it easy to be matey with them and rather hard to be sharp. One does have to be sharp a certain amount though, which I hate and cannot do it really well.

They told me when I started it's no good being nice to them you'll get no thanks for it. That may be so for the old stagers but three-quarters of our chaps are young and mainly "hostilities only," and even if they don't know how to say thanks in words they do so in behaviour, and it's worth it every time to be human with them. So I try to give a reason for everything, and when one has to be tough I let them know that I am being tough for the good of their characters. It is diffficult to get across that sort of stuff but I am still un-disillusioned so I still try.

He tried, but was he succeeding? He was bothered by doubts. "I wish I could be harder and fiercer," he wrote to Jane Howard. "I don't think I'll ever be a leader because I can't be. I can make men follow me in a crisis, but that isn't enough to make them efficient. They must have discipline for that, and discipline is fierce and unrelenting and I'm neither, and am faintly ridiculous when I try to be. If anyone produces any excuse at all I accept it. I'm obsessed with the danger of being unjust. That's all rather looked down on, I think, in the Service." Two small incidents suggest that he did succeed in winning the respect and even the affection of the men. When *Broke* returned to her base after a spell at sea, an Irish huckster would bring his rowboat alongside with a cargo of fresh butter; the sailors would throw their caps into the boat with the money, and the huckster hoist the caps back with the butter inside. This practice was forbidden. In the middle of one such transaction, the First Lieutenant appeared on the scene. The huckster cast off hastily and rowed away, taking with him the cap and money of a young able seaman. To mislay part of one's uniform—His Majesty's property—was not a trivial offence. The young seaman's heart sank to his boots; the First Lieutenant looked the other way. Fifty years later, the former able seaman remembered this incident.

Christmas 1940 was spent at sea; after singing carols as duets with the Captain on the bridge, Peter went below at four A.M. to find a sea-boot stocking hanging on a peg in his cabin. In it was a potato stuck with matches to resemble a pig, a carrot and onion, an old shoe, some chocolate, and a tin of shrimp paste. "Father Christmas is with the convoy," ran a note. "A happy Xmas and many more to come." Peter was deeply touched. Despite his lenient attitude he could be firm, even sharp, when necessary, but softened his reprimands with a touch of humor. Noting that dirty fingerprints had defaced the night order book, he wrote in it: "When the criminal tendencies of the ship's company demand that I should have a record of their fingerprints I will say so. Meanwhile more care is to be taken to keep this book clean."

But there was little time for such niceties as month after month went by with battering storms, monotony, and acute discomfort to contend with, and leaden fears as constant companions. Now there were no stirring adventures but "long awful watches in rain and wind when for four long hours there is nothing to see and yet one must look for it in case there is." Everything leaked, the ship rolled to an angle of 45 degrees each way, it was almost impossible to stay upright and quite impossible to stay dry. "I quite expected to put up a wisp of snipe when I came off watch this morning," he wrote to Winter. "A pair of skates would be useful in the flat outside my door," where about 4 inches of water lay on top of a layer of fuel oil. Waves 2 or 3 feet high washed over the deck, and it rained continuously. In his cabin, water ran down the side of the bunk to soak his bedclothes, and in the ward room everything that could be broken was.

One of the duties of the escorting warships was to pick up survivors, if any, of torpedoed vessels. To John Winter:

> There is no doubt that I do not care for seeing a lot of dead people, particularly when it is our job to take them out of the water and revive them for two hours when you know that they are dead good and proper and will only have to be buried. But some do come to life, so it is worth it. It's so dreadfully like punting after a big shot. You know—"this one's only wing-tipped, I wonder if it's worth trying to save him." And like escaping cripples—"if we go after that one, those two will get away." ... I find the only way is to think of them as numbers—there are only eight more to get—if we go there first and get those there'll be only five—that further one will be done long before we get there—and so on. Oh dear—what an ugly world it can be.

No wonder he added in another letter:

> I don't very much want to be torpedoed tonight. We lost our whaler in rescue work last trip and two of our Carley rafts have been damaged by the sea and one of the little Denton rafts has been washed overboard. We've got one compartment full of water we've been a-pumping and a-pumping all day. Added to which we're all alone—so I'd *much* rather not be torpedoed—not tonight.

At last there came a genuine adventure. On April 6, 1941 HMS *Comorin*, a former P&O liner of 15,000 tons converted into an armed merchant cruiser, was reported to be on fire about 600 miles out in the Atlantic, and *Broke* was dispatched to the scene. Two other destroyers had already picked up those men who had taken to the boats, but no boats were left and the rest of the crew were huddled together on the afterdeck of the burning vessel. It was dark, both ships were rolling heavily, and waves 50 to 70 feet high were breaking over them. The scene was lit by the orange glow of the fire which was spreading rapidly. Captain Scurfield decided that, despite the extreme difficulties and dangers, the only hope of saving the rest of *Comorin's* crew was to take *Broke* alongside her. This he did, with consummate seamanship. The ships were rolling so heavily that at one moment *Comorin's* afterdeck was 50 feet above *Broke's* fo'c'sle and at the next 10 feet below it; at one moment the two ships were touching, the next 40 feet apart. *Comorin's* men had to aim at jumping at the moment, almost a split second, when the ships were touching and when they were level.

Broke's crew padded the fo'c'sle with every cushion they could find and with their hammocks. It was impossible for *Comorin's* men to gauge exactly the right moment to jump; sometimes they dropped 25 feet or more, and many were injured. Peter's job was to organize stretcher parties and get the injured quickly off the fo'c'sle, then dash below with the shipwright to estimate the damage caused by the ships bumping together, then up to the bridge to report to the Captain and down again to the fo'c'sle ready for the next jump. The doctor was in bed with a temperature of 107 degrees but got up and worked through the night. Injuries to both men and destroyer mounted. One of *Comorin's* men was crushed between the two ships and fell into the water when they parted. The ship was badly holed, though mainly above water, and all the superstructure on the port side bent and flattened. The question was, how long could she remain seaworthy? And all the time the fire was spreading.

Comorin's Captain was the last to jump. As he did so *Broke's* fo'c'sle dropped away, he fell and got tangled in a rope with his feet on the wrong side of the rail. "It seemed certain that he would be deflected overboard," Peter wrote. "But no, he sat on the rail, balanced for a second and then rolled a neat back somersault on to the padded fo'c'sle. He was a man of 69—had served with my father in the '90s—but he landed with his cigarette still in his mouth and managed to fit his monocle into his eye quickly enough to pretend that he had jumped with it in. So at last the great ship was clear and we backed away and took stock of the situation." They had rescued 180 men.

It was an anxious voyage back to port pumping all the way, but the wind abated and *Broke* came "spinning in at twenty knots. Since then it has all been very nice." The Admiralty signalled congratulations, and Peter hoped that his Captain would get a DSO. As it turned out he got an OBE, and Peter himself his first mention in dispatches. One of the most successful of his wartime paintings depicted the dramatic scene of the rescue.

A spell of leave followed while *Broke* was being repaired. All through the autumn and winter of 1940–1 he and Jane had been writing to each other letters which became more and more committed. It was in the main a paper courtship; they met only briefly; they had fallen in love with an image of each other. Peter, by far the more experienced, realized this. "Do you still love me by any chance?"

he wrote just before he went on leave, "I mean really—not just reaction. I'll be happy if you feel inside you that particular sense of bubbling excitement and that it's I, rather than someone else, or the spring, or your art, who is responsible for it. Oh my dearest darling Jenny, how I'm longing to see you."

Jane was a student at a drama school evacuated from London to a house at Instow in Devon, and under the impractical management of Eileen Thorndike, a sister of Dame Sybil. Conditions were austere, with only one meal a day provided; for others, the students had to fend for themselves. As most of them were badly off, they often went hungry. "We all eat in the kitchen at the most extraordinary times," Jane wrote. "This morning we had breakfast at eleven and lunch at about three. Even then everyone comes in dressing gowns and no one is really conscious. Toward evening the air becomes thick with ambitions which is rather overpowering ... Only about one of us will ever reach the top and yet to see them all burning with ambition makes it very heartbreaking." (Only one did: Paul Scofield.) Jane herself also burned with ambition. She had written a play, and then re-written and re-re-written it, and hoped that Eileen Thorndike would put it on. She never did, although constantly planned to do so.

"What a lot we've got to discover about us," Peter wrote. "We're both fairly complex folk, I because I've had quite a long time in which to complicate my life and myself, you because you've not had long enough to unravel yourself yet. Jenny—d'you know I'm still rather scared of you! I am though—there's so much in you trying to burst out that I'm terrified by it all. And at the same time thrilled and proud." Behind her letters lay a fear that each of his might be the last; behind his, doubts about her youth and inexperience, his own shortcomings, and possibly a shadow cast before of how their different ambitions might pull them apart.

One evening, in his cabin while the ship plunged and rolled in a January gale, he wrote a short story, or what he called a short story; it was in truth a sort of alarm bell. It concerned a successful portrait painter called Nicholas whose charm, wit, and engaging manners masked a thoroughly despicable character—insincere, conceited and, in a word, bogus. He joined the RNVR, was posted to a destroyer and, in due course, told the narrator of the story that he was engaged to a girl of seventeen who was beautiful, romantic, and full of youth and music. Her name was Elizabeth and she was a childhood friend of the narrator, who was dismayed: Elizabeth, he believed, had been swept off her feet by Nicholas's bogus glamour and it was up to him to warn her parents. Before he could do so, Nicholas went down with his ship. The author added a note: "The story is a warning to a very young girl. More directly I cannot bring myself to warn. Is it cowardice or love? Who knows?" He sent the story to Elizabeth Jane Howard.

And she sent him her play, which also ended with a question mark. There were three acts. In the first, a young girl training to become a ballet dancer has just scored her first success, and is faced with the choice of either pursuing her career, or marrying a rich stockbroker. In the second act she has achieved fame and success as a dancer but at the cost of personal tragedy and, as the act ends, throws herself through a window to her death. In the third act, she has married the stockbroker, raised a family, settled into a bourgeois existence, and become a contented cabbage. Which course did she, and should she, take? The audience is left guessing, and the prophetic message is plain.

Peter proffered his opinion. The spelling was poor, the play uneven but—"Jenny, it is a good play. I'm absolutely staggered by bits of it. Some of them are really lovely, full of imagination and ever so subtle. Other bits aren't half as good." Her talent aggravated his sense of inadequacy. "I know you're an artist," he wrote in his next letter. "You want to be great and you can be. You must always create—compose, paint, write, act, do all these things and as many more as you can think of. It's right—it's right—I know it." It was curious that the course of his courtship reflected that of his father's: the object of Captain Scott's love had also been an artist whose talent had frightened him, and he had written to Kathleen tortured, self-deprecating letters. There was, of course, the critical difference that Kathleen had been a mature, sophisticated person, more so than her suitor, and Jane was a romantic seventeen-year-old.

When HMS *Broke* steamed up Lough Foyle to Londonderry to refuel and sometimes to refit, Peter was returning to a scene of his wildfowling adventures whose memory was assuming an increasingly golden hue. "The mountains are superb and the light is always so clear and winelike," he wrote to his mother. "It is all deep blue and deep brownish purple and deep rich green. What a glorious country it is. A good retired old Major with a fine old house and a rather charming wife has been my benefactor. He lends me a gun and takes me to little hidden marshes in the hills and great expanses of flooded rivers full of whooper swans, and home to a find old country house dinner and a big log fire after a grand day."

In July 1941 Bryan Scurfield left *Broke* to take command of a bigger and better destroyer, HMS *Bedouin*, which sailed for the Mediterranean to guard convoys supplying the armies fighting in North Africa. His replacement was an able and effficient officer but a stranger, with whom Peter was not at first at ease; but the ice was broken when *Broke* was involved in a collision with another destroyer, HMS *Verity*, while Peter was officer of the watch. There was a court of inquiry, and the threat of a court martial to follow. This hurt Peter's pride, and he feared that it might destroy his prospects of promotion. The Captain supported him, and the decision of the court was a relief. "They considered that the other chap was 'primarily to blame,'" Peter told his mother, but "some blame is also attached to me for not realizing that the other chap was bats." Both officers were warned "to exercise more care in future: a very mild rebuke which my Captain says 'will run like water off a duck's back—especially as you *are* almost a duck.'"

But it had been an anxious time, compounded by *Broke's* transfer to Liverpool, an infinitely less congenial base than Londonderry with no wildfowling, no hospitable Major, and dockyard foremen more concerned with restrictive practices than with winning the war. "God how I hate dockyards!" Peter exclaimed. Nor was the war at sea going well. Ever larger and more ferocious U-boat wolfpacks were ranging ever farther afield, long-range bombers were doing ever greater damage, Allied shipping losses were horrendous and rising. "If we lose the war at sea, we lose the war," Churchill wrote to Roosevelt. In darker moments, it looked as if this would happen. And "Hun airplanes can't go on missing us forever," Peter wrote.

War was changing him, as it changed many others, and yet turning him against change. More and more he was drawing memories of prewar years around him like a cloak, burying his head in its folds to keep out the present. The companionship of his close circle of sailing and wildfowling friends was very much part of that scene. "I'm not complaining," he wrote to John Winter after describing a particularly unpleasant ten days at sea in March 1941, "but recording my determination not to allow our lovely last five years before the war to go right away. You know you're the one thing that has gone solidly through all my loveliest memories of a life that was as full of enjoyment as anyone could wish a life to be. So whenever things aren't quite so nice which is fairly often now I find myself thinking of you and all our fun, and you just wouldn't believe how comforting it is. It is something unchanging and unchangeable to grasp, and fortunately the need of it is frequent enough to make sure that it won't go far away into the hidden corners of memory."

But change could not be cheated. Winter wrote that he had become engaged to be married; the close circle was broken; and Peter—unreasonably, it might be thought, in view of his own relationship with Jane—was dismayed. Winter, he wrote, had betrayed their friendship by giving him no warning of so important an event, and he disapproved, for various reasons, of Winter's choice. "I think," he wrote to his mother, "that if it were some girl who would really fit in I would approve at once although coming at this time when I keep up my spirits largely by reliving our past adventures together it would be an effort." The engagement came to nothing, and within the year Winter had formed a new attachment. This time Peter was enthusiastic. "I'm in favour of Rachel, who's a very charming and attractive girl," he wrote to Jane. "The only worry is that she has always lived in an enormous house with footmen and a dressing gong half an hour before dinner—you know. Shaped yew hedges 200 years old and no water supply." Of the three closest in the circle of friends—Peter, Winter, and Michael Bratby—Winter's marriage was the only one to survive.

During this second year of North Atlantic convoys, Peter experienced a crisis of self-confidence which may have purged his character of elements of conceit and arrogance born of privilege and almost unalloyed success. He walked no longer in the sun. He accused himself of being lazy, self-satisfied, content with mediocrity; "I amble about the ship doing nothing and pretending it is desperately tiring." Even his painting was a sham. "My standard has never been high enough for me to have become a painter. Jenny—do you think we could raise it—you and I—because I could only do it with your help—so's I could be a real painter and not just a talented quack."

His doubts extended to his future with Jane.

> I wonder if you will ever marry me? I don't really want you to have heaps of love affairs. I just want you to be sure that it is fat ugly old me that you love, and not being in love with someone who loves you, because being in love is just what a young girl should be in the spring. In short to be certain if it is me you love not love that you love. I do so hope it's me, but if you are going to discover that it isn't, I want the discovery to be made in time.

She, too, was uncertain, not about her own love but about his. "About getting married," she wrote, "I don't know, not meaning I wouldn't love it, but I just don't know.... I *do* love you. I wonder whether you love me. You do and you don't. Is that right ... And I adore you always." And for Peter, like the constant throbbing of a pulse beneath the skin, was the muted beat of fear. "I love you so desperately tonight," he wrote in November 1941, "because it's rather frightening going out these days and one clings so to life—and with life to love. The trouble is that it lasts so long. One can screw up one's nerves for the few hours of a bombing raid, but a fortnight of knowing that there may be at that very minute a whirring torpedo slipping toward you gets slightly depressing. I wouldn't like anyone else to know about it, because I like to pretend to be immune from such imaginings, but there it is."

During brief holidays from her drama school, Jane was invited to Fritton. An uneasy relationship prevailed between her and her prospective mother-in-law. Kathleen recognized Jane's qualities but thought her too young, and immature at that, to suit her son. The constant emphasis that Kathleen, and sometimes Peter, placed upon her immaturity irritated Jane, whose flippant response concealed a real resentment. "Please *darling* Peter pretend I'm not twelve, if you don't I shall come in plaits and a panama hat, and you'll have to buy me a schoolgirl's annual and keep on giving me ice creams even if it's snowing."

"What a lovely understanding person you are," Peter wrote to his mother, but she failed to understand his frame of mind when he came on leave seeking above all release from tension, and reassurance that his old life had not vanished forever. If her diary correctly describes his behavior, this did not match his protestations on paper. "Pete picked up Jane and brought her along," runs an entry in May 1941.

> He confined his whole attention to me and scarcely spoke to her at all until after I had gone to bed ... If that is being in love, the condition has greatly altered since I was young. (Or got old for that matter.) Jane is very pretty, very sweet, fairly nice man-nered, very childish and ignorant, and quite egotistic ... If she turns out well she might become a very interesting person.

As acquaintance ripened between the sixty-two-year-old woman and the eigh-teen-year-old girl, Kathleen's condescension grew into something like sympa-thy. In February 1942 she wrote in her diary:

> Pete has got up at four a.m. each day in order to be on the right marsh before dawn. There he lies in ecstasy under a white sheet in the snow, then perhaps creeps on his tummy for half a mile or so, then perhaps shoots a duck or two, and returns in time for a hot bath before lunch. He was usually out for eight and some-times nine hours ... He went to bed about 8.45 or 9 each evening. The rest of the day he painted. He didn't take much notice of poor little Jane, who poured out her woes to me after he had gone to bed. She has a lot to put up with. If Peter is in love with her he has a very quaint way of showing it.

Dote on him as she did, Kathleen could be critical of her son. "I tell him I will not advise. He keeps asking me ... A man of thirty-one should not be interfered with even at his own request." But she did give him one piece of advice. Hearing that he was somewhere close to the Howards' house in Sussex, she asked him why he didn't damn well go over and carry her off.

In the summer of 1941 Bomber Command launched a campaign of night at-tacks on industrial targets and railway yards in Germany. Casualties among the air crews were heavy. Peter's thirst for adventure had not been quenched by Atlantic storms, and when he met Air Commodore Sir Victor Goddard at the Royal Academy's summer exhibition, he asked whether he might go on one such raid as an observer. Goddard said that it might be arranged, and so it was.

On the last day of August 1941 Peter took off from Wyton near Huntingdon in a Stirling bomber with a crew of seven. Two hundred aircraft took part in the raid, and the target was Cologne's post office in the center of the city. Peter had already flown, about a fortnight earlier, in a raid on Kiel. He described the climax of the raid on Cologne to Stewart Morris.

We ran into our first trouble in the searchlight belt. We took a lot of avoiding action and lost a little height in it, and then suddenly a searchlight got us and held us, and at once six or seven more came on. We were badly dazzled and for two or three minutes we couldn't escape, in spite of aerobatics which I could not believe a Stirling was capable of. Meanwhile we awaited the arrival of the fighters. Our last wriggle and suddenly we were out and dropping away. Twenty seconds later two fighters streaked over our heads by 200 feet in a dive. They hadn't been able to see us at the last minute, and we'd got out just in time.

Over Cologne, the scene was like a gigantic firework display with gun flashes below, shells bursting all around, searchlights groping through the darkness, "rich prolonged red flashes of our bombs bursting," incendiaries exploding and lighting fires.

We let our bombs go in two sticks. You could feel them drop off with a jolt and a few seconds later an angry red flash lit the haze below … I saw one of our chaps falling in flames. The aircraft broke up into several bits before hitting the ground, where it went on burning as we went past. My pilot, who was a perfectly grand chap, very quiet and extraordinarily charming, amused me by saying, whenever the flack got close or we were illuminated, in a pained and surprised tone "Well! Fuck me!" Not very funny I suppose but it made me laugh at the time. About two hours later we were safely on the ground again and making our reports to the intelligence officer. It was an adventure I wouldn't have missed for the world.

Seven aircraft failed to return. Peter emerged from his adventure with a profound respect for the proficiency and morale of the air crews of Bomber Command, and with an axiom supplied by the second pilot of his Stirling, who was a Sikh. "When you are looking out of the window," he advised, "if you see something you don't like, look out of a different window." Peter's justification for his part in these raids, "that no better way could be found of fostering inter-Service relations," apparently satisfied the Air Commodore, but it might have been nearer the mark to say that it satisfied that nagging need to prove his own manliness and courage provoked by the story of his father.

It was while *Broke* was lying peacefully in dock at Liverpool in September 1941 that Peter had one of his many narrow escapes. On the other side of the dock lay a troopship, *Franconia*, full of soldiers, and a number of anti-aircraft rockets suddenly exploded on board. Peter responded quickly; he collected his Gunner, asked the Captain of a destroyer lying alongside Broke for the loan of his Gunner's Mate and, together with another sailor, went on board the troopship to find an ugly scene: seven men had been killed, several more badly injured and "bits and pieces of rockets were all in among bits and pieces of the seven." Also lying about the deck were several unexploded rockets, hot to the touch, some gently smoking and about at any moment to go off. The Gunner's Mate, Petty Officer Robinson, picked up four smoking rockets one by one and threw them overboard, Peter organized the rigging of a hose to flood the lockers where the rest were kept, and no more explosions occurred. Probably a good many men's lives were saved by this prompt action. Petty Officer Robinson won the George Cross for his bravery, and some believed that it was Peter's initiative and courage that earned him his MBE, rather than, or in conjunction with, his camouflage. He must have needed all his selfcontrol because of a weakness he kept strictly to himself: in his mother's words in her diary, "like his father, the sight of blood has always made him feel awful."

Then, in the stormy winter of 1941–2, it was back to convoy duty which sometimes took Broke to refuel near Reykjavik. The Icelandic capital had been taken over as a British base early in 1940, and Michael Bratby had been posted there as Intelligence Officer to the occupying force. (He wrote a short book on the birds of Iceland in his spare time.) The army had brought with it, Bratby related, a number of railway trucks, although Iceland had no railway. A visiting British officer, told of this as a good joke, stiffly replied: "I sent those trucks, and you'd have been damned angry if there *had* been a railway and I *hadn't* sent any trucks." When Bratby had asked for 1,000 maps of Iceland, the War Office had sent 750 maps of Ireland and 250 of Madagascar. So there was plenty to laugh about during Peter's brief visits to a country which was to play such an important part in his future life.

In February 1942 HMS Broke, considerably battered by her various escapades, was ordered into Portsmouth for a long refit, and her crew paid off and posted to other jobs. The destroyer's subsequent life was short. She was badly damaged in the action off Oran against the French fleet loyal to Petain's government, and sank while being towed away. Peter had served in her for two years and one day. He got his wish at last, his own command—but not of a destroyer. It was to be a steam gunboat, a larger and more heavily armed version of a motor torpedo boat, less inflammable than the MTBs, hopefully less vulnerable and even more aggressive. Great things were expected of the SGBs and Peter was delighted. His boat was still under construction at Cowes.

The time had come for a decision about Jane. Once more he consulted his mother. "You do set your family conundrums," she replied. "Do we mind? I should say the answer is no. I think we all probably agree that someone a wee bit older would have been better, but with things as they are we may all be dead before you have found just the perfect creature." What Kathleen wanted was a grandson, and Jane had said that there would be "no shirking," citing Sybil Thorndike's four children as proof that procreation could be combined with a career. "She seems to come from a very vigorous stock," Kathleen continued, "which probably you think unimportant in comparison with love but it *really* isn't." Her letter ended "Anyway if you give me the word that it really is your idea, I will rise to the occasion and jolly well see that everyone else does." Thus encouraged, Peter wrote to Jane that the family approved and "what do you know about that?"

> Only Peter is still cowardly [he added], not being quite sure that the war and the things that it has done to you and to him allow true values to hold sway. Whether for example he is unduly influenced by the long weeks at sea and by the feeling of insecurity and fleeting time: whether you are unduly influenced by the lack of "nice young men of your own age," and the difference between loving someone who is mostly far away upon an uncertain ocean instead of constantly around and about. And then too I wonder sometimes if I would not feel altogether different about war and would no longer rush madly towards my ultimate destruction whenever opportunity presents. If I ever came to feel that I didn't want to do that, I don't think I could go on enjoying life at all—but with a new responsibility I *would* have to reconsider all that part of it. No more trips to Cologne (well, I don't plan any of those because I think they'd be silly really)—but their equivalent in my own job. Then waves of love and adoration come and wash all those thoughts away and I just want you for keeps and for ever and ever.

So it was settled: the waves of love won. On April 2, 1942 Kathleen wrote in her diary, "Pete has just rung up to say he thinks he will do this deed ... He says he will come in later before going to bed. I shall have to be happy and excited. If she ever hurts him I shall kill her." Peter came in after midnight looking young and happy. "As I get used to the idea I know I must get to like it well enough not to act or grumble. I wrote Jane an adorable letter. I don't believe I'll ever have to kill her. She will be good." Jane had had her nineteenth birthday just a week before.

Once the decision had been made everyone entered into the nuptial spirit. Kathleen gave Jane a turquoise and diamond ring that had belonged to her Greek grandmother and forty clothes coupons (a very generous gift). The wedding was to be in London, and the Howards decided on a reception for about three hundred guests at Claridge's, which Kathleen thought too grand

and, in wartime, "rather unholy." The ceremony took place on April 28 at Christ Church, Paddington. In Kathleen's opinion, "the singing was poor, the organ mediocre, the flowers rotten, but Jane looked divinely beautiful, Peter tired and diffident." She added, "My sweet Pete, I think now he is in love with her and will be more so."

The honeymoon was spent at the Lacket. Primroses, violets, and anemones were out in the woods, the first bluebells were showing, willow wrens sang among the birches, and the sun shone from a cloudless sky. This was April as poets write of it, not as it usually is. No bombs fell or guns thundered over this corner of Wiltshire whose gentle beauty contrasted with the stress and tedium of war. "Our world is flooded with happiness," Peter wrote to Bill. "In the wind and sun Jane looks like a wild child and then in the firelight in her beautiful white gown with a blue feather pattern on it she looks like a grown-up dignified princess. And always, hour by hour, she grows lovelier and lovelier." They tired the sun with talking and sent him down the sky. "Our talk," he told his mother, "has the maddening habit of dashing on to the next subject almost before we have exhausted the last." Jane thanked Kathleen for her kindness, for her flowers and presents, and for "having the most perfect and wonderful and darling person who has ever existed for your son." She added, "I can't tell you that I love him more all the time, because yesterday, this morning, an hour ago I thought I couldn't love him more."

From the Lacket the couple went to a hotel in Cowes where Peter could oversee the building of his gunboat and then take part in her trials. His old friend Uffa Fox was also getting married, and Peter was his best man. It was rather an odd marriage; the bride was a French widow who spoke no English, and Uffa Fox had no French; however, they achieved a *modus vivendi* and the marriage was a success. The steam gunboat SGB9 was commissioned at the end of May 1942 and her trials completed in July; five weeks of "working up" followed, and by early August she was ready for battle. And into battle, almost immediately, she went.

CHAPTER TEN

The Battle of the Narrow Seas

Steam gunboats were an experiment. Nine were laid down, two destroyed by bombs when on the slips, seven completed. They were made of steel, whereas motor torpedo boats were made of wood, they were steam-powered and ran on diesel oil, they had a crew of thirty-five including three officers, a speed of nearly thirty-five knots, and were virtually miniature destroyers. Only four were ready when, on August 16, 1942 they were ordered to Portsmouth. Four days earlier, their commanding officers had received portfolios of charts, photographs, and plans for the SGBs' part in Operation Jubilee—the Dieppe raid.

By mid-1942 the Russian army was in full retreat, and pressure on the Allies to open a second front in the West was great and growing. On brick walls and railway bridges all over Britain "Second Front NOW" was being scrawled by Stalin's sympathizers, who were many. The Allies were sending convoys round the North Cape into Arctic seas to land supplies at Russian ports in the face of persistent attacks by enemy U-boats, bombers, and warships, but to land an army on the coast of France and breach the enemy's Atlantic Wall was still far beyond their capabilities.

Hit-and-run raids were a different matter. In March 1942 the water had been tested by an audacious raid on the port of St. Nazaire where, 5 miles up the estuary of the river Loire, the only dry dock large enough to take German battleships and cruisers in need of repair was situated. In the tradition set by Drake and followed at Zeebrugge by Admiral Roger Keyes in the First World War, a Commando force, escorted by destroyers and light Coastal Forces craft, sailed in to the Bay of Biscay and up the estuary, where an old ex-American destroyer, HMS *Campbeltown*, packed with three tons of high explosive in her bows, rammed the lock gates in the teeth of murderous fire. All but five of the landing party were killed or captured, and only three of the fifteen coastal craft returned. HMS *Campbeltown*, set with delayed fuses, blew up at noon the following day and destroyed not only the dock, but thirty or forty German officers who were on board. The dock remained out of action for the rest of the war.

Heartened by this success, urged on by the need to appear willing to Stalin and, most of all, to learn lessons essential to the planning of the eventual invasion, the Chiefs of Staff decided on an even more ambitious raid. No less than 237 vessels of various kinds—mostly landing craft, but including eight destroyers—were involved. Over six thousand soldiers with their weaponry, including 58 Churchill tanks, were to be landed on the Dieppe beaches, with the support of 67 RAF squadrons. Nearly five thousand of the soldiers were Canadians. Since the early days of the war, their regiments had been stationed in Britain awaiting their chance to do what they had volunteered to do, fight the Germans, but not a shot had been fired at the foe. They had grown impatient, and their commanders welcomed this opportunity to show the mettle of their men. About one thousand Commandos were also to take part.

The fleet set sail at nightfall on August 18 through a passage cleared by minesweepers. The element of surprise was lost when the landing craft on the most easterly flank ran into an escorted German convoy; an engagement followed, the enemy was alerted, and the land attack inevitably, and bloodily, failed.

The landings were timed to start just before dawn, but were late enough to sacrifice the cloak of darkness. In daylight, enemy bombers pounced on the ships which offered an array of sitting targets; the RAF responded, fierce battles took place overhead; SGB9 was crippled by a bomb and taken in tow by a sister gunboat. But only six minutes later the Flotilla Engineer Officer, James Grout, "appeared grinning and sweating on the bridge" to say that he had repaired the damage and got the engines going again. Rescuing the crews of stricken aircraft, whether German or British, who had parachuted down, was part of SGB9's job, but her principal role was somewhat unclear. In *The Battle of the Narrow Seas*, Peter explained that:

> It was very hard to know what was going on either ashore or afloat. From time to time signals came through calling for closer support. But how to do it, that was the question. The blanket of smoke between us and the shore was almost complete ... At 11:45 A.M. we made a signal to *Calpe* (HQ ship) "We have plenty of 3 inch ammo but no smoke, can we help?" to which we received the reply "Closer support is required, offer of help appreciated." A few minutes later we signalled to *Calpe* again "Can you

give us a bearing on which to lob shells?" but got no answer. There was a terrible feeling of helplessness at this time, and also a strange aloofness from the awful happenings so close to us but hidden by the thick white curtain.

The happenings on the beaches were awful indeed. On the eastern flank the Royal Regiment of Canada was cut to pieces on the beach—459 men killed, wounded or missing out of 515; on the western flank the South Saskatchewan Regiment and the Queen's Own Cameron Highlanders of Canada captured some of their objectives, but were stranded by the failure of the central assault, and the bulk of the attacking force never got off the Dieppe beaches. Despite murderous fire and mounting casualties, they fought on stubbornly, and soon after seven A.M. the Military Commander decided to throw in his reserves. The Fusiliers Mont-Royal, a crack French Canadian regiment, followed a little later by the Royal Marine Commando, went in. Some never reached the beaches, and those who did were met with devastating machine gun and mortar fire from the cliff tops. Acts of great gallantry could not avert disaster. This action was subsequently termed a modern equivalent of the Charge of the Light Brigade.

Evacuation from the main beaches was ordered at about eleven A.M. and RAF Bostons laid a curtain of smoke. Under very heavy fire, landing craft came in and men waded out to meet them; many of the craft were disabled, and dead and wounded choked the ramps. Nevertheless, over one thousand men were taken off and got back safely. They left behind 3,363 of the 4,961 Canadians and one quarter of the Commandos, many of them casualties but more of them prisoners. SGB9 was lucky; and her luck consisted partly at least in her Captain's quick reactions. On the way home, after leaving the convoy to pick up two shot-down pilots from their rubber dinghies, she was steaming, unprotected, to rejoin the convoy when a Dornier appeared out of the clouds. Many years later her coxswain, Petty Officer J. W. H. Stevens (DSM and bar), recalled what happened next:

> Going at a good speed to catch up with the convoy, we were attacked by an enemy bomber. In he came and dropped his stick of bombs. The Captain watched the bombs coming down, he gave the order "Full speed astern" which pulled us up dead in our tracks, the boat shaking like a jelly. The bombs dropped about fifty yards ahead with no ill effects. Had we gone on, the boat and all our crew would have been lost. That was the cool brain of that great gentleman.

SGB9's engines were failing, and she limped into Portsmouth in fits and starts at 12:45 A.M. to disembark two German and two Allied pilots, five men

from *Calpe* who had been blown overboard by an explosion, and eleven casualties taken off from landing craft under heavy fire. For "gallantry, daring and
skill" Peter was to receive his second mention in dispatches.

A post mortem on the raid identified the reasons for its failure. There
had been no preliminary air and sea bombardment; the Canadian troops, brave
as they were, lacked all combat experience; the plan was too rigid and complex, relying overmuch on strict adherence to a timetable—in fact, a planning
screwup. In Canada the shock, which turned to bitterness, was profound; men
who had waited for nearly three years for their chance, it was said, had been
sacrificed to the bungling of the British high command. Resentment went deep
and lasted long.

The raid had failed to take the town of Dieppe and destroy its installations, but it had taught the Allies lessons which helped to bring them victory on
Italian beaches and, in two years' time, on the beaches of Normandy. Captain J.
Hughes-Hallett, the Naval Force Commander, summed up the Navy's principal
lesson: "Next time we bring our harbor with us." The casualties were a heavy
price that had to be paid. Peter agreed. The raid had even helped Russia. The
strategy behind it, he said in a later broadcast, was "to hold down large defensive forces by the threat of more raids of its kind, any one of which might turn
out to be an invasion ... And it aimed to learn something about German methods of defending their Atlantic Wall. As it happened it did all those things, but
the cost was high and most people regarded it as a failure. Personally I think
they were wrong."

Soon after the raid, the Admiralty decided that the steam gunboats needed
more armored protection, and they were withdrawn one by one to have steel
plates fitted over their vulnerable steam pipes. SGB9's turn did not come at once
and she spent most of the winter of 1942–3 escorting convoys through the
English Channel.

For a while Peter was able to come ashore between spells of duty to join
Jane in the South Coast hotels in which she was bleakly living. At first, while the
steam gunboat was being built and "worked up," a tolerable married life had been
possible, and Jane had written joyfully to her mother-in-law. Peter was trying to
avoid having his hair washed and skimping his baths, but "I love him so much that
hardly anything else seems to matter. Sometimes we dance in our room. And we
do all our laughing there." They shared their room with a great many caterpillars.
Then they had rented a small house in Seaford with a garden and Jane had settled
into domesticity, making Peter steamed treacle puddings which he loved, but a
change of operational plan obliged them to give up the house after six weeks and
return to hotels, which she hated. Air raids were frequent, there was nothing to do
while he was at sea, and she was horribly lonely. And always, a ghost at her elbow,
was the fear that one day he would not return.

By now, Jane was pregnant. She wrote at the time that she was excited and even hoped for twins, but afterward affirmed that she had never wanted an immediate pregnancy; she wanted to get used to being married first. Peter's wish to pass on his genes before his own extinction was too strong a hope to be denied. Kathleen was delighted. Of course it would be a boy and would be called Falcon, Captain Scott's middle name.

The pregnancy got off to a bad start. In July Jane fainted twice in a single morning, once in a greengrocer's and once in the hotel. Peter carried her to bed and brought thick slices of bread and jam "and we ate them and thought how lovely Falcon would be." She added (to Kathleen): "Do you find loving one person makes you love everyone else a little bit more? I'm learning anyhow. He is a tremendously giving person. And taking too which makes it perfect." Her fainting fits led to the sensible decision to withdraw to The Beacon, her Sussex home, accompanied by ninety elephant hawkmoth caterpillars which escaped in the train. In December, Peter was able to take the lease of a house in London that had belonged to Jane's grandfather, Sir Arthur Somervell, who had been a distinguished musician, and Jane moved in. At last, at 105 Clifton Hill in St. John's Wood, they had a home of their own.

Falcon turned out to be Nicola, who was born in February 1943 in a nursing home where wartime exigencies made for dour conditions. Kathleen held up well to the disappointment. "It's a girl, well so is Jane and so was I and Pete loves us a bit, so I guess he'll love his daughter. I sent a telegram saying I was sending her 100 snowdrops and £100, as I like bairns to have a little independence." Peter was a jubilant father. "Nicola is quite the most beautiful creature in the world," he wrote to Lady Malise Graham (Rachael Holland's married name) three days after the birth. "She is very grown up and her Presence is a little awe-inspiring. I gave her her very first bath—at least I assisted at it, then dressed her and took her up myself, unassisted and unescorted, to show her to her mother when she was 3/4 hour old. It was Jane's first sight of her and a most memorable moment." Jane's memories of the occasion were less euphoric. She found the nursing home unfriendly, and "I never saw my child except when it screamed," she recalled. Peter returned to his duties; she was hurt that he had failed to send her flowers when she was in the nursing home.

His naval affairs were going remarkably well. In November 1942 the coveted half-stripe had come his way. It had taken him two years and three months to rise from the rank of Lieutenant to that of Lieutenant Commander: a meteoric rise, but he was still hoping for the command of a destroyer. Bryan Scurfield, writing in April from HMS *Bedouin* in the Mediterranean, took him gently to task for his impatience:

> I think perhaps you do not realise how much his first command
> means to a N.O. [Naval Officer] *de carriere* and how long he has

to serve as a rule to get it. In my case it took me fifteen years to get command of the *Skate* and I don't think I have had many greater moments than that when I first stood on her bridge, and a flame of blinding panic swept momentarily over me as I realised that nothing would happen until I said the word ... Do you remember that talk we had in the hotel in Falmouth one evening? It made me realise how difficult it must be for someone who has always had all he wanted to adjust himself to the humdrum monotonous life of the ordinary N.O. Only a very few can allow themselves the luxury of depression and a struggle for new surroundings when life gets a bit boring. (I've seen and spoken to two women on one occasion since 9th January last.)

He added that he hoped his remarks would not be taken amiss because "your friendship is the best thing that has come my way in the war and I value it greatly."

The need to resist all temptations to succumb to hubris was always present in Peter's mind, and he was never one for taking umbrage. Two months later came distressing news. Two British destroyers, *Bedouin* and *Partridge*, were escorting a convoy bound for Malta when they encountered a greatly superior force of Italian warships and torpedo-bombers. Although altogether outgunned, they unhesitatingly went into the attack and were as quickly disabled, and *Bedouin* sunk. Then came better news: Scurfield had been picked up and was a prisoner-of-war in Italy. His wife wrote cheerfully that he was undamaged and in touch with the Red Cross. (Their second child had recently been born and Peter was her godfather.) The story had a tragic ending. After Italy surrendered, the prisoners fell into German hands, and were being marched along a road when aircraft of the RAF machine-gunned the column, and Scurfield was killed.

Peter did not have long to wait for the command of his flotilla. In March 1943 he was appointed Senior Officer of the six steam gunboats—one had been sunk by E-boats off the coast of France. Their light armaments confined them to a defensive role, which was not at all to his liking; to "engage the enemy more closely," in the words of Nelson's famous signal, was his aim. While thicker protective plates were being fitted to the boats, he did a good deal of lobbying directed at the Admiralty's construction and ordnance departments, and got his way. Heavier guns were fitted, giving the boats the heftier punch that their Senior Officer wanted. In the spring of 1943 the refitted and re-armed SGBs went to sea.

Their new armaments were put to the test within a month. On the night of April 15–16Peter, on the bridge of SGB6 (SGB9 was still unready) led a small force consisting of his own boat and two (smaller) motor gunboats into the Baie de la Seine in search of enemy shipping. In bright moonlight they came upon three large armed trawlers whose fire-power was considerably greater than their own. There was a short, sharp exchange of gunfire—three midges attacking three wasps—in which SGB6's steering gear was jammed and one of the motor gunboats damaged. The attackers broke off the action to effect repairs, and when SGB6's hand steering gear had been rigged she set off together with one gunboat in pursuit of the trawlers, leaving the damaged gunboat behind. They came up with the trawlers going all out for Le Havre, and closed to about 1,200 yards. "I must own to a sinking feeling on sighting," Peter confessed to Jock Ritchie, second-in-command of the flotilla. "The moon was so bloody bright. Whilst there was a doubt about finding them, the cowardly subconscious was saying hopefully "Perhaps you won't" although the conscious went on working out every possibility to make sure that we did find them." Accurate firing by the two attackers silenced the leading trawler, stopped her, and set her on fire. Endeavoring to sink her, SGB6 ranged alongside the trawler and raked her from end to end with shells from the only gun still left in action. But suddenly the trawler came to life, fired back, and an incendiary shell exploded on SGB6's bridge, knocking down all five men standing on it but only wounding one, and that slightly. A fire was started among the ammunition boxes and the gunboat disengaged. With virtually no ammunition left and dawn about to break, the two boats made their best speed home. One man was killed in SGB6, and two wounded.

"I consider that Lt.-Commander Scott showed skill in the handling of his force," Admiral Sir Charles Little, C-in-C Portsmouth, reported to the Secretary of the Admiralty, "and great determination in his engagement, pursuit, and re-engagement of the enemy. Recommendations for awards will be forwarded in a separate submission." These were heeded. Peter received the Distinguished Service Cross.

For some time he had been concerned about the identity of his boats. Numbers, he thought, were too impersonal, uninspiring; the boats ought to have names, like proper warships. It was a question of esprit de corps; a man could take more pride in serving in HMS *Resolution* or *Revenge* than in AB9 or XY7. But there was an Admiralty rule: gunboats and torpedo-boats must have numbers, not names. The sacrosanctity of Admiralty rules was not to be questioned by temporary junior officers of the RNVR, but Peter decided to question this one, and sought out in the bowels of the Admiralty the secretary of the Ships Names Committee. This civil servant was friendly but firm: no boat under 130 feet long could have a name. Did that mean, Peter enquired, that any boat *over* 130 feet long could have one? The secretary supposed so. Steam gunboats, Peter pointed out, were 145 feet long; and so his case was won. The next step was to find suitable names. Inevitably, Peter thought of geese. To link them, he tried different kinds of geese; brent, snow, kelp, cackling, and so on. That did not sound right. Other combinations were tried—waders, ducks, finches, even butterflies. Peter's favorite wildfowling punt had been named *Grey Goose* and he wanted that to be among the six names. Perhaps the link could be not "goose," but "grey"? So it was decided, and the boats became *Grey Seal*, *Grey Fox*, *Grey Owl*, *Grey Shark*, *Grey Wolff*, and *Grey Goose*.

Throughout the summer of 1943 these boats went out on patrol two or three times a week. Sometimes they engaged the enemy and sometimes they drew blank. On the night of July 26–27 four of the gunboats set out in search of prey, and learned that an enemy force had been detected by radar making for Cherbourg. Although dawn was breaking, with only about fifteen minutes of darkness left, Peter, in *Grey Goose*, decided to give chase. When sighted, the enemy force appeared to consist of three armed trawlers and eight or nine R-boats, coastal minesweepers carrying 40 mm guns and used as patrol boats. The four steam gunboats raced toward, them, holding their fire until about 300 yards away when they let loose with everything they had.

> There seemed to be no end to the Germans [Peter wrote to Jock Ritchie]. They looked like a flock of wigeon with two or three geese amongst them. The sea was so glassy that you could see the reflection of stars … At least fifteen ships opened fire simultaneously and the air was thick with red and green and white streaks. They ripped away from our guns towards the enemy line, they fanned out of the enemy ships and came lobbing towards us and ripped past just over our heads singing as they went, they criss-crossed ahead and astern, they ricocheted off the water and popped as they exploded in the air, they thumped into us from time to time in a shower of sparks. It would all have been very beautiful if it had not been so dreadfully frightening. But for me, thank goodness, there was no time to be frightened.

The action, which lasted for thirty-six minutes, was ferocious, lethal and confused. *Grey Goose* was set on fire, *Grey Shark* disabled, *Grey Seal* and *Grey Wolf* collided while going to the rescue, and only a smoke screen laid by *Grey Goose* in the teeth of savage enemy fire saved the gunboats from total disaster. As it was, the little force suffered thirty-nine casualties, including ten seriously wounded and seven killed. In *Grey Shark* Lt.-Commander Howard Bradford was hit in the leg, his navigator was badly wounded, and his midshipman died on the way home. His coxswain, Petty Officer Hicks, himself wounded, attempted to amputate another man's leg with a razor blade in order to dress the wound—in vain, the man died. In *Grey Wolf*, Able Seaman Gray's leg was severed by a shell; standing on one leg, and supporting himself on his gun, he went on firing the gun for six minutes until the enemy boat disengaged, when he collapsed and died.

The verdict on the action was inconclusive. One German trawler and four R-boats had been severely damaged, but so had four British gunboats, and it would take between seven days and six weeks to repair them. Admiral Sir Charles Little, in forwarding his report to the Admiralty, observed: "The action of the Senior Officer in laying a smoke screen between the concentrating enemy and drawing fire on himself was a well judged and gallant action which met with the success that it deserved … I am satisfied with the determination and gallantry exhibited by the SGB flotilla and the manner in which it was led." Peter received his third mention in dispatches. The C-in-C had recommended a higher award.

Peter's feelings were mixed. He had brought his ships back safely, inflicted damage on the enemy, and won the Admiral's praise. But he had sunk no German vessel, and had lost some gallant men. To him fell the harrowing task of writing to relatives to give what comfort he could. "I know that when men were killed and wounded in his flotilla it hurt him much more than he showed," was the opinion of his coxswain. "If one of his crew was in trouble he would ask me all about the man's standing in the ship, his character, and he was very fair in his punishments, which was one duty as Captain he hated doing. He always said 'Thank you, cox'n, for your help' after every trip." Those who served under him did not expect an easy passage. It was said that he looked for trouble, but could get out of it if anyone could. "Cool, calm and collected he was," recalled Leading Seaman George Jennings, DSM, who sened with him in *Grey Goose* from Dieppe onwards. "I can only think of once when I witnessed him getting a little over-excited, and that was when, returning to Portsmouth after convoy duties with dawn breaking through, a flock of geese flew overhead, and Commander Scott jumped from his seat excitedly, dassifying the species. A many-sided man and for his service during the Second World War I for one of many thank God he was on our side."

Of the many actions in which he took part in the Channel, one more, which took place on the night of September 4–5, 1943, deserves a mention. Four "steamers"—*Grey Goose, Fox, Seal,* and *Owl*—went forth to attack an enemy convoy reported to be heading southward from Boulogne, and ran slap into a German patrol. "Here was a sudden opportunity, and I decided to take it." The four gunboats closed to within 500 yards and opened fire. *Grey Seal* fired a torpedo which hit its target and *Grey Goose* set on fire another patrol boat, but then an enemy shell shot away her steering and she started to go round in cirdes; several of her gun crews were wounded and one gun was jammed. Nevertheless *Grey Goose* closed to about 250 yards as she continued her circling, and fired with every gun still left in action. She was saved by a smoke screen laid down by one of her companions. "It was evident that we were in no condition to undertake any more fighting," Peter observed. Despite two large holes and many small ones in the ship's side and other damage, by marvels of improvisation the engine room crew managed to get her back to port under her own steam. Casualties were surprisingly light: one man killed, one died of wounds, and eleven wounded. For gallantry and skill in action, Peter was awarded a bar to his DSC.

Peter had been in his gunboats and mostly at sea, living in the boat even when she was in port, for almost two years, with only brief periods of leave. He was beginning to suffer from "operational fatigue." Despite having stung the enemy so often and so forcibly, the steam gunboats had not turned out to be a success. The armour needed to protect their vulnerable parts, and the guns that had been fitted to every available space on their decks, had slowed them down, and reduced their chances of carrying out surprise attacks. The decision had been taken to build no more. Peter's chances of promotion were therefore blocked in this direction, and he was still hoping for the command of a destroyer. Enquiries at the Admiralty were discouraging: no destroyer yet, and meanwhile he must do a stint as an instructor in HMS *Bee*, Coastal Forces training base, which had just been moved to Holyhead in Anglesey, where he could be reunited with his wife.

War is bad for marriages. Inevitably, their different lives were drawing Peter and Jane apart. His tunnel vision was fixed on one objective, to keep his flotilla at the peak of fitness as a fighting machine. Her part was to cope with domesticity and motherhood, neither of them congenial occupations and made more difficult by wartime conditions: rationing, coupons, blackouts, shortages, and so on. Living at 105 Clifton Hill became increasingly a matter of living without Peter. The house was fairly large and soon filled up with Jane's friends and relations and the friends of relations, who came as paying guests; among them was Lieutenant Christopher Dreyer, who stayed there for three months while writing a manual for the Admiralty. At Jane's home in Sussex there had been antlike activity, people coming and going, argument and music, and the pattern was repeated in St. John's Wood. The house must at times have been somewhat overcrowded. "This week we have a floating population of Barry, Doscha, me, Audrey, Wyndham, Sandra, Caroline, Robin, Bill and an unknown Wren of Johnnie's. So we should be gay." There was also Nicola and her nanny, who freed Jane to renew her contacts with the stage, experiment with writing, and go to concerts and theaters. War, for the time being, had receded to Italy, Russia, and the Far East, and there was a sparkle to life in a London full of men on leave seeking distraction, and entertainers of one sort and another willingly supplying it. Jane was rebuilding a life of her own.

In the winter of 1943–4, when Peter was instructing trainees at Holyhead in HMS *Bee* and Jane joined him there, the tensions that had been building up within their marriage came to a head. In marriage, runs a French proverb, there is always one who loves and one who is loved. In the beginning, Jane had been the one who had loved, but their times together had been as nothing to their times apart. "I loved you almost bitterly because I seemed so unnecessary," she wrote. He had taken her love too much for granted, she had begun to feel her growth as an individual and as a writer hampered by his engrossment in his own concerns. Not that he stood in the way of her career; on the contrary, he wrote: "I want you so terrifically to be happy and almost more still not to waste the brilliant talents that you have. You will be great. I know it as certainly as I can recognize a pinkfoot goose at a mile." Yet a crack had opened up between them in their attitudes to life. Put simplistically, she believed that understanding people was her most important aim, while his might be summed up in the word "achievement." The driving force in his nature to achieve could override everything else.

At Holyhead, in the intervals of putting on a performance of *The Importance of Being Earnest* which Jane produced, these differences came out into the open. It was not to be expected, given the assault of war on conventional morals, that Jane, like Penelope, would occupy herself with tapestry work while awaiting the return of her Odysseus. She had taken a lover. Peter was not a jealous man. "I do admire your tolerance," Jane wrote. But the compass was swinging toward Peter as the one who loved, Jane the one who was loved. The outcome was an agreement to patch things up and start again. In a letter written for her twenty-first birthday in March 1944 Peter hoped that "life is being easier without the strain of me being difficult and sad. But you know we are a good idea really—I mean basically we are. Say you think so too. We're both difficult people and we've got to learn not to make each other more difficult and then we've got to make each other work hard—and one day we'll be artists. Will we be happy? Well I think I shall and pray you will."

CHAPTER ELEVEN

End of a Marriage

When Peter's time at Holyhead was up, Jane returned to London and he, still hoping for the command of a destroyer, was directed instead to an underground tunnel near Portsmouth where the naval planners of Operation Overlord, the invasion of France, were installed. His friend Christopher Dreyer (DSO and DSC twice) had been appointed Senior Staff Officer to the Captain Coastal Forces (Channel), Captain Patrick McLaughlin, who was in charge of the deployment of all the Coastal Forces' craft that were to form part of the great invading fleet and its protective screen. Dreyer had asked the Admiralty for Peter as his right hand man. So, in March 1944, to Portsmouth Peter went, to spend a troglodyte existence for three months which he described as the most taxing of his career.

In the fort, which had been built at the time of the Napoleonic War, and in the network of tunnels and galleries cut deep into Portsdown Hill during the 1930s, was a cluster of offices known officially as Portsmouth Combined Headquarters. The staff, under Admiral Sir Charles Little, laid their plans to protect the armada of men and armaments that was to flow across the Channel on the chosen day through the Spout, a wide sea-lane whose flanks were to be guarded mainly by the ships of Coastal Forces. In the heart of this rabbit warren was the Plot. This consisted of a map of the Channel and its margins displayed on a 25,-foot-long table on which models of every ship afloat in the area, Allied or enemy, were moved about by Wrens armed with long sticks like billiard rests. The movements of all these ships were plotted by radar stations on Beachy Head, Ventnor in the Isle of Wight and on Portland Bill.

The planners in their strip-lighted, air-conditioned caves worked for up to eighteen hours a day. A staircase with ninety-eight steps led up to Fort Southwick on the hill where the Commander-in-Chief had his offices, and at first Christopher Dreyer and Peter clambered up them every day to have their lunch, a breath of fresh air, a smoke, and a game of "shove ha'penny" before returning to the tunnel; later, they found a way through tortuous galleries and steel gates to the hillside, where a steep path led to the fort, and they could enjoy the sight of wildflowers and butterflies as spring advanced into the month of June. The fort overlooked Portsmouth harbor where more and more ships gathered for the invasion, as they did in other south coastal ports, and it seemed impossible to suppose that the Germans did not know what was afoot. Captain McLaughlin and his team had known since mid-March the date and place fixed for the invasion, and so had a great many others; so many, in fact—cooks and clerks as well as Generals and Admirals—that in the tunnel a word was used to distinguish those who knew from those who didn't: bigot. People were "big-oted" or they were not, and most of those in the tunnel were.

Down in their warren Peter shared with five others an office "which is about the size of our bedroom at Clifton Hill, so it is pretty fair bedlam," he wrote to Jane. "But Christopher is one of the five so the party is very hilarious. We laugh almost continuously. Shortage of sleep is our chief problem." There were odd days of leave and away visits that offered rest and distraction, more often the latter when his mother was involved. "Pete said he might have to come up to the Admiralty, so I had a party, I believe in parties in anxious times," she wrote in April 1944. "It *was* a party, 52 people came and I had the place packed with rhodos, colossal tulips and azaleas. We fed them handsomely with eggs, asparagus, ham, sardines, plum cake and tartlets and had gin, rum, whiskey, beer, orangeade and lemonade ... Jane was *charmingly* dressed in grey. She took off her shoes and left them in the middle of the drawing room right in the doorway. I had to tell her to put them on." Kathleen had a way, intentional or not, of humiliating a daughter-in-law still uncertain of herself and barely twenty-one; perhaps with a twinge of conscience she added, "Oh dear, I hope I am not prim." A week later she observed: "Jane said she had had only one letter from Pete since he's been there [in the tunnel], about two months. I wonder if that is true. Anyway I suppose it is none of my business." The fact was that Peter's business was always hers as well.

Because of his hope and wish to save his marriage, he was able to stand back and see himself through Jane's eyes. "When I am foolish and touchy and hurt about things it is only because I mind so much whether you love me and feel with me and understand me," he wrote at this time. "So when I look sulky or say something cross knowing full well that your only reaction can be—God how *impossible* he is, yet not letting my reason prevail." He was doing his best, and asked her indulgence. "You have changed me a lot, and for the better I think, but I am not a different person all the same. You've cleaned off a lot of the bogus ornamentation—the gilt—but underneath I am much as I was, and I doubt if it can be altered much at 35. There are things in my bones like adventure and the country with a capital C (trees and marshes and things—not the State) and even wild geese and boats. One day I will make it that you understand why I love these things, even if you don't get to love them too."

Despite misgivings, and almost unbelievably, tactical surprise was achieved when D-Day on June 6 saw, in Churchill's words, "the greatest amphibious operation in history" successfully launched. "As dawn came and the ships, great and small, began to file into their pre-arranged positions for the assault, the scene might almost have been a review." (*The Second World War*, vol. IV). Upward of four thousand ships and several thousand smaller craft crossed the Channel, supported by eleven thousand aircraft. The lessons of Dieppe had been learned, and the navy took its harbor—"Mulberry"—with it.

That night the Plot was packed with models as the invading force poured down the Spout toward the Baie de le Seine. No enemy ships put in an appearance, no chance encounter alerted the defenders as had occurred at Dieppe. "So the Spout was a reality," Peter wrote. "Could it now be protected by the units of Coastal Forces deployed and controlled by the young officers sitting at their Plots and radar scans in the control frigates?" Most of the night was spent watching events unfold on the Plot. It was not until some time later that Peter heard the bad news: another of his wildfowling companions had been killed. David Haig Thomas, then with No. 4 Commando, who had been dropped with the 3rd Parachute Brigade on the night of D-Day near the river Orne, next morning ran into a German patrol and was instantly shot. Like Peter, he had loved the wild places of the earth and sought them out with even more determination; he had wintered twice in northern Greenland living with Eskimos and learned to harpoon seals, hunt polar bears, build kayaks, survive on seaweed and raw shellfish, and had sledded with dogs for over 1,000 miles. Lord Lovat, his commander, wrote of him that he inspired lesser men—"the enthusiast, *sans peur et sans reproche.*"

Inevitably, war was cutting down Peter's friends. Another killed in action had been Robert Hichens, a racing dinghy colleague who had competed against him for the Prince of Wales' cup. Like Peter, he had joined the RNVR, fought in gunboats with great dash and daring in the battle of the narrow seas, attained the rank of Lieutenant-Commander and won even more medals—the DSO twice and the DSC three times. His exploits were the stuff of legend and his qualities of leadership outstanding. Peter had made his story the centerpiece of a broadcast he gave on St. George's Day 1943; the vivid evocation of battles at sea made a deep impression on his listeners. His mother was deluged with congratulations, and the Master of Trinity College, George Trevelyan, told her that "it was a thing Trinity can be proud of."

Nine days after D-Day, Peter landed in a DUKW—an amphibious craft, colloquially a Duck—on a sandy beach in the British assault area. His task was to set up a small radar station on the higher ground of Normandy with a mini-Plot to cover operations in that part of the bay, and also to see whether some of the light coastal forces could be based in Normandy instead of at Portsmouth. To a large extent he was his own master, operating his Plot in a dugout near Courseuilles, varied by occasional nights on patrol in a frigate, to give the Captain a few hours rest and pick up some clean laundry in port. But this was not enough in the way of adventure. Furious land battles were going on around the stubbornly defended town of Caen, and Peter wanted to watch them even if he could not join in. He bought a khaki battledress, borrowed a jeep and, with three colleagues, drove into the captured part of the town along streets pitted with shell holes while snipers' bullets sang overhead. A few days later he went back to inspect a naval shipyard situated between the river Orne and a canal. The Germans still held the eastern bank of the river only 100 yards from the abandoned shipyard buildings, where a pair of black redstarts was nesting. A kingfisher flew over the basin, in which were lying scuttled ships of various kinds. Deciding to board one of them, Peter found a small raft and, using a plank for a paddle, went on board, half suspecting a trap. All he found was a stench of dead fish, the Captain's diary, and the First Lieutenant's jottings of suitable French phrases for addressing French girls (*Je vous aime*). He paddled back to the accompaniment of moorhens' squawkings which were soon exchanged for the *pieu-pieu* of bullets from across the river. During his absence, mortar shells had fallen on the building in which the redstarts were nesting.

There was one more sortie, when he and three fellow naval officers were forced to take refuge in a foxhole with shells bursting all around, and dead bodies lying about. Only Peter's proverbial luck enabled them to get back unscathed to their jeep and so away. Whether these ventures served any useful purpose in the prosecution of the war is open to question. Certainly it risked useful lives, some would say unnecessarily. It was Cologne over again. Peter's defense was the same, that morale was strengthened by increasing the respect felt by one branch of the Services for another. The afternoon's excursion was "not entirely wasted if it helped us to understand what the infantry have been standing up to on the battlefields of Normandy." Perhaps it was fortunate that he did not have to justify these adventures to a higher authority.

Early in August he was sent to Cherbourg to act as Coastal Forces liaison officer with the American Navy, and to help set up a radar Plot at their headquarters. A charming and compatible Lieutenant in the U.S. Navy invited him to share his comfortable quarters in a former German dugout, set in heathery moors above the cliffs, where he enjoyed two eggs for breakfast and other luxuries. His relations with his host, Maynard Fisher, could not have been happier, but this was by no means the case at higher levels in the naval hierarchy. The Americans were deeply suspicious of the Royal Navy, and Peter was never able to persuade their Admiral or his Chief of Staff to talk on the land line to their opposite numbers in Portsmouth; they communicated by signal, inharmoniously. It fell to Peter and a Lieutenant in Portsmouth to pour oil on troubled waters. Christopher Dreyer assessed Peter's aptitude at this task:

> He was fabulous at getting on with people, very competent, and he made use of his considerable fame. He was quite widely known from his books and as an artist, and of course as the son of Captain Scott. He was very good at making use of that without bragging. He just accepted the fact that everyone knew him and was keen to meet him and he used it. So he was a very useful salesman for us among the staffs. He did it awfully well.

Toward the end of July the Allies launched their decisive attack to drive the enemy from Normandy and Brittany, and almost a month later (August 25) they entered Paris. Meanwhile Peter had been summoned back to Portsmouth to write a full report. By September 1 the Channel had been cleared of enemy shipping and Coastal Forces' work there was virtually done. The staff completed their reports and left for other fields. While Peter had been working in the tunnel he had, in odd moments, covered the walls of the Coastal Forces' office with paintings typical of his art. When Dreyer returned to collect some papers about a fortnight after everyone had packed up, the plasterboard had been stripped from the walls of his office. Possibly Wrens had taken the paintings for souvenirs, since Peter had helped more than once those employed on coding the signals that directed Coastal Forces' craft when at sea. A former Wren, Veronica Owen, remembered that "Wrens rarely used these special codes, but were expected to know them. Quietly Peter Scott moved to stand behind them and whisper the code, which he knew by heart, over their shoulders. Speed was achieved and the Wrens got the credit. It was a most kindly action."

For some time Peter had been working in his spare moments on a history, commissioned by the Admiralty, of Coastal Forces' part in the war. The Admiralty had envisaged a handsome illustrated pamphlet, but it grew into a fat book. Peter decided that the men who had actually done the fighting, the young Lieutenants and Lieutenant-Commanders, would describe their exploits more vividly than anyone else could hope to do, and he collected a large number of firsthand accounts of actions at sea which he put together, and illustrated with many photographs, some reproductions in color of his paintings, and pencil portraits of a number of the much decorated young men. Many of these—Robert Hichens, Christopher Dreyer, Mark Arnold Forster, Peter Dickens, Donald

Bradford—were personal friends. The result was a compendium of tales of dash and daring and great courage, invaluable to future historians and poignant to those who had taken part, but possibly too detailed and repetitive to rivet the attention of the common reader. He completed it while on a training course in Scotland, and it was published by *Country Life* in 1945 as *The Battle of the Narrow Seas*. Kathleen was dismayed to hear that Peter had accepted a reduction in the promised royalties from 17 1/2 per cent to 10 per cent. "Pete is an absolute Parsifal about money." She went to see the publishers but got no change. The rewards were moderate: £600 for the first ten thousand copies, £900 if the printrun was fifteen thousand, both less standard income tax at 50 percent.

Although the war at sea was virtually over in European waters, it was far from over in the Pacific. British warships were to move to the Far East to reinforce the American fleet when Germany was finally defeated. Peter had never given up hope of getting command of a destroyer, and now the Admiralty redeemed its promise. They appointed him to command a frigate, HMS *Cardigan Bay*, building at Leith in Scotland. A frigate is smaller than a destroyer, but this new one was to carry the most up-to-date equipment, and its future commander was delighted—so much so that when, toward the end of his life, he was invited to make a list of the "things I am and have been most proud of," one of them was "being appointed to command a new frigate." He spent much of the winter of 1944 and early spring of 1945 taking courses that would fit him for his new command, and visiting the shipyard to see how *Cardigan Bay* was getting on.

All this traveling took him, as before, constantly away from home. On the surface, all was well domestically. The cloud of imminent danger to Peter's life had lifted, Jane had found a job at the BBC and begun work on a novel. But the underlying tensions had not gone away, nor had Kathleen's influence as an *eminence grise*. "If she hurts him, I will kill her," she had written. Hurt him, now, Jane had. Kathleen did not kill Jane, but she was quite prepared to kill the marriage. Peter was not. For once, there was open disagreement and an exchange of wounding words between him and his mother. "I am deeply sad that we cannot come to an agreement," he wrote to her on January 9, 1945, "and that our discussions about it achieve so little and are so unhappy." He implored her to see his point of view.

> I have married, I believe, someone very strange and rare and outstanding. I do not, nor ever did, suppose that it would be easy to be married to that sort of person. I was, and still am, prepared to meet all these difficulties for the sake of the good things that come out of being married to anyone so stimulating and exciting. When our first trouble arose a year ago I took a wrong course which put Jane and me much further apart than

we need have been, and prepared the way for the next trouble, which is now also over, and which might never have arisen if we had not been so far apart. The attitude, which was my mistake, is the attitude you have taken in your talks with Jane both then and on this second occasion, which leaves her with no one to turn to.

Now the point, darling, is this. I am taking a definite course, not just drifting or guessing. I am carrying forward a definite attitude which is perhaps best described as taming my wild animal and not caging it. You do not agree with that attitude, and I am trying to make you agree with it, but if I fail there is no reason at all why it should affect our relationship—yours and mine. Unfortunately if we talk about it, it does. So we must be especially careful when we talk about it, which is why I am writing this.

Whether you agree or not, you must let me give it a fair chance; that is to say you must not work against me, so as to make my plan more difficult. It was this which I deplored in your talks with Jane at Fritton. It is essential for her that she should have confidence, for example in her psychologist, and so you must not belittle or discredit this which she finds helpful ... There is one last thing to say, which is on the subject of loyalties. I don't want there to be any divided loyalties; on the other hand if there are, my loyalty must be with my Jane, who is my life now, rather than with my family ... I will come and have tea with you and we will be careful not to be so hurting to each other because I do love you so much, darling mummy, but my mind is so made up on the course I must take.

This was the nearest he ever came to a rift with his mother. She did not change her mind, and neither did he.

He persisted in his resolve to save his marriage. "It's a bitter irony, isn't it," he wrote to Jane, "that so much love cannot bring happiness." And "I will try so hard to be a more understanding husband, and not so soft and not so sentimental and not so selfish." The decision had been taken to move from Clifton Hill, and in the spring of 1945 they bought the lease of a terraced house in Edwardes Square, South Kensington, with a pleasant garden. Kathleen's comment was: "H'm. I hope it is going to be a success, because I did strive hard to find the money for him." Then, on May 8, 1945, came the German surrender. Jane was in the hospital having her tonsils out. She needed a change, and left with a friend for a holiday in the Scilly Isles.

"About a week ago," Kathleen wrote in June 1945, "Pete was sitting at his desk in his more or less unfinished new house when Sir Somebody Holbrook arrived out of the blue and asked him, 'Are you at all interested in politics?' to which Pete replied 'scarcely at all' and was told 'that's just what we want, will you come and stand for Rugby?' Rugby however had other ideas but the bug had entered under his skin and when the Conservative Central Office asked him if he would go on a list of eight, he agreed." He had less than twenty-four hours in which to make up his mind. His long desired ship was nearing completion; were he to take her over he would sail away to the Pacific for no one knew how long—years perhaps, for the atomic bomb and the Japanese surrender were quite unforeseen. It was unlikely that his marriage would survive. He consulted Jane by telephone. She, too, was faced with a difficult choice. She decided to give the marriage one more chance, advised him to stand for Parliament, and returned to London to take an active part in the election campaign.

Peter was adopted as Conservative candidate for a newly formed constituency, North Wembley. He was a war hero, election posters depicted him in uniform, his wife was young and elegant, and altogether the Tories believed that they were on to a good thing. Their candidate was the first to admit that he knew scarcely anything about politics and nothing at all about economics, but thought that he knew what kind of a future he had been fighting for. It was not one to be shaped by revolutionary ideas. He was a natural conservative. But war had generated questions in his and many other minds as to the kind of society they wanted to see, and would pass on to their children. As ever at election times, it would be a juster, happier, less class-ridden society with better opportunities and higher living standards for all. As long ago as 1940 he had written to Jane that he was developing a conscience, "a thing I never had or lost in early youth but am now visibly sprouting, and shall feel bound to try and help to rebuild the world. I don't really feel like a world rebuilder, but is that a good enough reason for sitting back at the end and not bothering?"

An imprecise desire to build a better world was a far cry from the cut and thrust of an election campaign in North Wembley. Sometimes he did not know what hecklers were on about, so he arranged a code with the agent, who indicated by signs whether the questioner was friend or foe. He summoned to his aid a galaxy of political stars such as Harold Macmillan, Quintin Hogg (later Lord Hailsham), Sir John Simon,m and A. P. Herbert. Despite his age—thirty-six—and plumpness, he turned a cartwheel on the rostrum of a church hall. All seemed set fair for success, but the 1945 election held one of those surprises that put politics in the same league as roulette. The party that had led the nation to victory with one of the world's greatest leaders at its head was swept from office in a landslide that left Labour under Clement Attlee in the seat of power. Peter, in losing by only 432 votes, did exceptionally well. Both he and Jane, who had canvassed as hard as he had, were sadly disappointed. He nursed the constituency for another two and a half years, but other interests soon extinguished his never robust political ambitions.

What would have been the outcome had the roulette ball come to rest at *rouge* instead of *noir?* Had Britain been deprived of a future Minister for the Environment tailor-made for the job? Certainly Peter would have gone on painting, cherishing ducks and geese, promoting causes, and pursuing aims. Whether he would have achieved more effectively inside Parliament those conservationist aims he was about to embrace in earnest is anybody's guess. It would not have saved his marriage.

Since leaving the Navy just before the election he had been painting busily at Edwardes Square, and his first postwar exhibition at Ackermann's gallery in November 1945 was a great success. Forty oil paintings and fourteen pencil drawings were on view, with prices ranging from 210 guineas (*Greylags on Flood Water*) to 25 guineas for the smallest canvases. Kathleen was triumphant when all the pictures sold, bar three, for a total of £4,000, less the gallery's commission and the cost of framing. The Queen bought "a rather yellowy goldy picture because it reminded her of Sandringham, and I got three dozen roses and made Jane present them to her. Then I made Pete walk round with her." He was also selling pictures on commission.

Now back in his stride as a professional painter, he decided to show his work again in New York. In April 1946 he and Jane sailed in the *Aquitania* for Halifax and proceeded to New York, where the exhibition at Harlow's galleries on East Fifty-seventh Street ran from April 10 to May 4 There were thirty-five oils and twenty-three small pencil drawings, but the latter did not sell well. This exhibition was more successful than the previous one had been, but considerably less so than those held in London, and for the same reasons: as a painter he was much less well known in New York, Americans were not as bird-minded as the English, and his mother's stagemanagement was missing. But he did conduct a useful piece of business. During the war Paul Gallico had published a short book, *The Snow Goose*, which drew its inspiration from the story of the wild pinkfooted goose Anabel. Gallico turned Anabel into a snow goose, Peter into an outcast hunchbank painter living in a lighthouse, added an innocent young lass called Fritha who befriended Philip the hunchback, and set the climax of the story at the time of the evacuation from Dunkirk. The hunchback perished while rescuing soldiers in his small sailing boat and the snow goose, after circling round his empty boat, flew back to Fritha. This unashamedly sentimental story touched a nerve and was a runaway success, selling over half a million copies. Now it was to be republished, and Peter was asked to illustrate the new edition. In Harlow's gallery he encountered Paul Gallico, who was looking for a new face that would fit the part of Fritha; in Peter's drawing of Jane he found exactly what he wanted, and it became the frontispiece of the British edition. The story, republished in Britain in 1946, leapt into the bestseller list and continued to sell lavishly for many years.

The zing and punch of New York, contrasted with blitzed and rationed London, was exhilarating. No clothes coupons and a feast of fashion in the city's department stores successfully led Jane into financial temptation, while Peter renewed acquaintance with Jean Delacour, who was in charge of the Bronx zoo, and asked him to take back to London an assortment of animals. Jane had brought with her a red notebook containing parts of the manuscript of her novel to show to publishers, but this got left behind in a taxi, and every effort to recover it failed. Though this was a blow at the time, when she had rewritten the novel she considered the second version to be better than the first.

Their departure in the *Queen Mary* was somewhat bizarre. Delacour had sent to the docks a generous consignment of terrapins, toads, tortoises, snakes, and sundry other creatures, including a case of alligators, but the dockers who loaded the passengers' baggage drew the line at these. Each box had been neatly labeled, and on the dock Peter was to be seen hastily crossing out "snakes," "toads" and similar descriptions and substituting "Fragile—Cabin Only." Luckily the cabin was a large one with a bathroom attached. After a day or two, Peter unpacked the snakes to exercise them in the bath and one of them, a garter snake, escaped down the drain. Where would it emerge? Their cabin was flanked by that of Lord and Lady Halifax on one side and of the Canadian prime minister and his wife on the other. Probably neither couple knew a harmless garter from a deadly asp. Fortunately the clever snake found its way back to the right bath. There were difficult moments, also, in the dining saloon, where they would ask for a whole lettuce without dressing, chopped cooked pork or raw mince. The stewards took these unusual requests with Jeeveslike composure.

Kathleen was at Southampton to welcome home her son, who (she wrote) had sold £3,000 worth of pictures and cleared £19. The cabin was crowded with boxes and "in every corner was a plate of raw meat and such. They had 31 packets to pass through the Customs, one being a gigantic wardrobe trunk and one a bird cage with a live bird. For 2 1/2 hours he never drew breath, but talked and talked about America." Just one month later she had "the great felicity of seeing my Pete standing up in naval uniform in a Duck, as he passed he was gallantly struggling with commentating for the BBC and saluting the King all in one." This was the victory parade in June 1946.

The New York expedition was the swan song of the Scotts' marriage. Jane had fallen out of love with Peter and into it with someone else. In the summer of 1947 she walked out of No. 8 Edwardes Square with £10, a suitcase containing her half-written novel, and some of her smart New York clothes. Nicola and her nanny remained behind. Jane had no plan except to look for somewhere to live, hunt for a job, finish her novel, and find a publisher. These objects she achieved. The novel became *The Beautiful Visit*, an immediate *succes d'estime* and winner of the John Llewellyn Rhys memorial prize. She did not return to Edwardes Square.

CHAPTER TWELVE

The Birth of the Wildfowl Trust

"I returned to my birds, Peter wrote, with a passionate delight." All he wanted, like most of his contemporaries, was to pick up the threads of his previous existence as if the war had never been. But the war had been. His lighthouse had gone, or rather the sea had gone, driven back by drainage schemes which had freed marshes for agriculture, and beyond the seawall lay crops of sugarbeet, corn, and potatoes. To re-establish his collection Peter must find for it another home.

He considered, and rejected, several possibilities. Then came a letter from an old acquaintance, a farmer living in the Severn Valley above Bristol, inviting him to inspect the immense flocks of whitefronted geese that came from Russia every year to winter on the saltings on the south bank of the river. So, in December 1945, he and John Winter met Howard Davis by the Patch bridge over the Sharpness and Gloucester Canal at the village of Slimbridge.

At this point the lesser whitefronted goose, *Anser erythropus*, enters the story. Peter had first made its acquaintance in Hungary when he had sent several wing-tipped birds of the species to join his lighthouse collection, and at the outbreak of war a pair had found sanctuary in Will Tinsley's orchard. Only one member of the species had previously been recorded in Britain, and that was in 1886 when a single bird had been shot in Northumberland. The lesser and the common whitefronted goose are so much alike that only an expert can tell them apart, and then only at close quarters. The lessers are only slightly smaller than their cousins, their bill is slightly smaller and pinker, and they have yellow eyelids.

In 1943 Will Tinsley had reported to Peter that a wild lesser whitefront had dropped down one December day to join the pinioned pair in his orchard. Might there, Peter wondered, be other occasions when lesser whitefronts had come, unrecognized, to Britain in the company of their larger Russian relatives? These thoughts were at the back of his mind when he accepted Howard Davis's invitation to see the whitefronts on the Severn estuary.

As a defense against Hitler's Panzer divisions, four concrete pillboxes had been built just to landward of the low seawall that protects the farmlands of the wide Severn valley from the river's high tides. Fortunately these pill-boxes had not been put to the test as military defenses, but they made useful hides for bird-watchers. You could approach them by crouching under the shelter of the seawall and so out of sight of the geese, who might be seen grazing between the seawall and the river on the saltmarsh, known as the Dumbles, perhaps only a few yards away. As an added bonus the winter sun, if any, would be at your back.

Peter, Howard Davis, and two companions ensconced themselves in one of the pillboxes and looked out at about two thousand wild and unsuspecting geese. That evening, Peter told Davis of his theory, so that when they returned next day to the pillbox both were on the lookout for a possible lesser whitefront. Sure enough, in less than an hour Davis spotted one: just one, mingling with the flock.

> It was first seen at 200 yards range [Peter wrote] amongst a crowd of [common] Whitefronts and it fed to within about 100 yards. In the bright sunshine the yellow eyelids were very distinct and called forth the remark that they were "shining like a golden sovereign." It was slightly darker than the surrounding Whitefronts and the base of the neck was noticeably more chestnut. The bill, which looked minute, was strikingly brighter pink, almost a coral pink ... . In conclusion, it seems reasonable to us [Davis and Scott] to suppose that A. *erythropus is* not really quite so rare as has hitherto been imagined.

In the afternoon they saw a second lesser whitefront in amongst the bigger birds. That settled it. Admitting that this observation hardly amounted to a world-shaking discovery, it was for Peter "a moment of unforgettable exultation—a major triumph, an epoch-making occurrence, a turning point." Then and there he made the decision to establish on the Severn estuary a center for the scientific study, public display, and conservation of the wildfowl of the world. The Dumbles where the wild geese wintered belonged, with much of the Berkeley vale, to Captain Robert Berkeley, whose family had held the nearby castle for some eight hundred years and still lived there, claiming descent from a Berkeley who adorned the court of Edward the Confessor (1042–1066). (The legend that the Berkeleys could ride from their castle on the Severn to their square in Mayfair without setting hoof off their own property is a half-truth; manors strategically dotted along the route were owned by members of the family, who could therefore leapfrog from one Berkeley property to another without necessarily owning all the land in between.) Outside the seawall, up to five thousand wild geese, mainly whitefronts (*Anser albifrons albifrons*) came regularly from Siberia, Greenland, and Iceland to winter on the Dumbles and on adjacent fields and marshes known as the New Grounds, because they had been drained in or about 1470. Both geese and their habitat were preserved, as they had been for centuries, by the Berkeley family, following correct principles of conservation while the word was still mainly confined to the preserving pan in the kitchen. Sport was the object, not study or display, but the result was the same: the geese flourished. "There were always at least three keepers on the New Grounds while the geese were in residence," wrote Captain Robert Berkeley. "We always had strict rules with regard to shooting which ensured that the geese were never driven off, nor did their numbers ever deteriorate because of shooting. The geese always had three months unmolested in order that they should look on the New Grounds as their home." Nevertheless, in recent years numbers *had* declined, for two reasons: the plow and the bomb. Both were wartime interruptions, and Captain Berkeley hoped that they would go away.

Peter's dream could not be realized, therefore, without Captain Berkeley's full agreement. This he secured. Early in 1946 the Berkeley Estates leased to him 23 acres of the New Grounds, together with two red-brick farm workers' cottages, one of them empty; a bungalow; and some ramshackle farm buildings. The lease reserved to the landlord the right to shoot over the property for not more than eight days a year, but in practice no more than three shoots, or at most four, had been held each winter in recent years. In 1949 the lease was renewed for twenty-five years at a rent of £65 a year.

A powerful eye of imagination was needed to see these flat, soggy fields from which, in wartime, crops of sugarbeet had been taken, as a happy home for Peter's new collection. No time was lost in attacking them with everything from spades to bulldozers. By a stroke of luck, there was a prisoner-of-war camp nearby, many of whose German inmates had not yet been repatriated, and Peter was able to engage a squad who proved excellent and willing workmen. Their first task was to enclose 17 acres in an 8-foot-high fox-proof fence, which still keeps out foxes more than forty years later. Then ponds were dug, paths laid out, reeds and brambles cleared, trees and shrubs planted; and so, with surprising speed, vision was translated into reality. One of the site's main attractions was an old duck decoy, overgrown and dilapidated, and this was brought into use for ringing. The first year's catch was hardly sensational—six mallards. Still, it was a beginning.

An experienced ornithologist, John Yealland, was Peter's first appointment. (He was later to become curator of birds at the London zoo.) Birds started
to arrive immediately, sometimes in advance of their pens' completion. One of
Peter's prewar friends and fellow collectors was Gavin Maxwell, soon to become famous for his tamed otters and his best-selling book about them, *Ring of
Bright Water.* Maxwell kept about forty or fifty pinioned geese at Monteith in
Wigtonshire, but had started to establish a fishing industry based on basking
sharks on the island of Soay, which left him no time to attend to his birds. Peter
arranged to take over the collection. Having satisfied himself that the pens and
pond designed for their reception would be finished in time, he traveled to
Wigtonshire with John Yealland to bring them back. Back they came, to find
the pens still unready. Birds being shipped from place to place often remain for
days, or even weeks, in their crates, but to keep them in these cramped conditions was not Peter's way. By then the bungalow was empty. Birds of each species had a room to themselves: greater snow geese in one bedroom, Ross's in
another, emperors in the kitchen and uplands in the pantry. Next day the pens
were completed, and the birds driven to their new homes.

Old avian friends from prewar days received a warm welcome. Will
Tinsley sent the pair of lesser whitefronts, and Dick Pilcher, a Lincolnshire surgeon, a pair of redbreasted geese, sole survivors of Peter's flock of nearly fifty. A
shipment from Spedan Lewis at Leckford included eight of the lighthouse con-
tingent: whitefronts, lesser whitefronts, a bean goose and a barred upland, a
pair of ruddyheads, and another of Abyssinian geese. From Canada, in the *Queen
Elizabeth,* came a pair of greater snow geese—"very quarrelsome birds"—and eggs
arrived from Iceland.

So the collection grew, as a rule through the usual methods of buying
and exchanging, but in one case by less conventional means. Among the drop-
pers-in at Edwardes Square was a young man Peter had first encountered when
punt-gunning in the Ribble estuary while on leave from HMS *Broke.* Keith
Shackleton, a distant cousin of the Antarctic explorer, was then an Oundle schoolboy who shared Peter's devotion both to shooting wildfowl and to painting
them in their surroundings; and when, after the war, he heard of the project to
preserve and breed them at Slimbridge, he attached himself to the enterprise in
an informal way. "We ought to have some diving ducks," he remarked one day
to Peter. "Tufted ducks for instance." Peter agreed. "There are lots in St. James's
Park. Why don't we go and catch a couple?" He continued:

> Peter said: "How on earth do we do that?" I said, "Well you know
> how tame they are, we could attract them with some breadcrumbs
> and when they get within reach, we'll grab one each." He thought
> that was a great idea, so into the pouring rain we went down to
> St. James's Park with a bag of stale cake etc., and fortunately

there was no one around, and it was dark, just the street lamps burning. We grabbed together. "Got one?" he said. I said "Yes." I pocketed them in an old raglan coat with a very large pocket each side. A policeman came along and Pete said "My God! There goes my peerage!" I said "It's alright, he didn't recognise you." We got them into a box and drove down the Mall and to Edwardes Square and put them in the bath.

By the autumn of 1946 the enterprise at Slimbridge had grown to a point where a regular, sustainable method of funding was needed. Peter's savings had melted away and been replaced by an overdraft. In October he wrote to Captain Berkeley:

> I am contemplating the formation of a Trust whose object would be the development of the ornithological and avicultural amenities of the place. It would be called the Severn Wildfowl Trust. Of course I would not consider proceeding without your full consent. But if you should agree that it is a good idea I would very much like you to be either one of the trustees or a member of our committee. The advantages of such a trust would be that my own contributions, if made by a seven year contract, would be doubled by reclaiming the income tax on them.1 Furthermore I could reasonably hope to get a fair contribution I think from a number of my friends and possibly also from the general public. The disadvantage is I suppose the danger of losing control of the place, but I don't think this is great, particularly if we are most careful in choosing the committee.

Peter took silence for assent, and two weeks later wrote: "Since you haven't sent a priority telegram saying that in no circumstances would you countenance the Severn Wildfowl Trust, I am hoping and supposing that, by and large, you approve. We have drawn up some rules and the Trust can come into existence as soon as we have a small meeting to pass them." The small meeting was held at the Patch Bridge guest house beside the Sharpness and Gloucester Canal on November 10. 1946. Captain Berkeley was there. The Kennet family solicitor, Keith Miller Jones, had drawn up some rules, and Peter had enlisted three friends as founding fathers of the Trust: Michael Bratby, James Robertson Justice, and the farmer-ornithologist Howard Davis. The meeting was short and to the point, and the Severn Wildfowl Trust came into being.

The next stage was to find a suitable president. He must be a man whose name would carry weight both with the public and in official circles, and he must be interested in birds. Fortunately such an individual existed in the shape of Field-Marshal Viscount Alanbrooke, who for four grueling years had fought the war on two fronts, against Germany as Chief of the Imperial General Staff and chairman of the Combined Chiefs of Staff committee, and against the wilder flights of fancy indulged in by a chief who at once infuriated and enchanted him. Without "Brookie's" incisive mind and steadying influence, some of those wilder flights would surely have led to disaster, just as without Churchill's leadership disaster would have surely come. The strain was very great. Alanbrooke's safety valve lay in photographing birds. He loved them with a passion almost as great as Peter's, and accepted the invitation without hesitation, only stipulating that he might not be able to give much time to his presidential duties. In fact, for fourteen years he never missed a council meeting, except on one or two occasions when he was ill.

In finding a treasurer, Peter again went to the top. Sir Archibald Jamieson had recently retired from the chairmanship of Vickers Ltd., the giant engineering firm; he was also a friend and Norfolk neighbor of the Kennets. Without, perhaps, fully foreseeing all the difficulties that stemmed from Peter's propensity for spending money first and raising it afterward, he, too, accepted. Sir Percy Lister, whose engineering works were in nearby Dursley, and Lord Dulverton, head of a generous family trust, agreed to serve as vice presidents, and Bill Kennet as a trustee. The other members of the council were: Max Nicholson, the least bureaucratic and most versatile of civil servants, soon to head the Nature Conservancy Council; Captain Berkeley; Howard Davis; Keith Miller Jones; James Robertson Justice; and two professional ornithologists, Phyllis Barclay-Smith, secretary of the British Ornithologists Union, and Bernard Tucker, editor of *British Birds*. Michael Bratby became the honorary secretary, and the honorary director was, of course, Peter Scott. The setting up of this new body eased financial pressures by attracting members who paid a guinea a head, and by securing contributions from one or two charitable trusts, but it was still a struggle to expand. Main water pipes and telephone lines were laid under the canal to reach the cottages; electricity did not come until much later. The decoy was completed and eight more hides built along the seawall. Peter indulged his love of gadgetry by designing an adjustable shutter which allowed the occupants of the hides to widen or narrow the slits through which they peered, according to the distance of the birds from their observers. He also designed elbow rests for users of binoculars, and foot rests for their comfort. By the end of 1947, he was able to claim that his collection of wildfowl was "certainly the most representative of its kind in the world."

As the collection grew so also did the need for people to look after it. Peter did not have to advertise: people turned up. An article in *Country Life* about Peter's plans caught the eye of a young man, recently demobilized, whose marriage and consequent baby had obliged him to abandon hopes of a medical career. "Is there any chance," Tommy Johnstone wrote to Peter, "of making a living with birds?"

To my amazement he wrote back and said yes, come and see me. So I went to Edwardes Square and was met at the door by a beautiful girl, Elizabeth Adams. She said, "Hello, I'm Peter Scott's secretary." So I said, how lucky for Peter, this gorgeous girl. Eventually Peter appeared. I thought he was a delightful chap. He was very vague about everything, but terribly nice. He said, you must go down and see the place. So Diana and I went down to find it . . .

The "gorgeous girl" so admired by Tommy Johnstone was in fact a friend of Wayland's whom he later married. As she put it, she was a "graduate temporary ex-WRNS full-time dogsbody there, part-running the house (put-upon cook, hysterical nanny), part being with Jane—who was on and off the boil about going; as best I could running Peter, whom Keith Shackleton was always 'ticing away from doing what he was supposed to be doing; running Douggie Eccleston and the office ... " Tommy Johnstone went to Slimbridge, trudged across some soggy fields and found John Yealland, who signed him on as assistant curator in charge of developments, and he stayed for thirty years. Eunice Overend, a young biology teacher at a school at Burnham-on-Crouch, heard through Howard Davis of the new project and came over to lend a hand. When the school year ended, she resigned her teaching post and signed on as assistant to Yealland for £6 a week.

By then there was a keeper, Mr. Cameron, living in the bungalow with his wife and two daughters, one of whom, Peggy—"tall and slim, with green eyes and a flaming mop of hair"—became adept at rearing birds, no easy matter with only a few antiquated paraffin-burning incubators to hatch the eggs, aided by a squad of unreliable broody hens. A gypsylike character who had made his living by catching eels and poaching salmon in the Severn joined the team and for a time worked the decoy. The way he caught eels was to string a lot of worms together, like a daisy-chain, roll them into a ball and drop the ball into the river, where the eel would swallow it and be drawn to the surface.

For the staff, life was spartan. Eunice Overend at first camped out in the empty cottage, curled up on a wooden settee until she borrowed a bed. A single tap in the yard served everyone's needs, but the yard in winter became a quagmire so deep that Eunice, after washing her labrador Blondel under the tap, had to carry him over her shoulder to the cottage or he would have again become encased in mud from nose to tail. A Rayburn in the cottage provided the only heating, paraffin lamps the lighting, and there was no bathroom or inside lavatory. The Johnstones found a cottage in the village no less devoid of comforts; if she wanted a bath, Diana had to walk with the baby to the guest house by Patch bridge, where Mrs. Hawkins charged a shilling a time.

To compound the discomforts, the winter of 1946–7 was exceptionally severe. The tap froze, ponds iced over, and snow blanketed the feeding grounds, to be cleared with shovels grasped in numbed hands. Feeding the birds became a major problem. Rationing was not relaxed for several years after the end of the war; indeed some shortages intensified. The corn ration allowed by the Ministry of Agriculture fell far short of the collection's needs. Peter was obliged to beg for tailings—grain too small or damaged to be milled—from his farmer friends, and to scrounge for anything else he could find. Most of the farmers helped him out, but not Mr. Fisher, the tenant of the land surrounding Peter's patch. Mr. Fisher resented the arrival in his midst of a number of strangers with peculiar ideas and unnecessary birds, and made his feelings plain. For several years a state of war prevailed, with Captain Berkeley called in now and then to restore a precarious peace. Mr. Fisher kept sheep and cattle on his part of the New Grounds, and after the wild geese had settled on them he would drive round in his Land Rover ostensibly to inspect his livestock; loud blasts on his horn caused the birds to take flight, and so disappoint visitors. Then he discovered the trick of making his vehicle backfire, so frightening away the geese even more effectively. This was to go on until Mr. Fisher, after a great deal of persuasion, agreed to take the tenancy of another farm.

Meanwhile, except on weekends, Peter was living in greater if congested comfort at No. 8 Edwardes Square. The dining room had become an office in which sat Elizabeth Adams and Douglas Eccleston, who had come to do the typing and filing from Bletchley Park in Buckinghamshire, where the geniuses who cracked the German code Enigma had played their crucial part in winning the Second World War. Nicola's ebullient white Pekinese Bushy would sometimes plunge downstairs to leap on desks and chairs and scatter documents in all directions. Michael Bratby was another regular visitor to Edwardes Square. He had had a successful war as a Major in the Intelligence branch of the army, and an unsuccessful marriage. He had married Brenda. After their wedding, Kathleen wrote: "How truly I pray it isn't, or won't be, as tragic as it seemed. It is quite clear she is still thinking of Pete. Why should she not be, but that will pass." Michael Bratby wrote that he was blissfully happy, but his kindness, which was great, was not enough. He was posted to America where she could not follow; she worked for an American colonel, and by the time the Wildfowl Trust came into being he and Brenda had parted. He resumed his stockbroking career, moved to London, and was spending his spare time in helping to establish the Trust. His services were free, but everyone else had to be paid, if not much, and Peter was the sole paymaster.

James Robertson Justice was another fairly frequent visitor. A friend of Peter's from punt-gunning days, he was one of those Falstaffian figures—portly, bold, rambunctious, and cheeky, with a bushy brown beard—who emerge from time to time from obscurity to become a legend while still alive. In 1947 his career in films was in its early stages; his big chance was to come in the following year when he played Petty Officer Evans in *Scott of the Antarctic*, with John Mills as the Captain and Diana Churchill as Kathleen. His varied career had included serving a spell in the Canadian Mounties, causing an international incident by shooting a Nazi in the leg in Germany, fighting with the International Brigade against Franco's forces in the Spanish civil war—he was said to have halted a charge by pointing to the sky and crying "Look! Greylag geese!"— and taking the Duke of Edinburgh punt-gunning on the Wash, to the disapproval, it was said, of the Queen, because of the danger. On the outbreak of the Second World War he joined the RNVR and found himself in the engineering branch, despite a total ignorance of anything to do with engines. He saw the war through with the straight gold braid stripes of an officer of the Royal Navy, instead of the insignia of the Wavy Navy—or so the story went, but he fathered many stories. He was a brilliant raconteur, indifferent to money, and so generous a host that when he gave a party at Wheeler's restaurant in London, the caviar was served in pudding bowls and the guests helped themselves with tablespoons. When the time came for him to play the part that made his name, the irascible, domineering but basically kindhearted consultant surgeon Sir Lancelot Spratt in *Doctor in the House* and other Doctor films, he had only to be himself to capture his audience.

Weekends were for the birds. Peter would drive at speed in his green Jaguar to Gloucestershire to review progress and re-energize everyone in sight. A neo-schoolboyish sense of fun pervaded these gatherings of middle-aged adults— Peter had his thirty-eighth birthday in September. He was the Commander, Bratby the Major, and the younger Keith Shackleton the Scapegoat, because he often got the blame for disturbing the wild geese. James Justice came over from Whitchurch in Hampshire, where he kept his falcons, and presented the Commander and the Major with a case of Founder's port (Sanderson 1917). The Camerons had a tame, or semi-tame, hare, who was standoffish toward strangers but let James Justice hold her while she nibbled his beard. During the summer of 1947, everyone got down to work hammering in stakes, digging out ponds, planting willows and, when the winter came, shivering in pillboxes counting geese. Peter's expertise lay in supervising, rather than in actually hammering in stakes.

Now he discovered a new talent, creating landscapes. In today's absence of wealthy landowners eager to lay out lakes, deer parks, follies, avenues, and ornamental fountains, he was lucky to have a piece of Gloucestershire, albeit flat, featureless, and muddy, on which to employ his skill. Amongst his papers are meticulous, detailed, and beautifully executed drawings of the layouts both of the Slimbridge venture and of others to come. Tommy Johnstone has de-

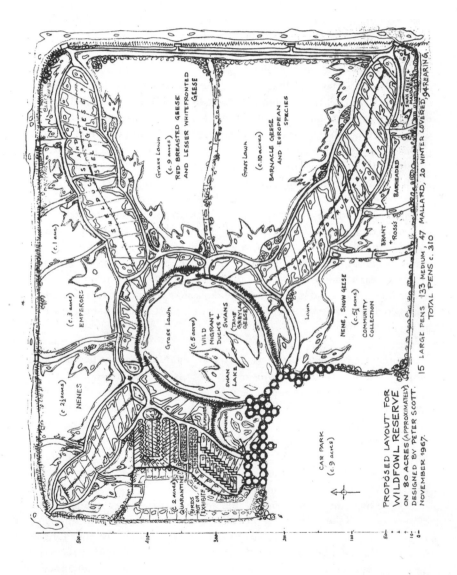

PROPOSED LAYOUT FOR
WILDFOWL RESERVE
ON 80 ACRES (APPROXIMATELY)
DESIGNED BY PETER SCOTT.
NOVEMBER 1967.

15 LARGE PENS, 133 MEDIUM, 47 MALLARD, 20 WINTER COVERED 94 REARING.
TOTAL PENS c. 310

scribed Peter's method of translating plans on paper into features on the ground. "He would walk round and mark out a pond like this—one foot in front of the other—and he had a chap behind him digging out the turfs with a space to make the shape of the pond." Then along came a digger or drag-line, and in a day or two there was the pond—that is, if the money held out. "Go in as deep as possible without getting stuck," Peter would say as he left for London, leaning from the window of his car, "and go on until the money runs out." It often did run out. "He'd go to the local nursery and buy two hundred laurel bushes, three hundred willows or whatever, then I'd get a phone message from London saying Tommy, you'd better hold that for the time being. Then he'd come down and say, we've got to get rid of some staff, we can't afford them. But we'd hardly *got* any staff! Really, he said, we must get rid of *something*. And in the end more staff were taken on." "He'd come down at the weekend," Eunice Overend added, "set up his easel in the cottage and paint two or three landscapes. Then he'd leave them to dry, come down the next weekend and put in the birds. He sold them for about £25 each and that kept us going for a bit longer."

Another source of income was the sale of surplus birds. Gasoline was still rationed, and the only transport available to get birds to the station, or to collect incoming ones, was provided by an elderly and self-opinionated mare called Mary who, with some reluctance, drew a cart. Mary had a phobia about trains. When approaching the station, her driver halted on a bridge and peered anxiously each way to make sure that no train was in sight. Even so, Mary generally panicked and had to be steered toward a wall at one end of the station that halted her cavalry charge, while crates of protesting ducks and geese rattled about in the cart.

The parentage of the wildfowl sanctuary at Slimbridge might be described as by Peter out of improvisation. Inevitably, things quite often went wrong. Self-restraint fostered by long hours spent in icy mud lying in wait for his quarry, and tempered by the storms and dangers of the North Atlantic, enabled him to cope with mishaps calmly. In thirty years, Tommy Johnstone said, he had only known Peter to lose his temper twice, and then only briefly. Once it was with Mr. Fisher who, on some particularly important occasion, had deliberately put to flight the wild geese. On the other occasion a youth employed as an assistant warden had thrown stones at pinioned birds.

Perhaps the impression created by this unshaken calm and self-discipline was one of the factors that provoked an unexpected reaction among some acquaintances. "One of the things I couldn't understand," Tommy Johnstone said, "was that people showed a sort of deference toward him. All sorts of distinguished people used to come to see him and you noticed that deference, that respect. Yet he was so natural, so reasonable, so kind and unaffected, he was just himself and never put on any act." An ability to concentrate on several things at once was a characteristic that impressed Diana Johnstone. "We all used to have Christmas dinner together with the children, our Carol, and Nicola who came from London with nanny Buss and the peke. We played games, and Peter joined in. At the same time he'd be making notes on a sheet of paper about some quite serious thing. But he heard every word we were saying."

At times it is hard to resist the feeling that Peter, as seen through the eyes of his colleagues, was almost too good to be true. Warts there must have been; his talent to inspire loyalty either blinded his staff to them, or there was nothing to see. "He hated sacking people," suggested a colleague. So does almost everyone else. "Yes, but he'd get others to do it if he possibly could." A man who had been eased out, if not actually sacked, resented this. "I understood the reason, but he should have told me himself." On occasion, he could intimidate. "If you went into his studio with muddy shoes" (this was later, when his house had been built) "he would say, very politely, 'Would you mind taking off your shoes?' And you'd feel diminished, though a seraphic smile removed the sting."

In November 1947, Peter made what he was to describe as the most important decision of his life. Elizabeth Adams had left Edwardes Square to marry his brother Wayland, and had passed on the news of the vacant post to Philippa Talbot-Ponsonby, who was looking for a job. Born in Bloemfontein in the Orange Free State, she was the daughter of a naval offficer who retired to South Africa to indulge his passion for creative gardening and breeding pedigree short-horn bulls. After his death in 1930 the family returned to England where Philippa had led the social life of an English county family, and satisfied her spirit of adventure by foxhunting in Hampshire and mountaineering in the Alps. Then came the war, spent first as a land girl and then in the Code and Cypher School at Bletchley Park, followed by a year in the British Embassy in Belgrade. Peter recalled "a shy, quiet girl, who sat before me looking small and neat and serious. The appointment was urgent and she got the job." It was to last, in one way or another, for forty-two years.

Despite the camaraderie of Slimbridge and the bustling days at Edwardes Square, Peter was lonely. The wound caused by the breakup of his marriage was still raw. Until the process of divorce had been started there might be hope, if only a glimmer, of reconciliation. From the cottage on the New Grounds, on a July evening in 1946, he wrote to Jane:

> Darling darling Jenny ... It is very *peaceful* here. I have just walked
> out on to the bridge over the canal, and along the banks were a
> dozen or more little twinkling stars amongst the grass. Glow-
> worms. I walked along the bank amongst them and bent down
> to watch them crawling up the grass stems, lit by the light of

their own green halo. Is it all right to mention them?—they aren't really worms at all, but the caterpillars of a beetle and they look like this [drawing], and the light shines from under their tails. It is amazingly bright. As I walked back and over the bridge and looked at them from across the canal I could still see the light from one of them at 100 yards ... My decoy is incredibly beautiful, with the tall willows silver grey in their full leaf. It is a lovely place and I am pleased to have it. ... I'm afraid it will not please you at all if I tell you how much I love you. *Embarras de richesse*—everyone loves you and why wouldn't they poor things.

The letter was never sent.

Peter still found solace in the company of his mother. In August 1946 he drove her to Lowestoft where he once more sailed a racing dinghy in the regatta. It was, he wrote, "less fun than usual." In June he and John Winter had taken *Thunder and Lightning* out of mothballs and sailed her once again in the Prince of Wales' Cup. Expecting to be outclassed by younger men, to their surprise they won the race by three minutes. It was his third win. "He is a queer lad," wrote his mother, probing, after nearly forty years, into a character she still found baffling.

> Whilst he is at a thing he is completely one-tracked. Last week he thought of nothing whatever but [dinghy] racing, he neither wrote nor received any letters, he did not read a paper. This week his single track will be this new wildfowl sanctuary. Next week the track will be the council of Olympic games in Switzerland, and the week after political meetings in Yorkshire. I think his strength lies in his quite extraordinary concentration on the matter in hand.

Once again, as in the days of the lighthouse, she found herself drawn into a world of mud and geese and rising in a dark and chilly dawn to trudge over marshes. In December 1946, a freezing one at that, she wrote:

> Oh dear me I do love going off with him for a lovely weekend. The geese were terrific, about 3,500 of them. The cold was terrific too but it was such fun and Pete is so like his dear old self that I wouldn't mind if it were ten times colder. We sat in hides behind the sea-wall for hours. *Really* hours, but the movement of the geese was enthralling—or at least Pete makes it seem so— anyway to me. And then the evenings back at the inn, very snug with a big wood fire, and then up early and back to the marsh.

Kathleen's health had been declining for some time. As long ago as 1940 she had suffered from constriction of the chest and throat which her doctor had said was due to old age (she was then sixty-one) plus a cold, but which turned out to be angina. Early in 1947 she contracted leukemia. As the disease progressed, the symptoms became so distressing that Peter, who gave his blood for transfusion to her, subsequently expressed a wish that no child of his should see him on his deathbed, or his body when he was dead. His mother was wholly realistic about the business of dying; she knew that her illness was incurable and was, in her son's words, "gay and carefree and magnificent until the very end." This came on July 24, 1947, when she was sixty-eight years old.

After her death, Bill found among her papers a letter addressed to Peter and written in 1923, when he was fourteen, just before the birth of Wayland which she had thought she might not survive.

> Little sweetheart: I want the person who tells you that I am dead to give you this letter. I am writing it before I die, because I am afraid I may. I want you to take it very sensibly. Don't be too miserable. I've had a *lovely* life, but I'm getting fairly old and it's very nice (since one must die sometime) to do so before one gets ill and blind and deaf and bored and tiresome. So let's all be quite cheerful about it. And remember that if I can see you in any way after I'm dead (though I don't think one can, but one can't be too sure) I shall want to see you gay and merry and funny—working hard and playing and keeping Hilton happy. No tears for me dearie! Only hurray, that your gay little mother stayed happy till she died.
>
> I'm not going to give you lots of good advice, only this: "Keep fit!" and I've taught you how to do this. I wouldn't learn to smoke or drink if I were you, but if you do, be moderate. Add to that "Be always kind." and with those two precepts you should be happy. If you feel sadly about me now, know that it will pass surprisingly soon. I shall not be unhappy, so you must not be. If you feel inclined to howl, go out and run violently and know that I am shouting "Bravo" to you. Bless you ever.

Peter kept to himself the hollow sense of loss that must follow the severance of a tie so close as that between himself and his mother. How faithfully did he follow her advice? Smoking and drinking: yes; he was moderate in his indulgence in both, more so in regard to alcohol than to smoking. Kindness: he was certainly kind to other humans, although the ghosts of many slaughtered geese and ducks might have risen up to question his kindness to them. When, years later, Keith Shackleton's son, who was a potter, designed and made a handsome platter as a christening present for Peter's grandson, an inscription was sought to go round the rim. Kathleen's advice came to mind. As always—or nearly always—Peter was a realist, and added a proviso: "Try always to be kind."

Kathleen, like her son, had been an uncommitted agnostic, and a conventional funeral service, with its emphasis on resurrection and a life everlasting, would not have been to her taste. She was cremated, and her ashes scattered at sea. Recalling her affection for the cottage at Sandwich, Bill and her two sons drove down there on a sunny day. The beach, Peter wrote to Winkie, was just as he remembered it, but the cottages had gone.

> The tide was out—there was a fisherman digging lugworms—a family bathing—there were some little Dunlins running about— the beach was just right, not deserted, not crowded, and the sea was superbly green. Wayland waded out with the old green pot- pourri jar which has been in our drawing-room for thirty years— do you remember it?—and scattered the ashes among the little wavelets. And then Bill said some Wordsworth and we came home. It was a happy occasion to see the old place again. We enjoyed our day and we felt that mummy would have approved of the idea. She wouldn't have tolerated any prolonged lament at the end of her full and exciting life. She'd have wanted us to rejoice that she managed to get so much out of it, and put so much back into it too.

Kathleen Kennet had chosen her own epitaph: "No happier woman ever lived."

ENDNOTES

[1] Standard income tax at this time was ten shillings in the pound, i.e., 50 per cent.

CHAPTER THIRTEEN

Travels in North America

Peter's objective for the next few years was to get the Trust established on a firm foundation, with a constantly expanding wildfowl collection, a reputation for successful breeding of rare species, and for respectable scientific research. Shortage of money remained the rub. The first year's expenditure was £5,640 12s 0d and income £2,761 0s 0d, hardly a recipe for happiness in Micawber's or anyone else's book. There were 854 full members paying one guinea a head, and the gate money, at the rate of one shilling a head, yielded £17 15s 4d. Peter's soaring aims were tethered to a shoestring.

He succeeded in getting several grants, mainly from the Carnegie, Pilgrim and Dulverton Trusts. At the end of 1947 an appeal for £5,000 launched at a luncheon in London brought in a bare £610. Peter simply could not paint enough pictures—he had no trouble in selling them—to fill an ever widening financial gap. He turned for reinforcement to the spoken word. He was known in Broadcasting House as a successful commentator, although a hiccup while covering the victory parade in 1946—he failed to find a quick, one-word description of what the *Times* called "a ceremonial erection" in the middle of Parliament Square—had caused a temporary loss of nerve. He recovered it in time to take up a position on the roof of St. Margaret's, Westminster, as one of the commentators at the wedding of the Duke of Edinburgh and Princess Elizabeth, whom he had met when he went to the palace to sketch the two princesses. At the royal wedding on November 20, 1947 his fluency was unimpeded despite an anxious moment when one of the BBC's staff stepped on an important junction box, temporarily cutting him off from the listening millions—250 million of them.

Accommodation was another problem at Slimbridge, and it grew more acute as staff, members, and important visitors increased in number. To meet the need, the Trust bought a narrowboat called *Beatrice* and moored her by the bridge over the canal. This marked the start of a long association between Peter and a movement to rescue and restore to use the network of canals that had been allowed to decay after the coming of the railways. The founder of this movement was Robert Aickman, who had a fire in his belly concerning canals that burned at least as fiercely as Peter's fire in relation to wildfowl. It has been said (by one John Smith) that "to further a cause, you have first to gain attention. There are two ways of doing this: you can cajole and influence and generally stroke the ears of those in authority, or you can attract a person's attention by punching him on the nose." Peter belonged to the first school of thought, Robert Aickman to the second.

Early in 1946, a few months before the Severn Wildfowl Trust was born, Aickman and his colleague Tom Rolt launched the Inland Waterways Association. While no one without second sight could have foreseen how the pursuit of leisure would swell into a monstrous industry that threatened to destroy the very peace and diversion its patrons sought, the pioneers of the canal rescue movement did foresee a growing need for the provision of interesting and, if possible, healthy pursuits for those enjoying longer holidays and more prosperity. What better than a cruise through beautiful and unscarred countryside, its peace mildly stirred by passages through locks and tunnels, with time to observe wildflowers growing on the banks, the splash of the water-vole, the flight of the heron? Peter became a waterways enthusiast, and vice president of the newly formed association, while Jane had become its part-time secretary at £2 10s 0d a week, and Aickman's wife Ray Gregorson joined Peter's staff as organizing secretary. Ray gave her husband unstinted support in his campaign, but had a good deal to put up with in her private life. Aickman's view of marriage was what might now be called permissive. "I saw women in terms of poetry and free love," he wrote, "not in terms of responsibility." Ray accepted the situation without complaint—or almost without complaint; she did once remark that while she didn't mind Robert and his current lover having an affair, she did draw the line at taking them breakfast in bed.

Beatrice had been converted into a cruiser by adding a superstructure that ran almost the whole length of the 70-foot boat. Rightly called narrow, she was only 7 feet wide; she was painted blue with red and white skirtings, and her doors were decorated with the traditional narrowboat design, a rose and a castle. Looking after her, Diana Johnstone said, was hard work.

> We had to pump out the bilge at intervals, and keep her polished up. Lord Alanbrooke came sometimes with other VIPs, and we had to give them lunch. All they had was hors d'oeuvres. One

morning I arrived to find Mrs. Flanagan, the manageress, in a terrible state. I said whatever is the matter? She said, I think I've killed them all. When I woke them they were all feeling ghastly.

Cooking was done on a stove with bottled gas, and a pipe had sprung a leak underneath the food cupboard. "All the meat had gone green. Luckily they didn't die but we watched them anxiously. We gave them aspirin and they never knew about the leak." It was lucky also that no one struck a match in the night.

Lecturing became an increasingly important part of Peter's fundraising activities. In 1949, at Robert Aickman's instigation, he planned a lecture tour in B*eatrice* through the Midlands and up to Liverpool, stopping en route to deliver talks in major cities. *Beatrice's* engines kept breaking down, the schedule got disorganized, and Peter had to hire taxis to drive for miles to keep his appointments. However, he discovered "a whole field of satisfaction" in navigating through the many locks without a bump or scratch, and then across the estuary of the Mersey, 15 miles of almost open sea. Beat*rice* was said to be the first converted narrowboat to make this crossing, which she did without mishap. But on the homeward journey, disaster nearly struck. The neglected canals were frequently blocked, and tunnels were especially unsafe. In the Harecastle tunnel, 1 1/2 miles long, they got stuck about halfway. Peter, who was steering, put the engine into reverse. Nothing happened. Part of the roof had collapsed, it was pitch dark, airless, and very frightening. The only way to free the boat was to lower her level in the water. Her crew had noticed a pile of dirty bricks stacked near the entrance to the tunnel, so they waded back along the towpath which was waist-deep in water, carried the bricks armful by armful, deposited them in the boat, and tried again. Beatrice edged forward but stuck once more—more than once, many times. Six and a half hours after they had entered the tunnel they emerged, black from head to toe, to encounter April snow. In a month they covered 450 miles, passed through 273 locks and netted for the Trust £484.

In August 1950 Robert Aickman organized a grand rally to draw public attention to his campaign. It was held at Market Harborough; 50,000 people and 120 narrowboats came, and the rally turned into an exuberant junket with massed bands, Scottish pipers, Polish dancers, and fancy dress competitions, as well as an exhibition of Peter's paintings and a play, *Springtime for Henry,* in which he gave "a rakish performance." But as a hostel *Beatrice* did not pay her way, and she had to be sold. Aickman had for some time been infatuated with Jane, and enjoyed with her a six-week cruise on the canals. It was a complicated situation, but everyone remained good friends. Ray eventually left her husband, reverted to her maiden name and, some years later, much to her friends' surprise, entered an Anglican convent in Hertfordshire; she became Sister Benedicta, and so remained until she died in 1983. Robert's dogged battle for the canals went on until he resigned from the Inland Waterways Association to become a writer, mainly of ghost stories, of which he published five volumes before he died in 1981. By then "this marvellous and most extraordinary man," as Peter called him, had overcome most of the obstacles to restoring the canals. Had he lived another ten years he would have scored his final triumph when the Queen opened the Kennet and Avon Canal.

One day, Peter wrote in his autobiography, while he was enjoying a goose shoot, a single bird came over and was hit. It fell on to the mudflats at an inaccessible spot, he does not say where or when. Its legs were broken, and it landed on its belly with its head up. The shooters adjourned to an excellent luncheon—he commended especially the cherry brandy—and in the afternoon it was still there with its head erect. It was there again next morning, its head poking up from the mud. By what right, Peter asked himself, did humans inflict that kind of suffering on a bird? He would not so treat his worst enemy, and the goose was not his enemy. So he saw the light and sold his guns. He followed up the story with his thoughts on the hunter's instinct as implanted in man, the evolutionary effect of hunting on the quarry—survival of the fittest—and the nature of suffering, different in quality in bird and in man.

As long ago as 1932 he had written to a friend, John Berry, who was to become Director of Nature Conservation in Scotland: "We shot far too many geese, in fact it was too easy ... I am determined next year to have a system of catching them alive perfected. What David [Haig Thomas] and I thought was, how marvellous to catch 208 live geese in a season instead of having distributed as many mouldering corpses." The seed of scruple was very slow to germinate. Possibly the war strengthened his doubts about the ethics of killing for sport, and by the end of it the youthful instinct of the hunter was waning. Maybe a natural reluctance to admit the advent of middle age and to lay aside his guns counterbalanced his ethical scruples. On February 19, 1949 he and Keith Shackleton took part in a shoot on the Wexford Slobs in Ireland's County Wexford. "We shot thirty-three geese between us," Shackleton recalled, "and had to carry them all home—we were absolutely festooned with geese. Pete said something like 'I don't know about you, but I feel like a murderer.' I said 'I'm absolutely with you, and they just don't look right, all broken.' Between us we were filled with remorse and I certainly never shot again, not for fun anyway." But Peter did. On December 15, 1951 he wrote to Kenzie Thorpe, "I am only just back from Ireland, where I had a wonderful day on the Wexford Slob, and shot 18 Greenland whitefronts." Less than two months later he wrote again to Kenzie:

> After having had a record season, you really ought to give the geese a rest. People won't think the better of you if you slaughter geese wholesale over decoys. Besides—like me—you've shot

enough geese now. Why not let them off for a bit. You must
have found, as I did, that when you get too good at it, it's too
easy, and not much fun any more.

Kenzie's reaction to this piece of advice was predictable. "After all the geese he's
shot, he's telling me to pack it up. I should say so."

On this evidence, it would seem that although Peter had for something
like twenty years seen the light flickering rather than blinding him, his final
conversion came during the winter of 1951–2, probably during one of the
annual Berkeley goose shoots on the New Grounds. Shooting had brought
him infinite pleasure over the years. Through it he had learned the ways of
wildfowl, and to understand the lonely marshes where they lived, the beauties
of their flight, their plangent music. Without this love and knowledge, he would
not have painted his birds so well. Wildfowling had stiffened his hardihood
and patience, and satisfied his need to take risks and to perfect physical skills,
so there were credits to set against the obvious ethical debits. After his change
of heart, he avoided the extreme reaction of the convert and did not openly con-
demn shooting, although he did try gentle persuasion, as with Kenzie; and whenever the Berkeley shoots took place on the New Grounds, he went away. The last
day's goosing was on January 31, 1983, when eight whitefronts were shot.

In 1948 the decision was made to sell No. 8 Edwardes Square and move the
Trust's headquarters to Slimbridge. Peter got £8,000 for the house, and the move
took place early in 1949. Like most moves, it was hard work and chaotic, and
was left to Philippa to organize, Peter having gone off to North America to look
at ducks and geese. At Slimbridge, Eunice Overend had taken over as curator
while Yealland had gone to Cameroon with Gerald Durrell on a collecting expedition. By this time there were thirty-eight hundred birds in the collection,
and all four pipes of the decoy had been brought into use.

To study wildfowl scientifically had, from the start, been one of Peter's
major aims. The British Trust for Ornithology and the International Council
for Bird Preservation had, for some years, been running a system of ringing
birds, recovering the rings of those killed or dead from accidental or natural
causes, and with this information mapping the migration routes of various species; but wild geese, being large and wary, were particularly difficult to catch,
and methods of doing so were unsatisfactory. Peter's prewar experiments had
been no more than a beginning in working out a sound technique. Even when
in the midst of planning the Allied invasion of France, his mind had reverted to
the matter of netting wild geese. In a letter to Jane dated February 2, 1944 from
his burrow in the Tunnel below Fort Southwick, Peter had written, "Christopher [Dreyer] and I have devised a new way of catching wild geese with a net
propelled by rockets! It sounds fantastic but is really quite practical." This was

followed by a drawing of the net with a flock of wild geese entangled in it. The idea came from a device to save the lives of drowning men: a lifebelt was propelled by a rocket to come to rest within reach of the man in the sea. This device had been developed by two brothers called Schermuly. After the Trust was well established, Peter had gone with James Justice and Lord Geoffrey Percy to their factory, and set them the task of adapting their device to propel a net instead of a life buoy. In February 1948 a trial of their adapted device was held on the New Grounds, where about thirteen hundred whitefronted geese had gathered. The team was made up of Mr A. J. Schermuly, Peter, Philippa, Keith Shackleton, Eunice Overend, Peggy Cameron, and a photographer from *Country Life*.

In darkness before dawn, armed with torches and a great deal of equipment, they laid the furled net on the edge of a field of young wheat where the whitefronts were accustomed to graze. They connected up the wires to a battery, loaded the rockets into their pistols, put up a hide, put out decoys (stuffed geese), and settled down to wait. It was freezing hard. With the dawn, the geese came flying in to feed, and as an orangey-red sun rose over the Cotswold hills, the great flock settled on the farthest part of the 100-acre wheatfield. Would they come closer—close enough? Tension in the hide rose to feverpitch as a party of geese took off and then settled within 40 yards of the area that would be covered by the net, and fed toward it. Would the birds see the net and take off? Would something unforeseen alarm them? Would the rockets work? The moment came, the rockets exploded, the net swung over and the whole flock took off with a roar of wings and cries as loud as the sound of a passing train. Thirty-two birds remained on the ground, flapping. "We had made the first great catch of geese alive for ringing," Peter wrote triumphantly. They were extricated from the net, ringed, and all but fifteen, which were kept for the collection, were released. Rocket-netting had come to stay, a refined tool for unraveling the secrets of the migrations and behavior of wild geese and swans. The technique called for almost as much hardihood and stamina as shooting geese, and the reward was a live and free-flying creature rather than a "mouldering corpse."

All his life, Peter was a traveler: not the kind who travels with a donkey but the kind who hurries between airports with a set purpose in view. The Trust was not quite two years old when he took off again, accompanied by seventy birds for sale or exchange in North America. His first stop was the Delta Wildfowl research station at the southern tip of Lake Manitoba. Delighted by the great array of ducks to be seen on the marshes, he caught a "beautiful full-plumaged bufflehead drake" with net and gong, Persian-style, and shot three bluebells and three lesser scaups "the first ducks I have shot for two years. I got quite excited and enjoyed it." It was the scientific research that most impressed him, both for its quality and for its method of funding: the firearms and ammunition industry provided most of the money, an arrangement unthinkable in Britain. "If this kind of fascinating work can be done in North America," he concluded, "why could not the same sort of research be started in Europe, and who better to do it than the Severn Wildfowl Trust?" As a result of this visit, 150 ducks, geese and swans traveled in the SS Aquitania from Canada to Britain in September 1948.

From Manitoba he flew on to the delta of the Great Bear River, which flows into the Great Salt Lake in Utah, to be amazed by the immensity of the Migratory Bird Refuge there: 64,000 acres of marsh, partially covered with samphire, and 39 miles of dykes. Here again he saw in action a partnership between shooters and conservers unknown in Britain, where the two groups were more often at loggerheads. Sixty percent of the area was a true refuge with no shooting allowed, and on the remaining 40 percent duckhunters could enjoy their sport within strict limits both of numbers and times of year. The average bag, on the day he was there, was only three ducks per gun. The great variety of species in the refuge astonished him as well as the numbers—over one thousand whistling swans—and not only migrants but also golden eagles and rough-legged buzzards, avocets and egrets, harriers and peregrines, all of which he listed with his usual exactitude. He took note also of a 100-foot-high tower at the center of the refuge, another suggestion to be followed up later on his home ground.

From the Great Bear River he went on to California to revisit the Federal refuge at Willows in the Sacramento Valley which he had seen in 1938. Both these refuges were, and are, part of a national network encompassing nearly 90 million acres, almost as large as the whole of the United Kingdom. It must have made his 23 acres of Gloucestershire seem pathetically small. Both these visits were brief but they gave him plenty of ideas. Britain, it was clear, lagged a long way behind the United States both in wildfowl research and in arousing public awareness of the need to conserve wildlife. By creating the Yellowstone National Park in 1872, Americans had started to redeem, insofar as this was possible, their crimes against nature in the previous century, when the tide of immigration had swept beavers from the rivers, bears from the forests, bison from the plains, and Native Americans everywhere from their tribal homelands. Chief Seattle, who died in 1866, in a letter to the President had summed up the message Peter was to spend the rest of his life trying to get across to the public. "What is man without the beasts? If all the beasts were gone, men would die from a great loneliness of spirit. For whatever happens to the beasts, soon happens to man. All things are connected. Whatever befalls the earth befalls the sons of the earth. Man did not weave the web of life, he is merely a strand in it."1

Ever since he had changed horses in the middle of the stream at Cambridge, science had pulled Peter in one direction and art in the other. As a painter he had made his name, but not yet as a scientist. He knew that in a sense he was a dropout from the world of science, and if there was one thing that he dreaded, and would go to almost any length to avoid, it was failure.

While he lacked formal qualifications, he became a self-taught field ornithologist and, later, ichthyologist, who commanded a full measure of respect from the professionals. In 1949 he appointed the first scientist to the staff of the Trust, a young man called Hugh Boyd who came for an experimental three months and stayed for nineteen years, with a starting salary of £200 a year. "As Peter didn't know when to stop," he remarked, "no one else knew when to stop either. It was all frightfully muddy and primitive and great fun." His first job was to goose-watch from the pillboxes on the seawall to note their behavior, then to monitor population changes in several species of ducks and geese in order to find out which species, if any, was declining in numbers to an unhealthy degree. For a young biologist it was a privilege when Konrad Lorenz, founder of the science of ethology, came from Germany to stay in the cottage in order to film ducks, and to lecture at Bristol University. He struck up a friendship with Peter which was to last for the rest of their lives. One of his major discoveries had been that of imprinting: that a newly hatched gosling will imprint upon the first object it sees, believing this to be its mother. Normally, of course, that object is its mother, but when eggs are hatched artificially it may be a human. In his book *King Solomon's Ring* Lorenz described how his hand-reared greylag goslings followed him about *en masse*, like Mary's lamb, even into the house where they fed from the hand, and ruined the carpets; the only way his long-suffering wife could keep them from doing the same to her flowerbeds was to spring at them with a frantic warcry and unfold a large red umbrella at the same time. Young birds could even be imprinted on an inanimate object, such as a hencoop. Lorenz used to say that Peter was a much better zoologist than he, Lorenz, ever claimed to be, because Peter's extraordinary eye for detail enabled him to see birds doing things that other people didn't see, and his ability to illustrate such actions made him unique. "It's a pity we can't squeeze him for his potential as a zoologist," Lorenz remarked. But Peter was too busy doing other things. Lorenz made a second visit to Slimbridge in 1953, bringing a copy of *King Solomon's Ring* with the graceful inscription: "I am so grateful, my dear Peter, for the wonderful opportunity to work not only *at* the Severn Wildfowl Trust, but *with* you."

Six months after his return from North America Peter was off again, this time as a member of a three-man expedition with a serious scientific aim. His companions were two American ornithologists, Paul Queneau, a former colonel in the U.S. Army and subsequently director of research for the International Nickel

Company of Canada, and Harold Hanson, a zoologist attached to the Illinois Natural History Survey. Their main object was to map the breeding grounds of Ross's goose (*Anser rossei*), which had only recently been found by one of the Hudson's Bay Company's post managers, Angus Gavin, to lie along the lower reaches and the delta of the Perry River, which flows into the Queen Maud Gulf about a hundred miles north of the Arctic circle. This was to be Peter's first experience of Arctic conditions. A spectral Captain Scott stood at his elbow more than once in their camp on a snowbound bog on the banks of the Perry River, where an Anson aircraft deposited them early in June 1949. The brief Arctic summer should have started, but it had not; lakes were still frozen over, snow stretched to the horizon, fog enveloped, and piercing winds assailed them and everything was cold and grey and bleak. Within his storm-bound tent, he wrote in his diary:

> These tuppenny ha'penny adventures of ours and this dash of bad weather cannot but cast a new light, for me, on the story I grew up with. And if I am enjoying the minor discomforts and difficulties—as indeed I am—then it serves to remind me particularly of one phrase in my father's diary which says "How much better this has been than lounging in too great comfort at home." It was good to be able to say that when death was imminent and inevitable. But in much lighter vein this phrase still applied to our days beside this Arctic river. However inclement the weather, I'm still glad I came.

Peter shared a tent just large enough for two with Paul Queneau. Although the sun never sank below the horizon, it seldom shone through blankets of thick cloud and driving rain or snowstorms. Some friction between three men living at close quarters in such conditions was inevitable. It was mainly between the two Americans. "Paul is consistently rude and patronizing which Harold much resents. When Paul is rude to me I put it down to constipation and leave it at that," he confided to his diary. "My principal role during the next six weeks will be peace-maker and pourer of oil on troubled waters."

There were other complications. As well as looking for the nests of Ross's geese, the members of the expedition were to bring back skins of birds and mammals, to identify intestinal parasites, take meteorological observations, and make contact with the local Inuit people. To skin the animals, preserve the skins, and study parasites was Hanson's job, while Peter was to sketch and paint the specimens, and also to shoot them. The most beautiful of all wildfowl was, he thought at that time, the king eider drake. He had to shoot two pairs of these birds.

It was a strange feeling as I went to pick them up. On the
one hand it was horrible to shoot these tame beautiful creatures
and to see themlying in the blood-stained snow. On the other
hand it was the first opportunity I had had to see at close quarters their surpassing beauty of colour and pattern. And since their
skins were needed it was useful to have got two pairs neatly so
that we need never fire at King Eiders again ... All the the same
it was a crime which brought inevitable remorse.

There was a scientific reward, of sorts. Hanson found a new worm in the intes-
tines of the king eider: "At least there is a chance that it will be a new one."
Science was insatiate. Peter's bag included several Canada geese, six lesser
whitefronts, three rare Sabine's gulls, three Ross's geese, two brents (sitting females) and other birds. Hanson found a small crane chick, reddish brown and
most appealing. Peter asked him to spare it, but he refused. "Science has no
heart, and its downy softness could not soften the scientist or divert him from
his purpose."

Hanson's demands for dead ducks, and the appeal of the downy crane
chick, aroused in Peter's mind questions that had not troubled him before. Must
science always be omnipotent at all costs? Must the classification of an intestinal worm always transcend compassion? What about Keats's "'Beauty is truth,
truth beauty,'—that is all/Ye know on earth and all ye need to know"? And has
not science been used as a stalking horse for man's ambition, even greed? Peter
did not address himself directly to these matters, at least on paper, but their
troubling presence may be discerned beneath the surface of his rational outlook. Meanwhile he went on shooting the birds that Hanson wanted, and feeling remorse. "When will the Arctic smile?" he asked, huddled in his bag at noon
with a gale blowing and reading Shakespeare; Hanson's wife had given him a
complete pocket edition, and he had got through the Sonnets, Richard II, and The
Tempest, and he completed Hamlet before the expedition ended. It smiled at last
on June 18, and a great change came over the valley. "What before looked grim
and forbidding suddenly looked smiling and friendly." A few days later they
found what they had come to seek. A family of amicable Eskimos arrived at the
camp. Communication by sign language, combined with Peter's drawings, got
across the message about looking for the nests of Ross's geese. After a long,
exhausting march over the tundra they reached the top of a hillock, and there
beneath them lay a great marsh, with an even greater lake beyond. From the
lake protruded five islands, each one covered with white dots: sitting geese
with their attendant ganders. Two hundred sixty pairs were counted. On their
maps the lake was nameless, and they called it Lake Arlone after Hanson's wife.
They went on naming lakes and rivers after members of their families in a manner that recalled explorers of a previous age; before the expedition ended this

section of the coast of northwest Canada had acquired, as well as Lake Arlone, Lakes Jane, Philippa, Nicola, Jamieson, Johnstone, Alanbrooke, Scott, and Easter after his first niece, as well as Keith, Aickman, and Currey islands, and Queneau, Yealland, and Bratby rivers.

Peter recorded in his usual meticulous detail every bird and insect seen, every meteorological reading, the habits of every ground squirrel. Much of this detail found its way into the book which resulted from the expedition, *Wild Geese and Eskimos*, based on his diaries, and probably there was too much detail in it for a public which did not always share the fascination that he felt for the minutiae of identification. *Country Life* published *Wild Geese and Eskimos* without demur but did not expect it to have the same wide appeal as his previous books, which were still selling well. But he had not been insensitive to the Arctic's beauties. "The whole scene was black and orange," he said in a broadcast after his return. "I took the canoe down over the rapids ... and then in the still waters below I paddled slowly on with an unforgettable feeling that this was the life as it should be lived—this was real—this was a peak of happiness."

He returned from the expedition with his first complete film, which was successful enough to form the mainstay of future lectures, and to find favor in the royal eye. In January 1950 he was invited to show it at Sandringham to King George VI and the royal family, and to take part in a shoot at the same time. Michael Adeane, an assistant private secretary and former Trinity College friend, lent Peter his guns. This was another occasion when scruple had to yield to conformity with social custom. In the afternoon he was flanked during a drive by the Queen on one side and Princess Margaret on the other, with the King as his neighboring gun. Tactfully, he refrained from firing at a woodcock that was heading for the monarch who, Peter noted with a trace of satisfaction, missed it with both barrels. "Fortunately, though I did not shoot especially well, I did not disgrace myself," he observed.

ENDNOTES

[1] Doubt has recently been cast on the authenticity of this letter, with the suggestion that it may have been a forgery. Even if it was, the message could hardly have been more tellingly expressed.

CHAPTER FOURTEEN

Rescuing the Nene

Middle age had now caught up with Peter. Wildfowling was over and done with, but he was to find that preserving geese, ducks, and swans took up a lot more time and effort than shooting them. He did not give up sailing, but was drawn increasingly into the administration of the sport instead of into the active pursuit of it. After he and John Winter had won the Prince of Wales' Cup in 1946, he was elected to the council of the Yacht Racing Association and, two years later, to the chair of the Association's Olympic committee, which was to organize the yachting events in the 1948 Olympic Games. These events were to be held at Torquay.

The Games were a social event as well as a sporting one, attended by several millionaires and by the Crown Prince Olaf of Norway. There was also an underclass of penniless young men who groomed the boats to bring them to the pitch of perfection. Inevitably, there was a social barrier between the sailors and the boatyard hands. One of the latter, Tom Hodgson, has recalled an incident which throws a light on Peter's character from an unusual angle.

> Our accommodation was awful. We were bedded down rather like horses in a dark, deserted, oily, former war-time factory. Straw mats on the floor and poor food and no money. We were young and broke. All the high life was going on around us. We were watching the rich enjoy their riches. After about four or five days, all of a sudden the door flew open, and I mean flew, bang, crash, and there was Scott. He'd heard about the situation. I sup-

pose we'd all grumbled. He was fully dressed for dinner, stiff white shirt, wing collar, the lot.

We looked at him in amazement. He looked at us on our straw pallets. He turned to the people who were with him and bawled, "Get these men food and beer and bedding—NOW!" And they did. And he came and sat with us and talked. I think this was the first time we'd ever seen leadership like this. His ability to lead men on those boats [steam gunboats] meant that he went into situations that most people never face, and we saw this in him. I mean if that man had turned to us and said, "This way, chaps, charge!" I swear we'd have got up, bare-footed, and charged. Our reception changed from that moment on. Next day I was even treated to champagne for the first time in my life. I didn't develop this taste, I still prefer beer, mild if possible.

I've been looking for people like that ever since. We could do with a few more like him. I suppose there just aren't many about. He didn't do too well at the sailing. I don't think that mattered. Obviously an extraordinary man.

As Tom Hodgson recalled, Peter's performance in the single-handed sailing event in a Firefly 12-foot dinghy "did not" in his own words, "impress the selectors." This left him free to devote himself to the management of the events. After the games were over he hosted a grand dinner party at which the guest of honor was the Crown Prince Olaf of Norway. It fell to Peter to propose the loyal toast, which he did in the words "The King." The Commodore of the Royal Yacht Squadron, Sir Ralph Gore, followed with the toast "His Majesty the King of Norway." Peter was horrified. Had he committed a fearful gaffe by omitting the words "His Majesty" before "The King"? His concern was typical both of his meticulous attention to detail and of his profound respect for royalty. It was not until some time later that he learned that it was all right: in formal toasts foreign monarchs were entitled to the prefix, "His Majesty," native ones were not. It was typical also of his self-deprecation that he described this incident as "an example of obsession with detail carried to a laughable extreme."

In ornithology as in sailing, middle age drew Peter more and more into the orbit of conferences and committees, although he never gave up his observations and adventures in the field. In the summer of 1950 he attended an International Ornithological Congress at Uppsala in Sweden, followed by excursions which took him to Lapland, together with several distinguished professionals including the director of the natural history museum in Reykjavik, Dr. Finnur Gudmundsson. The secretary of the Trust, Philippa Talbot-Ponsonby, went along too. They climbed a snowcapped mountain, danced round a maypole on midsummer's day and chugged across lakes to find the nests of interesting birds such as roughlegged buzzards and long-tailed skuas.

Peter wanted to catch three lesser whitefront ganders as mates for several hand-reared females in his collection. Guided by the stationmaster at Vassijaure on the Norwegian border, he and Philippa split off from the rest of the party and tramped over rugged and unpopulated country studded with lakes in search of the geese, flightless during their summer moult. One of these was chased "at lung-bursting speed up a hill and then down at breakneck speed, I after him, taking giant strides down the steep hillside. I ran all out for two hundred yards and overtook him only ten yards from a lake. We were both exhausted and I sank to the ground with the little gander in my arms." Peter and his companion visited a Lapp camp complete with reindeer, and "rowed in leaky boats and were devoured by mosquitoes; but above all we walked and walked over the fells and through birch woods. I was happier than I had been for years."

The contact with Dr. Finnur Gudmundsson of the Reykjavik Museum (a giant of a man, nearly 7 feet tall) was to prove fruitful. The pinkfooted geese that wintered in Britain were thought to breed somewhere in Iceland, but no one knew exactly where. No ornithologist had actually visited the breeding grounds, or if any had, he had left no record. There was a mystery here to be unlocked. The possibility of an expedition to unlock it was discussed with Dr. Gudmundsson and, after Peter's return home from Lapland, negotiations were set in motion to raise funds and organize an expedition.

This expedition began and ended in the British residency in Reykjavik in June 1951. There were four members: Dr. Gudmundsson, Peter, his friend James Fisher, and Philippa as cook and photographer. Fisher was a co-editor of the *New Naturalist* series which issued popular volumes on everything from butterflies to toadstools, wild orchids to British game—his own contribution was on the fulmar—and who "had the capacity," according to a friend, "of a great artist to cast a spell over vast audiences, while still remaining charming to the least of individuals. In conversation he was quick and sympathetic, widely read and learned, with an easy command of facts." He and Peter were to collaborate in many future ventures, such as the radio series *Nature Parliament*. While their interests coincided, there were differences of opinion: Fisher, for example, disagreed with Peter's use of the word "mystery" when applied to bird migration; it was a puzzle, he held, which meant that it could be solved, rather than a mystery which suggested some nonrational, even occult, force at work. As an ornithologist he was more of an academic than Peter. Roger Tory Peterson, the doyen of ornithology and a longstanding friend of Peter's, thought that "James had almost too much factual information at his disposal, while Peter boiled things down and came directly to the point."

There is a story that one day at Slimbridge, when the two friends were walking together in the grounds, a boy approached Peter with his autograph book, a not unusual occurrence. Peter took the pen and, turning rather red, gestured towards Fisher saying "This is the man whose autograph you should be getting, not mine." Fisher was to die tragically in a road accident in 1970, aged fifty-eight.

The members of the expedition set out from Reykjavik on June 22, 1951 in a large bus full of equipment, heading north for a farm where seventeen ponies and two guides were waiting for them. Their destination lay about 70 miles farther north and almost at the center of Iceland. Hofsjokul was a green oasis in a harsh desert of basalt and lava sand, with here and there patches of plant life which offered sustenance for the ponies, and beside them, very often, a small turf-roofed hut, or *kofi*, providing shelter for beasts and a ledge in the wall for shepherds to sleep on when they drove their flocks northward in the brief sub-Arctic summer to leave them there until the time came to drive them back again. Strong winds stirred the lava dust into gritty sandstorms. In the few hours of darkness a fierce cold gripped the members of the party in their tents, whereas in daytime, if it wasn't raining, they sunbathed and suffered from heat.

"We set off to a chorus of trilling whimbrels," Fisher wrote, "plaintive golden plovers, purring dunlins, across a patchwork quilt of desert and the dwarf campion *Silene acaulis*." On June 24 they saw through their binoculars a nest with a pinkfooted goose, "the gander standing close by, its bright summer-pink legs hardly showing through a dense mass of *Sedum roseum* (rose-root, midsummer-men), the fleshy green and yellow plant that grows richly on many Iceland cliff-edges." They knew then that they had come to the right place.

Each of the four was allotted a tough little pony for the strenuous journey across a treeless desert creased by tributaries of the Pjorsa, through which they had to wade. After three days they reached the Hofsjokul oasis, 2,000 feet above sea level. Streams flowing from the icecap cut it into meadows, each of which bore an evocative name: the meadow of the tarns, of the eagle's mountain, of the bogs. Wildflowers were everywhere in bloom, and in the dried mud were footprints of many birds including whooper swans, pinkfeet, skuas, ptarmigan, and the little meadow pippet. The party camped beside the river, and here the guides left them, taking the ponies and promising to return twelve days later with fresh supplies.

"What an extraordinarily congenial party we are," Peter wrote in his diary. "Finnur is a great success, very knowledgeable, charming and at times quite funny in a rather slow teddy-bearish way. James is an excellent companion, good-humoured, witty, practical and erudite. Phil has been wonderful, fitting in perfectly, and enjoying it all immensely." She was experimenting with cookery, and won praise for a risotto made of puffballs, rice, bacon, and dried peas. "As usual I over-ate," wrote Peter.

The expedition made an unexpected discovery: that of goosefolds. These were built of boulders, about 12 meters by 2, and had fallen into ruin, as they had not been used since some time in the seventeenth century. The translation of a passage in a Latin treatise published in 1638 by the Bishop of Skalholt in South Iceland describes how the wild geese :

> half grown, and exceedingly fat, and living for the most part in deserted places, have not yet become able to fly—the time when their parents are also unable to fly, having no strength left, and their wing feathers being moulted. Then our hunters are at hand; they prepare beforehand fixed fences, mounds or pens whither with no trouble they drive the flocks of birds like sheep to the slaughter; when they are shut up then they kill all they choose, since the geese have no chance left to them of escaping by the help of their wings.

Some three centuries later, this Anglo-Icelandic party revived an ancient technique, but with a difference: a ring on one leg instead of slaughter was to be the fate of the pinkfooted geese. After several failed attempts to drive them into the portable pen, made of netting secured by stakes, on July 25 came "the day of success" when, "as Peter breasted the ridge an amazing sight was disclosed. Coming towards him was a flock of about two hundred adult geese, and farther behind another flock of not less than three hundred mixed goslings and adults." The pen was ready; the trick was to drive geese and goslings into it, much as sheep are maneuvered by dogs at sheepdog trials, in this case with humans playing the part of the dogs. Slowly, cautiously, the birds were driven toward the pen until—as Scott and Fisher recorded in A Thousand Geese, a jointly written account of the expedition—"there in the middle of the V of the net all the birds stood, adults and goslings together!" It was not to be plain sailing, however. The weight of the geese pushed down the net and away ran all the birds down the hill. By means of bold cavalry maneuvers they were rounded up and held in a phalanx on the summit, while Peter and Philippa repaired the cage, and then once again edged the birds into it. This time the net held; each bird was caught amid a cacophony of screechings and flappings, then ringed and released. By the end of the operation 247 birds had been captured and ringed.

At the start of the expedition its members had agreed that if they ringed two hundred birds, they would be satisfied; five hundred would be accounted "a roaring success." The last roundup, on August 1, brought the final count to 1,151 birds—382 adults and 769 goslings. Next day they broke camp and set out for Reykjavik, leaving a cairn and a poem in a bottle. "What a marvelous, valuable and happy trip it has been!" was Peter's verdict. There were reasons beyond those of ornithology for his happiness.

When Peter and Philippa had been staying at the British Legation in Reykjavik at the start of the expedition the Minister, Jack Greenway, had spoken of his coming retirement. His only regret, he had said, was that he had never had an opportunity to conduct a marriage ceremony, as the heads of missions, like seacaptains, were (and are) entitled to do. "Peter and I felt that it was a pity to deprive him of his last ambition," Philippa wrote, "so we asked him if he would marry us." Not, however, on the spot. The law of divorce, recently liberalized by the almost single-handed efforts of A. P. Herbert, allowed desertion by either party to be cited as a ground for the dissolution of a marriage, in addition to the usual ground of adultery. Three years had to elapse between the decree nisi and the decree absolute. Barring some hitch, Peter's and Jane's decree would be made absolute in July 1951 and so, by the time the expedition had returned from the interior, he would be free to remarry. He telegraphed to the family solicitor asking him to send the legal document by air to Reykjavik as soon as it came. Philippa wrote to her mother to declare her intention, and to Mrs. Cameron, the keeper's wife at Slimbridge, to ask her to send a suitable dress (white broderie anglaise).

One might wonder, as some of their friends did, why they had taken so long to make up their minds. Everything seemed to fit together: age, background, temperament (complementary not matching), interests; although Philippa had no special knowledge of birds she had been brought up among animals and country sights and sounds. Since joining the Trust she had learned much about birds and had surrendered to their fascination. Companionship had been theirs from the start. Yet when someone remarked, "I suppose you're going to marry Peter Scott?" she had replied, "Good heavens no." "The spirit of independence still burnt strongly and I needed a life of my own," she added. It was Philippa who adapted to the life of Peter, not the other way round. She found her outlet within the orbit of his life and interests and, except for her photography, chose not to strike out on her own. Meanwhile love grew gently out of habit, rather than striking like a lightning flash. Perhaps both were suspicious. She had said to Michael Bratby, "Will he be faithful?" Bratby answered, "Yes, he will." "How can you be so sure?" she asked. "Because he was faithful to Jane." As for Peter, the wise saw "once bitten twice shy" no doubt applied. Except in money matters, he was a cautious rather than an impulsive man. His caution ended on March 28, 1951 on the occasion of the Trust's Annual General Meeting in London, which was followed by a formal dinner and a ball. The engagement was kept secret, as in those days it had to be until the divorce came through.

The British Minister in Reykjavik arranged an airdrop of mail and supplies to the expedition's camp on the Hofsjokul oasis at the end of July. It can be imagined with what mounting interest two of the party awaited the arrival of the airplane. At the last minute, something might have gone wrong with the decree absolute. At 6 P.M. on July 30—a rest day, with Finnur pressing flowers, James Fisher making maps, and Peter writing up his diary—a Catalina flying boat was heard. "Phil saw it first, through a crack in the tent door. It was much lower than usual. Could it be looking for our camp? It turned away, then back again, and passed far to the west; then suddenly it turned in again towards us, losing height." Two sacks were dropped right in the middle of the camp, coming to rest between two tents. The flying boat circled, the pilot waved, and away it went. "The packages contained the much-needed films," Peter wrote austerely, "twenty ciné magazines, our mail, cans of fruit juice, pate de foie gras and newspapers. This was a very exciting affair for us all." The decree absolute was in one of the bags.

Back in Reykjavik, Peter had his hair cut, bought a ring, and held a press conference at the museum. On August 7, 1951, after luncheon at the Legation, Jack Greenway married the pair, with Finnur Gudmundsson giving Philippa away. Photographs were taken, Peter looking tidy in a rather baggy suit with buttonhole and tie, Philippa youthful and happy with a bouquet of roses, and then they took off in bright sunshine for Akureyri. It was not, in any conventional sense, the most romantic start to a honeymoon. After dinner, a local taxidermist turned up at the hotel and invited them to his home. "We visited a good collection of mounted Icelandic birds and mammals," wrote Peter, "we had coffee and sweet cakes and talked of goose catching." Next day they filmed harlequin ducks, and four days later flew home, taking 3,000 feet of color film and 400 stills. Less than three months after their return, nine of the geese they had ringed in Iceland were caught in Scotland, and six more in the following year. It was like greeting old friends.

Peter returned to Iceland two years later, in 1953, with four British companions and three Icelanders, to ring more pinkfeet and possibly recover birds that had been caught and released in Scotland. This second expedition was "a success beyond expectation." In seven catches, no less than nine thousand birds were coaxed into pens, ringed, and released. By the end of the exercise, it could be claimed that probably one in five of the world population of pinkfooted geese carried a ring. And it had been established beyond doubt that most of the pinkfeet who wintered in England and Scotland bred in central Iceland. "Let us hope that its lovely and lonely headquarters below the edge of the white icecap," James Fisher wrote, "remains its sanctuary forever."

The honorary director and his wife returned to find the Trust's finances in their usual state of disarray. Membership was rising, and in 1953 the subscription was doubled, making it two guineas; more visitors were coming, but costs were rising even faster. At times the minutes of the Council breathed a sense almost of despair. "It was decided that stringent economy should be practised and that the secretary and the director should together attempt by charm and other methods to obtain the sum of £1,000 in the City, quoting the Treasurer's fine example." (Sir Archibald Jamieson had made the Trust an interest-free loan of £1,000.) Following the introduction of the National Health Service, "it is hoped that as the need for money to finance the hospitals ceases, old ladies will leave money to the Trust." Everyone heaved a sigh of relief when the Pilgrim Trust came up with £3,000 which was used to pay off the overdraft and several loans, but debts soon re-appeared.

"To meet the present gap between expenditure and income, the director offered to make a further donation of pictures." Such was the pressure he was under to earn money from his paintings that he sometimes promised more than he could deliver. There was the case of the Bermuda dinghy. Early in 1951 he accepted a commission from Mr. de Forest Trimingham of Bermuda to paint a picture of the dinghy in which Mr. Trimingham had sailed in the Prince of Wales' Cup. Reminders came in 1953, in 1955, and again in 1958, when Peter scribbled on the letter "I really must do this Phil. Help." Later in the same year Mr. Trimingham wrote that he was soon to be in London, and would there be "a snowball's chance that you have done the picture?" In 1959 "Dot and I are wondering how you are getting along with the painting as time seems to be slipping by." He was to be again in London in September, and "perhaps by that time we can pick up the picture, which I understand was practically finished when I left England in April." There was another scribbled note on the letter, this time to Peter's secretary. "Mike—I'll have to do this for him." Mr. Trimingham finally collected the picture eight years after it had been commissioned. Such hack work was uninspiring, but at least fees were rising. For a portrait of an emden gander who won first prize on six occasions at the national poultry show, Peter was paid one hundred guineas. He was in danger of being forced by financial pressure into a hack's corner, knowing that he was capable of finer work. In 1949 he had collected, and *Country Life* had published, a book of portraits in pencil and crayon: a far cry from dinghies and prize ganders, and it had pleased the critics.

Like many—most?—successful public speakers, he never really enjoyed lecturing, and suffered from the usual nervous symptoms before his talks began, but his reputation as a speaker was growing and so were his fees. In the year 1950–1 he gave thirty-one lectures for fees totalling £1,256 10s 5d after expenses, which worked out at just over £40 a time, and by 1955 one hundred guineas was his minimum fee. All these sums, or practically all, were handed over to the Trust. Gifts in kind were gladly accepted. Mr. John Tollemache (a brewer, who married one of Jamieson's daughters) presented some barrels in which to breed mosquitoes for ducklings to eat; Dr. Winch of Malmesbury gave two sacks of daffodil bulbs; and 12 tons of Blue Cross products were delivered free for food for the birds. On Peter's suggestion, £500 of his various loans was repaid by making ten of his godchildren life members of the Trust. At least this relieved him from the task of finding ten suitable birthday presents every year. Diana Johnstone started a small shop in a wooden hut beside the entrance where postcards and oddments added their mite to the coffers. This was to develop, under her efficient management, into a successful business and important source of funds.

Even if the Trust's finances were precarious, all was well amongst the birds. They were breeding happily, most of the young were surviving, and birds of more and more different species were arriving from distant lands. One species that Peter was particularly anxious to add to his collection was the nene, or Hawaiian goose (*Branta sandvicensis*), a smart, smallish animal with brown and black plumage and a dash of yellow on the neck, so acutely endangered that in 1950 there were reckoned to be only about thirty survivors in the wild, plus another thirteen in captivity. The story was a familiar one. The nene had coexisted easily enough with the native peoples of the islands, who kept their own population stable by such means, unacceptable today but formerly effective, as infanticide. The indigenous peoples were no more virtuous than the islands' subsequent invaders: they killed for meat and, in the case of birds, for gaudy feathers; they planted crops and cut down trees—there were simply many fewer of them, so the fauna and flora coped with their demands. Then came the invasion of the islands by alien traders, missionaries, sugar planters with their Asian laborers, plunderers and proselytizers all; men of many nations came to develop and destroy. With them came their cattle, horses, donkeys, goats, pigs, cats, and dogs, and then their pests: rats, rabbits, mongooses, and plants such as mesquite and thimble-berry. The native fauna came under siege, and retreated to the arid and inhospitable upper ranges of the island's volcanic mountains. In dwindling numbers the nene survived on the cold montane scrublands, its nests robbed by rats and mongooses, its food cropped by feral goats and pigs, until it appeared to have reached the point of no return.

Peter's interest in the species went back to his prewar lighthouse days, when he had read of its rarity and of a small flock kept on Hawaii island by a Mr. Herbert Shipman, to whom he had written. Mr. Shipman had promised him a pair if he would go and collect them. The outbreak of war prevented him from taking up the offer, but after the Trust was established he returned to the charge, corresponded with the Hawaiian Board of Agriculture and Forestry which had met with no success in captive breeding, and early in 1950 despatched John Yealland to investigate. (Two members of the Trust, Mrs. Carl Tucker and Mrs. Gladwin, paid the curator's fare.) In four months spent on the islands of Hawaii and Maui, Yealland saw only five birds in the wild and seventeen in captivity; but Herbert Shipman honored his promise and gave Yealland a pair.

In May 1950 Yealland returned to Slimbridge with the nenes who settled in nicely, and early in the following spring were watched hopefully for signs of nesting. Nest, indeed, they did, and laid eggs—both of them. There were red faces in Hawaii and in Gloucestershire. An urgent cable to Mr. Shipman was followed seven days later by the arrival of a gander, Kamehameha, who was in full moult and so infertile, and it was not until February 1952. that his two wives, Emma and Kaiulani, laid fertile eggs. (The geese were named after kings and queens of the Sandwich Islands, as the Hawaiian group was previously known.) Two of Emma's eggs hatched under bantams in a snowstorm, then three of Kaiulani's. Both geese had a second clutch and in all nineteen eggs were laid; nine goslings hatched and were successfully reared. Twenty percent of the world's population of nenes was then to be seen at Slimbridge: twelve birds. Barring disasters, the species had been saved at the eleventh hour from the fate of the dodo.

Some might say to this: so what? The world has got along without the dodo, and would doubtless do the same without the Hawaiian goose, and without the various other species that are threatened with extinction, or soon will be. But for Peter, and others of his mind, this was a matter of entrenched belief. As an agnostic, he did not believe that God had created the nene as it stood and that it was therefore flouting God's grand design to bring about its extinction, but he did believe that evolution by natural selection was a wonderful and mysterious process, and that to destroy forever any strand of, in his words, "the intricate and delicate web of life into which we have thrust the ham fist of civilization" was a crime against an undefined but immutable law of the universe. "My interest in the processes of evolution," he wrote, "has produced in me a kind of reverence for every living species. I personally believe that all other species of flora and fauna have as much right to their place on earth as does *Homo sapiens*. The prospect of the extinction of any existing species then appears as a potential disaster which man's conscience should urge him to avert." This belief could, in the widest sense, be called a religious conviction. Such convictions, fervently held, lead to crusades. Peter became a crusader, and was so to remain; but he was not dogmatic. He quoted Francis Bacon: "If a man will begin with certainties he will end in doubts, but if he will be content to begin with doubts he shall end in certainties." Content he may have been to begin with doubts, but whether he ended in certainties is in itself very doubtful. As a scientist, he looked for proof before accepting propositions which others might regard with the eye of faith. "Oh what a dusty answer gets the soul / When hot for certainties in this our world"— Meredith's comments may have more closely matched his philosophy than Bacon's. But he was too busy and too positive a man to brood for long over dusty answers. He held to one certainty at least, that destroying other species is wrong, and acted on his belief. Perhaps he remembered the words attributed to Chief Seattle.

Rocket-netting had now become the basis of the Trust's research into the populations and migrations of the *Anatidae*. Every October, barring some unavoidable engagement, Peter led a team to the north of England or to Scotland to catch and ring the birds. The Solway firth was a favorite catching ground. A stretch of marsh and bog along the river known as the merse attracted wildfowl in the tens of thousands, and from first light onwardsthe birds would fly out to the surrounding fields to feed. For the most part this was rough marginal land, owned or leased by small farmers who tolerated their uninvited guests partly from custom, partly because the wildfowl attracted shooters, bringing opportunities to increase their meager incomes. Many of the farmers were knowledgeable about the habits of the birds and helped the teams to choose the best places to set their nets.

After the initial experiments, techniques had greatly improved. The geese were marked by dipping the rear of each bird in a dye, and then putting them into portable cages to dry off before releasing them in batches, so as not to break up family parties which stayed united in their long migrations. As time went on, the number of birds captured in one year and recaptured in subsequent years increased, but most of the information came from dead birds whose rings were returned to the headquarters of the British Trust for Ornithology. Casualties were heavy but the birds' ability to survive was startling. A professor from the University of Missouri, Dr. L. H. Elder, who went out with the netting teams in 1953, found that 41 percent of captured adult pinkfeet and 37 percent of greylags carried shot in their bodies, some in positions where death would seem inevitable. One had a .303 armor-piercing bullet in its abdomen, another had nine BB pellets in its head and neck, some of which had flattened against vertebrae. Yet it "flew away strongly, as did all the others," and its weight was normal.

For the rocket-netting teams these sorties were tough, exciting, and also good fun. Peter, Philippa, Hugh Boyd, and one or two "regulars" such as Lord Geoffrey Percy formed their nucleus, and students and budding ornithologists joined as volunteers. After setting their furled nets the night before, together with the hide, decoys, and other apparatus, the teams settled down before dawn to wait. Then came plaintive calls as the first skeins flew in, mounting anxiety and excitement, maybe the triumph of a good catch, maybe disappointment and a long fruitless wait before packing up and returning to base, generally a village pub, cold, cramped, hungry, empty-handed. There were hilarious moments too, as when Peter and Philippa procured two smelly sheepskins and, armed with cameras and disguised as sheep, stalked a flock of geese feeding in a field. The geese saw through them.

Rocket-netting became for Peter "something very personal—the realisation of an early dream." It was also scientifically rewarding. By ringing and recovery it was possible to estimate the number of pinkfooted geese wintering in Britain and the number lost through shooting, accident, and other causes. From these statistics, an answer could be extracted to the question: "Is this loss too heavy for the populations to bear without endangering their survival?" About forty-three thousand pinkfeet, it was calculated, wintered in Britain; they sustained an overall mortality of 26 percent; this was "within the replacement capacity of the birds." In other words, pinkfooted geese were not endangered. Science, as Peter had written, has no heart but, when properly conducted, it is honest. The conclusion that "the notion of wildfowl as a natural resource which can be harvested like any other crop offers the best chance of peaceful co-existence between wildfowlers and bird-watchers" may not have pleased a post-conversion Peter, but it was printed in the Trust's annual report.

Travel had got into Peter's blood; perhaps the bug had been there since childhood. Now that wildfowl from every quarter of the globe swam and walked about at Slimbridge, he wanted to see as many as possible of the species on their home ground. South America was chosen as his next destination and the study of three rare species of duck in particular was his main objective. In this, as in nearly all his future expeditions, Philippa went too.

Leaving in February 1953, they flew first to the home in Georgia, U.S.A., of a plantation owner known as Biff and his wife Dixie. Colonel Biff was a martinet who ordered meals with the blast of a whistle. He took his guests quail hunting on horseback. When a dog "pointed" a covey hidden in long grass, two of the party (by a roster fixed by the Colonel) dismounted and advanced upon the quail. Peter borrowed Dixie's twenty-bore gun and "shot patchily," and possibly reluctantly. Joined at Biff's by the curator of the natural history museum in Cleveland, Ohio, the party flew to Santiago in Chile and   drove to a lake where at least two thousand ducks were feeding and resting among floating weeds. He searched for one of his three rarities, and "suddenly there it was, plain as a pikestaff, an unmistakable male Black-headed duck, the enigmatic and euphoniously named *Heteronetta atricapilla*"—enigmatic because it was believed to be a cuckoo-duck, laying its eggs in other ducks' nests.

Then on to Tierra del Fuego. They landed at Punta Arenas on Useless Bay and stayed with the British manager of a Chilean *estancia* covering 600,000 acres and carrying over 250,000 sheep. The sheep were in competition with rabbits, which honeycombed the pastures with their warrens and were "an awe-inspiring sight"—fecundity unlimited. Gales of up to a 100 miles an hour frequently swept across the "island of fire," so named by Magellan because of the many fires he saw burning as he sailed through the straits that bear his name: campfires of Tehuelche Indians. Their men were giants by Spanish standards and had enormous feet; hence, it is said, the word Patagonia, *pata* meaning foot in Spanish.[1]

The pampas might be bleak but there were open grassy marshes with pools and plenty of ducks where Peter searched for the bronze-winged species (*Anas specularis*), known locally as *pato perro*, the dog duck, because the female barked like a dog. His aim was to observe and film the many kinds of wildfowl, but Biff's intention was to shoot them, ostensibly to provide skins for the Cleveland museum. He despatched a kelp goose sitting peacefully on her nest, and then the gander standing faithfully by his mate. This was too much for Peter, who knew that the museum had plenty of kelp goose skins already. "I was rash enough to ask whether Biff had *enjoyed* walking up to the geese and knocking them over on the ground. The result was a certain coolness during the day." His good humor was restored when he filmed three bronze-winged ducks (*Anas specularis*) in the mountains south of Lago Fagnano—"a most spectacularly handsome animal," which obligingly swam toward him to investigate, then lost interest until he "squeaked at them," when they approached to within 10 yards.

The torrent duck (*Merganetta artnata*) remained the biggest prize, and the place to seek it was in Bolivia, in the high Andes. From La Paz they traveled over a pass at 16,000 feet where, they were told, a ship had been carried in sections by thirty-five prisoners walking in single file, whose shoulders had been rubbed bare to the bone. Near the southern tip of Lake Titicaca, which is shared between Bolivia and Peru, on the river Zongo, they found the elusive birds: five of them, swimming "down and across waterfalls with the greatest of ease ... leaping out and running up the waterfalls and along the tops of rocks with an easy gait." The females were a rich chestnut red on the chin and underparts, the rest dove grey, and both sexes had cherry-red bills. Unfortunately the light was poor when they found the ducks, and the film therefore indifferent, but Peter believed that it was the first ever taken of this "fascinating and mysterious bird."

To secure a pair of torrent ducks for Slimbridge became a fixed ambition. A few years later Gerald Durrell, about to set out for Argentina on one of his many expeditions to collect rare animals for his zoo in Jersey, asked Peter whether there was any species of duck or goose he particularly wanted. "He was, as always, wildly enthusiastic," Durrell remembered,

> and he begged me to obtain some Torrent ducks for him. Philippa tried to put a restraining leash on him by saying "Well, Torrent ducks will need a torrent." Whereupon Peter said "We'll build them one." Philippa said "Where will we get the money?" Peter said "Oh, that's easy to get. The important thing is to design the torrent properly." He talked so enthusiastically about the Torrent ducks that at one point I was under the impression that I had already got them for him, and he talked so enthusiastically about the torrent that I quite expected him, after lunch, to say

"Come and see the torrent." In the end, however, I unfortunately
did not manage to obtain any Torrent ducks for him.

Peter never did succeed in keeping torrent ducks at Slimbridge, one of his few
serious avicultural disappointments. "His enthusiasm for everything to do with
conservation or the animal world would warm you like a fire," was Gerald Durrell's
comment. "Half an hour's talk with Peter and you felt you could succeed in
realising your wildest dreams."

Although not commonly regarded as wildfowl, swans belong to the same *Anatidae*
family and so were kept at Slimbridge from the start of the Trust. The trumpeter
swan (*Cygnus cygnus buccinator*), the largest of the tribe, once bred all over North
America, but by the early 1950s its numbers had been pared to a few small,
widely scattered flocks in northern Canada and in the states of Montana and
Wyoming in the United States. Its world population was put at no more than
thirteen hundred. So, if not actually on the endangered list, it was rapidly heading that way. In 1950 Princess Elizabeth, while on a state visit to Canada, accepted a gift of six trumpeter swans, to be cared for at Slimbridge.

It was a case of first catch your swan. None of the species had ever
before been trapped in Canada. The task fell to the Canadian Wildlife Service
which had, as it were, taken the trumpeters under its wing by arranging feeds of
corn in winter to supplement their meager pickings on certain lakes and rivers.
The largest flock, numbering no more than about one hundred birds, wintered
on the aptly named Lonesome Lake in northern British Columbia, where a farmer
called Ralph Edwards and his daughter Trudie looked after them. Some 21 miles
of precipitous mountain footpath lay between the Edwards' homestead and the
nearest telegraph line, and Hagenborg, the closest "sizeable community," was
70 miles away. "When the temperature drops to −40°F or lower, and even the
swiftest parts of the river freeze over," wrote the wildlife officer in charge of the
project, R. H. Mackay, "it is an everyday occurrence for Trudie to take an axe
and punch holes in the ice for feeding places while the swans eagerly wait on
the ice nearby. The swans have thus come to recognise their benefactor, and
the bolder ones eat out of her hand."

Early in February 1952, Mackay and a colleague landed on Lonesome
Lake in a ski-equipped airplane, and the following morning Trudie enticed one
adult swan and seven cygnets into a trap set in a small creek. The adult and two
cygnets escaped, leaving five youngsters. The crated cygnets were flown to
Vancouver, then on to Montreal, across the Atlantic, and so to Slimbridge. And
there, on April 25, 1952, the Queen, as she had just become, accompanied by
Prince Philip, inspected her five young trumpeter swans. It seems a pity that
Trudie Edwards could not have come from Lonesome Lake to share in her cygnets' moment of glory.

"Her Majesty's gracious interest in the Trust's progress is, of course, a source of great gratification to all those who have our cause at heart," the Trust's director wrote, with some pomposity, in his annual report. Peter's excessive regard for royalty might be seen as a form of snobbery, and perhaps it was, but its roots lay in the romantic aspect of his nature. In the eyes of romantics, the mystique of royalty enfolded the royal personage, however fallible, like the cloak of many-colored feathers that adorned the kings of the Aztec empire, setting them apart from common humanity. "Not all the water in the rough rude sea / Can wash the balm from an anointed king." There can be no doubt as to which side Peter would have fought on in the English Civil War. In the year after this royal visit, 1953, he was appointed a Commander of the British Empire.

From the Trust's inception, Peter had had its shape and direction firmly fixed in his mind. Scientific research, education of the public, conservation of the birds—this was his trinity of aims. With the appointment of Hugh Boyd as resident biologist, the ball of scientific research had started to roll, and in 1953 enough money had been raised, or at any rate promised, to embark on a more ambitious program. Peter's first step was to invite a number of eminent scientists to plan and supervise such a program, and no less than twenty-eight agreed to serve on a proposed Scientific Advisory Committee. The list was sprinkled with the initials FRS as liberally as a winter holly tree with berries. Ornithologists abounded: Lack, Wynne-Edwards, Thorpe, Tinbergen, and Jean Delacour, then living in Los Angeles. Well-known ecologists, biologists, geneticists, veterinary authorities were there—Fraser Darling, C. M. Waddington, Ronald Fisher; zoologists such as Professors Harris and Hewer of Bristol; Sir Julian Huxley, biologist and supreme communicator; and the great Konrad Lorenz: Peter had spread his net widely and made a catch of really big fish.

The committee's first meeting was held at the New Grounds on midsummer's day in 1954, when Sir Landsborough Thomson was elected to the chair. This was the year in which the word "Severn" was dropped from the Trust's title, reflecting its widening horizons. The committee's first concern was to appoint a scientific director. The post was advertised (salary £1,000) and the choice fell on Dr. Geoffrey Matthews, a Cambridge man whose special study was the orientation and navigation of migrating birds. Dr. Matthews built up an impressive team of researchers, and was to remain first its scientific, later its deputy, director until he retired after a stint of thirty-three years.

Dr. Matthews did not start from scratch but took over a going concern which included the organization of national wildfowl counts. The object of these counts, formerly organized by an offshoot of the International Council for Bird Preservation, was to monitor population trends in the various species of ducks, geese, and swans in order to find out which species were declining or increasing, to study seasonal fluctuations, and generally to supply the basic information that must underlie any action to protect wildfowl. The scheme had been running for some time. At six hundred "count points" in the British Isles, on certain days, an army of unpaid volunteers counted wildfowl numbers, and observed their movements. All this basic field research was on the point of collapse, since the committee which organized the counts had been abolished. The first decision of the Trust's scientific committee was to take over these counts, then to start research into two diseases that had appeared among the birds in the collection, caused respectively by a worm that burrowed into the digestive system of ducklings, and by a fungus that infected their lungs.

One of Peter's aims in setting up a prestigious Scientific Advisory Committee had been to create a powerful advocate to support his case when he applied for grants. The collective voice, he hoped, of all those Fellows of the Royal Society and professors would surely penetrate the eardrums of such governmental agencies as the Nature Conservancy Council, as well as charitable trusts. He was correct in this assumption.

ENDNOTES

[1] Bruce Chatwin had a different theory. He suggested (In *Patagonia*) that Magellan might have read a book called *Primaleon of Greece*, published in Castile in 1512, which described a monster who lived on an island and had "the head of a dogge," the feet of a hart, and possessed human understanding. He was called "the Grand Patagon." He was captured and presented to the Queen of Spain, whose daughter Princess Zephira tamed him until he followed her about "like a spaniell." Chatwin further speculated that Shakespeare took the Grand Patagon as his model for Caliban in *The Tempest*, in which Trinculo says, "I shall laugh myself to death at this puppy-headed monster."

CHAPTER FIFTEEN

Faraway Look

The first television broadcasts in Britain went out from Alexandra Palace in 1936, but the service was closed down during the Second World War, and it was not until the early 1950s that antennas began to proliferate over the rooftops, and screens to move into the nation's living rooms. Peter was by then a well-established radio performer in the good books of the BBC. An internal memorandum in 1936 noted that he had "a very strong personality, a good voice and is very keen to do work of this sort," adding that he was also an expert yachtsman "and is soon starting across the Bay of Biscay in a canoe." In July, the sports editor commissioned a fifteen-minute talk on dinghy racing for transmission on August 21, for a fee of six guineas. Then came letters dated August 7, 13, 14, and 19 asking, with increasing fervor, for the script. At 3:40 P.M. on August 21 Peter sent a telegram: "Arriving 6.30 with dinghy talk have no fear Scott." The talk went out on time.

Charm, no doubt, as well as a good script, won forgiveness. A radio series on "Wild Britain" provided slots for talks on "Badgers and Animals of the Wiltshire Woods"—fee ten guineas—and similar topics. In October 1945 a talk on the subject of adventure made a considerable impact. War, for all its horrors, provided excitements; what could a peacetime existence offer to the sons and younger brothers of the men whose acts of bravery had lifted the heart of their fellow-countrymen and rekindled national pride? "So that's our problem: to bring forth those good things that courage and initiative and comradeship—in great works of construction instead of destruction; to satisfy the hunger for adventure in time of peace." It was an age-old question, to which no answer has as yet been found. Peter offered suggestions.

I believe that the spirit of adventure is not necessarily a craving
for physical thrills strung together in rapid succession. It is an
attitude of mind that can be applied to any field of human activity. It is the capacity to delight in the unexpected, to be un-
daunted by misfortune, to accept the challenge of "come-what-
may." You may find as much excitement catching butterflies in
Surrey as hunting tigers in the Indian jungle ...

So I would tell my adventure-seeking friend to find some
problem that needs elucidation. Then I would simply say "Go
off and find the answers." He will be adding something, however small, to the sum of human knowledge. If he has no money
it will be more fun finding out. He will need to exercise a little
ingenuity ... Above everything else he must be tremendously
excited about his mission. It must become for the time being the
dominating aim of his life. My great key to the enjoyment of
living is enthusiasm ...

It is not always necessary to leave home in search of excitement. Adventure is all around us, in art, perhaps, or science,
or sport. You may find it in a gentle quiet form, a sort of armchair adventure, as I have done, for example, in painting and
writing about birds. Or you may find it in rock-climbing, or diving, or sailing dinghies. There is no limit, because adventure is
an attitude of mind.

"Spell-binders are a lost tribe nowadays," wrote a radio critic in the *Observer*.
"A most potent spell-binder turned up on the air the other night and by the ca-
dence of his voice almost bewitched me of my reason ... He has a voice of delightful timbre and modulation and an eager manner of speech. These merits are forti-
fied by sincerity, a quality to which the microphone always seems immediately
sensitive. Here was a broadcast of exceptional power, a faultless model of composition and delivery." And yet the critic was not altogether bewitched. "Sailing small
boats or tumbling in northern snows are delights in themselves, yet as solutions to
the problems now besetting ex-fighter pilots or returned foot-soldiers they seem
invested with a sentimental unreality." Sentimental or not, the public loved it. The
BBC's appreciation index was eighty-seven, a very high rating indeed.

The BBC's *Children's Hour* was a national institution and its genial producer, Derek
McCulloch—"Uncle Mac"—was affectionately known by voice and personality to almost every child in the land, as well as to many adults. On January 22,
1946 the first broadcast took place of a *Children's Hour* feature that was to plant
the seed in many youthful minds of an awareness of nature, to enhance Peter's
reputation as a popular broadcaster, and to run for twenty-one years. This was

Nature Parliament. Derek McCulloch was in the chair, and the three regular members of the panel were Hugh Newman, who ran a butterfly farm in Kent, James Fisher, and Peter Scott. Often reinforced by an expert in some particular field, they answered questions sent in by children on such topics as how do bats see in the dark, can dogs distinguish colors, do birds eat snow, how do elephants drink, have penguins got teeth, and how do flies walk upside down on the ceiling? The program went out once a month and was a great success from the start. Peter's fee was eighteen guineas, exceptionally generous for the time.

Meanwhile, in Bristol, a young producer, Desmond Hawkins, was developing two radio programs which might be regarded as foundation stones of the Natural History Unit, now so esteemed throughout the television world. One was *The Naturalist,* chaired and edited at first by Brian Fitzgerald; the other, introduced by James Fisher, was *Birds in Britain.* Hawkins commissioned Ludwig Koch, the pioneer of sound recording, to record the calls of whitefronted geese on the New Grounds, and through Koch he heard of Peter's intention to make a sanctuary there for wild geese. "So when Peter arrived," he said,

> we quite soon met. Peter became a contributor to *The Naturalist* and *Birds in Britain,* and gradually he got used to coming to the Bristol studios and I got used to working with him, and that was that ... Yes, he was a good broadcaster, extremely good. He was a harder worker than one might have thought; he was so talented he often seemed just to slide through things without much effort. But all the time we were rehearsing, he was altering his script, making it more natural, easier for the listener.

Early in 1953 television came to Bristol in the shape of a mobile control room with all its equipment and attendant engineers. Making outside broadcasts was at first the unit's main activity, but soon the West of England light orchestra was turned out of its theater to make way for a television studio, primitive by modern standards, and here Peter made his debut as a television presenter, with a style and magnetism all his own.

At the outset of his lecturing career, it may be recollected, he had developed a gimmick designed to put the audience in a good humor from the start. He would approach a blackboard and, in silence, quickly sketch a duck, or goose, or some other bird. There must be humor in the drawing, such as to raise a laugh. One day he suggested to Desmond Hawkins that this routine might go down well on television. Hawkins was interested, and wanted to see how it worked. He persuaded the headmaster of Bristol Grammar School, where his eldest son was a pupil, to invite Peter to lecture there, which Peter agreed to do without a fee. It was a great success. The head of regional television then commissioned two or three experimental programs, as Hawkins recalled:

So we worked out a procedure in the studio, what Peter was to do in the way of sketching and so on, and then we began to look for film. Peter had some film, but he had shot it on to sixteen frames a second whereas television wants twenty-four, so that was a poser. We started with quite a small element of film and quite a large element of Peter drawing and talking, usually to a guest.

The first program that went out to this pattern was called "Painting Aloud." "A tour de force," a critic described it. "At a quarter to eight he had an empty canvas and some paints. By a quarter past he had painted a picture which I would be proud to see on my walls. And all the time with little brushes and whacking great big ones such as you and I use for distempering ceilings, he was making a stormy sunrise over a wild Welsh creek live before our eyes." (Actually it depicted wild geese flighting at dawn over the coast of Norfolk.) The BBC was inundated with offers to buy the painting, but it was not for sale. Desmond Hawkins continued:

We didn't call it *Look* then because we might have done our two or three programs and been told thank you very much we don't want any more. Then Peter went to an ornithological conference in Berne, and there he saw some remarkable film by a young German called Heinz Sielmann, about woodpeckers. Sielmann had managed to film the woodpeckers and their young inside the tree. This was a revolutionary piece of film technique, something no human eye could possibly have seen.

So Peter said you must get hold of this, I'm sure there's a wonderful program in it. It was only thirteen minutes long. I arranged terms with the Bavarian Ministry of Education in Munich by whom Sielmann was employed, and had James Fisher as Peter's guest. Sielmann explained how he had cut away the back of the tree, using infra-red light so as not to disturb the birds, and had found that they couldn't care less about what kind of light was used. So gradually he stepped up ordinary light without the woodpeckers minding, and got this remarkable film.

The program was a sensation. Next morning, Hawkins was rung up from Lime Grove (television's headquarters) to say that their switchboard had been jammed with appreciative calls for an hour and a half after the program had ended. When Sielmann went back to Germany next day the Customs officers said: "You're the woodpecker man, aren't you?" The program was made, and Peter's name with it.

So *Look* was born, the progenitor of a long line that was to embrace David Attenborough's costly and enthralling series. The BBC put in some fast footwork to keep Sielmann in their grip. The day after the program went out, someone from Granada television, which had just received its franchise, rang up—rather naively, one would think—to ask for Sielmann's address. Hawkins went hotfoot to Munich to secure a lien on Sielmann's future work in return for an undertaking to finance part of it.

If one single event can be picked out as a turning point in Peter's progress as a public figure, it is the launching of *Look*. As a lecturer, he could number his audience in thousands; as a radio performer in millions, but the broadcasts were sporadic; television brought him into the full view of millions as a flesh-and-blood individual every week. The first of the *Look* series proper went out on June 14, 1955 and was about foxes. It was seen by nearly six million viewers and its reaction index was eighty-two, classed as "very good." Peter's "easy delivery, nice sense of humour and obvious love of his subject," the BBC's audience research department reported, "made him, it was said [by viewers] the ideal personality for this type of program."

The principal difficulty faced by the *Look* team was to find enough film of high enough quality to sustain the weekly series. Virtually all such material as existed had been shot by amateurs, some of it good, but much of it indifferent or poor. After the program had been going out for two years material was running dry, and in July 1957 the series took off in a new direction under the title of *Faraway Look*. The great wide world, with all its wealth of plants and animals, was to be the field which Peter and his cameraman were to prospect for gems; and they were to go round the world to seek them.

The team was to consist of only three members. Peter with a sixteen-millimeter camera; Philippa taking stills with an Exacta; and a young cameraman, Charles Lagus, who had gained experience of wildlife photography in a very successful series named *Zoo Quest* presented by David Attenborough. When one considers the expense, teamwork and years of preparation needed for Attenborough's later wildlife programs, these three musketeers with their simple equipment seem remarkably intrepid. And, in the words of Chris Parsons, the series' producer in Bristol, material of high quality came "flooding back." The trio had to get on well together if the expedition was to be a success, so Charles Lagus was invited to spend a long weekend at Slimbridge to get to know the Scotts, and vice versa. "When I look back on my visit I am still amazed at the kindness and generosity of those two remarkable people," he recalled. "I was after all a very young cameraman chosen to film and direct a man who, among his many other achievements, had been a TV personality for many years, yet here was I being treated as a total equal and made to feel at ease and welcome. Even such details as the books by my bedside had been chosen with care to include subjects likely to interest me." Peter introduced Lagus to most of his staff and "managed to give both them and me the impression that here was the world's greatest natural history photographer."

In November 1956 the three of them flew to Melbourne via Darwin and the Northern Territories of Australia to be met by Harry Frith, head of the wildlife section of the Commonwealth Scientific and Industrial Research Organization, in Parsons's words "a small, freckled, forthright man suspicious of Poms who spoke in a drawl as flat and dry as the habitat of the mallee fowl on which he was the world's authority." Frith took the visitors to see fifteen hundred magpie geese on a rice project at Humpty Doo, and Peter climbed a pandanus tree to catch a lizard 2 1/2 feet long with a frill like a wide Elizabethan ruff round its neck. They went on to Melbourne, where Peter, as president of the International Yacht Racing Union, was to preside over the international jury at the 1957 Olympic Games, to be opened by the Duke of Edinburgh.

While Peter was attending to his duties, Lagus went off to find and film the rare pink-eared duck (*Malacorhynchus membranaceus*), guided by a young junior assistant from the CSIRO. After two days of search, some of these ducks were seen. The camera was in the back of the Land Rover. Lagus said to the young Australian, "I'll climb out on the off side, grab the camera and shoot." There was a semantic misunderstanding. Just as Lagus was about to press the button there was a "Bang! All I got was a close-up of a distintegrating duck." "Did you film it?" Peter asked when he heard the story. Lagus said no, and Peter was displeased; he thought the incident should be used, Lagus thought not. They argued, and next day there was a frosty silence at the breakfast table. But a day or so later Peter was all smiles. "You were right," he said. "We couldn't have used it. The trouble at Bristol is that they won't stand up to me. They do what I say. That's why the programs aren't as good as they ought to be. I may know about birds, but not about making TV programs." After that, all was amity. "I never ceased to wonder at his humility," Lagus said.

After more filming in New South Wales, the team flew on to the Furneaux group of islands off northeastern Tasmania to photograph a bird with a remarkable lifecycle. The mutton bird (*Puffinus tenuirostris*) nests in profusion in holes in the ground. On two islands of the group, Big Dog and Babel, there were reckoned to be at least one million nests. The female lays a single egg, never more, which each parent incubates in turn for thirteen days. Then, always in the first week in May, young and old alike set out on a migration lasting for five months which takes them round New Zealand, across the Pacific northward to the Bering Sea which touches Alaska, then down the coast of the Americas and so, 20,000 miles later, back in the last week in September to the Furneaux islands, and often to the very same nesting burrow, where they start the cycle over again.

But fewer than half of each season's hatch lived to take part in this great migration. At the end of March a mob of human "birders" invaded the islands, camped in sheds and shacks, caught the chicks, squeezed out the oil (used for suntan lotions) and processed the birds for export to the mainland's tables. In the past this uncontrolled slaughter had threatened the survival of these shear-waters, but by the time of the *Faraway Look* team's arrival it had been brought under control, though not stopped. Another localized bird, the Cape Barren goose (*Coreopsis novaehollandioe*), had been hunted almost to extinction, and the team succeeded in photographing a few of the survivors. Peter became a champion of this handsome bird, which was to be seen nowhere else in the world, and in due course a breeding pair found its way to Slimbridge.

And so back to Melbourne and a "royal occasion" with the rank and fashion of Australia watching the races from a bedecked launch. How far a commoner, not belonging to the Household, can ever claim true friendship with a member of the royal family is a delicate question. Perhaps there is always an element of thus far and no further. But there is also a fraternity of the sea, and Peter was gratified to be greeted by the Prince as an old sailing colleague, and set himself to pass on his enthusiasm for catamarans, then coming into fashion amid the usual controversy that surrounds any new idea—though scarcely new, since the idea of a craft consisting of logs bound together with twine goes back into the mists of time. Then came a "distasteful job"; Peter had to disqualify an Australian yachtsman who would otherwise have won a gold medal. The jury's meeting went on for so long that it was ten P.M. before, dinnerless, he reached a gathering of ornithologists who had been waiting for two hours to hear him lecture. After the lecture, over tea and cakes, he only just escaped into the cool night air to avoid a fainting fit. For once, he admitted in his diary, "I was very tired." A session with koala bears next day revived him.

Then followed a delectable ten days in New Guinea (the Papua was added later) in search of Salvadori's duck (*Anas waigiuensis*). The tropical color and profusion delighted Peter's artist's eye. It was, he wrote, an earthly paradise, however unparadisical was the behavior of a pair of mantises disovered inside his mosquito net. The male had gripped the female "like a vice" and was still copulating—minus his head—when the Scotts went to bed. His loss did not deter him; he was still copulating next morning, and going through the motions two days later, though by then understandably "sluggish." He had fifty-four hours of copulation, fifty of them without a head. No wonder *Faraway Look,* when shown in Britain, was such a success.

The search for Salvadori's duck took the team through narrow mountain passes and over hidden valleys in an antiquated machine to Wahgi Valley, where the river became a series of pools and swamps through which they squelched and plodded to a spot where "one of those great moments in ornithology" oc-curred "when two exciting things happen at once and there is not enough time to think of both." Two small ducks swam out from some rushes to pass beneath a tree where "a bird looking large and prominent and reddish" sat in a topmost branch—"a Red Bird of Paradise." The duck were grey teal (*Anas gibberifrons*), a rare species but not as rare as Salvadori's. The team had been looking in the wrong river. They did, however, see and photograph Salvadori's ducks in a private zoo at Nondugl.

Apart from the beauties of the flowering shrubs and trees and the prevalence of birds and insects, his deepest impression was of the harmony he sensed between man and landscape. "Nowhere can a dense human population blend more perfectly with its environment." A "singing" was arranged for them at which the dancers were resplendent in the plumes of many radiant birds: birds of paradise and ribbon-tailed, magnificent, blue and King of Saxony birds, as well as kingfishers, honey-eaters and parakeets. After the performance, Peter was given a bag of shillings to hand out to the dancers. He was dismayed.

> And so we had assisted, if even in a small way, in the degradation towards the white man's level of the Awahga natives. There is nothing that Australian civilisation (or indeed any civilisation) can do to make the New Guinea native remotely more happy than he was before his existence was discovered. There is only one way in which the white man could play absolutely fair with the New Guinea natives and that would be by declaring huge areas completely out of bounds to any white man at all and leaving them entirely alone. I have no doubt whatever that they are better without us. But as this would be putting the clock back, and as the grasping stupidity of man is such that for all his loudly proclaimed ideals he cannot resist exploiting new lands without thought for their original inhabitants, the natives of these lovely highlands will be spoiled, debauched and degraded by the processes of civilisation.

So, it seemed, Rousseau's Noble Savage had taken refuge in the mountains of New Guinea, free to head-hunt, dance, make love, and cultivate his garden; free also from missionaries, taxes, *Top of the Pops*, antibiotics, penicillin, repetitive stress, and AIDS. And so back to the mainland of Australia, and to the wonders of the Great Barrier Reef.

> 23rd–25th December, 1956
> For a part of these three days I have been in a new world. Nothing I have done in natural history in all my life has stirred me quite so sharply as my first experience of skin-diving on a coral reef ... The dramatic threshold which is crossed as soon as one

first puts one's face mask below the surface is, to a naturalist, nothing less than staggering in its impact ... The final effect was overwhelming ... I cannot see how I can escape from its lure. I am already an addict, and I have not yet used an aqualung.

Peter never did escape from the lure of skindiving. On this introduction to the underwater world his lips were badly bruised and lacerated by an ill-fitting mask, but so fascinated was he by this new experience, and so strong was his control of mind over matter, that he swam for hours on end oblivious of the pain.

The three of them stayed over Christmas at Cairns in Queensland and indulged in an orgy of snorkeling on the Great Barrier Reef. Charles Lagus already had some eight years' experience of underwater filming and therefore could identify a good many of the species of fish. These were legion: butterfly (fifteen species), parrot (green, blue, and red), blue (iridescent like a butterfly's wing), damsel, anemone (golden red and blue), razor (which swim standing on their heads), starfish, sand gobies, blennies, pig-snout triggers—the number of genera and species seemed infinite, the color patterns fantastic. And the coral gardens, with their ever-waving, softly tinted sea anemones and secret crevices in the reef, were as bewitching as the creatures they enfolded and sustained. Here was nature unconfined and, as yet, almost undisturbed by man: lavish, boundlessly inventive, in perpetual motion, and above all beautiful, and alive. For the coral itself was also quick with life. Tiny polyps, each no larger than a peppercorn, joined in untold numbers to form a reef 1,200 miles long and, in places, up to 10,000 feet deep, each polyp getting born, living, reproducing, dying, world without end. The reef was in a state of continuous creation, predation, and destruction, the largest assembly of living coral in the world.

Peter responded to this in two ways: delight in the reef's beauty, and a determination to identify each and every fish and provide it with its correct scientific label. He speculated in his diary on how all these wonders could have come about:

Then and since I have pondered on how all these different species of Butterfly fish can live on the same reefs, at the same depths, apparently with much the same feeding habits, and yet each with a different bold pattern of spots or stripes to assert its specific identity—each, so to speak, with its national flag. Can we suppose that an ancestral and perhaps ubiquitous Butterfly fish was hit many thousands of years ago by a large climatic change, and was only able to survive in a number of isolated patches perhaps on certain coral reefs? Each isolated population, subjected to slightly different conditions, might then have evolved upon slightly different lines so that, when a climatic amelioration came along and all the Butterfly fish were able to emerge from their geographical isolation, each population was unwilling to cross with its neighbour—had achieved reproductive isolation and therefore, by definition, specific status and proceeded to develop conspicuous "flag" patterns in order to avoid confusion. This mechanism was unlikely to be confined to Butterfly fish. And here the full significance of my new-found delight in fish-watching was revealed to me. Infinite possibilities stretched ahead.

After only three days over Christmas, they flew to New Zealand in search of a bird that had been written off as extinct until it was rediscovered as recently as 1948 in a remote part of the Murchison Mountains in South Island. This was the takahe *(Notornis mantelli)*, a large, plump rail with a vermilion bill, flightless like so many New Zealand species that had evolved in a land without predators. Peter and the biologist in charge of *Notornis* studies flew to Lake Orbell, and proceeded on foot through scrub and tussocky snow grass to the takahe's hiding place, where "a great dark bird crept across an open patch under a Turpentine bush. I had a brief glimpse of the heavy red bill and a suggestion of blue-green on the back and it was gone." They found a nest with the membrane of a hatched egg in it. That was all: but on the way back they came upon a family of blue ducks *(Hymenolaimus malacorhynchos)* which were not only rare, but lived in waterfalls like the torrent ducks in Bolivia that Peter still hoped to get for his collection.

In Wellington, he and Philippa bought snorkels and masks that fitted properly, and flew on to Fiji and more skindiving, which was even better than on the Barrier Reef.

> At breakfast I drew all the different fish that I could remember seeing and it came to twenty-two species. Once more, as on the Barrier Reef, I had the sudden joy of revelation. This new world, which can so easily be seen just by putting on a mask and dipping one's eyes below the surface, is a paradise. And immediately I began to see discoveries in the fields of animal behaviour, of genetics, which are so obviously there for the taking ... It would be interesting enough without the beauty, but to an artist the colour and form and movement were breath-taking, so that my cup was full.

At this stage he was still drawing his fish from memory. Later, he developed a new technique; he drew his fish under water on a plastic sheet pinned to a board, and with a special chinagraph pencil. Then next day, or at some convenient time, he painted them with every nuance of color in his notebooks. These drawings are remarkable for their accuracy and glowing color, like seventeenth and eighteenth century miniatures. Once he had mastered the skills of scuba diving, which he did in the Bahamas, it was nothing to identify and draw under water a hundred and fifty or more species in two or three hours. Later, he was to illustrate a fish-watcher's guide to match the field guides which are part of every bird-watcher's equipment.[1] It was printed on waterproof paper, illustrated with his colored drawings of 184 species of tropical fish, and dedicated to Konrad Lorenz, who had told him that if there was one thing he must do before he died, it was to skindive over coral reefs in tropical waters.

This pursuit was not without its dangers. There was the threat of exhaustion and of unsuspected currents, and by no means all the natives were friendly. There were sharks, large and small, and stinging rays, and very large carnivorous groupers. Charles Lagus has not forgotten that one evening in Fiji:

> Peter's lack of fear caused us considerable worry. We arrived late at a seaside hotel but Peter was stripped and ready to dive as the sun was setting, and with a small and not very water-proof torch he disappeared alone seaward. I pleaded fatigue after a long flight and secretly felt it was a little foolhardy to plunge into unknown waters, particularly in the coming dark when fish tend to do most of their feeding. I was also very unhappy about letting Peter go off on his own. He was gone for over two hours and Philippa and I grew increasingly worried on the beach. Eventually Peter emerged with the biggest lobster I have ever seen firmly clamped to his flipper, and we broke an oar getting it off, and the flipper itself was badly cut. Peter was ecstatic about what he had seen.

There was another adventure in their next port of call, Hawaii, where Peter identified sixty-five species during his first swim. Lagus reported:

> In a small bay off the island of Hawaii we spotted quite the biggest Grouper I have ever seen, or even heard described. He was well over six feet long and must have weighed at least four times my weight. This gigantic fish bore the scars of many battles and its open mouth could easily have accommodated my head. From a reasonable distance I watched with awe, and remembered the stories and dangerous reputation of larger members of the species. I was frantically signalling to Peter that we must keep clear, whether he saw me or not I don't know, he certainly took no notice, but swam right alongside the great beast gently

poking it here and there. Fortunately the fish showed no tendency towards aggression.

The purpose of the visit to Hawaii was to monitor the progress of the nene breeding project. It was Peter's first meeting with Mr. Herbert Shipman, who was something of an eccentric. A bachelor, he lived alone in a house hidden in thick and overpowering tropical vegetation, dark and damp. Three unmarried sisters lived not far away, in another part of the wood. His bedroom (Peter noted in his diary) was piled high with Christmas presents that he had never opened. He was a raconteur of melodramatic and unlikely stories, formal in manner, eschewing first names, and had a fine collection of Chinese pottery and bronzes. The number of nenes at the breeding station at Pohakuloa was increasing slowly, but they had failed to re-establish themselves in the inhospitable wilder parts of the island.

The snorkeling was wonderful; "anyone who has not done so has not lived." The only fly in the ointment was a distressing upward surge in Peter's weight graph. "I consumed a great quantity of Macadamia nuts with my whisky and grossly over-ate at the buffet supper," he admitted, but consoled himself by reflecting that a good layer of blubber was a valuable protection against cold when in the sea. Philippa's films were developed, and her husband wrote proudly: "Darling Phil has blossomed into a really brilliant photographer. The prize picture was a most beautiful shot of a pair of Salvadori's ducks with a background of reflected reeds. It is a great masterpiece of photography as well as perhaps the first colour picture ever taken of Salvadori's ducks." Then they traveled on to Los Angeles where they stayed with Jean Delacour, whose classic four-volume work on The *Wildfowl of the World* Peter had illustrated with much care and toil. Delacour had fulfilled, on a greater scale, his own abandoned ambition to write a monograph on *The Wild Geese of the World*.

And so, in early February 1957, the *Faraway Look* team returned home with 30,000 feet of film and 1,000 stills, having completed their circumnavigation of the earth and, in Peter's case, formed a lasting addiction. "Coral fishes," he wrote, "are simply under-water birds, but fish-watching is where bird-watching was fifty years ago."

The home to which the Scotts returned now had a nursery. In June 1952 their daughter had been born; she was christened Dafila, after the scientific name of the pintail duck. (It has since been renamed *Anas acuta acuta*.) Despite her parents' indifference to Christian ceremony, she was baptized by a Church of England clergyman, though not in a church. The event took place in *Discovery*, Captain Scott's ship, which was moored in the West India dock in London and had been kept in trim as a training vessel by the Sea Scouts. The ship's bell did duty as a font. A road accident on the way to the docks led to a rare breakdown in Peter's self-discipline. Both he and Philippa were smokers. Philippa had given it up while pregnant, and Peter had followed suit to offer moral support. The accident was not a serious one, but while waiting for the police to arrive they bought a packet of cigarettes to calm their nerves, and that was that. It was not until five years later when, during their travels, they took a dislike to Australian cigarettes, that they gave up smoking altogether. All three of Peter's children were christened in *Discovery*, Nicola in 1943, Dafila nine years later, and his son Falcon, born in June 1954.

Like many men whose muscular youth has mellowed into a more seden- tary middle age, Peter had developed a weight problem. Chubbiness became stoutness, and obesity threatened. He was not a tall man, about 5 feet 8 inches, and portly; by now baldness was approaching; he wore spectacles and looked benign. When his weight exceeded fifteen stone (210 pounds) and he found difficulty in tying his shoelaces, he decided that it was time to call a halt, indeed to go into reverse. Setting about the business with his customary thoroughness, he got some graph paper and drew a diagonal line to indicate the weekly loss he intended to achieve in order to reduce his weight to eleven and a half stone (161 pounds). Basing his diet on The *Slim Gourmet* by Martin Lederman, and starting in June 1955, he weighed himself every day and entered the weight on a chart which he kept going almost until the end of his life. There were bumpy passages. Cowes week sent the graph up, a visit to Sandringham in 1962 re- sulted in an increase of four pounds, and a healthy appetite generated by rocket- netting in October caused a significant rise. The road from Slimbridge to Lon- don led through Whitney, where a certain bakery sold lardy cakes, rich in fat, of an exceptionally tasty kind. It was not unknown for Peter to stop, emerge from the bakery feeling guilty, and devour a lardy cake as he drove on. Philippa took trouble to devise meals faithful to the diet, but now and then he would sprinkle sugar on a salad. It was not the sweetness, he said, so much as the gritty texture that he enjoyed. "Then try sand," Philippa advised. Despite setbacks, Peter shrank to such an extent that several viewers of *Look* wrote to express their concern at his wasted appearance. With ups and downs, he got his weight down to between eleven and eleven and a half stone (154–161 pounds) where it re- mained reasonably constant. But a weight problem never really went away.

The overcrowded, underequipped cottage at Slimbridge had become more and more inadequate, and in 1953 a new house, whose foundation was laid by Dafila, was built. It was connected by a passage with the old cottage and, beyond, the former farm buildings, which had already been converted into a hostel. A timely legacy enabled Philippa to pay for it, so it was their own and not the Trust's, although the land it stood on belonged to the Berkeley estate. While Peter employed an architect, the original plan was his own. One aspect of develop- ments at Slimbridge and, later, elsewhere, that he never delegated, was the design of buildings and grounds. More of the gimmicks that he enjoyed inventing were built into the new house. A sheet of plate glass was suspended from the ceiling over the bed, and he slipped behind it sketches of whatever project was in hand; then he could lie in bed of a morning pondering improvements. There was also a mirror so fixed as to enable him to watch the birds on the lake outside, while lying in bed. A big plate glass window, 10 feet by 8, modeled on the one he had seen in Quebec, was installed in the studio, and the Rushy Pen beyond it scooped out to make a lake where wildfowl swam, preened, courted, took on and off, and nested on islands and among reeds and shrubs and willows on the margins. Here he would sit, armed with a powerful pair of binoculars, watching the birds. Beside the window was his easel with a half-done painting resting on it and, on the wall, a shelf supported his paints and brushes. Above that hung a photograph of Captain Scott in naval uniform. One end of the studio was lined to the ceiling with books and here Peter had his desk; at the other end, in a kind of alcove, was Philippa's desk and her growing collection of photographs. Opening out of the studio was a heated conservatory where they bred insects, lizards of various kinds and, at one time, chameleons, for which Peter had a fascinated affection. Paintings were propped against the walls, books and binoculars lay about, plants and curios drew the eye; it was a spacious, comfortable, and very personal room, shared with the dog of the day.

Peter's personal staff at Slimbridge was minimal, with a core of Philippa, Douglas Eccleston, and one or two assistants who came and went. In 1955 Eccleston left for a holiday in Australia, and a young man was taken on as his temporary replacement. His name was Michael Garside and he stayed for twenty-five years.

Neither his pay, £5 a week, nor his accommodation, a bedroom in the hostel with a communal kitchen and dining room, can have been the attraction. The only transport was a battered Land Rover which went into Dursley once a week to fetch supplies. "If things ran out you did without," Garside said. "Tommy Johnstone used to dole out razor blades in an emergency." The telephone went at all hours, night and day, especially when Look was on the air. When Garside had worked for nine months without a break, he asked his employer for a week-end off. Peter appeared to be puzzled. "Why do you want to go away?" he asked. "Aren't you happy here?" Garside said yes, but he had some family business to attend to, and Peter rather grudgingly agreed. Inconsiderate? Selfish? Garside said no. "He wasn't selfish but selfless, two different things. What he wanted to achieve was so important to him that he thought it must be the same for everyone else and must overrule personal considerations."

If Mike Garside's job was exacting, it was seldom dull. Peter never carried a diary, and Garside made all his appointments, using for the purpose the largest diary he could find, too big to get lost. One day a telephone message came to say that the Countess of Ayr would like to see the grounds, and would arrive at about twelve thirty. Garside went to the car park to greet her and take her to the Director's house, where she was to have luncheon. He waited and waited, but no Countess came. Meanwhile, a little man turned up at the office and said he had an appointment with Peter. No one knew who he was. At last his patience ran out and he demanded "Am I to see Mr. Scott or aren't I?" "On what business?" "I'm the County Surveyor."

When Eccleston's return from Australia was imminent, Garside found a note on his bed saying that he could stay on if he liked. "He was an inveterate note writer," Garside said. "He'd rather write a note than tell you face to face." Some found this habit objectionable, especially if the message was unwelcome, such as the sack; but Garside defended it. "He hated hurting people's feelings. It saved embarrassment. He was basically kind. A perfectionist who knew exactly what he wanted to achieve. So long as you measured up, he made you feel on top of the world. A word of praise from him was magic." And if you didn't measure up? "You had to get it right. Sometimes we would go over the draft of a letter or article seven or eight times. We called it scotting over. He used the phrase himself. 'How many times has this been scotted over?' he would ask."

Mike Garside gave an example of Peter's kindness, which could be fool-hardy. One of Garside's duties was to keep his employer supplied with cash, no easy task at times. He sent his boss off to London one morning with an ample supply, but next day Peter came roaring back—he was a very fast driver—tapped on the window and said "Mike, I've got no money, why didn't you give me enough?" Garside found some more, and nothing further was said. But a few days later Peter explained. He had picked up a hitchhiker, a boy of eighteen or so who had left home after a quarrel with his father, intending to work his passage round the world. He had virtually no money. Peter pulled out his wallet and handed over all his banknotes. The boy, embarrassed, said he would repay the money when he'd found a job. "Don't do that," Peter told him, "but if you find someone in the same boat, do the same for him." Some time later, a letter came from Australia to say that the young man had found a job, and enclosed a donation to the Trust. Peter's action "was a quixotic thing to do," Garside commented, "but he knew by some kind of instinct that the boy was all right. He never thought of money as something to be husbanded or worried about, merely as something to be spent on things that mattered, such as birds or conservation or the future of a young man he'd picked up on the road."

Besides the small core of paid staff there was a periphery of willing volunteers working for Peter. Chief among these was Michael Bratby, first honorary secretary, then a shrewd councillor, who spent many weekends grappling with the Trust's affairs. After his divorce from Brenda he had remarried and found happiness with Joy, who had borne him two daughters. But his health had gone downhill. He was a heavy smoker, and in 1959 he died, a victim of lung cancer. So Peter's circle of close friends, already diminished by the war, was shrinking. Of the young punt-gunners who had gathered convivially at the Ship Inn on Brogden marsh, after Bratby's death only Winter, Dalgety, and the doctor Mervyn Ingram remained.

ENDNOTES

[1] *Fishwatcher's Guide to West Atlantic Coral Reefs*, by Charles C. G. Chaplin, illustrated by Peter Scott. ("Waterproof, Greaseproof, Washable.")

CHAPTER SIXTEEN

The Ocean of the Sky

In the summer of 1955, while listening to the news, Peter had heard a story about a glider pilot who had climbed to 23,000 feet in a thunderstorm over Hampshire. "I remember thinking as I listened, there's something I'd like to try—gliding." The opportunity came on All Fools' Day in the following year when a friend rang up to call his attention to the sight of gliders flying from the Cotswold escarpment a few miles away. The Bristol Gliding club had just moved to a site near the village of Nympsfield. Within half an hour Peter was there, and the club's chief flying instructor, John Parry Jones, offered him a flight in a training glider. They reached a height of 1,000 feet and stayed airborne for nineteen minutes. The trap was sprung, with Peter in it. "A whole new field of experience was about to open up," he wrote, "a new and, as it turned out, absolutely satisfying outlet for my occasional restlessness. To go sailing meant a long car journey from my home, but directly above it was, an ocean of sky waiting to be explored." And so he explored it.

Parry Jones explained to him the basic principle of gliding, that gravity is always pulling the glider down to earth, and the only way it can rise is to find air which is going up faster than gravity is pulling it down. The surface of the land heats up unevenly; towns, villages, factories warm the air; cornfields, for example, give out more heat than woods or water. Currents of warmer air, called thermals, rise from such areas and will take a glider with them. If they carry moisture, when they reach a certain height the moisture will condense and turn into clouds. So the glider pilot looks for clouds, gets underneath them and is carried upwards, circling as he goes. And there are other sources of lift that he must learn to look for. "In an up-current you are beating gravity," Peter wrote, "you are winning. By your own knowledge and cunning you are keeping yourself up, using natural power to do it. It is a gloriously uplifting feeling." A glider is a bird with rigid wings, soaring as a bird soars in upward air currents, and therein lay a main part of its attraction for Peter.

His previous experience of flying powered aircraft made it easy and quick for him to master the skills of gliding. His first flying lessons dated back to the last year of the war, but were cut short before he could get his licence. There was a flying school at Kidlington near Oxford, and when he was setting up the infant Trust from Edwardes Square and driving on weekends to the New Grounds, he sometimes stopped there en route to complete his training. Often Keith Shackleton went with him. Peter needed so little teaching that the instructor felt happier with Shackleton, who sometimes made mistakes. "You're one wing low, you're one wing low," the instructor would repeat. This led Shackleton to invent a Chinese aviator called Wun Wing Lo who sent postcards to Peter and Philippa, written top to bottom in Chinese style, recounting implausible adventures. In the summer of 1947 Peter got his license, but after that flew only intermittently, as a rule on wildfowl counts; flying in powered aircraft never appealed to him as gliding was to do. Engines, he thought, were noisy, smelly, and made of metal, which he disliked. He had a watch with a metal strap, and would sometimes rub a piece of orange peel over the strap and sniff it. He was particularly sensitive to smells, and Philippa kept the kitchen door shut when she was cooking.

Only ten weeks after his initial flight in a glider, on June 9, 1956, Peter flew his first solo.

> When people start gliding [wrote Derek Piggott, an experienced pilot] they are mainly absorbed with the techniques of flying and see very little of what goes on around them. But the more successful pilots see an enormous amount of detail. They see what even distant gliders are doing, they observe subtle changes in the clouds as they form and disperse, they see signs of activity such as wisps of smoke, ripples on the crops below, and birds soaring, which the average person wouldn't notice or realise was significant. Peter had the advantage of years of observing birds and other animals and had very developed powers of observation before he started to glide. He was a natural competitor, determined to be best and not content to do things half-heartedly.

Another champion glider pilot, Rear-Admiral Nicholas Goodhart, CB, RN, emphasized Peter's modesty when he set himself to learn a new technique.

Peter was not one simply to try to gain the necessary skills by trial and error. Instead he metaphorically sat at the feet of the current pundits asking innumerable questions and listening carefully to the answers. There was nothing he liked better than to get a group of pundits together and set them to discuss and analyse their methods. What impressed me most was his humility. Here was this great man who had reached the top in so many areas of human endeavour and yet he was fully prepared to accept that he could learn this particular speciality from lesser mortals whose achievements were insignificant compared with his.

Gliding provided plenty of time, often too much, for sitting at the feet of pundits. Many launches were abortive; the pilot, failing to find a lift, was back on the airfield within a few minutes to wait his turn for another launch. He could be launched by winch, or towed along a runway by a powerful car, or, best of all but much more expensive, towed by a light aircraft. In Peter's day, at Nympsfield, winching was the usual method. For a relaunch it was first come, first served, and the pilot might await his turn for the rest of the day; or it would rain, off and on, all day and there would be no gliding. Patience was demanded no less than skill, and demanded also of the staff at Slimbridge. A good weather forecast and a fine morning might tempt Peter from his desk or easel and no word would come from him all day, to the frustration of telephone callers with urgent messages, of his staff, and perhaps above all of his wife. Peter became quite bewitched by gliding.

His principal instructor was Peter Collier, whom he described as "a cynical young man who always wore a blue jersey and wrote novels which did not get finished. He had a devastating turn of phrase, took life as he found it and may yet be a great writer." It was said that he sat behind his pupils reading the *Financial Times* preparatory to playing the stock market, made a fortune, bought a yacht, disappeared in the general direction of the China Seas and came to rest in Majorca.

Just as, in his sailing days, Peter had to have the best make of dinghy, so he went for the best glider, in both cases regardless of expense (in 1939 the price of a high performance sailplane averaged about £350; by 1969, this had been multiplied by a factor of ten; by 1991, the cost would be about £30,000). The Uffa Fox of the gliding world was Fred Slingsby, who had flown in the first British championships in 1922 in a homemade contraption, and had gone on to design and manufacture gliders in Yorkshire. Peter bought from him a two-seated T42B Eagle, called it *Sea Eagle,* and in it completed a series of tests set by the International Aeronautical Federation which measured a pilot's ability to soar to a certain height, to stay airborne for a certain length of time, and to glide over a prescribed distance. He set himself at these fences with all the determination of a jockey whose one aim in life is to win the Grand National. Within seven weeks of his first solo flight he passed the first test by staying airborne for five hours, and throughout the summer of 1957 he was flying almost every week. He had no need to look beyond the gliding club at Nympsfield to satisfy his hunger for adventure. Dangers encountered in the ocean of the sky could be as menacing as those experienced at sea. A weak thermal could impose a forced landing, a strong one propel you far up into the sky at a terrifying speed, until, like a gale-tossed leaf, your glider spun downward out of control.

Several such adventures came Peter's way. In May 1959, coming in to land at Nympsfield, *Sea Eagle* was caught in a down current, fouled some telegraph wires and trees, and ended up as a heap of matchwood. By great good fortune Peter and his passenger were uninjured, but his self-esteem was badly dented; he told Garside to take the matchwood away to Slingsby's factory and said nothing about the mishap. It was not going to put him off gliding; he had passed all three tests by then for his "gold" badges, but still had three "diamonds" to tackle, the hardest of all to achieve.

The single-seater Olympia 419x, made in Newbury in Berkshire, was the last word in gliders, and he placed an immediate order. How to pay for it was a problem solved by a publisher's advance payment for his autobiography.

The trouble about his autobiography was that, having got the advance, he had to write it, and this was a time-consuming chore. One deadline passed and then another, and the ultimate one loomed. Jane Howard had agreed to edit the manuscript, and the final stages took place in her house in London, with Jane tapping out last-minute corrections, Philippa on the floor pasting them in, other helpers at hand numbering pages, and Peter presiding over it all. At five o'clock on the last day of the last deadline he left with the manuscript under his arm and delivered it to Hodder and Stoughton just as the partner in charge of the book was closing the office for the weekend. Such was the birth of *The Eye of the Wind.*

The accident to his Sea Eagle happened on May 31, 1959, and on July 19 he went to fetch his new machine, flew it for two hours and decided to try on the following day for his first "diamond," a flight of not less than 300 kilometers to a specified destination. On the way he spent some time circling in a thermal to study the layout of duck ponds on an estate near St. Neots. It was an uneventful flight, and he landed at the designated airfield with his first "diamond" achieved.

It was not until a year later, in May 1960, that he made an attempt on the second "diamond" badge, which called for a minimum flight of 500 kilometers; so hard was this to gain that only four pilots had hitherto succeeded. Thermals were weak; it was a patchy flight that seemed destined to end well short of the goal. He selected a field to land in but, as he approached it, passed over a small junkyard full of old cars.

> Perhaps it was the chimney of the adjoining workshop, or perhaps the old cars had retained some heat, but at 800 feet I picked up a very weak thermal. Scarcely rising at all I circled and circled and circled, until I saw two immature Lesser Black-backed gulls circling below me. They made much tighter turns than I could make, but were always in the best lift. All I had to do was to keep them in the middle of my circle and I knew I was in the most powerful part of the thermal. It pleased me a great deal to be using these birds as guides.

Reprieved by the junkyard and the immature gulls, he flew on slowly until he got into a powerful lift which carried him upward at the rate of 1,500 feet per minute until he reached 13,500 feet. Then came an alarming outbreak of turbulence. Lightning flashed, ice crystals poured into the cockpit, and frost formed on the backs of his hands. The lift tossed him to over 18,000 feet before he straightened out to meet more trouble; the ailerons were half frozen, his oxygen nearly finished, he was in thick cloud and had no idea where he was. At 11,000 feet there was a gap in the clouds and he recognized the coast beneath him north of Newcastle. He landed in a field near Cockburnspath just after six o'clock after flying for 298 miles, 14 miles short of the goal; but, with a height of 18,300 feet recorded on his barograph, the "diamond" badge for altitude was unexpectedly achieved. He also won the Wakefield trophy for the longest flight recorded in each year. "Mike Garside arrived with the trailer at 11.15 p.m. and the two of us drove back in two hour shifts, the other sleeping on a lilo [an air mattress] in the back. Breakfast at Cirencester and back at Nympsfield by 10.30 A.M., just twenty-three hours after we had both left."

"To frighten yourself just a little is an essential ingredient of adventure," Peter had written. Sometimes you frightened yourself quite a lot.

The "diamond" badge for distance still had to be achieved. Since gliding is an international sport, the rules in every country are the same. In January 1962 Peter and Philippa planned a combined holiday and wildlife reconnaissance in South Africa, and he arranged to make his attempt in that country in a borrowed glider. They reached Johannesburg in a Comet at 3 P.M. on Tuesday January 16; early next morning favorable weather conditions were reported and, disregarding jetlag, by nine o'clock Peter was at Baragwanath airfield, where he was to fly a Skylark IIIb belonging to an obliging and unknown Afrikaner called Boet Domisse. Perhaps it was a good omen that the borrowed glider's make was called after a bird. By 11:30 A.M. he was airborne, following a dogleg course southwest to Bloemhof and then back via Lindley, a distance of 325 miles. He had been used to flying over country almost every inch of which he knew; here everything was unfamiliar, even the instruments and the scale of the map, and the rarefied air meant "a good deal of wallowing." But he identified the turning point, took the necessary photographs, and reached his starting point at 6:24 P.M. after flying for just under seven hours. Given the strangeness of everything it was a brilliant flight. "I was glad to be on the ground," he wrote, "as Boet's glider had no plumbing and the polythene bags he gave me were not watertight." The photographs confirmed his success. Only six British pilots had won all three "diamonds" before him.

Next day he had his first sight of wild black ducks (*Anas sparsa*) on a dam, saw Shannon's portrait of his mother in Johannesburg's national gallery, and spent the weekend painting pictures for the gallery that handled his work. He and Philippa spent "a day of sheer delight" at her old home, Beauchamp in the Orange Free State; admired bushman paintings in Basutoland; saw their first wild greater kudu, their first sable antelope, their first tsessebie, their first leopard, and, off Lourenco Marques, recorded 112 species of fish. "Twenty years later I can see again the sunshine and the light playing on the kudu's horns, the brilliance of the blue that flashed on the back of the Angola kingfisher, the expression on the face of the sargassum fish *Histrio histrio* in a patch of weed on the edge of the Santa Maria reef."

Later that same year, 1962, in the summer, Peter attended an ornithological congress at Cornell University in Ithaca, New York, accompanied by Desmond Hawkins. The BBC was anxious to break into one or other of the American networks with nature films, and Hawkins hoped to see a vice-chairman of the Columbia Broadcasting System, George Wiegelheart, who was sympathetic to this suggestion. During the congress, there was an interval after each period of discussion when film transparencies were shown in a darkened room.

> Peter was chairman of a session [Desmond Hawkins recollected]. He introduced the man who was showing the transparencies, and the lights went down. I was called out for a phone call. It was to say that Uncle Gerald [George Wiegelheart] was being very helpful and we must get in touch with him at once. So back I went and thought, "I'll grab Peter the moment the speaker sits down." When he finished and the lights went up, the chairman's chair was empty. Peter had decided there'd be no useful discussion afterwards and slipped away.
>
> So I thought now where has he gone, what can I do? I went outside and suddenly I thought to myself—thermals! So I

went to the phone box, got on to the operator and said, "I'm a foreigner to your country, and I don't quite know how to use your system, but I want to get in touch with a gliding club if there is one within fifteen miles of this phone box." The girl was very helpful, and said, "Yes there is, I'll put you through." So she did, and I said, "Do you by any chance have an English visitor who's called in the last hour or so and is probably airborne by now?" "Yes," he said, "funny you should ask that, we do!" So I said, "Will you please ask him when he comes down to get in touch with me and that it's very urgent indeed."

Bless his heart, he did, and Peter said how the hell did you know where I was? I said well I know a thermal when I see one and I know what it does to you.

The story had a happy ending; the CBS vice-chairman was interested, Hawkins spent most of the night with the network's film editor putting a sequence together, and Peter gave an illustrated talk next morning on breakfast television.

The congress was interrupted by a weekend break, when delegates were conducted to places of interest. Peter was asked what he wanted to see; with many apologies, he asked to be excused. "I'm flying back on Friday night to skipper the King of Norway's yacht in a race in the Mediterranean," he explained. "I'll be back on Monday morning." And he was.

In 1963 came the year of gliding achievement. Peter made his fourth attempt to win the national championship, held in May at Lasham in Hampshire, still flying his Olympia 419. The start of the first day's competition was an apprehensive time for pilots. Often they had to hang about until the weather improved—if it did— and briefing could proceed in a tent. Keyed up, they fussed over their aircraft, chatted to their crews, strove to subdue the butterflies in their stomachs. Only one amongst them could be seen sitting in the shade of a wing of his glider with a sketchbook propped against his knee. The wooden gliders of those days were brightly painted for purposes of recognition, like jockeys' colors. Peter was drawing each one carefully, as he drew his birds, impervious to the tension around him, and ignoring press photographers' attempts to lure him out of the shade.

He was placed tenth on the first day, first on the second, and on the final day was running neck and neck with John Williamson (son of the author of Tarka the Otter).

As I came within sight of the aerodrome there was one tremendous question. Would John Willie [Williamson] who had started a few minutes before me, have arrived? Five gliders were on the ground. One was a red Olympia with white wings and day-glow strips on the tips. But there was no white panel on the fin and rudder. It was not John Willie's glider. This discovery must rank as one of the "golden moments" of my life.

He had won the British Open Championship (League I). He was fifty-three years old.

He might have been expected to rest on his laurels, but to win the championship again became an obsession and he made several more attempts, in each case buying a new and expensive glider. By the end of the 1960s the Germans had virtually cornered the market by making the machines of fiberglass instead of wood or metal, and almost every first-class sailplane was German made. Peter bought the best again, a BS-1, flew it in the national championship in 1968 and came second. This near miss persuaded him to have one more try. He was now one year short of sixty, the age of the senator not the gladiator; he had, in fact, become a senator in the gliding forum, indeed the Caesar, having been elected chairman of the British Gliding Association. Once again the weather was disheartening, so much so that all flying was cancelled on three out of the seven days. The last day saw Peter landing in a field near Didcot to find one of his principal rivals, George Burton, already there, with a bogged-down trailer that his retrieval crew had failed to extricate from the mud. Peter's crew arrived, joined Burton's pushers and got the trailer on the road. Burton offered to wait while his own crew did the same for his rival's trailer, but Peter, in the best sportsmanlike tradition, said no, you go ahead; so Burton did, and won the championship. Peter's place was eighth.

This was his seventh national championship and not a happy one. Fields were sodden, thermals fickle, clouds dense, drizzle pervasive, disappointments many. "Mike," he said to Garside when the championship was over, "sell the sailplanes (he had two by then) and build a swimming pool." This, in due course, came about, Philippa paying for the pool out of another legacy. Peter took no further part in gliding competitions. In 1970 he resigned as chairman of the British Gliding Association, giving as his reason the many commitments arising from the designation of 1970 as European Conservation Year. He was elected vice president and held that office until his death.

For nearly fifteen years gliding had given him excitement, the satisfaction of mastering a new skill and the delights of travel in "the ocean of the sky," with clouds as his companions and birds as his guides. His safety, survival even, had been in his own hands. Since his apprenticeship, various technological devices had been introduced, and while he made full use of them he half regretted their invention because they shifted the basis of success from the skill and resourcefulness of the man to the efficiency of the instrument. Writing to a friend about his newly fitted radio-telephone he concluded: "Oh dear! How complicated it is getting! And all I want to do is to fly like a bird."

In 1963, British gliding champion; in 1964, skipper of the yacht *Sovereign*, challenger for the America's Cup. The challenge was mounted by Anthony Boyden, a businessman who had made his pile in paper. He had his new 12-meter yacht designed by David Boyd, a leading naval architect and also the designer of *Sceptre*, the previous challenger which had failed to bring the cup back in 1958. Boyden was a yachtsman himself, but did not rate his own skills highly enough to take on the job of helmsman and skipper, so in the summer of 1963 he chose three candidates and put them through their paces at Cowes, sailing in *Sceptre* and his new *Sovereign*. Peter was one of the three. His experience had been mainly in smaller boats, but his sailing skills were highly esteemed in the yachting world and it was largely for his qualities of leadership that Mr. Boyden chose him. The helmsman must weld the crew together as well as skipper the boat.

From early April 1964 onward came a period of intensive training. The squad from which the eleven-man crew was to be selected gathered at Boyden's handsome Georgian house in Dorset, still being modernized and known affectionately as Mildew Manor, and for three months followed a strict routine. The day started at six-thirty with calisthenics and continued first at Weymouth, later at Portsmouth, sailing first against *Sceptre* and then against another 12 meter yacht designed by David Boyd and built on the Clyde. This was *Kurrewa V*, owned by two Australian sheep farming brothers, John and Frank Livingston. Rather ominously, Peter noted that *Sceptre* was unaccountably difficult to beat. Boyden's squad was rigorously trained; smoking and spirits were banned, though a *cordon bleu* chef was engaged and beer allowed. Four of the squad were rugby football players from the famous Harlequin club, whose will to win matched their brawn.

A member of *Sovereign's* crew, Paul Anderson, recalled that:

> one of Peter's greatest attributes was complete concentration—that, and attention to detail. I have never in all my life met anyone who paid so much attention to detail. Every day after the morning's sailing session we would sit down and he'd write down everything that had happened—every move and manoeuvre, every sail change, every alteration made in the rig, even microscopic adjustments. He was absolutely disciplined and his concentration was a hundred percent. I was the foredeck hand responsible to the skipper. Our working relationship was such that I could often anticipate what he wanted. We were both against shouting orders. He was a quiet man, decisive. There was great telepathy.

> One of the major criteria for a top class yachtsman is observing not just the boat, the sails, the rigging, the equipment and the tuning of the boat, but the sea conditions, the cloud

formations, the wind patterns, where the wind was coming from and going to. He had a tremendous grasp of all that. Much of it came from his great knowledge of birds. After all, the power of sailing is the wind. It's all developed round a wing which is the sail. Boats and birds are closely parallel. Peter was able to evaluate sails better than sail-makers. He used the wind in the same way that birds do. He knew which way a bird would go instinctively. He had the same instinct on water with a boat ... He was almost out of his time because technology was beginning to take over. Computers nowadays would do it all. Human navigation, the tides, the stars—all gone now. But Peter would have understood computers and made the best use of them.

When *Sovereign's* and *Kurrewa V's* crews and backup teams reached Newport, Rhode Island, the venue of the races, they saw for the first time the three boats, *Constellation*, *American Eagle*, and *Nefertiti*, which were to compete to be the Cup's defender. It was a sobering moment. "In refinement of detail," Peter wrote, "both *American Eagle* and *Constellation* were in quite a different class to *Sovereign* and *Kurrewa V*." If the British challengers knew from that moment in their hearts that victory was beyond them, they did not show it, reflecting no doubt that the unexpected often happens. First the two British boats had to fight it out for supremacy. This was a happy period, Peter wrote. The crew lived together in an old timber-built seaside "cottage" with twelve bedrooms and eight bathrooms, looked after by four of their wives. Philippa was detained in England by school holidays, but joined her husband just before the big race. Members of the crew wore red jerseys embroidered with the red rose of England, and admirers sent them bunches of the same flower. *Sovereign* was painted an attractive shade of dark blue. The elimination races, bedevilled by fog, were close and exciting, and *Sovereign* won by six races to two.

The first race of the series—the best of seven—took place on September 15, 1964, the day after Peter's fifty-fifth birthday. Within ten minutes of the start the crew of *Sovereign* knew that they were beaten. *Constellation* was simply a faster boat; in particular, she could sail considerably closer to the wind. The race was lost on the drawingboard. *Constellation* won the first race by five minutes and thirty-four seconds, a decisive defeat but not a humiliating one. That came with the second race, which *Sovereign* lost by over twenty minutes, the biggest margin of defeat in any America's Cup race since 1886. Two more races were to come. To keep up their spirits and the will to win in face of the certainty of defeat was an immensely testing ordeal for the crew. The British tradition of fighting best with backs to the wall came to their aid, and morale did not crack. *Constellation* won the third race by a less crushing margin, six minutes and thirty-four seconds, and the fourth and last by the melancholy one of nearly sixteen minutes. "Make no mistake," wrote a reporter, "Britain has had her oil-skin pants removed before the world."

In the post-mortem that followed, Peter identified what he believed to be the main reasons for defeat. *Sovereign's* sails were inferior to *Constellation's;* her mast and rigging were heavier aloft, her instruments less efficient. He blamed himself for two shortcomings. His choice of spinnaker had been faulty; and when normal sailing methods were getting nowhere, he had tried one or two experiments that might have improved *Sovereign's* performance, but had not. He added: "The mind is numbed by the enormity of being so far behind in an America's Cup race. This applied to quickness and soundness of thinking rather than to speed of action, and caused some foolish mistakes. Crew morale was high all through and except for the numbness already mentioned, their spirits and cohesion as a team remained astonishingly good." His final conclusion went to the heart of the matter. "I revert, with greater conviction than before, to my 1958 dictum that without a designer of comparable genius to Olin Stephens [designer of *Constellation*] the odds against any challenge succeeding are very great indeed ... There seems no indication that such a designer exists at present in Britain."

Most of all, Peter felt responsibility toward *Sovereign's* owner, who had spent three years and a considerable fortune in mounting the challenge. On his return home he wrote this letter:

> My dear Tony, it hasn't been possible to say, and perhaps it isn't now possible to write what I feel about the 19th challenge— except that I wouldn't have missed it for anything in the world. It was a great and "enlarging" experience. You deserved so much better than your team were able to give you—though want of trying was not one of the shortcomings. I suppose the fact that *Sceptre* could ever beat *Sovereign* was the writing on the wall that we all read, yet refused to believe. But I am far from satisfied with my own part and the losses off the wind must be laid fairly and squarely at my door ...
>
> Meanwhile, Tony, I want to thank you for so many things. For making the whole wonderful summer possible, for giving me the chance to sail the boat, for backing me so loyally when things went wrong, for taking the final disaster in such a constructive and philosophical way and for being so understanding and help- ful during the difficult time immediately afterwards. Such re- grets as I have are for the others involved—for you and David Boyd and all the boys, and our multitude of backers. For myself none; I just hate to have let others down.

The press reported the defeat as it might have done had Britain lost the battle of Trafalgar. So many friends wrote to Peter to express their sympathy that he sent a round-robin reply:

> Of course *Sovereign's* defeat by so wide a margin was a terrible disappointment, and it is distressing to be even partly responsible. But it would have been wrong to have gone into the challenge at all without a back broad enough to carry that kind of failure ... We did our very best and it wasn't nearly good enough. We're sadder but wiser, and on balance I'm glad to have had the chance of trying. As for me personally, I'm in good shape, very fit and well, and feeling fairly philosophical about it. It may have involved national prestige and all that—but after all it was only a series of yacht races. I mind most for Tony Boyden, for David Boyd, for my crew who did so well and for all the people who put their faith in us and thought we should win. For myself I mind not at all. My darling Phil was marvellous during the gloomy days and helped me to keep a sense of proportion. Periodical failures are quite good for the character. This wasn't my first and it is unlikely to be my last.

A few days later he was off to Tokyo, with Philippa, to preside again over the jury of the International Yacht Racing Union at the Olympic Games. Then back to Slimbridge and his painting, and to "give a fresh push to the Wildfowl Trust and World Wildlife Fund."

CHAPTER SEVENTEEN

Tortoises, Family Life and Bewick's Swans

On October 5, 1948, at a conference held at Fontainebleau, there had come into existence a body with the unwieldy name of the International Union for the Conservation of Nature and Natural Resources, IUCN for short. Its parentage was Swiss, its gestation prolonged, and representatives of eighteen nations, seven international organizations, and one hundred and seven independent bodies signed the instrument that set it up with a set of objectives which, if realized, would have gone a long way toward re-creating the state of affairs that had prevailed in the Garden of Eden before the Fall. Preservation of wildlife and the natural environment throughout the world; creation of national parks and wildlife refuges; scientific research; spread of public enlightenment; protection of endangered species; no good environmental cause was omitted. There were two main weaknesses. The human population explosion, which was to throw its calculations out of balance, was totally ignored; and the financial cupboard was almost bare. Every signatory of the instrument was supposed to contribute something; in practice, some did and some did not, and the amounts were very small. The strength of the IUCN, whose headquarters was at Morges in Switzerland, was that it attracted the services of many distinguished scientists and public figures, generally without reward.

Peter had already been elected to the IUCN's council when a proposal was made to celebrate the centenary of the publication of Charles Darwin's *Origin of Species* in a practical way. It was in the Galápagos Islands that the seeds of the theory of evolution by means of natural selection had been sown in the mind of the twenty-six-year-old naturalist attached to HMS *Beagle*. This group of fifteen major islands, plus a lot of little ones, lying off the coast of Ecuador, possessed a flora and fauna quite unique, quite extraordinary, and in danger of being obliterated by what is generally known as civilization. The suggestion was that a Charles Darwin research station should be set up to study the natural history of the archipelago, and to breed in captivity some of the most threatened species in order to re-establish them on the islands. Peter welcomed this proposal with enthusiasm. To him, Darwin was more or less a secular god. The *Origin of Species* had been the only book that Captain Scott had packed into his kit on his first sled journey toward the South Pole.

Peter joined a committee set up under Julian Huxley's chairmanship to frame plans for the research station, with money to come in the first place from United Nations Educational, Scientific and Cultural Organization— UNESCO—of which Huxley was director-general. Here was an opportunity to gather fresh material for *Faraway Look* and, at the same time, to win publicity for the research project. The BBC agreed to send Peter and Philippa to the islands in January 1959 with Tony Soper as their cameraman.

The attractions of the Enchanted Islands, as they have been called, lay in the strangeness of their creatures. The islands had risen from the sea as a result of volcanic eruptions some three million years ago, and active volcanoes were still spewing out lava from time to time. There they had lain out in the Pacific Ocean, barren rocks streaked with lava floes, lifeless until, gradually, seeds dropped by birds, and plants brought on floating rafts of vegetation, found crevices in the weathering rocks in which they could germinate and take root. Then came the first animals, no one knows precisely when or whence, including ancestral tortoises and giant lizards known as iguanas, which evolved into forms known nowhere else in the world. Birds found their own way, stayed to nest and, like the reptiles, evolved into different races, each of which filled a particular niche in the environment.

It was here that Darwin noted slight differences in the shape of the bill and in the habits of the Galápagos finches, small brownish birds prevalent on the islands, during his five-week visit in September and October 1835. The bill of one race had adapted to eating small, soft seeds, another to cracking the very hardest ones. The bill of a further race was slim and tapered for probing into cactus flowers and pads, whereas the strong, pointed bill of the aptly named woodpecker finch was able to dig into soft wood to discover insect burrows. And so on. Similarly, each of the fifteen major islands had its own race of tortoises, each slightly different from the other. It was this variation in the bills and behavior of the finches, and in certain chracteristics of the giant tortoises, that led Darwin to the conclusion that in each case a single species had modified its original shape and habit to meet the circumstances peculiar to each island— evolution by means of natural selection.

These islands and their plenteous fauna lay uninhabited and undisturbed by man until the Bishop of Panama, so far as is known the first human to report on the islands' wonders, arrived in 1535. He found the giant tortoises so abundant that it "looked as if God had caused it to rain stones." In the eighteenth and nineteenth centuries came the whalers, who loaded tortoises into their vessels by the thousand to provide meat for their crews. As the tortoises could survive for many months without food or water and were defenseless, they were a perfect source of victuals for the whalers, who ate out the entire tortoise population of three of the islands (Charles, Jervis, and Barrington). Even worse, from the point of view of the tortoises, they introduced goats to the islands, and in time others of man's familiars—pigs, cattle, donkeys, rats—which devoured or trampled on the native fauna's eggs and young. It was the story of the Hawaiian goose over again. Darwin had foreseen "what havoc the introduction of any new beast of prey must cause in a country before the instincts of the indigenous inhabitants have become adapted to the strangers' craft and power." It has taken them a long time to adapt. Tortoises still make no protest when humans ride on their backs; boys may sit beside a pool and knock doves on the head with a stick as they come to drink; and Peter found the veranda of a house in which he stayed "covered with small marine iguanas, the little ones sitting in a geranium pot on the balustrade eating bananas, and curled up in a corner was a half-grown sea lion."

After Ecuador claimed the islands in 1832, settlers came with more domestic animals and made further depredations. Nor should the scientists be overlooked. An expedition sent by the Californian Academy of Sciences in 1905 collected 8,691 specimens of birds, 266 giant tortoises, and a lot of other animals besides. Whether it is to be eaten or its remains put on view in a museum makes no difference to a species' chances of survival.

A launch belonging to the Ecuadorian navy took the Scotts and Tony Soper to Santa Cruz Island where the research station was to be. They climbed with rucksacks to the interior to stay the night with an elderly Norwegian gentleman, Mr. Hornemann, who spent his time reading philosophy, and his German wife who looked after the plantation of bananas and citrus fruit with the help of their thirteen-year-old son who was fluent in five languages. This was the jumping-off place for the inaccessible mountain forests of the interior, to which survivors of the once great tortoise population had retreated. The team walked for four hours before they found their first tortoise, a small one not worth filming. Two hours later they came upon a slightly bigger one, and finally an even larger one which was feeding but which withdrew into its shell when disturbed. Heavy rain impeded the photography. The team slept out in jungle hammocks, and next morning the tortoise was still in the same position. "We stood half under the trunks of trees waiting for the rain to stop, and when it was no more than a drizzle we made a shot of Phil climbing on the tortoise's back." To such small remnants had the population sunk. Wild pigs had eaten the eggs and wild dogs the newly hatched young. The team arrived back at Academy Bay at nightfall, after seven hours of strenuous walking along twisting, muddy, overgrown paths. Next day, on Fernandina Island, they tackled the marine iguanas which lay about in masses on the grey lava-sand beaches, themselves grey and justifying the description given them of "imps of darkness." To film an iguana actually laying an egg was their objective. They dug several holes in the sand to encourage gravid females; two iguanas obliged, and both were filmed laying eggs at regular 8 minute intervals.

Five weeks packed with new impressions lavishly recorded on film ended in Academy Bay with Peter painting three hawk-moth caterpillars while Philippa packed the gear. He felt guilty about:

> painting my last caterpillar until the very last moment. Somehow I can never see why it is upsetting to go on doing things until the last moment. But I know that it is so, yet I was so very keen to get the pattern of that last caterpillar on to paper before we left and it seemed the only important thing at the time. Phil says it is simple—I should have started earlier. She is quite right.

They left Ecuador on March 14, 1959 and on July 7 the Charles Darwin Foundation was set up under Belgian law, with Peter as a member of the executive council, of which Julian Huxley was chairman.

With the support of the government of Ecuador and money from UNESCO the project went ahead, and the research station was officially opened in January 1964. Its first task was to tackle the pests that had already wiped out completely five of the fifteen races of giant tortoise, and endangered seven more; on Hood island, in 1963, only a single tortoise could be found. Over one thousand goats on Pinta Island had been destroyed, but on Santiago an estimated one hundred thousand remained, as well as twenty thousand pigs. The government of Ecuador issued a decree declaring all uninhabited parts of all the islands to be national parks. As the small human population was confined to a few areas, over ninety-six percent of the archipelago then enjoyed protected status—on paper. As ever, cash was lacking to pay for wardens and their equipment, and to enforce the law. It was to be sixteen years before the first captive-bred tortoises—seventeen of them, then five years old—were released on Espanola Island, on which only fifteen adults, which had not bred for possibly a century, had survived. The last goats were eliminated on Espanola island three years later.

Almost thirty years after the foundation of the research station, the thousandth captive-bred giant tortoise was released into its ancestral island. So the giant tortoise, as well as three species of land iguana, have been saved from extinction, one may hope forever; but there will always be a question mark.

Two years after the Scotts' first sight of the Galápagos Islands—they were to make three more visits—they were off once more, in February 1961, on their travels, first to the Murchison (now Kabalega) National Park in Uganda.

This was their second visit; during their first, in 1956, their host, Ralph Dresfield, who was chairman of the national parks, had introduced them to mangoes, which they had liked so much that they bought an extra supply and, following local advice as to the best way to deal with this delicious but intractable fruit, ate them in the bath. They stayed on both occasions in the lodge in Paraa, where the White Nile squeezes through a cleft in the rocks less than 7 meters wide to roar amid clouds of spume into a crocodile-infested pool, then widens out to enter Lake Albert (now Mobutu Sese Seko) and so on through Sudan to Egypt and the sea. Here Peter and Philippa saw their first wild elephant herds, "so intensely the proper inhabitants of this green vastness," in Juliette Huxley's words, "they were like whales in the sea, there in their own unquestionable right." So at home with humans had they become that they had taken to overturning trash cans to investigate the contents, and one, called Nellie, accustomed to being offered bananas from car windows, picked up a small automobile and shook it, hoping to dislodge a bunch. She had gone too far, and was shot. In the last resort she was there for human entertainment, not in her own right.

It was the birds that most delighted the Scotts: the goliath heron, 6 feet tall and with a 6-foot wingspan; fish eagles swooping swiftly to grab fish in their claws; malachite kingfishers glowing like gems; carmine bee-eaters; three kinds of ibis; martial eades; hovering sunbirds; and elegant lily-trotters with long slender legs picking their way across floating leaves.

Then they did the rounds of Kenya's parks and reserves conducted by the director, Menyn Cowie. It was mainly due to his perseverance and vision that the first national park in East Africa had been established in 1946 on the outskirts of Nairobi, to be followed by twenty-three others which now attract tourists by the hundreds of thousands from all over the world. Mervyn Cowie described their journey to the Amboseli park bordering on Tanzania:

> We left early in the morning to travel 150 miles and reached Amboseli well after dark. That means we averaged about twelve miles an hour. We stopped every few miles to examine a weaver bird's nest, or to watch a rare cuckoo, or to see a mole-rat throwing soil up from its tunnel under the road, or to collect some resin from a frankincense tree (Browellia). In each case Peter described in detail all the interesting features of what we had

stopped to see. He had the knack of being able to make any journey a fascinating experience, however dull the scenery might seem to be.

It was in Nairobi's small but species-rich park that Philippa found a Jackson's three-horned chameleon, which accompanied the Scotts to Slimbridge where it spent the summer, to be returned the following September to its home— a privileged chameleon, having shot out its tongue to take a blowfly from a royal finger, that of Prince Charles.

The object of this second African visit was to open a new national park, that which enclosed Lake Nakuru with its immense flocks of lesser flamingos, at times over a million strong. On February 15, 1961 (Peter wrote) he and Philippa with two guides

> waded nearly up to the top of borrowed wellingtons through soft mud and a bed of tall reed mace till we emerged at the edge into a hessian hide. From its large "window" was a sight of incredible beauty and interest. The sun had not yet topped the hill behind us. The far shore of the lake was already sunlit but the uncountable masses of flamingos, which stretched from the far distance to within twenty yards of us, glowed pink in the blue shadow . . . As the sun rose from behind the hill the colour became more and more brilliant. Streams of flamingos came in from far out on the lake, a triangular patch of bright scarlet under their wings lit by the low sunlight. There can be no more remarkable ornithological sight in the world.

One result of this African visit was the publication of *Animals in Africa*, illustrated by Philippa's photographs. And almost every bird and beast, every fish or feather, insect or tree, was recorded in Peter's diary with exactitude of line and color. Every expedition stocked his mind with fresh images and observations of nature. All this might be seen as a preparation for the days immediately ahead when his first crusade, to protect and sustain the world's wildfowl, broadened out into his second crusade, to protect and sustain all wild animals everywhere.

The decade of the 1960s opened with the death of Bill. Until the last year or two of his life he had shared Leinster Corner with Wayland and Elizabeth and their growing family, pursuing hobbies such as church music and calligraphy while maintaining his Ciq interests and his devotion to birds and to Spinoza. His daughter-in-law remembers him being driven in his ancient Baby Austin by a retired six-foot-odd Guardsman who couldn't wear his cap while driving because there wasn't room for it. He stayed sometimes at Trinity with his old friend George Trevelyan and gave suave little dinner parties in the Old Guest Room—I remember him working out the menus—and innumerable young men, Cambridge graduate students and undergraduates, came to visit him at the Lacket when he went there to live in the last few years of his life.

He died of a heart attack at the Lacket, after calling for a glass of sherry, at the age of eighty-one. Wayland inherited the Lacket and the house in the Bayswater Road, where once a seal, rescued by Peter from some unpleasant fate, had spent a week in a bath.

Peter's frequent absences from home left him with all too little time to spend with his children. Dafila and Falcon were joined in the school holidays by their half-sister Nicola whose pony, on which her life was largely centered, was kept at Slimbridge. Peter was an indulgent father rather than a disciplinarian, yet there was an air of authority; no liberties were taken. He was not demonstrative, yet sometimes felt he ought to be. His affection for Dafila was to be reinforced by pride in her achievements, but with his son there was less rapport.

From an early age Falcon had struck out on an unusual line of his own. At the age of eight or nine he built a church out of willow poles which he cut, carried, and bound together himself. This was followed by a tower, 30 feet high, also made of willow poles, straw, and wire. There was a platform on top, and on the tower's completion the family climbed up a ladder to enjoy a celebratory picnic. Falcon's third tower was more ambitious still. Peter had taken the family on holiday in Africa, and in Zambia Falcon had observed the use of bamboo poles as scaffolding; willows, he reckoned, would do as well. He was fourteen or fifteen at the time. He resolved to build a tower higher than any already erected at Slimbridge for goose watching on the Dumbles; the highest was 51 feet, and his was to be 3 feet higher. Possibly this ambition was an expression of the adolescent's determination to do as well as, or better than, his father, a rather desperate aim in his case. If Peter sometimes felt the shadow of his father lying heavily across his path, how much more oppressive must have been the double shadow of two famous forebears? Falcon's parents did not ridicule his tower but ordered breeze-blocks, cement, sand, and other needed materials, and left him to get on with it. He taught himself by trial and error. The tower reached its goal of 54 feet, but before it was completed a gale removed its top. It was rebuilt to 45 feet and still stands, the Falcon Tower overlooking the Rushy Pen.

Then came Falcon's chef d'oeuvre as a builder. At Millfield school in Somerset, where he was a reluctant boarder, he and two companions excavated an underground retreat. On the pretext of exercising the headmaster's dog, they took possession of a hut in the grounds and dug beneath it, carrying out the soil in buckets, until they had a room 4 feet by 6 feet and deep enough to stand up in. They laid on electricity and piped water and then dug out a second, slightly larger room, one for a kitchen and the other for a sittingroom; they even installed a television. The boys believed that the headmaster knew nothing of all this, but he must have. Falcon was from youth a builder at heart, and remained so, meeting with considerable success in the practical if mundane aspects of the construction industry, while seeing in his mind's eye castles, towers, bridges, cathedrals even. Possibly a gene tending toward eccentricity might be traced in his heredity; he and his great-uncle Rosslyn, breeder of green mice, would have had much in common. All three of Peter's children agreed that they had learned one lesson in particular from their father, and learned it by example, not by being told. This was the importance of setting an objective, and pursuing it through thick and thin and never giving up.

Among Peter's more unusual appointments was that of Admiral of the Manx fishing fleet, whose flag sported the three legs of Man with two herrings rampant on a red ground. The first Manx Admiral was piped aboard his ship in 1610; the post subsequently lapsed, to be revived in the 1960s by Sir Ronald Garvey, the island's Lieutenant Governor, who offered Peter the post, with a tenure of three years. The Admiral's salary was only £5 a year, but he had a perk in the form of a comfortable cottage called New Admiralty House, with a telescope on the roof and a bottle of rum in the locker. A condition of the appointment was that he must spend at least a week on the island, and in 1962 the Admiral, wearing a red knitted cap with the Legs of Man embroidered on it, accompanied by his wife in a red track suit and by the children, enjoyed a holiday on the island, sailing, gathering scallops, and going to lunch at Government House.

When the children were somewhat older, for their holidays the Scotts shared a house in the south of France with John and Rachel Winter and their three children. The adults took turns doing the cooking, each person providing one course. (Peter, as he acknowledged, could not boil an egg, nor carve a joint or bird; once, when Prince Philip spent a night in the Director's house at Slimbridge, it fell to the Prince to carve the chicken, Philippa having not yet mastered the art; she did so later.) There was much speculation as to what Peter's contribution to the meal would be. He shut himself into a bedroom and spent much of a morning peeling peaches and dropping the halves into a bowl of brandy, thus neatly avoiding confrontation with the kitchen stove. Through the closed door could be heard the stanzas of The Hunting of the Snark.

Two Easter holidays were spent in the Bahamas, where the family was lent a house near Nassau, with the sea at the bottom of the garden and a reef about 150 yards out. Here Peter was in his element, diving and drawing and classifying fish, and Dafila, aged twelve or thirteen, proved an apt pupil. Her father decided to explore the reef at night. Taking an ineffectual torch, the four of them swam out toward the reef until Falcon and Philippa got cold and turned back. Father and daughter swam on. Then, in the feeble torchlight, a very large black shape loomed immediately ahead, close enough to touch: a 7-foot shark. The torch went out. Dafila thought that the shark had bitten off her father's arm which was holding it, but the shark had not; they turned and swam back as fast as possible, but steadily, trying not to splash. "I wasn't sure how worried he was by this situation," said Dafila, "but I knew when we got back, because both he and my mother had a large brandy."

An even more ambitious holiday came in 1969: a month in Zambia— Dafila armed with a guitar—among the leaping lechwes and long-legged storks of the Kafue flats; the Victoria Falls; lunch with President Kaunda; then the Maasai-Mara game reserve in Kenya, a visit timed so they could see the awe-inspiring wildebeest and zebra migration. Peter was tireless in pointing out every living creature to his children; while most adults appreciated this, a fifteen-year-old boy could find it tedious. "We had to keep stopping and looking at birds that were miles away which looked much the same as other birds we'd seen," Falcon observed. Their father's calmness in every circumstance impressed both children; placid was Falcon's word. At Entebbe, the family were packed and ready for the flight back to London, waiting for Peter to join them in the hotel. He arrived still in his dirty bush clothes. "The next thing we knew, we heard the bath running," Falcon said. "We had about five minutes, and he had to have a bath, and there was nothing we could do to rush him. He had his bath, and he was ready, and we didn't miss the plane. Most women would have got completely mad at him, but I think my mother knew he'd make it all right. Even if we'd missed the plane, he wouldn't have worried. He'd have seen it as an opportunity to do something else. He was never negative, always positive, and I think that's the greatest inspiration he could have given to anybody."

With the birth of Nicola's first child Daniel in 1964 Peter became a grandfather. At the age of twenty, Nicola had married Kip Asquith, a great-grandson of the Liberal prime minister (later the Earl of Oxford), Kathleen's close friend and model, whose sessions in her studio the young Peter had once disturbed with an overenthusiastic performance on the pianola.

That same year saw the start of the saga of the Bewick's swans (Cygnus columbianus bewickii). The preface to the story goes back to the winter of 1948, when a single male of the species dropped down into one of the pens at Slimbridge which was occupied by pinioned whistling swans. He was captured, named Noah, and a wife acquired for him from the Rotterdam Zoo. Mrs. Noah hatched the first Bewick's cygnets known to have been born in captivity, and continued to breed regularly for thirty-two years until she died of old age in 1982, having successfully reared twenty-seven cygnets. Mr. and Mrs. Noah, together with the pinioned whistling swans, attracted small parties of wild Bewick's who were passing from their Arctic breeding grounds to their winter quarters in Somerset and southern Ireland. Peter decided to make a serious study of these birds. He moved the pinioned whistling swans from their enclosure to Swan Lake, outside his studio, where he could observe them through his plateglass window. One of the wild Bewick's females had become attached to a pinioned whistling male; she was named Maud, after one of the painter Whistler's lady friends. The day after the move, a single wild Bewick's female came down to join the small party outside the studio window. She should have been Maud returning to join her whistling friend, but she was not. She had more yellow, Peter noticed, on her black-and-yellow bill. This simple observation, made in February 1964, started the study, which continues to this day, of the life histories and behavior of some sixty-seven hundred individual swans which are told apart by the pattern of the black and yellow on their bills. Each individual has a different pattern, like human fingerprints and zebra's stripes, and no two are exactly alike.

The Bewick's study became a family affair. Peter sketched the head and bill of each swan, Philippa photographed it from three angles, and from the age of eleven Dafila took so close an interest that she could, her father claimed, carry the names and faces of up to a thousand individual swans in her head. It was another of Peter's lucky breaks that his daugher grew up to share his devotion to the *Anatidae* and to become a distinguished ornithologist in her own right.

The more puritanical among scientists studying animal behavior disapprove of giving names to the animals they study. Name an animal, they say, and it becomes an individual with a character of its own; personal bias, even the heresy of anthropomorphism, may creep in. Their study animals are given numbers instead. Peter would have none of that. To him, birds *were* individuals with characters of their own. In any case, naming them was fun. There were Owl and Pussycat, Porgy and Bess, Lancelot and Victoria, Peasant and Gypsy, Prongy and Porcupine, and many others. Three newcomers who flew in at teatime on the Trust's twenty-fifth birthday were named Jammy, Honey, and Butter. There was no divorce amongst swans, although the death of a partner was often followed by remarriage. After a trap was constructed to catch, ring, and examine a sample of birds, it was distressing to find how many carried shot in their bodies, although they enjoyed legal protection from shooting everywhere along their migration route. Lancelot, who first arrived in 1964 and returned every winter for twenty-three years, lost two wives; his third, Elaine, survived him.

The first swans started to arrive from Arctic Russia, some 2,300 miles away, in late October, and left, in small parties, in March. For about five months the lake outside the studio window was alive with these graceful, snow-white birds coming and going, some roosting on its islands like (Peter wrote) great white tea cosies, and gathering morning and evening for meals of corn flung out along the margins of the lake. As darkness fell, on came the floodlights, which had been originally installed to please Prince Philip; the birds had minded not at all, and so the floodlights remained. There was magic in the rippling, shadow-riven scene with its constant motion, the drama of sharply contrasting light and shade. The wildfowl "look on us as friends who know us well by sight, as individual humans whom they can trust not to be predators," Peter wrote. "That these birds should be drawn back after their 5,000 mile round trip to this tiny pond, seventy yards long by forty yards wide, lying under the wall of my house, gives me a feeling of wonder and delight that is hard to describe."

When Dafila was about sixteen, having won a scholarship to Millfield School, she found herself sitting at luncheon next to the headmaster, Mr. Jack Meyer, who asked her where the swans went to feed and rest after they left Slimbridge on their way to northern Russia. Probably to Holland, she replied. Was she certain? No. "Then why not find out?" said the headmaster, and offered to give her £200 to pay for a visit to the Netherlands. So in the following spring she went, driven by a Dutch schoolteacher who enlisted the interest of several professional ornithologists. These scientists were understandably sceptical about the ability of a seventeen-year-old schoolgirl to identify the birds simply by the markings on their bills.

Two days after the start of the search, at the end of March 1970, in fields bordering the river Yssel, she spotted two familiar faces: those of Peasant and Gypsy, last seen at Slimbridge. Four days later she saw them again farther up the river together with another swan called Booster. Only by checking the number on the birds' rings could their identity be established to the satisfaction of the Dutch ornithologists, but the swans remained obstinately afloat with their legs under water, obliging Dafila and her companions to endure a long, cold wait until at last Booster up-ended to reveal the number on his ring which confirmed his identity. The Dutch scientists were convinced. Two years later Dafila, by then an undergraduate at Cambridge, returned to Holland with a fellow ornithologist, Mary Evans, and again saw Peasant and Gypsy, with a family of cygnets, on the floodwaters of the River Yssel. Dafila and Mary Evans then proceeded to search among a flock of some fourteen hundred birds on the estuary of the river Elbe in Germany— and there were Peasant and Gypsy again, with their family, having moved on toward their destination. It was to be eleven years before the Scott family was able to reach that destination, and see for themselves the breeding grounds of the swans they counted as personal friends. To gain permission to visit regions off the Intourist track in the Soviet Union was very hard indeed, and Siberia was a no-go area even for Soviet citizens. But ornithology has its freemasonry, and Peter's regular attendance at conferences for many years, and all the contacts he had made, brought its rewards.

Early in July 1978 he, Philippa, and Dafila were camped on the Yamal peninsula, about 170 miles north of the Arctic circle, conducted thither by a congenial and knowledgeable Russian ornithologist called Vladimir Flint. With them were four young assistants, an interpreter, a reindeer carcass to be refrigerated in the snow, and a great deal of vodka. Would they, on this windswept tundra, encounter familiar faces—Peasant and Gypsy perhaps, Grimes and Grizelda, Caesar and Calpurnia, or any of the other pairs who made the long journey to that small pool at Slimbridge year after year? Five gaily colored tents were pitched beside a tributary of the Yuribei river. At first, in hot sunshine, they saw a quantity of brent geese, many waterfowl and other birds and a phenomenal number of mosquitoes; the crowns of their wide-brimmed hats became black with the insects. On their second day they sighted eighty-three Bewick's swans, and found an empty nest.

July 18 was one of Peter's red letter days. After crossing the river Yuribei, 350 yards wide, in a rubber boat, and walking round a large lake, they found a Bewick's nest with the shells of two recently hatched eggs. "It did not matter so much that the birds were not there," Peter wrote. "Dafila had seen one of them the day before, we had seen his [the cob's] footprints in the river mud, I had his feathers in my pocket and we could study what had been his outlook for the nest-building and incubation period." They had come a few weeks too late in the year to find the birds on their nests: a disappointment, but not a crushing one. Peter's verdict was that the organization of the expedition had been first class, Vladimir Flint's leadership outstanding, the supporting team "superlatively competent," and the food good but rather fattening.

It was all a long way from the Cold War, still so very much a fact of life in Moscow and at the Berlin W3all. Only in a refusal to allow a cameraman to join the expedition did Soviet restrictions frustrate Peter's plans. Anglia Television had hoped to make a documentary of the expedition with Peter as its compère. He was by then closely associated with this company, which his old friend Aubrey Buxton, with three other Norfolk gentlemen, had started in a disused agricultural hall in Norwich back in 1958. By the early 1960s the BBC's *Look* program was running out of steam, and when the Corporation decided, a little abruptly, to change the format and move to a more up-to-date style of presentation, Peter's feelings had been rather bruised; but Aubrey (now Lord) Buxton invited him to join Anglia's board, and to introduce some of the *Survival* films which were to become a speciality of that company. So the Soviet ban was a disappointment, but it was a rare privilege to get into Siberia at all, and they had been allowed to take their still cameras. "We now know in what kind of ecosystem the British-wintering Bewick's breed, and we have made a preliminary list of the flora and fauna in the Bewick's habitats," was Peter's summing-up. "But we failed to recognize any of the known and named individual swans that had wintered in Britain."

CHAPTER EIGHTEEN

World Wildlife Fund

In December 1960 Julian Huxley and his wife got back from a tour undertaken on behalf of UNESCO to report on "the conservation of wildlife and natural habitats in Central and East Africa." In three articles in the *Observer* Sir Julian wrote trenchantly of the urgent need to safeguard habitats being rapidly destroyed, and to rescue many African species from extinction. Among the letters called forth by these articles was one from a naturalized British subject, Mr. Victor Stolan, who wrote:

> There must be a way to the conscience and heart and pride and vanity of the very rich people to persuade them to sink their hands in their pockets and thus serve a cause which is greater and nobler than any other one ... A single and uninhibited mind must take charge of such a world-embracing situation. I hasten to add that I am not such a person. However, I have some ideas as to how to collect substantial donations but nobody of sufficient importance to speak to.

Would Sir Julian put him in touch with such a person, "with whom ideas can be developed and speedily directed towards accumulating millions of pounds without mobilising commissions, committees etc., as there is no time for Victorian procedures."

Julian Huxley consulted Max Nicholson who welcomed the idea and discussed it with Peter and with Guy Mountfort, a businessman who was also an ornithologist of international repute. Soon Mr. Stolan's suggestion was crystallizing into a plan, with Max Nicholson the catalyst. Nicholson wanted to form an "Ark club" to be joined by six hundred "leaders of opinion" worldwide, each contributing £1,000. He also outlined a structure on which the future organization would be based, that of an international core located at the IUCN's headquarters in Morges in Switzerland, with separate national appeals launched in each participating country: an ambitious structure for an ambitious scheme.

Peter, Nicholson, and Mountfort flew to Switzerland late in April 1961 to present these ideas to the IUCN's executive board, of which Peter was a member, as well as having been a vice president of this Union since 1953. The board endorsed them eagerly—not surprisingly, as they did not know where the money was to come from to pay the next month's wages. They issued a resounding call to action signed by sixteen prominent scientists from twelve countries which became known as the Morges Manifesto. "Skilful and devoted men, and admirable organisations, are struggling to save the world's wildlife. They have the ability and the will to do it, but they tragically lack the support and resources ... They need above all money to carry out mercy missions and to meet conservation emergencies by acquiring land where wildlife treasures are threatened, and in many other ways." Peter was among the signatories. This manifesto attracted plenty of publicity, but no money. At an informal meeting in May 1961 Mountfort, Nicholson, Huxley, Peter, and one or two others, including Aubrey Buxton and Lord Hurcomb of the Fauna Preservation Society, agreed on a name, World Wildlife Fund, and also a logo, the giant panda designed by Peter from a sketch by Gerald Watterson, a former secretary-general of the IUCN. The panda was chosen partly for its cuddly appeal, and partly because, being black and white, it would reproduce in print easily and cheaply.

The committee endorsed three aims summarized by Guy Mountfort:

> One was [put forward by] Peter Scott, who said quite casually "We must raise at least £5 millions a year." We had not yet raised a penny, but nobody thought him outrageously ambitious because we shared a common faith that WWF would succeed. The second was by Max Nicholson: "We must be strictly non-political and truly international: the West, the East and the Third World, a kind of United Nations for conservation." The third was anonymous: "Our work must be scientifically valid and free from sentimentality or bias."

A small sub-committee was formed, consisting of Nicholson, Mountfort, Peter, and a vigorous, red-bearded Scot recruited from industry, Ian MacPhail. Mr. Stolan's hope of raising money without committees and "Victorian procedures" had proved to be vain.

A name, an aim, a logo: the next need was a president, someone famous, prestigious, and more than a figurehead. There was only one answer to that. Peter left a short dossier about the proposal at Buckingham Palace with a request: would the Prince become the first president? It so happened that the council of the International Yacht Racing Union was to meet at the Palace with the Prince in the chair. At the meeting Prince Philip handed back the papers to Peter saying "I'll do it," but what he agreed to do was to be president of the British national appeal, not of the international one. That evening he telephoned to Peter. "Prince Bernhard [of the Netherlands] came to tea, he's interested, if you go to Claridge's you may catch him before he goes out to dinner." Peter got to Claridge's just as Prince Bernhard was getting into a taxi, and got in too. Prince Bernhard accepted the international presidency in the taxi. "Two Princes in one day!" Peter exulted. It proved to be a fortunate double.

Two Princes, but still no money. An anonymous interest-free loan of £3,000 opened the bank account. Half of this came from Nicholson and half from Peter. Then a businessman, Mr. Jack Cotton, made an outright gift of £10,000. WWF was in business. Even before the bank account had opened, an urgent plea had come in to buy land in order to protect the great nature reserve in Spain, the Coto Donana. Ian MacPhail was engaged as international campaign manager, and on October 10, 1961 WWF was registered as a charity in Zurich. Peter and Dr. Luc Hoffmann of France were appointed vice presidents. Guy Mountfort took on the job of honorary treasurer, and a young Swiss businessman who had worked for the Red Cross during the Hungarian rebellion, Dr. Fritz Vollmar, became the first secretary-general. He set up his office in the Chateau des Uttins, a private house converted into offices in Morges, on the shores of Lac Leman. On November 23, 1961 the British national appeal was launched, with Peter as its chairman.

In August 1961 the focus of attention shifted, temporarily, to Africa. The IUCN had organized a conference at Arusha in Tanganyika (later Tanzania), which gave birth to another manifesto, signed by forty-three "leaders in the field of conservation" from eighteen countries, echoing the note of urgency sounded by the manifesto of Morges:

> We ... feel it is our duty formally to declare to all whom it may concern that unless conservation measures are taken *immediately* a State of Emergency will arise from the wildlife of the world. We urgently request the utmost support for a special campaign which will shortly be launched to bring into operation effective rescue measures before it is too late.

The special campaign was, of course, that to be launched by WWF, whose formation was announced at the conference to loud applause. The manifesto was backed by a declaration considered by some to be even more significant, since it was issued in the name of the president-to-be of Tanganyika, Dr. Julius Nyerere, who pinned his colors, and those of "all of us in Africa," to the mast of conservation of Africa's wildlife, "a source of wonder and inspiration" and also a valuable natural resource. In the sparkling highland air of Arusha euphoria blossomed. "I believe it [the conference] will be a turning point for Africa's threatened wildlife and perhaps even a turning point in Africa's whole future," Peter prophesied in a broadcast, and Julian Huxley affirmed that it was "one of the most successful conferences I have ever attended." Back in London, euphoria had to contend with reality; WWF's temporary nook in the garret of the Nature Conservancy's Council's offices leaked so badly that three buckets were needed to catch the water when it rained.

From Arusha Peter went on, as one of the group of seven, to the Ngorongoro crater to suggest a management policy which would halt severe erosion on the crater's rim caused by Masai tribesmen cutting down the forest to make way for their proliferating herds of small humped cattle. In a later speech, he claimed that this had been the occasion when "the penny dropped for me." On the floor of this crater he saw those great concentrations of wild animals that have enthralled all who have observed them, and he also saw the ugly reality of advancing threats to their survival—soil erosion, burnt and cut-down trees, dried up rivers, scorched pastures, a land where vultures thrived. There were only four rhinos left, and one of these was speared by poachers on the day of his visit. "Here the world is young and fragile" ran an inscription on a board beside one of the entrances to the Serengeti National Park. It was the land's fragility that made the penny drop.

From Tanzania Peter flew direct to Ecuador to see its president about the rescue of wildlife in the Galapagos Islands, but was back in time to speak at a dinner on September 26, 1961 at the Royal Society of Arts when the birth of WWF was publicly announced, and an ambitious eight-point World Wildlife charter read and adopted.

In October, Ian MacPhail brought off a coup. He persuaded Hugh Cudlipp, editor of the *Daily Mirror* and an old friend, to bring out a "shock issue" in which seven pages were devoted wholly to the threat to wildlife. Across the front page was spread a picture of a rhino and her calf, "DOOMED," the page shouted, "to disappear from the face of the earth due to man's FOLLY NEGLECT AND GREED UNLESS"—unless readers supported WWF; and there was the panda logo in the bottom right-hand corner. Few charities can have had such a powerful sendoff.

For the next two days [wrote MacPhail] we awaited the results
with bated breath but nothing happened! Hugh Cudlipp and I
could hardly believe that the pulling power of one of the world's
most powerful and popular newspapers had failed. But next day
ten mailbags arrived at our temporary office, twelve bags the
next day, then twenty and so on and so forth ... The mailbags
accumulated and I had to take them home for security reasons
and relays of friendly neighbours sat up until all hours of the
morning to help. Eventually the *Daily Mirror* raised £50,000 and
the new Ark was well and truly launched and on its way.

The Ark was afloat on British waters; the next stage was to launch it on
international ones. The United States appeal was registered in December 1961,
though not launched until the following June at a glittering banquet at which
both Peter's Princes spoke, as well as Peter himself. General Eisenhower had
agreed to be its prestigious president and Dr. Ira Gabrielson its effective one,
with Harold Coolidge as an influential director. The Swiss appeal was registered a week after the American one, followed by national appeals in Holland,
West Germany, and Austria. In Britain, enthusiasts like Nicholson, Mountfort,
Peter, and Huxley had succeeded in turning the campaign into a crusade, but in
the rest of Europe animals, whether wild or tame, were less highly regarded, so
it proved a good deal more difficult to untie the people's moneybags.

The untying process continued unabated in Britain. In November 1962
another banquet was held, this time at the Mansion House in London, attended
by both Princes. Realizing that WWF might well be criticized for spending a
lot of money on champagne and expensive food to please the palates of already
well-fed, often overfed, guests, instead of on beleaguered animals, the organiz-
ers found a sponsor willing to pay for the dinner, provided he remained anonymous. "If you can get a prestigious venue and Prince Philip and Prince Bernhard
and the leading businessmen of Europe and possibly America I will pay for the
banquet," he said, "but I don't want anyone to know I'm doing it especially my
wife." He was the Marquis of Willingdon, president of the Fauna Preservation
Society. The inventive brain of Ian MacPhail, who appeared at such functions
in the kilt, spawned a bright idea: he persuaded the managing director of Josiah
Wedgwood and Sons to make a set of plates decorated with paintings of six
African wild animals and stamped with the date, which made them into collectors' items. It was hoped that rich businessmen, touched by this gesture, would
respond in an appropriate way. "We aren't allowed to pass round the plate in the
Mansion House," it was announced at the end of the banquet, "so we're going to
give you the plates from which you ate your dinner here tonight. They'll be
waiting for you downstairs, each in a plastic bag." Mr. J. Paul Getty, "like an
albino bloodhound," said MacPhail, "walked across the room on the arm of his

lawyer/girlfriend and in his grating voice said to me: 'Congratulations young man on a splendid occasion—any chance of another plate?'" MacPhail had to surrender his own. However, Mr. Getty made amends some years later when he gave a $50,000 conservation prize, equivalent to $25,000 a plate. Mr. Getty was then in the hospital, and Peter went to offer thanks for the gesture, and to attempt to arouse the billionaire's interest in a scheme to set up a conservation foundation that would make awards on the lines of Nobel prizes. Mr. Getty listened in silence until, at the end of the interview and after a pause, he observed: "Romans competed for laurel leaves."

Relations between the IUCN and WWF were both symbiotic and complex. The IUCN, advised by scientists from all over the world, was supposed to pass on to WWF news of endangered species and places: which ones were threatened, how severely, and what might be done about it. WWF would then allocate funds. By the same token, WWF was supposed to submit to the IUCN the applications it received, and ask for expert advice. This arrangement was complicated by a decision to divide the money raised by each national appeal into three parts, one to be spent in the country that had raised it, one to be handed over to the international fund, and one to be spent on whatever project seemed most urgent, wherever it might be. Obviously this was a situation fraught with possibilities for misunderstandings, for personality clashes, and for simply ignoring decisions, and all these occurred. It fell to Peter, as vice president of the IUCN and chairman of WWF, to smooth down ruffled feathers.

Besides being a vice president of the IUCN's executive board, in 1963 he became chairman of one of the six commissions into which its activities were channelled. This was the Survival Service Commission (later the Species Survival Commission) which, as its name implies, dealt with all endangered species everywhere, whether plant or animal; with the measures that might be taken to prevent their extinction; and with the degeneration of their habitat—an enormous task, which was to grow more formidable as the threats to survival multiplied. Peter was to remain chairman of this commission for seventeen onerous years. This complicated setup looked neat on paper but suffered from a crippling disability, a lack of funds. The IUCN and its commissions could advise, but not perform. It was like a head without a body; to supply that body was the original purpose of WWF.

The new chairman of the Survival Service Commission soon brought in major reforms. There were to be regular meetings three or four times a year, and the commission was to be advised by a number of specialist groups, each concerned with a single species or with a group of allied ones. Flights of letters went out from Morges inviting scientists prominent in every field to form such groups and recruit members. The groups were to deal with everything from apes to turtles, whales to parrots, marsupials to lemurs, polar bears to spotted cats. Their tasks were to assess the status of all the animals within that group's remit and grade them into five categories: very rare and getting rarer; less rare but threatened; stable; unknown; and a small but hopeful category, "formerly rare, now no longer in danger." The hope was to transfer more and more species from the top of the scale down the ladder to the bottom, but it was a consummation only very seldom brought about.

Peter's major achievement while working for the IUCN was the creation of the Red Data books. Members of all his specialist groups were invited to send to Morges particulars about each species in their stable: its numbers, if known; degree of endangerment; state of the habitat; measures being taken to protect it; and so on. These particulars were summarized on one or two sheets of loose-leaf paper to be slotted into the appropriate Red Data book. Initially there was one book for mammals and one for birds, the latter compiled by the International Council for Bird Preservation; reptiles and amphibians, fishes, insects, and plants were to follow later. Thanks to their loose-leaf format, the information could be continually updated. These books were to become, and to remain, indispensable tools for everyone involved in conservation. Peter devised the format, and to compile them he had two aides: Jack Vincent, formerly director of Natal's national parks, and Noel Simon who compiled the book on mammals.

The IUCN staff at Morges suffered from chronic fund starvation, and one of Peter's self-imposed tasks was to stiffen their morale. "Do I detect a hint of defeatism?" he wrote on one of Vincent's minutes. "Keep your pecker up! We shan't save all but we'll save a jolly lot more than if we'd never existed. And the Fred Karno outfit at Morges will have played an *amazingly* big part in it." Soon afterward, Vincent resigned to return to a life of active conservation in Natal. "It is a bitter thing to know," Peter wrote to him, "that this is my own fault, that the failure of WWF to come up to expectations has been my failure." Yet no one could have tried harder or more persistently to feed the insatiate cormorant of demands. "On our little shoestring," he wrote of his commission,

> we have created an organisation with a quite surprising international power and influence ... One day perhaps we shall wake up to find that our ship has come home, and that at last we can hire the help we need at the various levels at which we so badly need it. Anyway I shall go on trying to raise enough funds to see that the remarkable array of specialist experts we've gradually drawn together are reasonably well served in follow-up and action.

All these experts gave their services free and had to pay their own expenses. It was in the follow-up, doing in the field what they recommended on paper, that the shoe of poverty really pinched. There were even discussions as to whether the commission could afford to send out its agendas by air mail; its minutes went by sea. Peter never allowed his doubts and frustrations to surface in public but in private, especially toward the end of his life, they did find expression. "I'm not at all sure that the international conservation movement has got it right even now," he wrote a few days before his death in 1989. "We're swimming a bit faster against the stream than we used to, but we'll probably go down the plug-hole just the same. The Green movement is about fifty years too late, but we have to keep swimming!" Those last five words summed up his last message to the world.

If, as he said, Peter disliked making speeches, after the launching of WWF he was a real martyr to the cause. In speech after speech he strove to strike sparks of enthusiasm in the public mind, often resting his case on what he called the "four pillars" of conservation. The first pillar was ethical. Man has no justification for wiping out other species which share the planet with him; they have a right to live just as he has. The second pillar was aesthetic: the works of nature are no less noble than the works of man; if it is wrong to destroy great paintings, great buildings, and other works of art, it is no less wrong to destroy nature's equally beautiful creations which, once gone, are gone forever. This pillar had a buttress; with increasing leisure, people increasingly seek refreshment in nature's wilder places and among her wild creatures; to destroy them is to impoverish humanity by denying it the spiritual renewal that it needs. The third was the scientific pillar: many of the plants and animals that inhabit the forests, lakes, and rivers of the planet are still unknown to science; some might—almost certainly would—have vital uses for mankind; to exterminate a plant or animal before it even has a scientific name is an act of vandalism. Finally there was the economic pillar: people of richer countries flock to see the wildlife of poorer ones and so create tourist industries which keep many of the latter afloat.

In presenting these arguments, Peter was hoping to counter the "man versus animals" attitude ingrained in many minds. He was appealing for money; better, many people thought, to give it to a cause aimed at the relief of human suffering, than to keep in existence a kind of turtle on a distant beach, or an antelope scarcely anyone would ever see in the deserts of Arabia. Peter's aim was to convince people that man and animals are on the same side.

As time went on, the argument widened out. Well before such matters as global warming, ozone holes, acid rain, pollution, and chlorofluorocarbons made the headlines, Peter had become convinced that habitat destruction threatened not only its plants and wild animals but man himself. He was not, of course, the only one to see this gathering cloud and to utter dire warnings, but with his skill in communication and his public stance he could put across with special authority the unpalatable idea that mankind, overreacting to the divine command to increase and multiply, was digging its own grave by destroying the resources by which men lived.

Apart from making speeches, he wrote personally to a number of millionaires, heads of companies and foundations, politicians, and others thought to have some influence on events. One such was the medical missionary, theologian, and philosopher Albert Schweitzer, once described as "the noblest figure of the twentieth century." At Lambarene in Gabon, then part of French Equatorial Africa, he had established a hospital, and practiced the philosophy of "reverence for life" in all its forms, a principle at times at variance with the normal hospital practice of destroying certain forms of life, such as rats, lice, bacteria, and malaria-carrying mosquitoes. Peter appealed not for money but for Dr. Schweitzer's blessing. In February 1962 he wrote:

> Recently I have begun to understand that man's own future is bound up with his right assessment of the use of land. His survival must depend not only on his capacity to avoid blowing himself up, but also on his capacity to stop making deserts and dust-bowls, to preserve and replant forests, to husband the earth's renewable resources, to consider carefully the relationship between water, soil, plants, animals and men. So at one end of the scale our campaign is nothing less than the ecology of man. At the other it is the preservation from extinction of certain animal species which have taken hundreds of thousands of years to evolve their unique adaptations to their environment and which, if nothing is done, will be wiped out in a few decades. Conservation in nearly all parts of the world is hampered for the want of comparatively small sums of money. We are aiming to raise annually for conservation in all the countries of the world £500,000 which is the cost of one present-day jet fighter aircraft. If we cannot raise this money species extinction—an irreversible process—will continue at its present headlong rate. Nearly a hundred kinds of bird alone have become extinct in the last hundred years ... I know from what I have read, and from a delightful series of drawings of animals made at Lambarene a few years ago, that wild creatures have a place in your philosophy. If you think we are aiming in the right direction, and that what we are trying to do is a worthwhile enterprise, will you consider sending us a message? Your opinion, stemming from your wisdom and your great humanity, could immeasurably help our cause.

He received no reply. The letter was posted in Tanganyika, and perhaps never arrived.

If the wings of the conservation movement were so often clipped for lack of money, there were solid achievements on the credit side to sustain morale and generate hope. One such was the rescue of the Coto Doñana in Spain. This was an area of marsh, scrub, and woodland, with sand dunes 30 or 40 miles long, adjacent to the estuary of the river Guadalquivir and lying mainly between Seville and the sea. For nearly four centuries it had been preserved in its wild state as a hunting reserve for the dukes of Medina Sidonia. It was considered to be the most important wildlife sanctuary in Europe, offering shelter to about half the species of European birds and to such rarities as flamingos, purple gallinules, and four species of eagle. This wildlife oasis had been sold to a consortium of Spanish capitalists looking for profit. Moreover, much of the marismas, the marshes bordering the reserve, had been drained and planted to rice and other crops; roads had been constructed, pollution of the Guadalquivir contaminated the water supplies of the former hunting reserve, and the coast with its sand dunes was threatened by plans to build holiday homes, hotels, and everything that goes with modern tourism.

No sooner was WWF established than an application came in for money to buy about 16,000 acres of marismas called Las Nuevas, an area that received great flocks of migrating wildfowl in winter. Guy Mountfort had led three expeditions to the Coto Doñana in the 1950s to assess its importance as a wildlife refuge, so WWF was fully apprised of the threats to its survival; but the asking price for Las Nuevas was beyond its means. A series of prolonged and complicated negotiations followed between the Spanish government, the owners, and Mountfort and Luc Hoffmann for WWF. Eventually the Spanish government agreed to put up one third of the money. That still left two thirds. The credibility of WWF was at stake; if it failed in its first major enterprise, it would fail to win worldwide support. Prince Bernhard's help was enlisted; he had a word with General Franco, the Spanish government increased its grant, the rest of the money was found through donations and loans, and the Coto Doñana was saved—for the time being; since 1963, when an agency of the Spanish government took over control of the reserve, which became a national park in 1968, new threats have arisen and old ones re-emerged. The hosts of Midian still prowl and prowl around.

Nevertheless it was a success story, and so was that of Operation Oryx to which WWF gave financial support. For many centuries the Arabian oryx— a handsome cream-colored antelope with long, slender horns which probably gave rise to the legend of the unicorn—coexisted with the nomadic Bedouin, matching its wariness, keen eyesight, and swift-footedness against the camel-mounted tribesmen's craftiness and antiquated and unreliable guns. Then came jeeps, automatic rifles, and the wealth of oil. The sheikhs and their henchmen hunted the oryx to the brink of extinction, and what they left, the poachers took. By 1960 there were reckoned to be about one hundred oryx left, scattered throughout most of Arabia.

Then, in 1961, came news of a massacre of forty-eight oryx, about half the surviving population. The Fauna (now Fauna and Flora) Preservation Society, on whose council Peter sat, launched Operation Oryx to save what they could of the remaining animals. The only way to do this, experts reckoned, was by captive breeding, with a view to the ultimate re-introduction of the oryx into the deserts of Arabia if and when these could be made secure. First a few must be caught. Kenya's chief game warden, Ian Grimwood, set out to look for them in about 10,000 square kilometers of rock, wadi, and dune. His aircraft proved useless and his vehicles broke down; nevertheless one female and two males were caught. After an interlude in northern Kenya, they ended their journey at the Arizona Zoological Society's zoo at Phoenix, Arizona, where they were joined by another female, Caroline, from the London zoo. A year later, mated to Tomatum, one of the wild Arabian males, she gave birth to a calf, unfortunately a male. The "world herd" was in existence, to be increased by presents from the rulers of Kuwait and Saudi Arabia, who had their own private zoos. With the discovery in 1972 of the remains of three dead animals and evidence that others had been shot or captured, the Arabian oryx was believed to have become extinct in the wild.

But its numbers were building up in the Arizona and, later, in the San Diego and Los Angeles zoos. Sixteen years after the founders of the world herd had arrived in Arizona, the first four captive-bred animals were returned to Arabia—not to the wild, but to pens built for them in the Shaumari Wildlife Reserve in Jordan. The true wild was still a danger zone; only if the ruler of one of the Arabian nations took the oryx under his personal protection would the animals be reasonably safe. The Sultan of Oman stepped in. In 1981, after a year's acclimatization in pens, ten captive-bred oryx, including four with radio-collars, were released, a large enough number to establish a herd.

How wild was the wild? Geographically, truly wild; and fears that animals bred in zoos might have lost their ability to live for months without drinking proved unfounded. Politically, it was not wild at all. Members of a small nomadic tribe called the Harasis were detailed by the Sultan to act as guardians of the oryx, so as to protect them against poachers. The Harasis have protected them well. Calves have been born and more animals released; all has gone according to plan, and should continue to do so—so long as the Sultan's protection endures.

Success has not attended all attempts to remove a species from the IUCN's "severely endangered" category to the happier one of "formerly rare, now no longer in danger." The rhino is a case in point. There are five species, three found in Asia and two in Africa, the white or square-lipped and the black. These had lived in profusion in most of sub-Saharan Africa since the Pleistocene Age until the advent of automatic weapons, four-wheel drive vehicles and organized poaching reduced both species to a few pockets of creatures under continuous threat. A chain of demand led from the poacher with his gun or poisoned arrows to a network of dealers throughout China and Southeast Asia who sold the powdered horn to practitioners of traditional Chinese medicine, and to the *jeunesse doree* of Yemen who wore dagger handles carved from the horn in their belts. As rhinos grew rarer, their horns grew more expensive, and trade in them very lucrative indeed, tempting those in high places to join in the bonanza. So anti-poaching measures became impossible to enforce.

In 1980 WWF mounted an international "Save the Rhino" campaign aimed at all five species, and directed mainly at persuading governments to outlaw the trade in horn. Through the IUCN and other bodies, pressure was brought to bear on them to sign the Convention on the International Trade in Endangered Species—CITES—if they had not already done so, and to make serious attempts to enforce its rules, which aimed at altogether banning trade in severely threatened species, if they had. Meanwhile an intrepid WWF emissary based in Nairobi, Dr. Esmond Bradley Martin, traveled about the countries of Southeast Asia and those bordering the Red Sea and the Persian Gulf, trying to convince politicians, traders, carvers, Chinese doctors, and everyone concerned that if rhinos were wiped out there would be no more rhino horn, and that they had better look elsewhere for their fever-curing potions and elaborate dagger handles; the saiga, a fairly common Russian antelope, and the wild water buffalo were suggested alternatives for the latter. At first this campaign scotched the snake, but never killed it; poaching and smuggling still goes on, and genuinely wild rhinos, apart from those under close protection in reserves and parks, are almost extinct.

Finally, the tiger. In 1969 Guy Mountfort presented a report on the status of these animals to a joint meeting of WWF and the IUCN's executive board. It was gloomy. There had been eight races of tiger; two of these were already extinct and a third, the Javan, reduced to five survivors. The only race still numerous enough to make the effort of saving it worthwhile was the Indian, and that had been reduced to between two and three thousand animals. Mountfort failed to convince the joint board that they should take immediate steps to try to save the Indian tiger. They could not launch any project without the goodwill and cooperation of the government concerned, and the Indian government's attitude was uncertain. Many Indians believed that their country would be better off without any tigers, which took the peasants' cattle and sometimes the peasants themselves.

So Guy Mountfort went back to India, Bangladesh, and Nepal. He called first on India's prime minister, and Mrs. Indira Gandhi set up a Tiger Task Force next day. The prime minister of Bangladesh was equally helpful. The plan was to set up a number of tiger reserves from which cattle would be excluded, and such villages as lay within them moved elsewhere. A census carried out in 1970 showed that Mountfort had underestimated the tiger's decline; only 1,827 were left. In 1930 the estimated number had been thirty thousand, so there was no time to lose. Mountfort committed WWF to raising a million dollars, and the Indian government eventually contributed more than four times that sum. Nine tiger reserves were set aside, later increased to sixteen.

So, in 1972, WWF launched Operation Tiger, and raised $1,750,000 within eighteen months. By 1980, the number of tigers within the reserves had doubled, and continued to rise. Other forest animals such as swamp deer and water buffaloes also increased in numbers, and vegetation recovered from its former overgrazing by cattle. This encouraged streams and rivers to flow all the year round as they had in Mowgli's day, instead of only seasonally. On the debit side must be put the fact that in certain areas, especially in and around one particular reserve, tigers have eaten people, mainly trespassers in search of firewood, honey, or meat. This has naturally led to criticism of the preserve-the-tiger policy, but has been partially overcome by an ingenious device. It has been said that a tiger will not attack a man who looks him squarely in the eye, and this seems to be the case. When wardens and others working in the reserve fix a mask to their backs, tigers approaching from behind, confronted by a human-looking glare, desist from their attacks. So the survival of the Indian tiger looked secure but, as in all such projects, the threats were contained for the time being rather than eliminated. The tiger's future still hangs in the balance, and the story's end is yet to come.

These few random examples of how WWF has gone about its business can only skim the surface; before the end of Peter's life a legion of projects, great and small, had been tackled in 130 countries; over 177 million Swiss francs had been raised and spent internationally, in addition to money raised by twenty-eight national appeals. Such great undertakings as ensuring the survival of major nature reserves and of species like tigers and pandas are the flagships, and a host of lesser craft have followed in their wake. Captive breeding of the Madagascan ploughshare tortoise; campaigns to save the Brazilian manatee and the few surviving fur seals sheltering in undersea caves on Robinson Crusoe's island off Chile; surveys of fruit bats in Borneo which pollinate many useful plants; attempts to save fir forests in Mexico in which monarch butterflies over-winter after flying 5,000 kilometers from Canada; training Peruvian staff to manage Lake Titicaca as a nature reserve—the list seems endless, and cries for help escalate year by year as pressure on the environment grows. The emphasis is increasingly being laid on convincing the local people and their governments that their native plants and animals are worth saving: in this lies the only long-term hope.

CHAPTER NINETEEN

Nessie and Antarctica

When Peter flew to Ecuador from Arusha in 1961 to interview the president about Galapagos tortoises, he carried with him the greetings of the University of Aberdeen to the University of Quito. In November 1960 the Aberdonian students had chosen him as Rector, an office whose origins go back to the Middle Ages and to the constitution of the University of Paris. In the United Kingdom only Scottish universities have Rectors. Four candidates besides Peter contested for the office: Cliff Michelmore, the broadcaster; Sir Colin Anderson, a shipping magnate; Sir Donald Campbell, an engineering tycoon; and Hugh McDiarmid (whose real name was Christopher Murray Grieve), the Scottish nationalist and much revered poet, said by the University's newspaper to "rank with Burns as one of Scotland's greatest literary figures," and the obvious favorite. The election was conducted with the aid of such weapons as fish heads and guts, bags of soot, overripe fruit, and almost anything non-lethally throwable, and it came as a surprise to everyone when Peter won by forty-nine votes, materially assisted by members of the University's rugby football team. The Rector was the students' choice, not that of the academic governing bodies, and was supposed to represent their interests in an unspecified way. He had the right to chair the meetings of the University Court, the supreme governing body, and Peter was to do so on two occasions.

The installation ceremony called for an inaugural address, and the Rector took a lot of trouble to strike the right note. He kept a book of "funnies," and noted which joke he had used on which occasion so as to minimize the risk of telling the same joke or story twice to the same audience. Read in cold blood, it must be admitted that some of the jokes lack effervescence, but, as every actor knows, it is the timing that matters. Peter timed his jokes professionally and nearly always got his laugh. In his legible and shapely handwriting he jotted down, in red and black ink and on separate cards, the headlines of his themes, and as often as not he introduced a self-deprecating note that pleased his audience.

He ended his rectorial address, which dealt with conservation issues, in a lighter vein by suggesting that the possible existence of a large, unidentified and maybe prehistoric animal, or group of animals, in the depths of Loch Ness, should be taken seriously enough to justify a proper scientific study. It was on a tramcar in Warsaw that his interest in the Loch Ness Monster had first been aroused. He was in Poland for a meeting of the General Assembly of the IUCN in June 1960, and traveling back to his hotel with Richard Fitter, at that time the *Observer's* scientific correspondent. Richard Fitter had been reading a book which had revived public interest in the Nessie question: *More than a Legend*, written by a surgeon, Mrs. Constance Whyte, whose husband was manager of the Caledonian Canal and whose credentials were impeccable. Mrs. Whyte, who had never herself seen the elusive creature, had collected firsthand reportings from 117 sightings of the so-called Monster, made by people with no axe to grind, whose bona fides she had investigated, and who, far from seeking publicity, had often been reluctant to talk about their sightings for fear of ridicule. "There is a Monster in Loch Ness," she concluded, and it should be scientifically investigated.

There was nothing new about the Monster. The first recorded sighting of *an Niseag* (whence the loch, and therefore Nessie, had derived their names) was made in the sixth century by Saint Columba, who also saw a *a'Mhorag* in Loch Morar and a *t'Seileag* in Loch Shiel, and called them water-horses. Ever since, and doubtless before, the natives of those parts had taken for granted the existence of something unaccountable, and best to be avoided, in each of their lochs. Little attention had been paid to these shadowy tales until, in 1933, a narrow winding lane along the north shore of Loch Ness was widened and realigned to become the A82, bringing tourists in ever mounting numbers to within sight of the loch. It was not long before sightings of Nessie increased dramatically, in some cases backed up by photographs which, though their interpretations might be disputed, could not be dismissed as hoaxes. The story offered, of course, heaven-sent—or rather media-sent—opportunities for hoaxers to move in. Many did so, obscuring the hard core of serious sightings in a fuzz of rumor, invention, and fantasy, and turning the whole subject into a music-hall joke.

It was this jocular approach to a scientific puzzle that prompted those who took seriously the possibility of the survival of a prehistoric animal in the very deep and not yet fully probed waters of the loch to call for a scientific investigation. It was, after all, only in recent times that the coelacanth, believed by scientists to have been extinct for seventy million years, had reappeared, in the Indian Ocean in 1938, on the end of a fisherman's line. Other animals believed to be extinct, such as the giant panda rediscovered in 1869, or the okapi in 1901, had been quietly existing in inaccessible spots. Why not Nessie? Believers questioned whether all the sightings, adding up to something like three thousand over the years, had been hoaxes or illusions or mistakes. Descriptions of the creature broadly agreed with each other. N, and two protuberances on the forehead. It was ugly, silent, had a good turn of speed, and had been seen chasing salmon on which it might be presumed to live. There must be several of them, or the creatures could not have survived. It might be amphibious; there were several sightings of the creature on land, in one case crossing the road to devour a sheep, but these sightings were taken with several grains of salt.

Influenced by Mrs. Whyte's book, by several other authorities and a number of photographs, Peter became convinced that, true or false, the phenomenon should be thoroughly looked into. At this stage he had an open mind. While the scientific establishment metaphorically withdrew the hem of its garment from a subject tainted with ridicule, a number of people of good faith began to investigate the matter for themselves. In 1934 a London surgeon, Lieutenant-Colonel R. K. Wilson, had secured a picture which appeared to show a head and long neck emerging from the waters; and in 1960 Mr. Tim Dinsdale, an aeronautical engineer who subsequently devoted his life to the search, caught on film a dark humped object, corresponding to descriptions of the Monster, submerging into the loch. An active Conservative Member of Parliament, David James, took up the cause of Nessie; Richard Fitter and Peter became involved; together with others, they agreed to assemble a small panel of biologists to review the evidence, and to decide whether it justified further study.

The guardian of the tabernacle of such sciences, the British Museum (Natural History), had taken a firm line about Nessie from the start. The Loch Ness Monster did not exist, and reports that it did were either hoaxes or hallucinations. They even went to the length of dismissing one of their staff, a Canadian ichthyologist and world authority on eels called Dr. Denys Tucker, who had rashly asserted that the presence of an unknown animal in the loch, although unlikely, was not impossible, and who had encouraged a team of volunteers from Oxford and Cambridge Universities to search for evidence at first hand.

Eventually the panel of biologists was recruited and assembled at Burlington House, with Peter in the chair. The professors of zoology at Oxford and Cambridge Universities were members, as was the Curator of Mammals and Fishes at the London Zoo, together with Dr. Desmond Morris, Dr. Geoffrey Matthews, and others. The meeting was held in secret. To join the panel took some courage, in view of the hostility of the British Museum (Natural History) and of other superior scientists, with caricaturists ever ready to pounce. The panel concluded that there was a *prima facie* case for investigating the presence of something in the loch that could be explained as a large unknown animal. But the panel had no funds.

Partly to meet this situation, in December 1961 Peter, David James, Richard Fitter, and Constance Whyte met at the House of Commons and agreed to set up the Loch Ness Investigation Bureau as a registered charity. "The heat of the day," Richard Fitter has written, "was borne throughout by David James. It was he who recruited Norman Collins, deputy chairman of the television company ATV and soon to become a director of the Bureau, who provided the essential initial finance—one could do a lot with £500 in those days." David James was no run-of-the-mill MP; in the Second World War he had twice escaped from a prisoner-of-war camp in Germany, the second time successfully in the guise of Lieutenant Ivan Buggeroff of the Bulgarian navy. For nearly twenty years he organized annual expeditions to the shores of Loch Ness with naval exactitude. Ten sites along the loch shore were manned day and night for a fortnight by volunteers equipped with searchlights, radar, and the last word in underwater cameras and sonar devices. A major obstacle was the peaty nature of the loch which makes its waters dark and murky, so that visibility drops almost to nil a few meters below the surface. Another obstacle was its size, nearly 22 miles long, about 2 miles wide, and in places over 750 feet deep. It was a needle-in-a-haystack situation and the Monster or Monsters remained unseen.

While organized teams failed to spot the Monster, sightings continued by unorganized, casual individuals. In October 1962 seven witnesses saw "a long, low, indeterminate shape giving chase to a shoal of salmon," and in 1963 there were over forty sightings, all examined by the Bureau and believed to be genuine. But sceptics were unconvinced. Dr. Maurice Burton, formerly of the zoology department of the British Museum (Natural History) opined that "a large sheet of hessian wallowing in the waves" could account for the "gigantic improbable animal." Peter replied: "I still find it difficult to account for the photographs in terms of inanimate objects ... But believe me, I do not underestimate the gigantic improbability of a gigantic undescribed animal." Later, Dr. Burton settled for a pair of playful otters. A floating tree trunk, a dead bullock and even a Viking ship were other suggestions.

In 1971 came an important new development: Dr. Robert Rines appeared on the scene. Dr. Rines, a patent lawyer with a degree in physics from the Massachusetts Institute of Technology, had founded the Academy of Applied Sciences in Boston, which set out to bridge the gap between technology on the one hand and academic institutions such as universities on the other. It also had the wide and worthy aim of "identifying people and teams making a significant contribution to human progress and national security." Whether or not a solution of the Loch Ness puzzle would make a significant contribution to human progress, Dr. Rines had become personally intrigued by the Nessie saga. He got in touch with the Bureau and brought to Scotland a small team equipped with technologically advanced equipment designed to detect underwater objects. For the next ten years his visits to Scotland became an annual routine.

Until then, photographs had been taken of the animal, or what was believed to be the animal, only when it had surfaced, presumably to breathe. Rines and his team hoped to record the creature underwater, using a technique involving sonar transducers and time-lapse cameras with strobe flash, 45 feet down, deployed in Urquhart Bay. Excitement was great when, in 1972, two frames out of two thousand taken one minute apart revealed a spearhead-shaped object construed to be a flipper, 6 to 8 feet long; and the sonar recorded two very large echoes just in front of the camera as the pictures were shot. Here was the "diamond shaped fin" that Peter was to portray in his imaginary portrait of a pair of Nessies which became widely known. The photographs were computer-enhanced by the Jet Propulsion laboratory at the California Institute of Technology at Pasadena, a process that makes the image clearer but cannot change its shape. The result, "though lacking in clarity, does suggest quite strongly the presence of two animals," Dr. Rines concluded.

Dr. Rines and his team had to wait three years before their underwater cameras secured two more pictures which suggested, though they did not prove, that a large aquatic animal did indeed exist. On the night of June 19–20, 1975 a single camera with a strobe flash was suspended about 40 feet beneath a moored boat, again in Urquhart Bay. At about four-thirty A.M. what appeared to be a large animal was recorded on film. One picture, which became known as the gargoyle shot, could be interpreted as that of a head with hornlike protrusions and possibly an open mouth. It was hideous. The other was a good deal clearer. It showed what could be construed to be a creature with a long neck attached to a slightly bulbous body, and two appendages which might be flippers.

Announcement of these findings naturally created a sensation in zoological circles, and an element of farce, which never entirely deserted the Nessie story, now entered in. Peter flew to Boston early in October 1975 to see the photographs, which so convinced him that he publicly committed himself, for the first time, to the statement that "there are indeed large animals in Loch Ness. My own guess is that they might look rather like plesiosaurs. I felt that there was ample new evidence to justify a scientific meeting to discuss it." Dr. Rines agreed to keep the photographs under wraps until a suitably august gathering of scientists had been convened to consider the photographs and all the other evidence.

The Royal Society of Edinburgh agreed to arrange a symposium, in which the Universities of Edinburgh and of Heriot Watt would also participate. Meanwhile Peter took the photographs to the British Museum (Natural History), whose zoologists remained suspicious and aloof. They agreed, however, to consider the new evidence, and to keep the photographs embargoed until the meeting in Edinburgh on December 9 and 10, 1975.

Things went wrong. A young journalist called Nicholas Witchell had written a book, *The Loch Ness Story*, whose paperback edition was in the press and being printed in Reading. He had described the photographs in a supplementary chapter, but the paperback was not due to appear until after the Edinburgh meeting. In mid-November a bet was placed with Ladbroke's in the Reading area that Nessie would be authenticated within the coming year, at odds of a hundred to one. Betting quickly spread, and the odds shortened to six to one. The press sniffed out the story, rumors gathered force, and the *Glasgow Record* got hold of a confidential draft of the agenda of the Edinburgh symposium and published the story, including the existence of the photographs. In Peter's words:

> The British Museum (Natural History) chaps read in the press that they were "impressed with the photographs" when they were not, and issued a statement (in breach of confidentiality) that they "proved nothing," before they had heard the supporting evidence. The magazine which had made an offer for the pictures (money to be spent on further research in the loch) withdrew. The Royal Society of Edinburgh, together with the University of Edinburgh and Heriot Watt, took fright, panicked and, without consulting me, withdrew their sponsorship of the symposium. Thus the opportunity to show the original photographs and spend a day discussing them and other evidence was denied.

So the symposium was cancelled, but two other events, arranged to follow it, went ahead. One was the showing of the photographs at the House of Commons on the evening of December 10, 1975 to a large gathering of MPs and other interested parties, including those scientists prepared to attend. Dr. Rines had assembled a number of Americans of undisputed reputation and authority. Dr. Edgerton, who flew from Greece where he had been working in Jacques Cousteau's vessel *Calypso;* Dr. George Zug, Curator of Reptiles and Amphibians at the Smithsonian Institution in Washington; Professor Crompton of Harvard; and Dr. McGowan of the Royal Ontario Museum were among those who gathered in the Palace of Westminster to attend the meeting, presided over by Lord Craigton, chairman of the all-party committee on wildlife conservation. Dr. Rines and his associates outlined the story up to date and then the photographs were shown.

The audience, wrote Nicholas Witchell, was "for a moment stunned into complete silence ... After this momentary silence there were audible gasps and exclamations from the audience. An MP who was sitting next to me (who was, admittedly, slightly drunk) dropped his cigarette and left it to smoulder on the floor." Eminent scientists from the United States and Canada addressed the meeting in guarded tones, but left no doubt that Nessie could no longer be dismissed as a joke, an illusion, or even a floating log. There was sufficient weight of evidence, one of them concluded, "to support the proposition that there is an unexplained phenomenon of considerable interest in Loch Ness and that the evidence suggests the presence of large aquatic animals." The zoologists of the British Museum (Natural History) remained unmoved. "We have no reason to alter our main conclusion, namely that the photographs do not constitute acceptable evidence of the existence of a large living animal."

The other event timed to follow the cancelled symposium was publication in the scientific journal *Nature* of an article written jointly by Peter and Rines conferring on Nessie a scientific name, *Nessiteras rhombopteryx*, meaning "the monster of Ness with the diamond fin." This was a rash thing to do, and was to tarnish Peter's reputation in some scientific circles. To name a creature whose existence had never been proved was considered by many to be ill-advised; at the least, it was prejudging an issue still very much in doubt. Peter, however, had a valid reason. Without such an identification, the creature, if found, could enjoy no protection and be killed with impunity, whereas once scientifically recognized it would be protected by the newly enacted Conservation of Wild Creatures and Wild Plants Act. If Nessies existed, the population must be small, and the loss of even one individual might seriously affect it. There would be plenty of people after its blood. "As a biologist," one such had said, "I want a body, or bones." The naming was an open invitation to the jokers, never far away. The *Daily Telegraph* quickly found an anagram in *Nessiteras rhombopteryx*: "Monster hoax by Sir Peter S." (It was said, rightly or wrongly, that Sir John Sparrow, Warden of All Souls, had discovered the anagram.) Rines, not to be outdone, retorted with another: "Yes, both pix are monsters."

In an article in the magazine *Wildlife*, Peter made his own position clear in a typically balanced and moderate manner:

> It can never be proved that there are no large animals in Loch Ness except by draining the loch, and that will never be done. There is a threshold for each of us which makes us believe or not believe in Nessie. There should be no "fixed positions" on either side of the threshold. Whichever view we hold we should keep our minds open to new evidence and new aspects of existing evidence. Each one of us has a right to admit that he might be mistaken if anyone can show him convincingly where his reasoning went wrong. Meanwhile I still believe that the evidence

adds up to a population of large animals in Loch Ness. None of the events I have described has cast any doubt in my mind on the validity of that evidence.

On Christmas Eve 1975 he wrote to a friend: "My own view is that the 1975 pictures *could* conceivably be gnarled tree trunks floating round in mid-water, which the 1972 flippers could not. On the other hand some and perhaps all of the 1972 pix *could* be part of an animal ... So we are left with tree trunks or an animal. In my view the 1972 flippers can only be an animal."

December 1975 was a watershed in the Nessie story. Soon afterward the Loch Ness Investigation Bureau was wound up. Dr. Rines continued his researches with increasingly refined tools, which were to have included two camera-carrying dolphins, but one of them died before their training had been completed and the project was cancelled. Peter never lost interest in the Loch Ness puzzle, and never either retracted or reaffirmed his faith in the possibility of Nessie's existence. Several more attempts by Dr. Rines and his colleagues failed to find conclusive proof. In 1977 Peter and Philippa joined the American party at their headquarters on the loch; Peter donned his wetsuit and dived again into the murky waters; he and Dr. Rines presented the evidence for Nessie and chaired a discussion held at the Eden Court Theatre in Inverness in aid of World Wildlife Fund. Despite patient watchfulness and sophisticated equipment, nothing conclusive came to light during the next fifteen years, and attention shifted from a search for prehistoric animals to a scientific study of the whole loch's ecology in all its aspects: its structure, its geology, and all forms of its aquatic life. With scientific backs turned on Nessie, biologists from the British Museum (Natural History) withdrew their objections and took part. Much of interest will emerge, if Nessie does not; but, as Peter observed, only if the loch were to be drained could everyone be absolutely sure that Nessie is only a legend.

The pursuit of Nessie was only a sideline in Peter's work-crammed life during the 1960s and 1970s. A topic of greater consequence took up more of his attention and time.

During the first half of his adult life he had deliberately avoided the topic of the Antarctic. As part of his intention to walk free of the shadow of his father he did not talk, write or think about it, let alone make an effort to get there. When he was fifty-seven years old a proposal came to make a documentary film about the return of the son to the scene of his father's exploits and tragedy; he decided that his attitude had been a "rather pointless vanity" and fell in with the suggestion. The film was to be made by the BBC with Christopher Ralling as producer and Charles Lagus the cameraman.

In January 1966 the three men flew from Christchurch in New Zealand to the Ross Ice Shelf, and thence by helicopter to McMurdo City near Hut Point, where in 1902 the crew of *Discovery* had erected a wooden bungalow to be used mainly as a recreation center while they lived in the ship. Now McMurdo City, an unlovely frontier-type town which in summer held up to one thousand people, was an outpost of the United States. Peter was naturally prepared for great changes, but found the sprawl of McMurdo City depressing. The hymn-writer's lament, "Where every prospect pleases / And only man is vile," was never more applicable. Against the grandeur of unsullied mountains, the gemlike splendors of ice floes, the overwhelming sense of freedom and immensity and the cleanliness of the Antarctic's creatures, the strident angularity of man's buildings, his discarded rusting machinery, the sordid litter of his middens, was deeply offensive. It could have been then and there that the idea first came to him of preserving Antarctica's integrity by keeping the humans there on a much tighter rein.

After some initial filming, dogs, sleds, and a tent were assembled and they made a camp, as like as possible to Captain Scott's, 4 miles from the base, "all for show—as if we had been doing it for months in some long and rugged journey. It is bogus, and hard not to feel a charlatan." A few days later they flew to the Pole in a Hercules, which can make the journey in less than three hours; Captain Scott and his companions had trudged on foot, hauling their sleds, for forty-seven days. Ironically, Peter's principal discomfort was being much too hot; he had piled on clothing suitable for polar rigors and the temperature in the airplane was 27°C. They broke their journey at the Russian base at Vostock. The Cold War was then in an especially chilly phase and they wondered what reception they would get. It was tremendous: the Russians hugged and kissed them and each other like victorious footballers, and vodka flowed. Lagus wished to film the scene but, during the short walk from aircraft to hut in a temperature of −50°C, the camera had become a ball of ice.

> There was nothing for it [Lagus recalled] but to take the large risk of wrecking it for good, or fail to get this unique occasion, so I put it in the oven of the large old-fashioned iron range. Out came the food, in went the camera, spitting and hissing as the water ran off. Ten minutes later we were in business and running and the Russians needed little persuasion to start kissing and hugging and toasting us all over again. Enormous quantities of vodka and pirozhki were consumed and Peter was persuaded to give a brief impromptu speech on the importance of international cooperation in the Antarctic—it was a most moving occasion, full of optimism.

"What a way to arrive!" Peter exclaimed when they touched down at the Amundsen-Scott base at the South Pole. "Sweaty hot in an overheated aircraft." The base was equipped with all the comforts expected by Americans engaged on business of national importance; in their underground bunkers were kitchens and canteens, bars and flush lavatories, computers and telephones, a generator, a cinema, a post office. Next day they trundled in a Nodwell, successor to the motorized sleds that had failed Captain Scott, to the site of the Pole.

> We took stills [Peter wrote in his diary] and we shot film, I shook hands with Griffin [the base commander], I looked up at the American flag which now flies over the Pole, I stood in front of it, alone and in various groups—a photographic bonanza. I remembered that fifty-four years ago my father had also been involved in taking photographs at the Pole. It made the whole distasteful business a fraction more bearable ... Away to the horizon in every direction the snow is flat and unbroken but for the masts and buildings round the station. "Great God, this is an awful place," my father had said. And awful it must have been with a prospect of 800 miles to walk back—and Amundsen's tent already there. For us with 400 yards to walk back to a snug overheated camp under the snow it was not awful. Yet it had a certain wonder born of its immense isolation.

Three Hercules came in on skis while they were filming; eighty-six had landed at the Pole during the previous month. "Who can guess what further developments there may be at this spot, in man's never-ending pursuit of knowledge?" Peter wondered. "But I doubt if anyone here will ever know the desolation of spirit which that small band of men must have felt when they got here in 1911, and during the two months of their unsuccessful return journey."

Back at Cape Evans, the Scott base run by New Zealanders was much cooler and more to the liking of the British trio. There was more filming in the simple but substantial wooden hut in which the crew of *Terra Nova* had spent their last Antarctic winter in 1911. Here Captain Scott had sat in his alcove, writing up his diary and making his plans; and here his son sat at the father's table, writing in his diary in his turn.

> Peter was hardly ever visibly emotional [Lagus noted], but there was a pause and a moment of silence and reflection when I asked him to pose at the head of the dining table in his father's place. It was a strange feeling in there, shelves stacked with tins of still edible food, beds with blankets. It didn't need much imagination to hear the crunch of men's boots and the hiss of sledges, the

door flying open with a rush of wind and a flurry of snow as a party returned. Soon the hut would be warm and full of noise and talk again with those famous larger-than-life ghosts from the past.

Peter also found the atmosphere of the hut surprisingly buoyant. The men who trudged away had lived here hopefully, and, it seemed to these visitors, left some of their spirit behind.

> Goodbye to the Antarctic [he wrote]. I wonder if I shall see it again. I wonder if I could have kept away from it if I had allowed myself to go there as a young man. There is no denying its tremendous appeal. Cold and inhospitable it may be, but Oh the exquisite beauty of it and the challenge that is still there.

Peter was to see the Antarctic again on four occasions, the next time only two years after his visit to the South Pole. He had been put in touch with an enterprising Swedish American, Lars Eric Lindblad, who was launching a travel business with a difference. He was building a ship in Finland which would penetrate into regions where tourists did not usually go. Peter and his wife joined the *Lindblad Explorer* for twenty-six expeditions, he in the capacity of guest lecturer. Known affectionately as "the little red ship," she had a displacement of 2,500 tons, accommodation for ninety-two passengers, a mainly Swedish crew, and was equipped with every comfort that affluent tourists might expect. She carried a number of inflatable rubber boats with outboard motors called zodiaks, which were used to enable passengers to penetrate into distant creeks and to land on inaccessible beaches. A happy atmosphere built up on board which made the Scotts feel at home each time they took possession of their usual cabin, where Peter assembled what he called his toys: pencils and brushes, paints and notebooks, sunglasses and lotions, kept in a self-designed and home-made box.

The "little red ship" was still under construction when the Scotts' first Lindblad expedition took place in 1968. A Chilean vessel, the *Navarino*, was chartered to take the party first to the Falkland Islands, then down the western side of the Antarctic peninsula as far south as the Lemaire channel, which was almost choked by icebergs carved into fantastic shapes, whose luminous greens and blues shone with dramatic splendor in a world of black and white. Penguin rookeries were everywhere, the birds in places staining the snow pink with their krill-tinted droppings—rockhopper and macaroni, chinstrap, gentoo, and adelie. Wildlife was abundant: dolphins and seals, the wandering and blackbrowed albatross, fulmars and shags. The voyage covered over 4,000 miles. Once again the beauty, the purity and the immensity of it all beguiled Peter's senses, and inspection of an abandoned whaling station brought home the contrast between the works of nature and the works of commercial man.

In 1971 another Lindblad tour took him back to Cape Evans and the *Terra Nova* hut, this time with his wife, Dafila, and Keith Shackleton. On the way they landed on Enderby Island, where Dafila looked into a deserted hut to find it full of baby seals sleeping in rows, and Peter and Roger Tory Peterson, a fellow lecturer on board the ship, spotted a penguin they could not immediately identify. Was it a snares or a fiordland penguin, which look much alike? "I jumped out of the zodiak with my Nikon flashing," Peterson recalled, "while Peter just sat there with his sketchpad and drew the bird. He said that he would merely have to get back to the ship to identify it from a reference book, whereas I would have to wait until my films were processed back home in Connecticut, which would take several weeks. He was quite right. When he got back to the ship's library we found that it was indeed the fiordland penguin far from home. Peter's drawing accurately showed the white marks on the cheek, and the lack of bare pink skin at the base of the bill … He had a genius for portraying all wild things visually."

On Campbell Island the party climbed 5 miles through rain and fog to inspect a pair of royal albatrosses—"vast and friendly-looking, sitting on flamingo-like nests and surrounded by red-coated tourists clicking cameras at them … but their immense dignity was never seriously compromised." (When in the Antarctic, Lindblad tourists wore red anoraks and so could be more easily spotted if they went astray.) At Cape Evans everyone converged in zodiaks on the *Terra Nova* hut, "but even the milling LE passengers," Peter wrote, "could not spoil this enchanted place which has seen so many moods, in which men have been happy and bored, hopeful and heartbroken." Keith Shackleton felt the same sense of almost mystical enchantment, as if a spell had been laid on the place.

Peter's third Antarctic expedition came in 1978 when he and Philippa, again joined by Keith Shackleton as a fellow lecturer, flew to Ushuaia in Tierra del Fuego to join the *Lindblad Explorer:* "It is like a happy family," Peter wrote. The family was a particularly affluent one on this occasion. Among those on board was Prince Bernhard of The Netherlands, president of WWF International and also of the 1001 Club, a number of whose members were of the party. Most of them were millionaires, often several times over.

This club had originated in a conversation held in 1970 between two South African businessmen: Dr. Anton Rupert, the tobacco tycoon, and his associate Mr. Charles de Haes. Peter had invited Dr. Rupert to raise $10 million for WWF. Too busy to undertake the task himself, Dr. Rupert had offered to second Mr. de Haes to take it on, paying the expenses. Charles de Haes had never heard of WWF but he agreed to the suggestion. A meeting was held at Slimbridge, and in the car driving back to London an idea sparked in their minds: there would be one thousand subscribers each paying $10,000, and one over who would be their president, Prince Bernhard; and it would be called the 1001 Club. By the time they saw the Prince in Holland three days later, a letter for his signature had been drafted and three members had already joined; Dr. Rupert, Charles de Haes, and a business associate. None of them knew of the suggestion made seventeen years earlier by Max Nicholson, when WWF was conceived, to create a club of six hundred members each paying £1,000, so the resemblance was coincidental. To secure Prince Bernhard as president was a brilliant stroke which ensured its success.

Charles de Haes spent three years calling on millionaires in all parts of the world in his capacity as honorary assistant to Prince Bernhard, with no mention of WWF on his visiting card. The royal name unlocked many doors. By the end of the three years he had raised even more than the stipulated $10 million. Out of this money a fund was set aside to pay the administrative expenses of WWF International; so, when it appealed to the public for money to save whales, rhinos, lemurs, tortoises, or whatever, it could truthfully say that every penny would go to the cause and none to paying salaries, company cars, and telephone bills. This put WWF in a unique position. Most charities, faced with ever rising costs of administration, must deduct ever increasing proportions of the sums they raise to pay for their own existence.

The 1001 Club had no clubhouse but, through WWF, arrangements were made for periodic excursions, receptions at palaces and castles, and other events where gold-plated shoulders could rub together, generally in the presence of a prince of the blood. Many (though not all) of the passengers in the *Lindblad Explorer's* Antarctic cruise in 1978 were members; had she sunk with all hands, stock markets throughout the world would have trembled. Nature smiled upon the millionaires: the seas of the Drake passage, often so tempestuous, were placid; skies were cloudless, winds zephyrlike, sunshine perpetual; the passengers played football on the ice in the Lemaire channel and "the superlative beauty wherever one looked was almost overwhelming," Peter noted. "This was unspoiled, untouched nature at its most sublime." Then it was back to the treadmill: appointments in Morges, meetings in Portugal, problems to sort out at Slimbridge.

One more Antarctic expedition was to come, in the following year. Again the Scotts joined the *Lindblad Explorer* at Ushuaia, this time to circumnavigate the continent and end up in New Zealand. On the way they made landfall in the Falkland Islands, where too many sheep and rabbits had led to overgrazing, erosion, and a degradation of the land which threatened colonies of rockhopper and macaroni penguins that nested there. A "conservation delegation" from several agencies arrived on the islands at the same time as the *Lindblad Explorer* anchored there, and Peter was drawn into discussions about the islands' future.

"While watching penguins," he wrote, "and walking back, I put forward the idea of a Falkland Islands Conservation Foundation on the lines of the Charles Darwin Foundation for the Galapagos Islands." This would go far beyond its starting point of resuscitating the islands' ecology and safeguarding the penguin rookeries; it would aim to protect all forms of wildlife in the islands, of which there are 780, as well as historical monuments such as the wrecks of old sailing ships; it would encourage research, create conservation areas, regulate tourism—virtually manage the islands, in fact, as a conservation showpiece. Peter had let his imagination rip. Among the members of the delegation was an American lawyer, Michael Wright. "How soon can we bring a foundation of this kind into being?" Peter asked Mr. Wright. "We could do it today," was the reply. During luncheon on board the *Lindblad Explorer*, Michael Wright drew up a document which, he said, could come into force as soon as it had six signatures. "As there were six of us present, the Foundation was born as soon as the document, typed by Judy Marshall, the hostess on board, had been duly signed." This was on January 16, 1979. The approval of the Governor of the Falklands was sought and obtained. Back in Britain, the process of registering a charity proved to be a good deal more complicated, and had barely been completed before the Argentine flag was run up in Port Stanley on April 2, 1982.

This act of Argentine aggression came as no surprise to Peter. Six months earlier, in September 1981, he had written to the prime minister asking her to reconsider her government's decision to withdraw the survey ship HMS *Endurance* from Antarctic waters.

> Having travelled in Argentina [he wrote] and visited their bases on the Antarctic peninsula, where contrary to the Treaty military uniform is worn by all personnel, and having been invited to hold the first baby to be born on the Antarctic continent (then ten days old, whose mother had been flown in, when pregnant, for the purpose), I am well aware of Argentine ambitions in that part of the world.

And, he added, he was also well aware of the loyalty of the people of the Falklands, "who clearly wish to remain British. In this equation HMS *Endurance* is a vital, if symbolic, factor." Mrs. Thatcher sent a full but regretful reply; the decision had not been taken lightly, and must stand. Peter wrote asking her to think again but her reply was a foregone conclusion. Undeterred, three weeks after the war began he wrote to express concern about "unnecessary damage" that might be inflicted on penguin, albatross, and seal colonies by the military, and suggesting a signal from the Commander-in-Chief to alert British forces to the risk. At a time like that, he wrote, the suggestion might sound frivolous; if it did, she refrained from saying so, but replied that she could "understand your concern for the wildlife on the Islands, and I shall certainly make sure the Ministry of Defence are aware of it." This did not end the correspondence. Before the war was over, on June 1, 1982, he sent the prime minister a paper embodying his thoughts about the islands' future:

> Their rich wildlife—152 species of bird, including nine of penguins and huge breeding colonies of albatrosses—could form the basis of a thriving tourist industry, and the whole group of islands, including a 200-mile zone around them, should be declared an area of outstanding biological significance, protected under a World Heritage convention as a World Park.

By this time the Falklands Foundation was in being with an office in London, Peter as chairman and Lord Shackleton as vice-chairman, an income in 1982 of £4,525 and an ambitious program of future research into the ecology of the islands. Many of them had been covered by tussac or tussock grass, which can grow to 12 feet high, and provided a wonderfully secure habitat for birds of many species and for other forms of wildlife, but 80 percent of the tussock had been destroyed, mainly to make way for sheep. Over three-quarters of the world's population of black-browed albatrosses nested in the islands and needed protection. The Foundation also set out to rescue and preserve the many wrecks of square-rigged sailing ships that were rotting away in creeks and harbors, including the *Jhelum*, possibly the last surviving Eastindiaman, built in Liverpool in 1849. Peter stayed on as chairman of the Falklands Foundation until 1986, when he handed over to Sir Rex Hunt, but remained president until his death. By that time it had changed its name to Falklands Conservation and moved to Edinburgh.

CHAPTER TWENTY

Saving the Whales

After leaving behind the Falkland Islands in January 1979, the *Lindblad Explorer* sailed on round the Antarctic continent, experiencing atrocious weather which made a landing at the Scott base in McMurdo Sound impossible, so the ship set course for Lyttleton in New Zealand. On February 8, 1979 Peter noted that two minke whales were playing like dolphins round the ship's bows. A few days later he saw minke whales again but in a less playful mood. A Russian whale-catching ship was stalking a pod of these small baleen animals, with a factory ship in attendance waiting for the kill. He described what happened next in *Observations of Wildlife*.

> As we were approaching, we saw the harpoon fired and one of the whales hit. For four and a half minutes it surfaced occasionally, spouting blood, then it sounded, diving deep. Eight minutes after being struck it was hauled up to the surface tail first and seemed to be dead. The whale-catcher already had two dead Minke whales lying alongside. By this time we were within a hundred yards. Every camera on our ship had recorded the scene. Every passenger had seen the death of a whale at first hand. It was something I had never seen before. Thinking of all those speeches I had made on behalf of WWF to the International Whaling Commission down the years, telling them what damage they had done to the populations of the great whales, I now realised how much their impact had suffered because I had never seen the real thing.

Now that he had, a more impassioned note colored his future speeches—and they were to be many—urging civilized nations to renounce this cruel and outdated industry.

His next experience of whales was a great deal pleasanter. He and Philippa broke their journey home from New Zealand in Hawaii for more underwater swimming, this time to look not only at coral fish but at humpback whales, one of the three most seriously endangered species. (The other two were the right and the great blue whale, the largest animal that has ever lived on earth, larger than the biggest dinosaur; a blue whale may be over 100 feet long and may weigh 160 tons, the weight of two thousand men; its heart is as large as a bull, its arteries wide enough for a child to crawl through, its tongue as big as an elephant, and its young drink half a ton of milk a day.) Holding hands the better to communicate, Peter and Philippa dived together, the latter with her camera.

> It was intensely exciting just to be with these fifty-foot crea-
> tures. They passed us by and very quickly disappeared with lazy
> tail flaps. As soon as they had gone, we saw people in the boat
> pointing again, and almost at once another pair came in sight
> ... And then the [pair of] whales crossed slowly ahead of us,
> rolling slightly away from us to take a good look. I gazed into
> the eye of the nearer, smaller whale—it may have been twenty
> feet away and the end of the pectoral fin was a good deal closer.
> As they passed ahead of Phil I saw the eye move away from me
> to her and a crescent of white showed just behind the brown
> iris. That the animal was close enough to see the white of its eye
> immediately struck me.

They saw in all five humpbacks, possibly seven, and the closeness of these mighty creatures, totally without ill will toward interlopers whose species had so long persecuted theirs, and whom they could have obliterated with a flick of the tail, was "one of the most stirring experiences of my life. Talk about euphoria—we were walking on air!"

Far from walking on air, for most of Peter's long involvement with whales he had been plodding through a slough of despond. In 1963, as chairman of the Survival Service Commission, he had raised the matter of the population crash of the blue whale, and had set up a Whale Group to ferret out the facts about existing stocks of the ten species of these cetaceans, eight of which had been hunted, stage by stage, to the point of extinction.

In the long, unfinished story of man's beastliness to beasts there can be no more horrible chapter than that which tells of the hunting of the whale. It is a story not only of cruelty and greed, but of stupidity as well. Stage by stage,

the whaling nations killed the goose that laid the golden egg. At first the hunters went out in rowboats to harpoon their prey and tow it to their sailing ships,
there to be cut up and the oil drained into barrels; only those species which
floated when dead—some species sank—could be hunted, and the faster ones
could get away. Steam power brought wider-ranging vessels, and harpoons with
explosive heads that enabled shrapnel to riddle the whales' bodies; then came
factory ships equipped to process the animals quickly and efficiently; and, finally, helicopters and sonar techniques. Wide as are the oceans, for whales there
was no hiding place.

Commercial extinction, when so few animals remain that it no longer
pays to hunt them, comes before biological extinction, which is final. By the
1920s, humpback stocks had been destroyed; by the 1940s blue whales had
followed; next came the turn first of the fin and then of the sei species; by the
1960s only the much smaller minke whale remained worth plundering. As each
species became commercially extinct its survivors were protected, but by then
they might be too few and far between to meet and breed, and so their recovery
was problematical.

Did the whalers, one may ask, fold their hands and watch their industry
run out of whales and so perish? For centuries they took that road, ignoring
warnings; their business was in international waters and there was no authority
to impose control. It was not until 1946 that the International Whaling Commission was set up with the object of setting for each species an annual killable
quota, and giving protection to those heading toward extinction. The job of
setting quotas was entrusted to a scientific committee whose members were
appointed by the Commission itself. So in effect it was a butcher's club, whose
members decided on the size of the kill. Far from achieving its ostensible aim of
curbing overhunting, an annual catch of all species of around forty thousand in
the 1930s rose to sixty-seven thousand in 1962. No resolution could be passed
by the International Whaling Commission without a majority of three-quarters, and any member could invalidate a resolution merely by lodging an objection within ninety days. In other words not only did the Commission have no
teeth, it had no bark either, because it did not want one.

It had, however, an Achilles heel. Any nation could join the Commission if it wished to do so, merely by agreeing to the rules and paying the dues.
There was no need to possess a whaling fleet. Also representatives of bodies
called in the turgid jargon of the international network NGOs, or Non-Governmental Organizations, might attend the Commission's meetings and speak,
but not vote. WWF was one such NGO, and from 1965 onward Peter became
its spokesman at the Commission's meetings. "It was a new kind of jungle to
me," he wrote. "It was almost pure politics with frequent mentions of 'the freedom of the seas' and 'the rights of sovereign states' and all that guff. There is no
doubt that what is going on is a world scandal of considerable magnitude." For

the next twenty years he addressed himself to exposing this scandal, and to maneuvering the whaling nations, of which the USSR, Norway, Iceland, and Japan were the most committed, into mending their ways. He was not, of course, the only campaigner nor, especially after Greenpeace entered the fray, the most forceful; as always, he preferred persuasion to confrontation, the net to the trident; but his emotions were deeply engaged and a fair slice of his time and energy went to the anti-whaling cause.

From the 1960s onward the conservation movement was gathering momentum and spawning many bodies, from local clubs and charities through pressure groups and NGOs up to United Nations level. Peter had a say in the direction of many of these, either through his membership of their boards and councils, or through his network of personal contacts with the great and good. All were potential allies of the whales. And his own Survival Service Commission kept up a steady pressure on the scientific committee of the Whaling Commission, whose members had, in his view, been more servile than scientific when fixing quotas.

He was criticized for empire-building. In March 1972 John Hillaby, renowned for his long walks, wrote in the *New Scientist*:

> Through some inner drive that still intrigues and, occasionally, depresses me, Peter has forged ahead, glueing one organisation on to another until nowadays I sometimes have the feeling you can't see Peter because his latest hat is so big ... Listen Peter, as you know better than most, the great whales are in deadly danger; the blue whale, the biggest animal the world has ever seen, might even be already extinct. The IWC meets in London in June. If you can hurl a harpoon into *that* gang of double-talkers—or even stop cat and dog food manufacturers buying whale meat—in this column I will sing of thee and thy multifarious hats like unto a bulbul in the courts of Kubla Khan.

Two months later, in June 1972, the United Nations convened a Conference on the Human Environment held in Stockholm which passed unanimously a resolution calling for an immediate moratorium on commercial whaling. Peter wrote to Hillaby suggesting that he should start to practise his bulbul warble. He claimed that he personally had managed to get seven or eight of the delegates to the conference in Stockholm to change their votes, and had persuaded the management of a major pet food firm to stop using whale meat.

Two weeks later came the meeting of the International Whaling Commission at which Peter gave the opening speech. He stepped up his criticism of the scientific committee, whose members had estimated the whale population of the southern oceans to be between eighty thousand and three hundred thousand—a gap so wide as to prove nothing but the ignorance of the scientific members and the folly of building a plan of action on such a quicksand. It had been discovered that whales could communicate with each other by means of "songs," which had been recorded; how much more could we find out about them if we could learn their language, and lose if we killed them off before this could be done? To the charge that he was reacting emotionally he made a spirited reply. Whether we like it or not, man is an emotional creature, and without emotions would be only half a man, and the least estimable half at that. "Decisions made without taking emotions into account are likely to be unrealistic decisions, and unrealistic decisions are bad decisions." World opinion, he believed, had turned against whaling, and the path of those who defied "the collective conscience of mankind" led only to a deadend.

The fourteen members of the Commission present at the meeting were unimpressed. Only four voted for a moratorium. Whaling based on unrealistic and excessive quotas went on, although whaling had become repugnant to a growing number of people both because it was cruel and because it had become redundant. In its earlier days, it had met a need by providing oil for lamps and whalebone for ladies' corsets; electricity and fashion between them had put an end to those requirements. As for its current uses—shoe polish, soap, cosmetics, pet food, and so on—there were plenty of substitutes. The Japanese claim that the meat was a necessary part of their diet was flimsy, to say the least; whale meat accounted for less than one tenth of 1 percent of their protein intake, and anyway would have priced itself out of the market without a government subsidy.

Peter was informed that most of the whale meat was eaten by Japanese children, convicts, and soldiers, but as it was expensive this seemed unlikely, and further enquiries revealed that minke meat especially was a luxury to be consumed with whiskey, rather as smoked salmon was enjoyed in Western countries, though generally without the whiskey. He recognized that smoked salmon eaters in the West would not welcome a campaign to ban their delicacy because it was unkind to fish, and became more understanding of the Japanese position, but this did not deflect him from his purpose.

For the next ten years the anti-whalers kept up a persistent campaign in the media, on the platform, and at sea. Greenpeace activists drove their zodiaks between catching ships and their prey, and in 1978, with the help of a grant from the Netherlands branch of WWF, launched their ship *Rainbow Warrior*, whose stormy career ended when she was sunk in a New Zealand harbor by the French. Peter's approach was more crafty. His strategy could be described as one of encirclement. If a sufficient number of right-minded nations could be persuaded to join the International Whaling Commission, they would be able to out-vote the hard-core members, and a vote in favor of a moratorium could be achieved. As he jetted about the world, he seized every opportunity to urge heads of states to join the Commission, and so frustrate the knavish tricks of the whaling nations.

Among the independent sovereign states that joined the Commission was the Seychelles, that group of small islands in the Indian Ocean with a population of some fifty-seven thousand, whose waters possess a superb variety of coral fish, and whose government an interest in their conservation. Peter, with his wife and Dafila, had visited these islands in the *Lindblad Explorer,* clocked up 216 species of fish and studied the courtship of *Anthias squamipinnis* whose male changed the color of his head as he saw off rivals in his underwater territory. The Seychelles' zeal to put an end to whaling in the southern oceans so perturbed the Japanese that they offered the islands first a ship, then an aid package worth $40 millions; both were refused. Other member nations of the Commission were less circumspect, and some delegates known to support the moratorium proposal were unexpectedly recalled shortly before a meeting, to be replaced by representatives who duly voted against it.

The Seychelles then put forward a proposal to declare the whole of the Indian Ocean a whale sanctuary, and won support among other delegates. In January 1980 Peter and Lyall Watson, a biologist, zoo-man and sometime fellow lecturer on the *Lindblad Explorer,* flew to Mahe Island to congratulate the Seychelles president, M. Albert Rene, on his stand, and to suggest that he should call a conference of states bordering on the Indian Ocean to bring into being the proposed sanctuary. M. Rene, a man after Peter's heart, listened carefully, said "I agree, let's do it," and started to discuss dates. In April Peter was back in Mahe to take the chair at the conference of fifteen Indian Ocean coastal states. It went smoothly; all that now remained was to secure the agreement of the International Whaling Commission to respect the sanctuary's boundaries. Membership of the Commission was growing fast. How far this was due to Peter's personal efforts no one can say, but undoubtedly they played a part. In February 1980 a telephone call from him in Beijing informed the WWF that China had agreed to join the Commission, followed in July by a cable from Oman to say that the Sultan had made the same decision. Mrs. Indira Gandhi had already brought India into the fold, and Australia had decided to withdraw from whaling. By the early 1980s, the number of member nations of the Commission had increased from the original seventeen to forty-one.

A few weeks after he had swum with humpback whales off Hawaii in February 1979, Peter addressed a rally of one thousand people in Trafalgar Square on the eve of the International Whaling Commission's annual meeting. His appeal was overtly emotional. "What we have done to the great whales in the sacred name of commerce," he said, "is an affront to human dignity." What would you think if you went into a field and saw someone hurl a harpoon into a cow's rump, and then watched its prolonged death agonies? Whales were intelligent and sensitive to pain—how intelligent we were only just beginning to understand.[1] He called for a two-minute silence, which was broken by a recording of the humpback's song. The withers of the Commission were unwrung. Rejecting a moratorium, they did concede the Indian Ocean as a sanctuary, for the time being. Three more years were to pass before the breakthrough came at last. At the thirty-fourth annual meeting of the Commission in 1982 the necessary majority was secured to proclaim a moratorium on whaling. So, wrote Peter:

> After more than twenty years of concern for whales, and ten years after the moratorium vote at the Stockholm conference on the human environment, after year after year of speeches by me and others that were always ignored by the whalers—after year after year of quotas proposed by the scientific committee being systematically exceeded, and one whale population after another being brought to commercial extinction ... after all that, *we have won*. It seems to be a great victory in one of my lifetime's battles, and I feel a great lift.

"It seems to be"—did doubts already underlie the note of triumph? The major whaling nations, Japan, Norway, and the USSR, voted against the resolution, backed up by Iceland, Peru, South Korea, and Brazil. There was to be a three-year stay of execution; the moratorium was not to take effect until 1985. There could be a review at any time, by 1990 at the latest. Worst of all, "scientific whaling" was to continue, and this was not so much a loophole as a gap wide enough for a factory ship to steam through. Moreover the Americans had weakened their anti-whaling stance by allowing their Eskimos to kill more, rather than fewer, bowhead whales. Only a year later, Peter noted that a heavy price had been paid for the moratorium. More pirate ships were operating, ignoring the ban; minke catches were higher than ever; whales killed for "scientific" purposes were, in reality, meat for the Japanese. When the International Whaling Commission met in Bournemouth in 1985 many of its members made no secret of their determination to carry on regardless, and the advice of their scientific committee, by now reinforced by genuinely impartial scientists, was again ignored.

It is a sad, continuing story of greed subduing compassion and even common sense, since overexploitation of the oceans threatens unforeseen consequences. Perhaps compassion has no place in commerce; nor awe of "that great Leviathan;" nor curiosity about its songs, its ways, the uses of its brain; nor respect for its grandeur. An American marine biologist, Mr. Victor Shaffer, put the matter in a nutshell: "Whales are different. They live in families, they play in the moonlight, they talk to one another, they care for one another in distress."

The United Nations conference on the Human Environment held in 1972 in Stockholm, and organized by Dr. Maurice Strong, had done its best for whales, but in another of the battles Peter was fighting on several fronts it had evaded the issue. Mountains of paper, oceans of ink, clouds of cogitation had gone into preparation for this gathering of delegates from 121 nations, charged with nothing less than drawing up a blueprint for the future of mankind—a species seen, almost suddenly, to be approaching the endangered status: in Mrs. Indira Gandhi's words, "in poverty threatened by malnutrition and disease, in weakness by war, in richness by the pollution brought about by his own prosperity." Peter attended this conference as a representative of WWF, one of the 150 Non-Governmental Organizations that had been invited.

His brother Wayland was there too. As a member of the House of Lords on the Labour side—he had been Parliamentary Secretary to the Minister of Housing and Local Government—he had been one of the first of Britain's legislators to foresee the growing threat of environmental pollution, and it was partly through his efforts that a permanent Royal Commission (still in being) on that topic was set up by the Labour government shortly before its defeat in the general election of 1970. At the time of the Stockholm conference he was chairman of the International Parliamentary Conferences on the Environment and it was in that capacity that he took part in its deliberations.

Peter had two objectives: to save the whales, and to get the human population explosion recognized as the root cause of the world's ecological troubles. The population question was a hornet's nest. Family planners faced not only the stings of Roman Catholics, but those of the developing countries whose populations were increasing at an apparently unstoppable rate. World population was out of control; already it had reached about five billion, it was on course to double in the next thirty or forty years, and nearly all that increase was in the developing countries, where 90 percent of the four hundred thousand babies being born *every day* were first drawing breath. The governments of these countries resented being preached at by richer nations whose populations, however stable, were using up a very much greater share of the world's resources, and were therefore causing most of the overexploitation and pollution themselves. Behind this resentment lay hard lessons of experience. Ever since mankind evolved, its struggle had been to rear enough replacements, with an extra margin to consolidate a fragile hold on the environment, so that the desire to breed unchecked had become an inborn compulsion. Nature had arranged in every species for a generous margin to allow for the many dangers faced by the young contending with a hostile world. More than a single generation and a lot of persuasion was needed to quench and then to reverse this compulsion. "To the very poor," Mrs. Gandhi said in her speech to the conference, "every child is an earner and a helper." Except, she might have added, when there are no ways to earn money and no land on which to grow food.

Peter was quite prepared to brave the stings of hornets, but had to be content with chairing a "side meeting" organized by the International Planned Parenthood Federation, a matter of preaching to the converted. When it came to drawing up the final list of recommendations, of which there were 109, not one dealt with the population question. Peter took some comfort from nine which endorsed the need to maintain "genetic diversity," threatened by the ever rising toll of species heading for extinction. The conference agreed on an "action plan," and the goal was summed up as the realization of a world community "in which man makes an ally of the natural world in achieving that better life in larger freedom which is the hope and promise of all mankind." Fine words butter no parsnips, Peter might have thought; but he was encouraged by the fact that the cause he had embraced when it was unrecognized and ignored had become the focus of world attention. "After Stockholm," he wrote in a foreword to a booklet *Did We Save the Earth at Stockholm?,*

> we may be listened to with more attention than before, and no longer be regarded as freaks or other-worldly eccentrics, more interested in animals and plants than in people. Maybe it will be recognized that the quality of human life is connected with the welfare of all life on earth. *Did* we save the earth at Stockholm? I think we took a first step, but unless the United Nations World Population conference is at least as successful as Stockholm, then the earth may yet be lost.

Peter was in his sixty-fourth year when he acquired a handle to his name. Since he fell into none of the categories of those normally knighted at the appropriate stage of their careers, it took some time for those who advise the monarch on such matters to decide that "services to conservation" would be the right citation, and in 1973 he became the first person to receive that honor for promoting that cause. He and Philippa jointly decided that a title was to make no difference to their way of life. He sent a note round to his staff to say that they would go on being Peter and Phil to everyone working for the Trust, from Council members to groundsmen and cleaning women, as was the custom at Slimbridge.

Another honor followed in the knighthood's wake. Toward the end of that same year, he was invited to become Chancellor of the University of Birmingham, and in May 1974 was installed amid the pomp and ceremony traditional to the office, although in this case the tradition was not much more than a century old. Only three Chancellors had preceded him: Joseph Chamberlain, Lord Cecil of Chelworth, and Anthony Eden. First he received an honorary degree of Laws (*honoris causa*) from the Vice-Chancellor, Dr. Robert (later Lord) Hunter, and donned one set of robes; then he retired to change into the even grander robes of Chancellor. Preceded by four trumpeters of the Royal

Artillery, he returned to the podium to confer, in his turn, honorary degrees on five individuals of his choice, who included Konrad Lorenz and Sir Landsborough Thomson. Into this elaborate ceremony he introduced a note of his own: beneath his gold embroidered robe, a pair of red socks could be seen. Red socks had become a hallmark, an ice-breaker, perhaps a gentle snook cocked at the Establishment of which he knew himself to be a part. "I know I'm a bit square, but they want me to be a whole lot squarer," he was to write some years later of his publishers, who had wanted him to cut out most of the light-hearted touches he had worked into his latest book. On one occasion his red socks led him into trouble. He and Philippa had been invited to a grand dinner at Windsor Castle to mark the engagement of Princess Alexandra to Mr. Angus Ogilvy. On unpacking his bag at the hotel he found that his black evening socks had been left behind. His red ones would scarcely be *comme il faut* with white tie and tails, and it was too late to buy a new pair. He appealed to the receptionist, who succeeded in borrowing a pair of thick woollen ones from the chef, who wanted them back in time to wear them on a fishing expedition very early next morning. Thick woollen socks were uncomfortable with evening pumps, but honor was saved and the chef got them back, duly washed, in time to go fishing.

Peter took his duties as Chancellor seriously. These included awarding degrees to students twice a year; despite his very frequent travels he missed few of these events, and reckoned that by the end of his ten years as Chancellor he had shaken five thousand hands. In 1975 a symposium on Man and his Environment was held at the University; Peter was in Zaire attending an assembly of the IUCN but flew back in time to deliver the closing address, a rousing exhortation on now familiar lines. More and more he was coming to stress the non-material and ethical basis of conservation: it was not only economically suicidal to destroy the earth's resources but, like eating people, it was morally wrong. As an optimist he believed that humanity would find the will to limit its own increase, as it had already found the means, but time was running out. On relinquishing his post as Chancellor in 1983 he conferred three more honorary degrees on distinguished individuals of his choice: he chose Max Nicholson, Keith Shackleton, and Sir Max Williams.

It has been said that Peter was too easily persuaded to join almost any charity or other worthy body that approached him, and therefore took on too much. Sometimes he did refuse. Invited to become vice president of the Friends of Birmingham Cathedral he replied: "It is not really my subject, as I am an agnostic." Agnostic though he was, as old age approached questions hitherto submerged beneath a tide of action began to surface in his mind, sometimes seemingly at odds with his belief in Darwinian evolution. Since his early childhood, butterflies and moths had fascinated him—the image of a hawkmoth, it may be recollected, had once mesmerized his mind to the exclusion of severe pain; and he believed that a study of the oleander hawkmoth, made in 1981, was the best oil painting he ever did. In the early 1970s one of the founders of the British Butterfly Conservation Society, Robert Goodden, invited him to become its first president, and at the Gooddens' butterfly farm in Dorset showed him rare specimens of these resplendent insects. Peter was intrigued by mimicry, and saw species pretending to be twigs, thorns, or bits of tree bark, or poisonous grubs, or nasty-tasting flowers, in order to escape detection or to warn off predators. He was particularly struck by the giant Edwards atlas moth, which had evolved an intricate pattern of two snakes, their threatening heads at the tip of each wing. "When one considers the evolutionary steps by which these amazing facsimiles are finally reached, the mind can only boggle," he wrote in his diary. "The answer has to be time. The genetic plasticity must be there, but so must the millennia." Faith remained unshaken, but a hint of perplexity remained.

An experience that disturbed him deeply brought such questions sharply to his mind. A young landowner-cum-farmer, Rodney Dawson, had been fired by the conservation message Peter had put across in one of his lectures. Afterward he had introduced himself to the lecturer, and the two men, despite the difference in age, had become good friends. Peter became Dawson's guru, Dawson a disciple who took to heart the guru's teaching, including that of population control. Never, he resolved, would he add another being to an overcrowded and polluted world, and his wife at first agreed. They had bought a semi-derelict farm on the island of Islay in the Hebrides, Easter Ellister, partly because of their interest in the greylag geese which bred there. In the winter of 1972 Peter and Philippa, with their friends the Pilchers, stayed at Easter Ellister for a day or two of goose-watching. The farmhouse was partially roofless and water came from a pump; Jane Dawson was mortified when, bringing in a jug of drinking water, a shrimp was seen to be swimming about. She started to remove the jug but Peter stopped her. "Don't take it away, we haven't identified it yet," he said.

That evening, looking by moonlight over the rugged and romantic landscape, Peter remarked to his host, "It seems a pity to live in such a lovely place and have no children to share it with." The remark sank home. Within a year, the first of two daughters was born. Easter Ellister flourished, but Rodney Dawson did not. He contracted cancer. One day in 1977 a message came to Slimbridge that he was in the hospital in Glasgow with not long to live, and had asked to see his friend again; so next morning Peter caught the shuttle to Glasgow and found his way to Rodney Dawson's bedside.

> He was propped up in bed in a sitting position bare to the waist,
> head drooping a little and breathing was evidently difficult. His

face and body were without colour, his chest and abdomen criss-crossed with operation scars and stitch marks. A tear-stained Jane got up and greeted me, and then left us alone together. I stood by the bed and took his hand. My other was still holding my brief-case. Rod's voice was scarcely audible, in part because of an earlier operation which had affected his vocal chords. He whispered my name and then said: "I can't see you very well," but his hand closed over mine in recognition. "It's the place ... tell them ...' I listened intently but couldn't hear what to tell them. My hand rested in his left hand. He was having great diffficulty in breathing. Then the breathing just stopped and his head dropped forward a little. I stood there for a minute or more. Then a nurse went past to the opposite curtained corner of the ward. As she came back she saw me standing there. "I'm afraid he's gone," I whispered. She took one glance and immediately pulled the curtain across. I had been in the ward for no more than five minutes . . .

So I had arrived just in time. In time for what? To give a shaft of recognition and perhaps pleasure in the last moments of a too-short lifetime? To wave goodbye to a departing spirit? To be deeply moved by the witness of death? To be struck by an inescapable feeling that there was some meaning in that incredible coincidental timing? He was just thirty-four—with a wife and two small children, an estate in Islay and another in Lincolnshire, a passion for birds and deep convictions about conservation and the long-term future of planet earth. He had fought illness with the utmost bravery for a second time, and this time he had lost.

To witness death was no new experience for Peter, but war was different; a casualty in battle was not a close friend dying with his hand in yours. Questions that had lain dormant for many years arose to perplex him. Perhaps to exorcise the demon, he put them into the shape of a poem which is really more of a creed. One of the "funnies" in his joke book concerned a child who drew a picture of God, and he began his composition with the same image. "What are you drawing?" the child was asked. "A picture of God." "But no one knows what God looks like." "Well they do now," was the reply. This led on to questions that have challenged theologians and philosophers throughout the ages: if God is just, why does so much injustice persist in his world? If God loves his people, why does he permit the innocent to suffer so much grief and pain? And, Peter asked:

> Who contrived the patterns in the bark of a tree,
> The structure of crystals, the frost on the window,
> The exquisite intricacy of hyper-parasitism,
> The amazing mechanisms of mimicry?
> The flight of wild swans against a leaden sky?
> The beauty of a spider's web loaded with dew?
> Is Nature the God in whom I can put my faith?
> And how much do I need faith anyway?

Perhaps, he continued to speculate, his life had been so fortunate that religious faith had been unnecessary; perhaps if he had suffered more he would have needed more spiritual support. And if disasters were yet to come, would he have the inner strength to face them? "For I am in love and my love loves me, And no one of us can live forever." He ended on a note suggesting that the stark creed of the agnostic left him or her with not only unanswered questions but an unsatisfied spirit.

> Life holds an infinite complexity of patterns;
> Do not these patterns add up to a Grand Design?
> And does not a Grand Design postulate a Designer?
> Is this the ultimate Deity—the Master of the Universe?
> Does he encompass all that is incomprehensible to all men?
> And is he the same God as the good in the spirit of man?

Peter was not an atheist, who says "There is no God;" he was an agnostic, who says "I don't know." He went on asking these eternal questions, and to him, as to the Walrus, the Carpenter, and the Oysters, answer came there none.

ENDNOTES

[1] It had been discovered that the brain of the Beluga whale possessed nearly twice as many cells in the temporal lobe, the seat of learning and memory, as the brain of a human—1,650,000 cells to 964,000. What advantage this conferred upon the whale, and what use was made of it, was in Peter's view a great unsolved puzzle of evolutionary biology, and it would be tragic if whales were exterminated before a solution could be found.

CHAPTER TWENTY-ONE

The Wildfowl Trust Spreads Its Wings

THE ENTERPRISE AT Slimbridge, like its birds, was breeding. As long ago as April 1957 a second center, as these satellites were called, had been opened at Peakirk in Cambridgeshire, 3 miles from the Borough Fen decoy; in fact it was mainly to help pay the costs of keeping this decoy in operation as a ringing station that the Wildfowl Trust had bought 14 acres nearby and taken over the lease of the decoy itself. At first its financial shoestring was even frailer than Slimbridge's had been, as Tony Cook, its future warden, recalled:

> My first job was to put up the perimeter fence. Two of us did that, nearly a mile. We all tried to save money and we scrounged here and there. We bought a lot of scrap timber and on a wet day we hauled the nails out of it with pliers and straightened them for use another day. There were two of us outside and a girl in the gate-house, we had an honesty-box outside in case she wasn't there and visitors put in their half-crowns. I think most people were pretty honest in those days.

Then an anonymous donor gave £10,000 which put the center on its feet. Captive geese, ducks, and swans bred happily in these quiet, shaded surroundings with plenty of trees and scooped-out ponds, and Chilean flamingos added a flash of color. Peter's memories of his youthful visits to the decoy, when he had learned the decoyman's art from Billy Williams, gave this Centre a special place in his affections. Billy, aged seventy-five, was still operating the decoy, thankful that he no longer had to kill the birds but only to ring them. (He had been so proficient at killing them swiftly and painlessly that a merchant had remarked: "Mr Williams, your birds always look as though they had died in their sleep.") He became the center's first curator, but only for a year, for he died in 1958, the last of seven generations of decoymen. His wife Annie, a cousin, lived on in a cottage in the village but had no children, and so the line died out.

Three years after the Peakirk Centre opened, Lord Alanbrooke resigned as president of the Trust. As well as being a firm and decisive chairman, through his influential contacts he had been a most successful fundraiser. For Peter and Philippa he had become a personal friend, keeping them enthralled with candid stories about the conduct of the war at Cabinet level and the behavior of his unpredictable, indomitable, infuriating, and captivating chief.

> When Lord Alanbrooke visits the grounds [his biographer noted] he stays with the Scotts, fitting easily and happily into their simple life ... He has become a familiar figure in gaily colored braces, breeches and long cavalry boots, setting off with his cine camera and all its paraphernalia of tripods, filters etc., then spending hours in mud and water photographing ... For flying shots the Field-Marshal mounts his camera on a special "gun stock" made for him in America and the only one of its kind in this country ... Peter Scott once spent a whole day trying to get wild geese up to the hide where Lord Alanbrooke was, they only gave up when Scott got stuck in mud up to his eyebrows and Lord Alanbrooke had to pull him out.

It was ironical that after surviving many wartime dangers on land and sea he escaped death by a mere whisker when he was electrocuted at his home by a defective hedge-trimmer. He recovered, but died only three years after giving up the presidency of the Trust, to be succeeded by Prince Philip.

The next center to open was near Welney in the Fens, and this was different. There was to be no collection of captive birds and no breeding programs. It was to be a refuge for wild birds, especially the wildfowl that wintered on the Ouse Washes. During the drainage of the Fens, Dutch engineers had dug out a new river, straight as a ruler for over 20 miles and called the New Bedford River or Hundred Foot, to shorten the flow of the Old Bedford River to the sea, and between this and the Old Bedford River lay the Ouse Washes. When winter floods subsided these Washes provided rich grazing for livestock, as well as nesting grounds for native wetland-loving birds. It could be said that the longtailed godwit started the movement to save part of these washes from threatened developments. In 1952 the nest of a pair of these birds was discovered, and kept a closely guarded secret until, in 1964, the land on which the birds regularly nested came on the market, and was bought by the Royal Society for the Protection of Birds. The Cambridgeshire and Isle of Ely Naturalists' Trust bought a block of adjoining marshland in the following year. Peter kept an eye on these marshes, only 35 miles from Peakirk, and when just over 100 acres came up for sale in 1967 he was determined to buy it for the Trust. Yet another of Peter's anonymous donors came forward, and the land was theirs for £4,000. The first warden was Josh Scott, one of the last of the "Fen Tigers"; his punt with its long barrel now stands in a corner of the visitors' reception room at the Welney Centre. The present warden, Don Revett, remembers that:

> Peter came down and looked out and said, "That's the beginning, we're going to build a great bridge over the marsh and we'll have an observatory right out over the marshes and make a lake so it'll be surrounded by water, and we'll have a big plate-glass window and floodlights and people can watch the swans and geese and ducks in winter, they'll all be wild, and winter here." He came in for a lot of ridicule. You can't build a bridge without any money, people said, and wild birds won't come near a great floodlit plate-glass object stuck out right in the middle of a lake. But of course he knew what he was doing. It had worked at Slimbridge and it would work here. He paid no attention when people said "you can't." He was very patient. He didn't bully people into giving money. Some people do that, and it puts backs up. He would always listen. He never shut his ears to arguments against his ideas. He would listen carefully and sometimes change his ideas, but never the main direction, he would change his tactics sometimes and work his way round objections. As a result he was very much admired, not only by his staff but by local farmers, he got on with them extremely well.

By 1967 Peter's contacts with well-disposed trustees of well-endowed trusts were many, and the Condor Trust, created and managed by a friend and fellow glider Robin Cole, provided materials for the bridge, while the Royal Engineers put it up for nothing. More interest-free loans and grants from charitable trusts came to the rescue, and the observatory arose, as it were, from the bosom of the lake, equipped with heating, a plate-glass window, and floodlights phased to come on and fade out gradually. Shallow lagoons were made to attract waders, and banks built up to shield visitors. Bit by bit, the Trust's holding was increased to 850 acres. Between them, the three charities came into possession of about 3,500 acres offering a refuge for the birds, which still faced gunshot dangers on the rest of the Washes. As Peter observed, if you create the right habitat, birds will find it. In the winter of 1951–2, seven Bewick's swans wintered here; in 1966–7, 855; by 1991 numbers had built up to 3,500. (It was here that Dafila did much of her research on the behavior of the swans that gained her a Ph.D.) The wild birds were given corn to supplement their normal diet. Some said that this compromised their wildness, but corn drew them toward the hides and the observatory where they offered a spectacle comparable, he suggested, in avian terms, to the great herds of wildebeest and zebras inhabiting the Serengeti plains. The Welney Centre was opened in 1970 by Mrs. Ernest Kleinwort, wife of one of the Trust's most generous benefactors.

Soon after the Trust had bought the land, and before anything had been done to turn it into a center, Peter wrote a letter to an imaginary friend about an imaginary visit to the refuge seven years later. He described in detail the hides, the banks, the observatory, the swan-trap, the geese taking off into the sunset, wigeon "whistling and churring and sweeping around." Seven years later, his vision had become reality almost to the last detail. In the words of the imaginary visitor:

> I was conscious of a tremendous feeling of satisfaction. For a day we had been in amongst the birds, yet few of them had seen us. We had watched them intimately without harming them or even frightening them. Somehow this was a proper relationship between man and animal, and the way in which this refuge had been planned and laid out to maintain and foster this relationship seemed infinitely imaginative and splendid.

On Peter's last visit, a few months before he died, he sat in the observatory with Don Revett and watched the swans flighting in from the fields. It was a beautiful March evening. "I'd never before seen so many birds coming so close to the observatory," said Don Revett. "We watched the dusk falling and Peter was as entranced as he had been when he was an undergraduate. I thought it was almost as if the birds knew he was there and were coming to say hello, or perhaps goodbye. Of course it was all imagination, but I just thought it rather strange."

The next center to take shape after Welney was Martin Mere in Lancashire, beside the estuary of the river Ribble. The actual mere, into which Sir Bedivere, according to local legend, had hurled King Arthur's sword Excalibur, had been drained for wartime cultivation and subsequently became more or less a wasteland, given over to rough shooting, to skating in hard winters, and to poaching all the year round. A local farmer's son, Ronnie Barker, remembered it from his boyhood when it had been a marsh frequented by wildfowl, the sky full of larks and swifts feeding on insects that formed into upward-spiraling columns so dense as to put him in mind of poplar trees. He had first encountered Peter with the rocket-netting teams, and the two had agreed that the former mere and its surroundings would make an excellent wildlife sanctuary, in particular for pinkfooted geese which fed on arable fields inland. In 1968 part of it came up for sale; as usual, the Wildfowl Trust had no money with which to buy it.

One of Peter's friends and fellow ornithologists was Peter Gladstone, who was living in Shrewsbury as a housemaster at the school, with his own small collection of birds. The idea of establishing a sanctuary beside the Ribble so excited his enthusiasm that he resigned from his teaching job and, early in 1972, spent three months raising money and negotiating for the purchase of the 363-acre farm, which included part of the ancient mere. When price, terms and all the details had been agreed, the Trust's Council met in London to decide whether to clinch the deal or to withdraw. The coffers were empty, and the Council decided to withdraw. Peter Gladstone was enraged. He had secured promises to cover the whole of the purchase price, £52,000, but not the cost of its development, which, in an expansive mood, Peter had put at £400,000. Gladstone walked out of the meeting in disgust, but

> a little later Peter came out of the meeting [Gladstone wrote] to say that he was sorry, but that was what councils were for. "I think you see them as a lot of fuddy-duddies," he said, and I replied "No—a lot of bigots and geriatrics," which was unfair. Peter went back to the meeting and a few minutes later a message came to say that I wasn't to wait, as they'd be a long time. That evening he phoned me to say that they had "reconsidered it"—meaning that Peter had got his own way—and that I was to go ahead with the purchase. What news! So I did.

Martin Mere, Peter and his council decided, was to be a bigger and better center than its parent. There was to be a wild area for wild birds and a landscaped area for tame ones, and the wild birds must be shown to the public, not hidden from them. Since wild birds were shy and liked their privacy, the trick was to conceal the public from them with the high banks, topped by shrubs, which were thrown up at every center at the start of operations. Then came hides, and a central observatory with comfortable chairs, efficient heating, and the big plate-glass window which was to become a hallmark of the Trust. All this luxury provoked criticism from those to whom a tough, out-in-all-weathers-in-wellies-and-padded-jackets approach to bird-watching was *de rigueur*. Peter refuted this: the elderly, infirm, and handicapped had as much right to enjoy the birds, in his view, as the fit and active.

Peter Gladstone, Martin Mere's first curator, had to cope with conditions similar to those that had faced Tommy Johnstone at Slimbridge twenty-five years before. He took up residence with a bride of a few months in a trailer, and set to work dredging out a lake, putting up a perimeter fence, pegging out paths, and generally turning a stretch of overgrown and soggy wasteland into a sanctuary for birds and a pleasure ground for people. Then came the usual manna from heaven, an anonymous gift, spent on a log building which arrived from Norway with every log numbered, and went up in three weeks. Tame birds arrived from other collections and the lake was soon discovered, first by whooper's swans and then by Bewick's; in 1978 six of these swans arrived to spend the winter. Their numbers mounted year by year until, in 1991, the thousandth Bewick's flew in.

One evening, when Peter was looking out of the plate-glass window with Dr. Janet Kear—Gladstone's successor—and Keith Shackleton, a pair of pinkfooted geese few in and landed nearby. "D'you know," Peter mused, "I could have dropped that pair with a choke barrel." "Let's face it, Commander," Shackleton observed, "that's a foetid bubble oozing up from your past."

Three centers opened in 1975: Martin Mere, Washington and Arundel. The least financially demanding was Washington, near Newcastle-upon-Tyne, because the Washington Development Corporation invited the Trust to lay out a waterfowl park on 100 acres of farmland beside the river Wear, and on the edge of a new industrial estate. The Corporation put up the bulk of the capital and the Trust's staff drew the plans and supervised the construction; the result was an oasis in an industrial landscape which was soon discovered by migratory wildfowl; tame birds were also on display and bred well.

At Arundel in Sussex the Trust leased 60 acres of water meadow beside the river Arun from the Duke of Norfolk and Peter landscaped it, leaving a marshy area to revert to its pristine wildness and offer nesting sites to native wetland-loving birds. Andrew Dawney, curator from the start, translated these plans into realities, following Peter's principles: no paths must be straight, all paths must wind about among the vegetation so that visitors did not feel crowded; hides must be placed with the sun behind them so as not to dazzle visitors' eyes; and all the birds, whether breeding or not, must be seen, nothing held back. Wildflowers such as golden kingcups and marsh-marigolds, purple loosestrife and ragged robin line paths made of railway sleepers, and dragonflies and butterflies hover. The rare New Zealand Blue duck, which breeds nowhere else outside its native land, has raised its young in a pool provided with a waterfall. The buildings, designed by Neil Holland, a local architect, seem to crouch in a comfortable and unobtrusive manner beneath a steep, wooded hangar bearing on its crest the stern baronial castle of the Duke of Norfolk.

Meanwhile work was proceeding on the Trust's only Scottish center, Caerlaverock on the Solway Firth. Three species of geese winter on these quiet, green, undulating farmlands beside the softly flowing river: greylag, pinkfooted, and barnacle. The latter, a smallish, dark, and wary bird, breeds in Spitzbergen and had formerly been numerous enough, but by the early 1950s its numbers had fallen to less than five hundred. In this case it was shooting, not loss of habitat, that had decimated the birds.

These barnacles roost on the marsh bordering the tidal river and feed on the surrounding farms, most of which belonged to Bernard, Duke of Norfolk, who in 1970 had succeeded Prince Philip as president of the Trust. (Later, the Duke made over this land to his daughter, Lady Anne Fitzalan Howard.) The decline of the barnacle had concerned the Nature Conservancy Council, which had for some time been persevering with a plan to set up national wildfowl refuges on the lines of those already successfully established in other countries such as the United States. Max Nicholson, the director, had to persevere because these proposals were at first opposed by the Wildfowlers Association of Great Britain and Ireland, whose members feared that their sport might be severely restricted if favorite wildfowl habitats were barred to their guns.

To bring both sides together—WAGBI on the one hand and several conservationist bodies, including the Wildfowl Trust, on the other—Nicholson called a series of informal meetings at which, over tea and biscuits, differences were thrashed out. Peter had seen for himself how well the refuge system worked in the United States and played a key part in these discussions, for he could understand the wildfowlers' point of view as well as the conservationists'. "There seems something agreeably English," Max Nicholson concluded, "in resorting to tea-parties to bring about, with complete success, a peaceful revolution through a meeting of minds when several eminent committees and the combined efforts of both Houses of Parliament had failed to produce a workable means for naturalists and wildfowlers to get along together." As a result of the tea-parties, a joint Wildfowl Conservation Committee was set up and the first three sanctuaries established, one on the estuary of the Humber, another at Southport in Lancashire, and the third at Caerlaverock in Dumfriesshire, where, in 1957, about 1,500 acres of marsh was declared a National Nature Reserve.

Peter knew this region well, having punt-gunned on the Solway while still an undergraduate at Cambridge and, later, rocket-netted on the surrounding farmland. In 1970 Eastpark Farm, bordering on the Solway, came in hand; the Trust secured a twenty-five years' lease of 235 acres of arable and pasture and 600 acres of tidal merse, and started to turn it into a center. Here scientists and students came to study, in particular, the habits of the barnacle goose, which had puzzled enquiring minds for many centuries. Where did the birds come from, early naturalists had asked, so mysteriously appearing as winter approached and as suddenly disappearing, no one knew whither, as it drew to a close? It was one such early naturalist who gave the bird its name. In 1597 Dr. Gerard wrote in his famous *Herball* that in northern Scotland and adjacent islands there are found "certain trees, whereupon do growe certaine shell fishes of a white colour tending to russet; wherein are contained little living creatures, which ... falling into the water, doe become fowles, whom we call Barnakles." The creatures that emerged from the "shell fishes" must obviously be classed as fish, so good Roman Catholics could eat barnacle geese on Fridays without incurring the displeasure of their priests.

It was not until the end of the nineteenth century that the first nests of the barnacle goose were found in Greenland, and others, later, in Spitzbergen and Arctic Russia. Toward the end of the twentieth century scientists were still finding out more about these geese. In 1974 a six-man expedition from Caerlaverock disembarked off Spitzbergen with two fiberglass boats and five weeks' supplies to catch and ring flightless birds, together with their newly hatched goslings, that nested on the jagged cliffs and mountain slopes of this inhospitable island. The birds took to the sea—goslings can swim almost as soon as they emerge from the egg—pursued in boats by the young scientists, who drove them back ashore and into pens, to catch, ring and release them. The catchers had a narrow escape when, searching in their boats for nesting sites, they were overwhelmed by a ferocious storm with mountainous waves and nearly crushed by an enormous iceberg. Ornithology can still offer adventure.

The Caerlaverock Centre is wild, watery, and beautiful with a hint of the sea on the air. From an observatory on top of the tower, skein after skein of geese can be seen flighting in at dawn to settle nervously on the surrounding fields. Two more farms have been added to Eastpark's 800 acres and, thus protected, the barnacle population has built up in less than twenty years to twelve thousand birds or even more. The speed with which a once-threatened population can multiply, sometimes to a level which may in turn threaten its environment, is a factor not always taken into account. Canada geese should have taught everyone that lesson. There can be a limit to the tolerance extended by farmers to birds feeding on their fields.

The creation of six new centers placed the Trust's finances under a very severe strain. Its Council members grew more and more alarmed, and its sailor president (Prince Philip) talked of battening down the hatches. The Controller, Steven Goodall, took on the unenviable task of telling the honorary director that the time had come to call a halt to expansion and to abandon several cherished schemes. It was high summer, and he found the director sunbathing in his trunks beside the swimming pool. Peter listened carefully to the Controller's tale of woe, said nothing, and walked indoors to make two telephone calls. Within six minutes, he had won promises of £60,000. (The donors were Ernest Kleinwort and Jack Hayward.) Programs at the new centers went ahead. "They talk of charming birds off trees," remarked Steven Goodall, "but he could charm money out of millionaires, which is just about as difficult. He knew everyone— dukes and dustmen, lords and ladies, tycoons, sheikhs, kings and princes, bankers, scientists, Field-Marshals and Vice-Chancellors, television stars, the lot."

The Controller had been lucky to catch Peter beside the swimming pool; he was much more often to be found driving to and from airports. "I always seem to be writing to Mrs. Gandhi on the way to Heathrow," he noted in his diary—attending conferences, or presiding over meetings. In late middle age he had almost become a perpetual chairman. He had the right touch, friendly and genial, yet with a bedrock of authority that enabled him to win compliance without giving offense. It was said by some that he allowed speakers to waffle on for too long and stray off the point, but his justification was that people who had come a long way and given their time without reward deserved some indulgence. He had his own antidote to the boredom that must at times affflict most chairmen of committees: he doodled. His were no ordinary doodles, they were beautifully executed pen-and-ink drawings, mainly of animals of many kinds, voles and vultures, caterpillars and chameleons, as well as ducks and geese, with an occasional glider thrown in. Fellow councillors sometimes cast acquisitive eyes at these works of art, but at the end of the meetings Peter slipped his papers back into his briefcase and bore them away. No doubt many are still to be found in the vast array of files at Slimbridge, but one or two, duly framed, hang on a wall at Buckingham Palace.

After Peter became chairman of the Survival Service Commission of the IUCN he seldom missed a meeting, although flights to far-flung destinations became increasingly tiring, and Philippa could not always go too. Now and again, he was able to combine his official duties with some enquiry of his own. Ever since he had sought in vain the wintering grounds of the redbreasted goose in the Danube delta, he had puzzled over its migrations. The species had become "a kind of mystery bird for me," he wrote. So, on his way back from a meeting of the IUCN's general assembly in New Delhi in December 1969 he flew via Beirut and Istanbul to Bucharest to rendezvous with a Dutch ornithologist, Tom LeBret, and make another attempt to find the answer.

From Bucharest they set out in pouring rain and icy blasts and in a lame-duck car for Sinoe by the Danube's delta on the Black Sea, and settled into a cold and smoky cottage used by archaeologists excavating an ancient Greek citadel. "What a day of days!" underlined in Peter's diary, signalled triumph two days later. They squelched along a cart track to reach a tree in whose branches they could rest LeBret's telescope:

> through it I could see that the main flocks on the green wheat fields were Redbreasted Geese. There were thousands of them. Perhaps three thousand ... In front of us was a field in which maize stalks still stood, affording cover for an approach to the geese in the stubble ahead ... We came to the edge of a sand quarry, jumped down it and walked across ... Then came the business of assessing their numbers. The same total was reached three times over, it was between 3,000 and 4,000 Redbreasted Geese. In four days with the Redbreasts I shall never forget the unparalleled thrill of discovering that we had thousands in front of us.

He could not keep away from this enticing scene, and made three more visits. On the first of these, in November 1971, the party included Philippa and Sir Max Williams, a sagacious member of the Wildfowl Trust's council and a former president of the Law Society. The Romanian Academy of Sciences provided them with maps and with a pair of unreliable Volkswagen Beetles. The redbreasts did not disappoint. On the second day a gathering of between nine and ten thousand geese was seen, one third of them redbreasts, the rest mainly whitefronts. "It is impossible," Peter wrote, "to describe the excitement of just spending time in the presence of Redbreasts ... It is an experience of deep emotional significance to me."

The geese were wary, vigilant, and easily disturbed, so guile was needed in approaching them. The stalkers converted their little cars into hides by covering them with camouflage netting stuffed with maize straw. Max Williams had brought along two army surplus walkie-talkie machines so that members of the party, deployed in different cars, could report to each other sightings and movements of the geese. Peter set off in his car, taking one of the walkie-talkies, to reconnoiter ahead, leaving Max Williams and Philippa in their car with the other machine. They arranged that Williams would call up Peter every hour, using Peter's code Sunray Major, while Williams's code was Sunray Minor.

> Off he went [wrote Max Williams] and at the agreed time I called him up. "Hello! Sunray Major—how are you getting on? Have you seen anything interesting?" But no response. I continued for a few minutes and then switched off. "Obviously," I said to Phil, "he's forgotten to switch on the machine." One hour later, I started again. "Hello Sunray Major—what goes on? Any sign of our friends?" Silence—so I muttered about naval inefficiency and that as a former gunnery officer I took communication much more seriously. An hour later, just after I had made a third attempt, Peter appeared, driving at great speed. "Get in your car and follow me," he shouted.
>
> In due course we stopped, slightly worried about his pretty strange behaviour. And then we got the story. He had arrived at the spot, parked his car by a hedge and then covered it with mealie stooks. Very close by was a large stack of straw. Leaving the car, he climbed the stack to look for the geese. A few minutes later, a convoy of army vehicles appeared and Peter found that he was in the middle of manoeuvres by the Romanian army. And then on the hour from the car—he had left the walkie-talkie on the seat with full volume on—came "Hello Sunray Major, how are you getting on? Seen anything interesting?"

Happily the soldiers were too busy with their own affairs to notice the call for Sunray Major. The soldiers settled down for lunch around the stack. As the minutes ticked away for the next call by a rather loud Sunray Minor—irritated by the nil response from Sunray Major—Peter considered his position. The Romanian authorities were particularly sensitive about national security—he recalled that two British plane spotters had recently been sent to prison for being near an aerodrome with cameras and binoculars. [This was during the Ceausescu regime.] And here he was in the centre of army manoeuvres with a camouflaged vehicle plus cameras and binoculars. To crown it all there was someone operating a British army walkie-talkie who in a loud voice was asking if Sunray Major had seen anything of interest! His anxiety increased as the second hour approached. Happily and to his immense relief, as "Sunray Major" came across from the hedge, the army decided to pack up and move on. All the noise drowned the remainder of the broadcast.

I think he felt that we had all failed to appreciate the stress and strain of his position, particularly as that evening at dinner we presented him with the wooden spoon. It is to be found in the downstairs loo of the director's house at Slimbridge. The next morning Peter confiscated the walkie-talkies—I never saw them again—I suspect he chucked them into the Danube.

Two more Romanian visits were to come, the last in December 1977 when, with Philippa and Tom LeBret, Peter reckoned that they saw about seventeen thousand geese, mixed redbreasteds and whitefronts, taking to flight when a helicopter disturbed them:

Great skeins streamed off to the west and south-west. There was a great scattering and none returned to our field ... Today was the first time we had been within sixty yards of wild Redbreasts— and the sun was shining. Nothing can take away the breathless excitement of those few moments before the birds were aware of our presence.

He had at last succeeded in what he set out to do—as he nearly always did in the end.

Peter's life in the late 1970s, when he was approaching seventy years of age, became more restless than ever. After his return from Romania with Philippa at the end of 1977 there was an interlude at home, with visits to all six other centers, followed by the Siberian quest for Bewick's swans in July 1978. Only sixteen days after their return, Peter and Philippa set out on a two months' journey that was to take them from Hong Kong to China and Mongolia, on to Japan, then back to Hong Kong to join the *Lindblad Explorer* for a cruise through the south China seas and among the Philippine islands. "I decided to start my day at six because I had three letters to write to Prince Philip," began the account in his diary; there was also a letter to Prince Charles. He dictated letters all the way to Heathrow as usual. Here they joined a Lindblad tour of twenty-four people for their first visit to Mongolia.

A clean and comfortable train took them from Beijing across the Gobi Desert to Ulan Bator, capital of the People's Republic of Mongolia, whence they went by coach to a region of mountains and sparse woodland full of marvelous wildflowers—Peter listed over fifty kinds, and painted beautiful gentians in his diary. They visited a horse farm where they drank fermented mare's milk and ate mare's milk cheese, and slept a night in a *ger*—a felt tent hung inside with lace and needlework, with grey felt home-woven rugs and five large mirrors. Finally they were taken to the site of Genghis Khan's capital, built in 1236 and burned down in 1388. On the way back by train to Beijing, unfriendly customs officers at the frontier confiscated books and films at midnight; Philippa handed over the film in her camera but did not draw attention to some thirty in her suitcase, and Peter surrendered his *Field Guide to the Birds of South East Asia*.

They had a week to spare before they were due in Hong Kong to join the *Lindblad Explorer*, and the Scotts decided to spend it in Japan, checklisting birds again but also securing from the Minister for the Environment an undertaking that Japan would ratify the Ramsar convention on the conservation of wetlands throughout the world. (This convention was signed initially in 1971 at Ramsar on the Caspian Sea, and has since been ratified by seventy nations.) Also they had an audience with the Crown Prince to whom Peter offered a choice of Slimbridge ties; the Crown Princess made the choice for him. Two more princes were added to Peter's collection. Then they returned to Hong Kong and the familiar ship, on which he spent his sixty-ninth birthday anchored off Zamboanga on the western tip of the Philippine archipelago.

Next day, on the north coast of Sabah, the Scotts were able to see in the flesh the orphaned orangutans whose rehabilitation his Survival Service Commission had supported. The Sepilok rehabilitation center, started by Mrs. Barbara Harrison, was on the edge of what little primeval forest was left in Sabah, and when the young orangutans, orphaned as a rule by poachers, had learned to fend for themselves they could swing off into the forest, and return to a feeding station when they felt inclined. On Turtle Island the Scotts stayed in a cabin on stilts among palm trees where, in bright moonlight, they watched a green turtle scoop a hollow in the sand and lay her eggs—plop, plop, plop into the hollow; then she scuffed back sand to cover them and waddled out to sea, never to see her young. Next day her eggs were dug up and reburied in a hatchery, protected against predators by wire netting enclosures. At night, armed with torches, Peter and Philippa watched a clutch of baby turtles emerge from the sand, about one every two minutes, "milling around and over each other in a struggling mass." Soon a warden arrived with a basket to carry them, each one tagged for future study, down to the sea.

From Sabah they flew via Singapore across the Indian subcontinent and Afghanistan to Moscow where they spent a single, and uncomfortable night, then backtracked across the USSR to Ashkhabad near the Iranian border. They arrived at one A.M., and at nine o'clock Peter was chairing a meeting of the Survival Service Commission; two days later came a full meeting of the IUCN's general assembly which endorsed his demand for a moratorium on commercial whaling. Its main business was to consider a draft of the World Conservation Strategy on which the IUCN, together with various other international bodies, had been working. This was, in Peter's words, "a document for signature by all nations recognizing that, if human development is to be sustainable, it must be linked to the conservation of living resources; the World Conservation Strategy sets out guidelines for how this can be achieved." He considered that this strategy was having "an extremely beneficial effect in drawing everyone together to convert the strategy into action." Drawing people together was the problem; at the conference, the six North Korean delegates intimidated the three South Koreans to such an extent that the Americans had to go to the rescue.

The strain of all this nonstop activity on a man in his seventieth year whose health was already beginning to cause anxiety was severe, but he would brook no restraint. After flying home in October, in January 1979 he and Philippa were away on their expedition to the Falklands and Antarctica; then in April came a hectic four weeks in Australia to launch the World Wildlife Fund there. This time he had started out alone. "Oh how I *hate* being without my wonderful Phil," he lamented. "I refuse, I positively refuse, to travel without her ever again." She joined him later. He was coming to rely more and more on her support and companionship, given without stint—perhaps a reflection of the relationship with his mother which had ruled so large a share of his emotional life into middle age. With old age approaching and despite the armor of success, he retreated into the comfortable stockade provided first by a dominant mother, now by a supportive wife who had, in that sense, replaced her.

His Australian visit was more demanding than ever, with meetings and speeches in Sydney, Melbourne, Adelaide, Perth, and Brisbane, all in ten days. It started with a grand dinner in Sydney's Opera House on the evening of his arrival, jet lag or no, followed by the usual speechifying which still gave rise to self doubts. "I wish I were a more polished and fluent speaker," he wrote in his diary. "I get plenty of practice these days but don't seem to get much better at it and continue to dread having to do it." Yet he was to be remembered almost without a dissenting voice as a competent and polished speaker. He had to leave a conference in Sydney halfway through to catch a plane to Kuala Lumpur via Singapore, but managed to fit in a bird-watching session in south Australia when he clocked up fifty-eight species. He need not have worried about his speechmaking. At a grand dinner and ball in Malaysia, attended by most of the expatriates in the country and at least one prince, his audience laughed so much that his speech lasted for twenty-one minutes instead of the allotted ten, and ended by everyone calling for more. It was a fresh audience for his "funnies" and he told them well.

CHAPTER TWENTY-TWO

No Pot of Gold in Arabia

The financial bases of both the Wildfowl Trust and World Wildlife Fund rested on the public's fancy, the money coming from appeals, from membership fees, from other charities, from gate money, and from unpredictable sources such as grants and legacies. What Peter dearly longed to see was a massive fund, such as the J. Paul Getty, Ford, and Nuffield Foundations, which would do away with the begging bowl and with the nagging anxiety resulting from a hand-to-mouth conduct of affairs. He searched persistently for a wealthy individual who would do for conservation what others had done for art, medicine, education, and other worthy causes, and so secure the donor's name in perpetuity. In the early 1970s the proposition that it was not merely the survival of various animals and plants that was under threat but the habitat of man himself, the planet Earth, was generally regarded as a crack-brained notion only held by shaggy characters in beards and sandals, so not only must Peter find another Getty, Ford, or Nuffield, but he must first make a convert of his benefactor.

Where was such a person to be found? Peter looked first toward the United States. One likely prospect invited him to a lavish reception at his home in Connecticut to put his case before a gathering of fellow millionaires. Peter and Philippa flew over for forty-eight hours, received the full Cadillac treatment and attended the dinner; by the time Peter stood up to speak, conviviality was so far advanced that the seed fell upon ground not so much stony as sodden, and failed to germinate.

The other noted habitat of multimullionaires lay in the states bordering the Persian Gulf. In August 1974 Peter flew to Jeddah with Prince Bernhard, who had agreed to lend his support, with the aim of persuading King Faisal of Saudi Arabia to set up a foundation with a capital of £90 million. The British ambassador thought that they would be lucky if they got a promise of £250,000. An audience with the King proved impossible to arrange; Prince Bernhard flew away and Peter was obliged to leave behind in Riyadh with one of the King's many brothers a written submission. He flew home empty-handed, but was back in November after marshalling his forces more thoroughly and securing the promise of an audience with the King. He took with him a letter of greeting from Prince Philip and, in this land of princes, messages of support from all the other royals he could muster: Prince Bernhard, King Carl Gustav of Sweden, Prince Harald of Norway, Prince Hendrik of Denmark, and Prince Juan Carlos of Spain. His aim was still the £90 million. This was "the biggest conservation mission I have ever undertaken," he wrote, feeling very nervous about it all.

They flew direct to Riyadh, to be received with courtesy by the department of Royal Protocol. Then came the royal audience:

> After a while we were led from the side building with an imposing portico with pillars panelled in shiny black marble. The hall inside was richly decorated in red and black and white with a lot of velvet. Sitting cross-legged around the walls were twenty or more guards with scabbarded sabres on their knees. We were led to a smallish ante-room where we sat down on comfortable chairs upholstered in velvet. [An interpreter came in.] Then in we went. The King was entirely alone in the large room with its chairs all around the walls. Each of us shook hands and murmured "Your Majesty." The King's face remained completely impassive. He motioned us to the chairs beyond him ... I was very nervous, but set off with my piece about bringing greetings from Prince Bernhard and a letter from Prince Philip. The King said he was grateful ... During the audience we had coffee (strongly aromatic in tiny cups) and sweet tea, and again coffee which is the sign of departure.

"Nature is a gift of God. To administer it wisely is the solemn responsibility of mankind," Peter's script began. It would ill become mankind, as God's steward, to allow His creation to be impaired and even destroyed. Peter drew attention to an extract from the Koran (Sura 6.39): "No kind of beast is there on earth nor fowl that flieth with its wings but is a folk like you," and went on to present the conservation message as succinctly as long practice had fitted him to do. As the King shook hands on the visitors' departure, he said: "We wish your venture every success, and we will play our part alongside others." This

Peter took to mean that the King would make a contribution but would not take the lead, still less put up the £90 million. So his mission was only a very partial success. He and his companion were referred to the Minister for Agriculture and Water, who got down to brass tacks. "What do you want?" the Minister enquired. "I had to say money." The Minister asked for detailed estimates of his conservation projects, which Peter could not supply: in the usual rush of departure, a vital folder had been left behind.

That was in November 1974; in the following April he flew again to Riyadh; during the interval, in February 1975, King Faisal had been assassinated. The King had been the victim of no political revolt but of a sad tale of fanaticism and revenge. Ten years earlier a nephew, Prince Faisal bin Musa bin Abdulaziz, had led an attack on a newly opened television station that had been authorized by the King, and had been shot dead by the police. His younger brother, educated in the United States, had held the King, as head of state, responsible for Prince Faisal bin Musa's death; as custom demanded he had taken his revenge, and his execution had inevitably followed. King Faisal was universally mourned. This ill wind Peter hoped to direct to the advantage of his cause. He took with him a detailed conservation scheme for Saudi Arabia, and the outline of a grand design to set up a King Faisal Memorial Philanthropic Trust for World Conservation, with a King Faisal World Conservation Centre in Geneva, King Faisal chairs in ecology and conservation in one hundred major universities, King Faisal awards to selected international agencies, and several other ventures besides. It was indeed the vision splendid: destined to fade, like many another, into the light of common day.

The Minister of Agriculture, Sheikh Hassan Mashari, was sympathetic, and with him Peter established a rapport. Nothing was said about the Memorial Trust to King Faisal, but the Sheikh reported that the submission Peter had left behind with the late King in November had been referred to a committee whose chairman, Prince Fahad, had said: "OK, go ahead, we will join your organisation [the IUCN] and will give it support." Encouraging, but there was no mention of money. Once again Peter returned empty-handed, leaving both his conservation proposals for the Kingdom and his grand design on the Sheikh's desk. There was a consolation prize. At Heathrow he was met by Mike Garside with the news that Sir Charles Hayward had promised £80,000 to expand the Martin Mere and Arundel centers.

Four months later Prince Bernhard again took up the cudgels, with Peter once more at his right hand. It was August, and extremely hot. Now it was King Khalid who received them both. The £90 million had been scaled down to £4 million "this year, and if possible some plan for continued help." The King, "a large and rather handsome man" who was a half-brother of the late King Faisal, listened attentively.

When Prince Bernhard said that world leaders were becoming increasingly concerned about the environment, the King replied that a stork with a Dutch ring had been recovered in Saudi Arabia. When he went on to talk about wise land-use policies as an essential element in economic development, the King said "Yes, and a sakar falcon has been taken quite close to Jeddah which had been ringed near Moscow." The King would like to bring wild animals from Africa and India and let them loose in Saudi Arabia.

Peter presented the King with two small pictures, one of a sakar and one of a peregrine falcon. Nothing was said about the £4 million. "And so back to Jeddah and straight to the Netherlands Embassy at eight-forty for a dinner party. I ate and drank too much." Next day he flew to Kinshasa in Zaire via Addis Ababa for the twelfth general assembly of the IUCN; and "it was a terribly sad thing to spend two weeks in tropical Africa without seeing any wild creature." Soon after he got home, he was invited to dinner at No. 10 Downing Street to meet the Crown Prince of Saudi Arabia, who went on to a gambling club and staked £200,000. "It would have been nice," Peter commented, "if he had given it to WWF." Nothing came of the proposal for a King Faisal Memorial Philanthropic Trust for World Conservation, but only a year after Peter had left his proposals with Sheikh Hassan Mashari, it was announced in Riyadh that the King's eight sons were to set up a King Faisal Philanthropic Foundation "to honour excellence in the fields of service to Islam, Islamic studies and Arabic literature." Three years later, awards on the lines of Nobel prizes for services to medicine and science were to be added, and the great majority of these were to go to non-Islamic scientists from Europe and America. But there was nothing, specifically, for conservation. The connection, if there was one, between Peter's vision splendid and the King Faisal Foundation—the word Philanthropic was dropped—will probably never be known.

The government of Saudi Arabia made good Prince Fahad's promise to join the IUCN, and contributed £50,000. Peter still had his sights on £4 million, and early in 1976 he was back in Riyadh for his sixth visit. This time he failed to get an audience either with the King or with three of his brothers, but did secure the King's consent to be patron of the national appeal which WWF was about to launch in Saudi Arabia, with a great array of princes and sheikhs on the board. This was some consolation: and so was two days' snorkeling in the Red Sea among its 780 species of fish.

This was not the end of his hopeful endeavors. On February 14, 1976, less than three weeks after his return from Saudi Arabia, he left home for two days' meetings in Morges, then flew on to Rome where, after a long wait, he boarded a "part-worn Boeing 7206 of Somalia Air" that set him down in Jeddah at four A.M., after only about forty minutes' sleep. This was his seventh visit to the Kingdom, visits all the tougher because Philippa had to be left behind. After a lot of telephoning and frustrations—as in many hot countries, offices closed at about two P.M.—he delivered to the Minister of Agriculture a box of seeds of the jojoba bush (*Simmondsia chinenso*), containing a substance that can be substituted for sperm whale oil. He had not forgotten the plight of the whales. There was an interlude in a camp on the shores of the Red Sea, with a meal of the customary whole sheep and platters of rice; he declined the sheep's eye, but a companion from the British Embassy ate four. Then, leaving Riyadh on March 4, 1976, he flew to Tehran accompanied by Aubrey Buxton. Anglia Television hoped to make a film in Iran, and Lord Buxton had arranged an audience with the Shah. The British Foreign Minister, Jim (later Lord) Callaghan and a party from the Foreign Office were also on the plane, paying an official visit. As the aircraft taxied to a halt, the Foreign Secretary's party prepared to disembark for their official reception; the rest of the passengers were to continue in the airplane to the main terminal. In Lord Buxton's words:

> As soon as the door opened a very important General covered with gold braid and ribbons entered the aircraft, marched smartly past Callaghan and straight down to us and saluted. We were taken swiftly off the aircraft on to a red carpet and then a limousine, while the aircraft door shut and the Foreign Secretary and all the passengers were taken to the airport buildings. He was just going to see the Foreign Minister, but Peter and I were going to see the Shah!

Their audience followed. They walked

> out and along a high wide passage to an enormous room [Peter wrote]. From far across it came the slight figure of HM the Shah. We seemed to walk endlessly towards each other, with the slight problem of when to start speaking, bowing, holding out one's hand. I started my bow too soon, Aubrey's was a good deal more polished. The Shah was very courteous and charming and we had a long talk.

Soon afterward Reza Mohammed Shah was ousted and forced into exile, so the talk did not bear fruit.

There was to be one more visit—Peter's eighth—to Saudi Arabia in search of the pot of gold. The formation of the King Faisal Memorial Foundation had

been announced, and in October 1976 Peter, undismayed by past prevarica-
tions, flew out again to stake a claim for conservationist causes. A general assembly of WWF was to be held in San Francisco in November; what better time
to announce a substantial contribution from the new Foundation, which would
enhance the Kingdom's prestige?

"We are wrecked," he wrote two days after his arrival, "by the summit
conference on the Lebanese civil war, to be followed by a further summit in
Cairo." Everyone of importance was tied up, there was an atmosphere of uncertainty and crisis. He spent his time waiting for telephone calls that never came—
"nine days of frustration." Then there was a sudden change of fortune. He was
ushered into the presence of Prince Abdullah bin Abdul Aziz, the King's half-
brother, deputy prime minister and commander of the National Guard, who
was friendly and attentive—"a rather successful encounter." The secretary of
the new Foundation said that, while no grants would be made for another eighteen months to two years, "conservation would certainly fall within its scope."
Once again it was coffee and promises, and the pursestrings did not slacken.
Tangibly, Peter's £90 million target had shrunk to £50,000; intangibly, he had
established good relations on which others might in future build.

That was the end of Peter's long, frustrating assault on the citadel of
Riyadh; but there were to be three more visits to the Gulf, all to Oman. The
first was in 1976 with the object of seeing on the ground a project he had
approved on paper, a study of a small, shaggy kind of goat, the Arabian tahr,
which was severely endangered. From Riyadh he flew to Muscat and thence by
helicopter to an outpost in the desert where a young zoologist was camped.
There was a goat for dinner with the customary rice and dates with goat's milk
butter, all eaten with the hands; Peter felt ashamed of his earlier squeamishness
over the sheep's eye, and swallowed the eye of the goat. Finally, the skull was
cracked to apportion the brains. "Through the door, I watched a desert lark"—
possibly a relief. He got home in time to meet Prince Khalid al Faisal, director
general of the King Faisal Foundation. The end of the rainbow was in the Carlton
Towers Hotel in London, and there was no pot of gold. The Prince told him
that the Foundation's funds would be devoted to Islamic projects only. "Is conservation to be a subject acceptable to the trustees of the KFPF?" Peter rumi-
nated in his diary. "Probably not." There was no time to repine. Two days later
he was off again for a conference of the International Wildfowl Research Bureau
in the Crimea.

The Sultan of Oman was a generous supporter of the IUCN, and in
1983 he called a conference to consider ways of sustaining and improving his
country's environment. After it was over Peter, this time with Philippa, went on
to see the herd of captive-bred oryx that had been successfully released into the
desert. It then consisted of eleven animals, four of them born in the wild since
the release—"the first time in history that a species has been saved from extinc-

tion by captive breeding and reintroduced into the wild where it had become totally extinct." They inspected armed warriors of the Harassis tribe who would have made short work of would-be poachers. A zoologist, Mark Stanley Price, who had carried out in stages the tricky task of reintroduction, still supervised the herd. The operation had taken twenty years and a lot of money—"a major conservation milestone" in Peter's words.

His third and final visit to Oman came in 1987. The Sultan had commissioned the IUCN to draw up a comprehensive plan to safeguard and develop the country's natural resources; the report had taken two years to complete and the time had come for its presentation to the Sultan's government. The Sultan invited Peter to an audience on the day before the presentation, together with Philippa and Ralph Daley, adviser to the government in Muscat on the country's environment. A helicopter took them to Sohar, the Sultan's desert retreat. When the heat of the day was over, they were conducted to a table set on a splendid carpet in the middle of a lawn. The Sultan, whose black beard contrasted with his white hair on cheeks and temple, greeted them warmly and talked on subjects ranging from the future of the human species to conservation projects, on which he was excellently informed. The food was delicious, plentiful, mostly sweet and therefore fattening, and there were no sheep's eyes; the drink, pomegranate juice, was ambrosial. Next day the "Programme for a System of Nature Conservation Areas in the Sultanate of Oman" was formally presented to the Diwan and other Ministers at the al Buston Palace Hotel. This was the kind of cooperation between independent nations and international conservationists that Peter and his colleagues had always hoped to see.

"Off to China" runs a note in his diary dated September 17, 1979. Not directly; first there was a meeting in Cambridge to launch a Survival Service monitoring unit, followed by another in London of WWF executive committee, and then a seventieth birthday luncheon attended by Prince Bernhard when he was presented with a check for £5,710 for the Wildfowl Trust. There was still more to do before he actually left, including a visit to a training college for partially handicapped youngsters which brought forth the comment, "Perhaps I *should* pay more attention to the misfortunate." Then came a quick look at a newly hatched brown violet-eared hummingbird learning to catch fruitflies in the tropical house at Slimbridge, followed by a second birthday luncheon given by staff and friends, which he attended in a brown wig. He had taken to wearing wigs now and then, partly to amuse his family and friends and partly to escape recognition by the public when he strolled round the Slimbridge grounds. Perhaps there was also, at the back of his mind, a sensitivity to his baldness, and an impulse to defy the senatorial image that was pinned to his person. Anyway, it raised a laugh.

At last he really was off to Beijing, to his great regret without Philippa. She was to handle awkward negotiations about a book that was highly, and as he thought unfairly, critical of Captain Scott: it made him out to be an indecisive, irritable, incompetent, humorless, and stupid individual as unfit to lead an expedition to the South Pole as to command a battleship. Peter was both angry and hurt, especially as he had given the author access to private papers. Wayland had done the same. Eventually Peter brought a lawsuit which was settled in his favor out of court, and the damages were paid over to the Wildfowl Trust.

The major aim of Peter's venture into China was to persuade the People's Republic to join a cluster of bodies whose acronyms are now familiar to the reader— IUCN, WWF, CITES, IWC, and so on—as well as to make contact with people in authority concerned with the environment. Arrangements for the visit had been made by Nancy Nash, an enterprising and dynamic freelance journalist in Hong Kong, who was also a keen supporter of WWF. Through her Chinese friends she secured an official invitation from the Environment Protection Offfice, which was, Peter wrote, "slightly *above* most of the government departments and ministries," having the last word on pollution and kindred matters. Its director, Li Chaobo, was their host. This was the first invitation to any non-official body extended by the Chinese government since the Cultural Revolution. Peter joined the other members of the delegation—Charles de Haes, director-general of WWF, Lee Talbot, and David Mitchell, respectively its conservation and its public relations directors, and Nancy Nash herself—in Beijing.

Next morning, at a formal meeting, the delegates were astonished and delighted by Li Chaobo's announcement that the People's Republic had agreed to join forthwith the IUCN and adhere to the CITES convention. "Two of our major objectives in the bag without any effort on our part!" Peter exulted. Four days later he was able to announce that the People's Republic and WWF had signed a conservation agreement, and that a joint committee would be formed, consisting of three members of the Chinese Academy of Sciences and three from WWF, to coordinate China's conservation plans with those of other nations. Moreover it emerged that a law had just been passed requiring an "environment impact assessment" before any land development could go ahead—a provision still awaited in the United Kingdom—and that it had come into force on Peter's seventieth birthday. His age then became a subject of frequent and admiring comment among his hosts, and something of a joke among his colleagues. As if to demonstrate that age had not withered him, he galloped upstairs—and there were many stairs in China—two if not three at a time. His host prefaced the toasts obligatory at every banquet—dinners were always banquets—with the words "You are so old!" a compliment among Chinese, but rather an irritant to Peter. "He was very teasable," a colleague observed, and he was submitted to a good deal of teasing. "Oh Peter, you are so old!" became a recurrent greeting.

The delegation's hosts laid on a trip to northern China, formerly Man-churia, where lakes and rivers near the borders of the USSR and of North Korea offered a refuge for wildfowl of many kinds. Peter had let it be known that of the world's 247 species of wildfowl, he had seen all but two; one was the Brazil-ian merganser and the other the Chinese scalysided merganser (*Mergus squamatus*). The visitors were taken to a reservoir in the Changbai Mountain reserve where, in the far distance, three specks were seen: mergansers, Peter felt sure, but were they the redbreasted species, or the genuine scalysided *Mergus squamatus*? As the only way to tell the two species apart for certain was by the position of the nostril in relation to the tip of the bill, it was not surprising that, at a distance of about a quarter of a mile, he could not be absolutely sure. His Chinese hosts tried to convince him that he had indeed achieved his aim, and by the end of the outing he agreed that he had, but retrospective doubts could not be stifled. "It was a great moment," he wrote, "although I shall never know how great a part in the diagnosis was played by good manners and by my wish to please our hosts." So it was not quite a red letter day. He drew a splendid pair, male and female, in his diary.

From the start of the visit, which lasted only thirteen days, an *entente cordiale* prevailed between British and Chinese. The spirits of Marx and Lenin, though no doubt present in the background, seemed content to remain there, yielding to spirits poured at banquets into tiny cups which were frequently replenished. There were hilarious moments, as when Charles de Haes and Peter stacked the furniture in the former's bedroom to clear it for a meeting, with a glass-topped table on top, and the whole pile collapsed, shattering glass in all directions, just as the first Chinese delegate came through the door; and light-hearted ones, when they skipped with Chinese children at the zoo for the ben-efit of a film unit. On the more serious side there was the task of explaining the World Conservation Strategy, shortly to be launched, to which they hoped the Chinese government would adhere.

Less than six months after this visit, in February 1980, Peter was back in Beijing for an official launch of this strategy, not an easy concept to put across in a popular way. There was a television interview in Beijing, then a shuttle to Hong Kong for a similar performance, then back to Beijing for a press confer-ence and subsequent banquet, and finally an interview in the Great Hall of the People with Vice-Premier Gu Mu, a member of the central committee of the Communist party but a "quiet, gentle little man." Everything was harmonious but exhausting, all the more so because of his own doubts about the weighty document he was attempting to sell. He thought the plan too materialistic, resting the case for world conservation on self-interest and material gain, and underplaying the ethical and aesthetic sides of the argument. "To me the final document seems to lack a soul. We are told it will be periodically updated. A soul needs to be breathed into it, and this could still be done. I wonder if it will."

Before leaving China he was able to meet several fellow painters, who had emerged from the dark night of the Cultural Revolution when they had been despised as intellectuals, to be humiliated, starved, and often tortured. One such was Huan Zhou, whose small flat in a seedy tenement was crowded with prints, pottery, trees in pots, and free-flying birds. He had been famous for his drawings of donkeys, and had been told: "You draw donkeys—now you can work like one." So he was harnessed to a cart, with a board hung round his neck proclaiming him to be a useless artist. After ten years of hauling his cart, often in wet conditions, for up to 35 kilometers a day, he was crippled by arthritis and could only walk with sticks, yet Peter described him as an ebullient character full of jokes who insisted on paying for lunch at a hotel with plenty of toasts and calls of mao tai, *gambei!* meaning "bottoms up." Peter gave him two small drawings, and he responded with one of a shrimp. "My lasting impression," Peter wrote, "is that he is a great man." On the way home Peter bought a small carpet for Philippa in Karachi. "I hope she will like it."

Only two months later, in May 1980, he was yet again in Beijing, once more on behalf of WWF and mainly about pandas. The Giant panda was (and is) severely endangered. In 1980 between four hundred and one thousand were thought to survive in China's mountainous bamboo forests; as the panda is a secretive animal dwelling in thick vegetation, this was necessarily a guess. Only by catching some pandas and fitting them with radio collars to determine the extent of their travels could a better guess be made. The danger was that—as with whales—populations had become too isolated and widely dispersed to breed effectively.

After the Cultural Revolution ended, plans were laid for a major WWF panda project, and in due course the People's Republic invited a delegation to visit the main panda stronghold in the Wolong Nature Reserve, in the Sichuan province of western China. The delegation included the Scotts and George Schaller, a distinguished American zoologist who had studied lions in Africa and snow leopards in the Himalayas and who was to manage the project. In Chengdu, the capital of Sichuan province, Peter and Philippa joined Schaller and Nancy Nash, who was once again the intermediary, together with Mrs. Ma the chief interpreter, the deputy governor of the province, and a number of other officials, and proceeded to the Wolong Reserve, where they stayed in a guest house in the mountains at an altitude of over 6,000 feet. Next day they set out on a strenuous three-hour climb up a steep mountain trail in search of pandas; they saw panda droppings, chewed bamboo leaves, and other traces of the animals, but no pandas. They also learned about the Chinese plans for the project.

These were exceedingly ambitious. A research center was to be built in the Wolong Reserve with laboratories, captive breeding pens, staff houses, experimental plots for different strains of bamboo, even a bridge over a river, and much more. WWF was to pay half the cost, put at two million U.S. dollars. Schaller and Peter tried to convince their Chinese hosts that a much simpler program would achieve just as good, or probably better, results. They argued in vain. From Chengdu they flew back to Beijing, and reported by telephone to WWF headquarters in Switzerland. WWF was faced with a dilemma. Their policy was clear: it was to supply expertise, personnel, and sometimes equipment, but not to invest in bricks and mortar; this the recipient countries must provide for themselves. One million dollars was a great deal of money to spend on any project, but to invest it in one which, they believed, might turn out to be a white elephant would be irresponsible to say the least. On the other hand, their team on the spot—Peter and Schaller—believed that if the Chinese did not get their one million dollars they would withdraw from the panda project altogether, and might even renege on their promise to join the IUCN, the International Whaling Commission, and the CITES convention as well. A door that had been edged ajar would shut. The million dollars would therefore be the price not only of trying to save the panda but of Chinese cooperation in the whole conservation drive. Although neither Peter nor Schaller believed that a costly research center out in the sticks was necessary, Chinese cooperation was; so WWF agreed to pay the million dollars in installments, and there were smiles, and toasts, all round. Subsequently, in Gland, the headquarters of WWF and the IUCN from September 1979, a good deal of reluctance on the part of the executive committee had to be overcome.

In due course the research center with its adjuncts was built in the Wolong Reserve, Schaller returned to the United States and a Chinese survey team scoured the bamboo forests to estimate just how many giant pandas were left: they concluded that numbers had declined by about a third between 1981 and 1985. It looked as if only captive breeding would ensure the animal's survival, but the pandas were reluctant to oblige. It was not until 1986 that, after a good many disappointments, the first baby was born at the research center, to be named Lan Tian—Blue Sky—by Prince Philip during one of his tours of inspection carried out as WWF's international president. In ten years, two captive-bred pandas have been born, and only one has survived. So Peter's and Schaller's doubts were not unfounded; but the People's Republic in due course joined WWF, the IUCN, CITES, and the International Whaling Commission, and endorsed the World Conservation Strategy. There is a price for everything. On May 23, 1980 Peter flew home.

CHAPTER TWENTY-THREE

Finale

"My perpetual concern is that life is too short for all the things I want to do," Peter had said in a broadcast back in 1953. "Perhaps," he had added, "I should do some of them better if I didn't try to do so many." In the last decade of his life he was still trying to cram his eagle-sized aims into the sparrow-sized cage of a man's life.

Despite his resolve never to travel without his wife, he had to do so fairly often. Sometimes Philippa's knowledge of the Trust's affairs, which stretched back by now for thirty years, was needed at home; she had never cared for flying, and lacked his ability to snatch a few hours' sleep in an airplane or in transit. When he was at home she acted as a filter between her husband and the innumerable demands made upon him by people asking him to support their causes, make speeches, grant interviews, write articles and forewords, and do a hundred other things. She performed her task firmly and sometimes even fiercely when this approach was needed to repel invaders of his time. Also she looked after his financial affairs. "Without her," he wrote, "I'd be lost—and bankrupt."

In August 1980 Dafila, to everyone's approval, married Tim Clutton-Brock, a young Cambridge zoologist, one of whose concerns had been to supervise the reintroduction of the white-tailed sea eagle into the island of Rhum. Shared interests were to underpin their marriage, as it did that of her parents, and in due course two more grandchildren, Amber and Peter, were added to the Scotts' tally, which had begun with the birth of Nicola's son in 1964. Nicola had two further children with Kip Asquith, and a fourth by a second marriage to Eliott Starks, and Falcon contributed one daughter. These seven grandchildren brought to Peter and Philippa in full measure the perhaps slightly smug satisfaction of almost every grandparent.

On January 2 Peter penned—he always wrote in longhand—the last words of the manuscript of *Observations of Wildlife*, which was due to be delivered to its publishers in Oxford next day. He was sitting on his favorite perch, the top of a square, red-brick tower built on to a corner of the house, and commanding a view over Swan Lake and the Rushy Pen with the Tack Piece and the Severn estuary beyond, and the gentle blue hills of the Forest of Dean beyond that, the waters in the foreground quivering with swans and geese and ducks splashing and diving, swimming in family parties, clustering on islands, and soaring overhead. In 1977 he had been awarded the International Pahlavi Environment prize, worth $50,000, for "the most outstanding contribution in the field of the environment," which had been presented by the Shah of Iran's younger brother Prince Abdorreza Pahlavi. Peter shared the prize with Jacques Cousteau, pioneer of scuba diving and active in the campaign to save the whales. In his speech of acceptance, Peter pledged nine-tenths of his share to conservation causes and the remainder to "a few small comforts for our home"; he put the money toward building a long hoped-for tower. He loved towers, a trait he had possibly passed on to his son, and one of his aims, not achieved in his lifetime, was to build a tower with a lift at Slimbridge, so that disabled visitors could enjoy the panorama of birds.

For the first seventy years of his life his health had seldom troubled him, but a few days after his seventy-first birthday, in September 1980, cancer of the prostate gland was diagnosed. "A sudden coldness took hold of me," he wrote in his diary. "A time limit on life which had until that moment seemed limitless. It was quite unreasonable to be shocked when I so often say with bravado that survival after such a good life is of only minor importance." Radiation treatment was advised, and in the meantime he flew to Florida for a meeting of the Species Survival Commission, followed by an "unforgettable day with the Mermaids," seen from a little Piper Cub flying just above the water to observe manatees in lagoons. In November 1981 he went into a hospital in Bristol for the treatment which lasted for five weeks. Many engagements had to be cancelled, but one he was determined to keep was to preside over a lecture to be delivered at Birmingham University. The difficulty was that the treatment included drinking a lot of liquid, with consequent effects on the bladder. He persuaded his doctors to fit him with an "appliance," and duly presided over the lecture. "There is no doubt," he concluded, "that it is *fascinating* to be standing in a crowded room with Lord Mayors and other dignitaries and be quietly pee-ing away into a plastic bag unbeknown to everyone." The treatment did not cure the trouble, and he had to have his prostate gland removed—successfully, for the cancer did not return.

The next few years of Peter's life were as busy as ever. There was a holiday in the Aegean, then a visit to India and Nepal, which started with him putting a redbreasted goose in the back of the car for delivery to Buckingham Palace. After a meeting of the Species Survival Commission and another cordial interview with Mrs. Gandhi, they went on to a tiger reserve where they watched a long-horned rhino wallowing in mud, but saw no tigers. Then came a break in "a beautiful unspoiled island where we could walk all day and see only birds and trees"; this was an island off Bergen in Norway where the Svanoy Foundation had a nature reserve, frequented by the white-tailed sea eagle.

In June 1981 they were in Zimbabwe, then they traveled on to Johannesburg to enlist South Africa's support for the anti-whaling campaign. In a major speech Peter introduced the theme of the three ugly sisters, Pop, Pol, and Pov—population, pollution, and poverty—and took by the horns the bull he had introduced into the arena at Stockholm, that of the escalating human population. The resources of the world being finite, it did not take much imagination to foresee what would happen unless something was done, and done quickly. "I believe," he said, "that the time has come to make all aid to developing countries conditional on a vigorous and well organized family planning programme," a statement with which most unbiased people in the business of aid agreed, but which no one in authority had dared to say in public. The year, no more crowded than any other, ended with a few days in Hong Kong to monitor a project to turn part of the Mai Po marshes into a nature reserve, and a meeting of the general assembly of the IUCN in Christchurch, New Zealand, with a week's fish-watching on the Great Barrier Reef on the way.

Had tropical fish ousted birds from the center of his nonmarital affections? It could be said that while he remained wedded to his first and feather-clad love, he had taken as his mistress the glittering and alluring community of the scales. The wonder and delight that had first hit him like a punch-blow in 1957 had intensified rather than faded over the years. "I think that keeping still among a profusion of fish on a coral reef is a magical experience, one of the most totally enjoyable things I have ever done," he wrote. "My day was in Elisium. I remain in a dream world." He stressed in other entries in his diaries the magical, Circean nature of this underwater pageant, quite detached from the mundane world around us, like a world of fairies, and its surpassing beauty, as if a host of jewels was in perpetual motion among coral cliffs and caves and waving coral gardens. He never ceased to marvel at the infinite variety, the sheer exuberance, the inventiveness of the process of evolution that had brought it all about.

But there was more to it than wonder and delight. While to identify each observed object is the naturalist's first commandment, Peter seemed at times to carry his compliance to extremes. Why was it so important to measure every minute spent on or under water, and to record every species of fish? He himself puzzled over the answer:

Is it the appeal of saying to oneself "Aha! I know you!"? Is it the solid satisfaction of new knowledge acquired in such exquisite surroundings? Is it—perish the thought!—the kudos to be gained by being able to name fish from the descriptions of others who have seen them? ... And then there are the conundrums—the convergent resemblances, the unmasking of mimics, the glimpses of new aspects of fish behaviour. And there are doubts too. Am I putting my underwater time and experience to any useful scientific purpose, am I advancing our knowledge of evolutionary processes?

He very much hoped that he was.[1] But if the pursuit of knowledge was, as he believed, in itself virtuous, it scarcely mattered if the purpose to which such knowledge might be put was obscure.

The lure of the fish took Peter and Philippa again and again into tropical waters lying between the eastern shores of Asia and the strung-out chain of archipelagos, islands, and atolls that stretch from Papua New Guinea, past the long swath of islands that comprise Indonesia, past Borneo and Brunei, past the seventy-one hundred volcanic islands of the Philippine Republic, past Taiwan, to the northernmost extremities of Japan. Many were the primitive islands they set foot on, the scarcely known inlets they explored, the contrasts they witnessed that led to renewed questions in Peter's mind about the virtues of Western civilization compared with a simpler existence in long houses entered on all fours, or in palm-thatched dwellings on stilts on the edge of lagoons, where goats, pigs, poultry, and people dwelt together in an amiable jumble, regaled by song and dance. Tall, magnificently savage-looking paddlers in war canoes and dancers caked in ginger mud entertained the passengers; and so did Peter, when a chameleon he had rescued from wanton boys who were beating it to death climbed up him in the bus and sat on his bald head. On Rodrigues island they saw the world's rarest tree—one solitary specimen; and in Mauritius the native kestrel whose numbers had been down to seven, but had been restored by captive breeding to fifty.

In February 1984 the Scotts left Slimbridge for Sri Lanka to swim with blue whales off Trincomalee. On the eve of their departure he wrote: "As the years go by there is a 'Look thy last' syndrome. Shall I ever see this beautiful place again? ... Does adventure beckon as irresistibly as it always has done? Perhaps we should simply cancel it all and stay at home." Of course they did not. Was this a presentiment, or merely a sign of advancing years? Off Trincomalee blue whales, reduced now to perhaps a thousand in all the world's oceans, could be seen blowing, and Peter was dropped from a zodiac about 30 feet from one of them, but the water was so murky that he could not see it. They flew on to Fiji for a cruise among the Solomon Islands, and one night

Peter suffered severe pains in his chest. It was angina pectoris. The doctor forbade him to scuba dive and he had to be content with snorkeling. Back home in May, he had a mild coronary attack. Angina pains continued, and in September a hernia was found. In November there was a trip to Israel to fish-watch off Eilat, and Peter fainted on arrival at the airport. Disobeying doctor's orders he scubadived and recorded 203 species.

If 1984 was a poor year for Peter's health, it was a good one for his painting. He had another one-man show at Ackermann's, his fifteenth, and discovered that the public had not lost its taste for his work. His top price was £6,750. Most of the larger oils were priced at between £4,000 and £5,000, and on the first day seven such oils were sold for a total of £27,000. Including pencil drawings and small sketches, eighty-two works were on view. Nine years had passed since his last exhibition, but even so it was a respectable tally, considering the many pictures he had painted on commission or as illustrations for books.

He did not overrate his paintings, and had moments of regret. There had been little time to see the work of contemporary painters, but in 1985 he went to an exhibition by James Renny. "He has become a slave to his market as I to mine," Peter commented. "I remember the lovely abstract paintings of his early career and find myself sighing sadly—perhaps for us both." By then it was too late to make experiments, and over twenty years since, in a painting he called *The Natural World of Man,* he had attempted "to represent man's dilemma in his relationship with nature. I saw the problem as triangular," he explained. Animals facing extinction, rivers and seas threatened by pollution, symbols of man's destructive ingenuity—a rocket, factory chimneys, a mushroom cloud— were assembled in a triangle within a sphere, with fish in the sea below and an orange moon overhead. It was a composition to provoke thought rather than to stun with beauty.

"I know my paintings are extremely unlikely to be admired by future generations," he wrote. It was as a landscape painter that he would have wished to excel, with Constable as his master; the swirl and subtleties of light fascinated him, at dawn and dusk over estuaries and marshes. "I like most to paint a picture in which I am looking into the source of light—and if it is reflected in water, so much the better," he wrote. The greatest challenge in painting birds, he believed, lay in mastering the depiction of movement. Liljefors had met it by blurring slightly the edges of the wings as photographs do, but Peter preferred to rely on the bird's attitude and on the whole composition to suggest movement. After nearly fifty years of painting wildfowl, had the subject staled a little? Possibly. He had devised a labor-saving scheme: neat little stiff paper cutouts of geese in flight in various postures, that could be fixed to the canvas to make a satisfactory pattern.

There was to be one more exhibition at Ackermann's now-defunct gallery; this was opened in March 1989 by Prince Philip, who bought a picture. The exhibition was so successful that only four pictures remained unsold at the end of the first day.

Birds, if not as popular as flowers, are a favorite subject for amateur painters, some of whom wrote to Peter for critical advice. He found time to give it whenever he could. To one such lady he advised:

> I think you make them [the birds] too hairy. Looking at your birds I feel that they all look slightly sick! Birds' feathers when they are in good condition flow beautifully round the contours with very few sticking up in the wrong places. ... The wren's bill when open does not look like that. The lower mandible would be more parallel at the base with the upper. I have the feeling that all your birds look rather flat without enough shading ... My final word would be to keep at it, to look at birds more carefully and not be afraid to use the sorts of photographs in the Collins bird guide, in order to see what birds look like in nature.

Below his signature was a neat little drawing of a wren. Not every man of such distinction and considerable age would have taken so much trouble over a stranger's request.

In April that year (1986), he had taken part in a small ceremony that had given him more pleasure than many grander ones he had attended. The East Lighthouse on the banks of the Nene had fallen into a sorry state after the war, empty and vandalized, windows smashed, timbers rotted, battered by gales, roof half blown away. One day in 1985 Commander David Joel RN, an admirer of Peter's, had been sent an advertisement offering the place for sale. He had driven immediately to the agents', inspected the property, bought it on the spot, and set about the business of repair. His aim was not just to make it habitable, but to put it back as exactly as possible into the state it had been in when Peter had lived there. Local builders restored it and painted it white. Commander Joel uncovered a frieze of ducks Peter had made over the fireplace, collected memorabilia such as a set of cigarette cards he had painted, hung original pictures on the walls and set up an easel, and made a pond outside the studio window for a new collection of free-flying ducks and geese. The only thing he couldn't do was to put back the sea. When the place, inside and out, was pretty much as it had been in the 1930s, Peter and Philippa were invited to a reopening party, together with local notables and a few old friends. The lighthouse had become a kind of memorial put together in his lifetime, and Peter was glad and touched. Three years later, Commander Joel was to invite him again, this time to a party to unveil a blue plaque over the door and to open a

Peter Scott Walk, nine miles along the shore to West Lynn, which the local county councils had made and would maintain. Peter's failing health obliged him to refuse this invitation.

In Peter's late seventies the harvest of a lifetime's labor was being gathered in. In September 1986 he flew with Philippa to the United States to receive the Getty prize of $50,000 presented to him at the Smithsonian Institution in Washington, D.C. Quoting a couplet from Edward Young (1683–1765), he admitted in his address that "The love of praise, howe'er concealed by art / Reigns, more or less, and glows in every heart," but he was determined not to be puffed up about it. He pledged the whole of his prize money to conservationist causes; this time there were to be no "small comforts for our home." A fortnight later he was presented with the Gold Medal of WWF, its highest award. He had already received similar prestigious medals from the RSPB and the IUCN.

WWF's presentation took place at Assisi, and he flew there in an airplane of the Queen's Flight with Prince Philip at the controls. It was the Prince's idea to celebrate the twenty-fifth anniversary of WWF's foundation by holding an ecumenical service at the birthplace of St. Francis, who on September 14—Peter's birthdate—had preached to the birds in 1224. Five religions—Buddhism, Christianity, Hinduism, Islam, and Judaism—were to take part. On a bright, sunny September morning a procession headed by the Prince wound its way into the Franciscan basilica, after a call to reflection by a muezzin and to the chanting of the 148th Psalm by a Franciscan choir. The Jewish *shofar*, a ram's horn, called all peoples, faiths, and cultures to repentance for the crimes committed by man against nature. Then followed readings from their holy books by rabbis, priests, monks, imams, and others, canticles intoned by choristers, trumpets, and horns, a Hindu dance and finally the tying on of *rakshahs* to the wrists of leaders of each faith, *rakshahs* being bracelets fixed by Hindu girls to the wrists of their male protectors, symbolizing in this case the need for all peoples of all faiths to care for each other and to care for nature. Although it was scarcely his scene, Peter found the ceremony "hugely impressive." It was not the first time that he had taken part in an attempt to enlist the forces of religion into the ranks of conservation. In 1969 Pope Paul VI had received the board of trustees of WWF, of which Peter was one, and blessed their enterprise. Nothing had been said about family planning.

Some years earlier, Peter had fixed a mirror opposite the entrance to the Slimbridge Centre, so that every visitor was confronted with a reflection of himself in a cage; underneath was a caption saying that the visitor was looking at the most dangerous animal on earth. Peter held two conflicting views on human nature. Although he had sailed under the flag of the Church of England, as he had said in a broadcast back in 1953,

> my picture of the power and glory that unites humanity is not
> the Bible's picture. I believe in the basic greatness and goodness
> of man. I believe in a lot of simple things, beliefs which are com-
> mon to most of us—that good deeds don't justify bad means,
> that love and tolerance and kindness make the world go round—
> kindness, how important that is!—and above all, and this I be-
> lieve implicitly, that good must ultimately triumph over evil. If I
> didn't believe that I should be a much less happy man than I am.

Over the years these beliefs had got a little frayed about the edges, but the
garment had remained intact.

Ever since his first visit to Antarctica in 1966, Peter had pursued the aim of
getting international protection for this last unsullied wilderness by declaring it
a World Park where all forms of human activity, save for scientific research and
a limited, controlled amount of tourism, would be permanently banned. He
knew that a lot of international self-denial would be needed to achieve this,
since under a deep covering of ice lay deposits of useful minerals and probably
oil. That the "opening up" of Antarctica, for mining and all that goes with it,
would destroy the solitude, the wonder, and the wildlife of this great continent
(twice the size of Australia) was, to conservationists, self-evident. Airfields would
come, and so would sprawling hideous towns like that at McMurdo Sound. The
litter that humans accumulate and spew out around their settlements would not
break down and decay in Antarctica as it does in temperate climes. If exploita-
tion would disfigure the land, it would pollute the sea even more. Enormous
icebergs, some of them hundreds of square miles in size, were continually breaking off from ice shelves to threaten shipping, and the inevitable oil spills could
be at least as disastrous as the *Exxon Valdez* spill had been in Alaska. For these
and other reasons, especially the emotional pull that drew him to the Antarctic
through his father's story, to see the continent and its surrounding oceans preserved for all time became Peter's last crusade.

He was not alone in this, of course. Greenpeace spearheaded the movement under its forceful leader David McTaggart, and was the only non-official
body to set up its own research station in the region. WWF threw its weight
and some of its money behind the campaign, and other conservationist bodies
joined in. Ranged on the other side were powerful forces. In Antarctica there
were minerals, oil, and krill, the latter present in such astronomical quantities
that swarms might be several kilometers long and light up at night as with a
blue-green flame. Krill fishing—these crustaceans are rich in protein—had begun and was gathering impetus. It might be thought that the sea's resources
were so vast as to be inexhaustible: people had thought that about rain forests,
and they had been wrong. Minerals, oil, and krill: Antarctica belonged to no

one, and had no government. Seven nations had staked out limited territorial claims. To avert international rivalry and possibly wars, in 1959 these seven nations, together with five others and later joined by fifteen more, signed the Antarctic Treaty which bound them, as "Consultative Parties," to make no further territorial claims and to keep the continent as a scientific preserve. "Antarctica shall be used for peaceful purposes only," said the Treaty, "and there should be no nuclear explosions or nuclear waste." The parties to the Treaty met, virtually in secret, only once every two years. The Treaty had not said that there would be no mining. In 1988, after long negotiations, the Consultative Parties agreed to an Antarctic Mining Convention which laid down strict rules to protect the environment from harm if and when mining took place. This might be thought to be an excellent agreement, but in conservationists' view it was not, because it gave legal recognition to the possibility that one day mining *would take place—the thin edge of a lethally destructive wedge.*

The Mining Convention could not come into operation until sixteen out of the twenty-five nations concerned had ratified it, and at first it looked as if most of them would. Lobbying on both sides became intense. The turning point came in 1989 when Australia's prime minister, Bob Hawke, announced that his country would not sign the Convention. France followed suit; Jacques Cousteau had secured over one million French signatures to a declaration in support of making Antarctica a World Park. Peter was overjoyed. "Australia's magnificent stance," he wrote to Hawke, "may well at one brilliant stroke have ensured the future of the last virtually pristine wilderness continent on earth. This wonderful initiative gives us all new hope for the future of the planet."

But the battle was not yet won. The United States, Britain, and several other countries were still in favor of the Mining Convention. A spokesman for the British Foreign Office had said, "There is no way the UK is going to agree that conservation is the paramount issue in the Antarctic." At the biennial meeting of the treaty parties held in October 1989 in Paris, lobbying reached a new pitch. It took place during coffee breaks and whenever a delegate emerged from the conference room, because meetings were held behind closed doors and observers were not allowed in. The observer for WWF was Cassandra Phillips, Peter's colleague and tireless fighter in the cause both of saving whales and declaring Antarctica a World Park. The meeting in Paris was inconclusive, but in April 1991, following a sudden and last minute turnabout by the United States and Britain, agreement was reached by all the treaty parties to ban mining and drilling in Antarctica for at least fifty years, which conservationists hoped would be forever. The ban was confirmed later in 1991, on the thirtieth anniversary of the signing of the Antarctic Treaty. Peter did not live to see this famous victory. "I hope he is dancing in his grave," Cassandra Phillips said.

The year 1986 also saw the Trust's fortieth birthday. In those forty years, 17 acres of scooped-out ponds and muddy paths had grown into over 100 fenced-in acres set with many shrubs and trees, dotted with hides and towers, and home to between three and four thousand captive birds, plus many more that came and went. Another 760 acres were rented from the Berkeley estate to be managed in the joint interests of farming practice and over-wintering geese. Six more centers had taken root like suckers from a parent tree, each developing its special character, and two more were planned. An annual budget that had started with two small loans and an overdraft had grown to one of £3 1/2 million, and an appeal was shortly to be launched for £6 million for expansion. During the year, over half a million visitors had passed through the turnstiles.

It had been Peter's intention from the start to return to their native habitat, or to such of it as survived, as many as possible of the species of wildfowl the Trust was breeding. The nene was the classic example. From the original two females and one gander, over three thousand birds had been bred, many to be distributed to zoos and collections in several countries, others to be seen at most of the centers, importuning—begging would be an unkind word—food from visitors, and charming children by eating out of their hands. A number of consignments had been sent to the island of Maui in Hawaii to be released, in stages, in the Haleakala crater, but feral pigs, goats, and mongooses preyed upon the eggs and young, so that the nene's re-introduction had so far been only a partial success.

Other reintroductions were by now in progress. One concerned the white-headed duck (Oxyura leucocephala), once common in many parts of Europe but decimated by the drainage of marshland and by uncurbed shooting. It had died out altogether in Hungary by 1958. Eggs laid by captive birds at Slimbridge were sent to that country to be hatched out by the Hungarian Ornithological Society, and the resulting birds released in the Kiskunsag National Park. In November Peter, Philippa, and Slimbridge's curator, Mike Ounsted, went to see them; there were fifty-eight, all doing well. Then the Hungarians laid on a surprise. They took their visitors to the *csarda* near Hortabagy where Peter had stayed in 1935 to shoot a prodigious number of whitefronted geese and to search in vain for redbreasted ones, and where a gypsy band had composed a song for him about his passion for that elusive bird. The *csarda* had scarcely changed at all; another gypsy band played Peter's tune, which brought back to him the days of his youth.

But the rescue of the white-headed duck in Europe subsequently ran into trouble. During the late 1940s one of the *Anatidae* species Peter had added to his collection had been the North American ruddy duck (Oxyura jamaicaiencis), a smallish russet bird whose drakes have blue bills. They had bred at Slimbridge, but because ducklings hatched from eggs in incubators had not thrived satisfactorily in breeding pens, some adults had been allowed to find their own nesting sites in the grounds, and to rear their own young. Wardens had regularly patrolled the grounds in order to find any such nests, and to clip the ducklings' wings in order to prevent them from escaping when fully fledged. But one of the pinioned ruddy ducks had concealed her nest so near the margin of Swan Lake that the young had jumped into the water before they were discovered, to grow up full-winged, and fly away to nest in reservoirs and gravel pits, and so begin a feral population, which by the late 1970s numbered about thirty-five hundred birds. They did no harm, and bird-watchers liked them so well that the West Midlands Bird Club chose them as the club's emblem.

Unfortunately they crossed the Channel and made themselves at home in Sweden, France, the Netherlands, and other European countries; here again, no one raised objections until the birds reached Spain. It was in Spain that the last remnants of the European population of the white-headed duck had taken refuge, reduced in numbers by 1977 to twenty-two. The government of Andalucia was engaged on an expensive project, costing some £2.5 million, to rescue the species; numbers were building up again (to 790 in 1992) and the duck was extending its range. The first of the ruddy ducks that had originally escaped from Britain reached Andalucia in 1986, and the drakes, which were more aggressive than the white-headed ones, mated with white-headed females; their offspring were fertile, and soon the white-headed species was in danger again, this time from hybridization. The Spanish authorities saw their ambitious rescue project being undone, authorized the shooting of ruddy ducks in Spain, and pressed for their extermination in Britain and in the other European countries they had invaded. Peter ruefully admitted his responsibility. In a foreword to his friend Sir Christopher Lever's book *Naturalized Animals of the British Isles*, he wrote: "I really should not have allowed them to fly out into the countryside—although they look delightful in flight." It is hard to see how he could have prevented their escape, unless by not bringing them over from North America in the first place. They had been distributed to other collections, from some of which, as well as from Slimbridge, they had no doubt escaped. The drakes obeyed the law of nature that the race is to the swiftest and the battle to the strongest, in breeding as in other matters. This was not the first occasion on which a native animal's survival has been threatened by a foreign species introduced by man.

The rescue of threatened species, and their reinforcement by captive breeding, are never simple matters, but are cornerstones of conservation; and the Wildfowl Trust, with its long experience, is often called in to help and advise, not only about birds but on conservation matters generally. The Malay Nature Society in Singapore, for example, was concerned about a mangrove swamp, all that was left of a forest of mangroves now covered with concrete. Slimbridge's current curator, Mike Ounsted, was consulted, and in three days drew up a plan to turn the surviving swamp into a reserve for wildlife and a recreational center for people; this was immediately accepted, and put into effect at a cost of nine million dollars. The Trust has formed a Wetland Advisory Service to act as consultants to any body, anywhere, seeking to manage or develop wetlands; these are no longer written off as wastelands, but are gaining recognition as important elements in the planet's ecology.

"The curious part is that I don't *feel* old, but am aware that I must seem so to those I meet," Peter wrote in January 1987. By then he had suffered three coronary attacks, none of them very serious but all of them warnings, and frequent angina pains brought on, as he believed, by his old enemy, over-eating. In Malmo, in June 1986, his resolve to eat a really light evening meal had succumbed: "The onion soup was superb, so was the sole, and I failed to resist the strawberry flan." As a result he spent the night propped up in a corner of his room taking glyceril trinitrate pills every twenty minutes. He was even worse when he got home, and was taken to hospital and treated in intensive care. "I'll fight hard to keep alive," he wrote, "because I have things to do in painting, maybe in conservation and writing. So he [the consultant] had better keep me going."

He did: and six months later Peter and Philippa set out once more for a cruise and fish-watching session among the Indonesian islands, staying on the way with their friends Sir Percy McNeice and his Chinese wife Peng, who gave the Peng Swan Observatory to Slimbridge. There was a red letter day among fish so tame that Peter's hand could have touched them: they had "no experience of the darker side of human nature; for me, this was a most blissful thing." Discarding prudence, he scuba dived, and on another occasion stayed for over three hours in the water watching courtship displays by parrot fish, among other things. "There were hardly any fish I couldn't put a name to," he observed, and he painted fifty-seven species in their different forms and phases in his diaries.

This voyage ended in Cairns in February 1987, and in August another one took them via Singapore to Bali and thence to Ambon in Indonesia. "I expect I should be careful not to overdo things," he conceded, "on the other hand it doesn't matter too much if I die ... I'm not at all afraid of death—but I don't like being a nuisance to people ... Whatever happens I'm still the happiest man I know—and the luckiest." He was echoing almost to the letter the words his mother had chosen as her epitaph, "No happier woman ever lived."

He was home in time to attend the unveiling of a bust of himself by Jacqueline Shackleton at Martin Mere—one was already in position at Slimbridge. Plans had been drawn for an imposing new building at the Trust's headquarters to be called the Scott Conservation Centre, but Peter turned them down, preferring a much simpler design which would present "a delightful meandering of single-storey buildings, so as not to interfere with swans flying in and out, rather than a pretentious building whose architecture would soon be out of date." The Trust's president, Prince Charles, no doubt agreed, but the new building did have two stories.

In June 1987 Peter reached, in terms of public recognition, the peak of his career. He was appointed by the Queen a Companion of Honour—"How pleased my mother would have been!" he exclaimed—and elected a Fellow of the Royal Society under Rule 12, which allows one individual in each year to put the coveted letters FRS after his or her name for rendering conspicuous service to the cause of science, or in other fields of value to science and to the world. "It is all very gratifying," he observed, "but I must take it with a pinch of salt. I am determined not to get pleased with myself. I think it's all because I'm old." This award pleased him more than any other. To be taken seriously as a scientist had always been his hope and aim—his obsessive resolve to name and record each and every fish was an expression of this aspiration—and he thought he had achieved it; then Nessie severely dented his credibility among the scientific sages. He had kept his feelings to himself, but they had been badly bruised. Now, on the ebb tide of his career, recognition was restored to him. It was a deeply satisfying moment. He was already an honorary Doctor of Law five times over, from the Universities of Exeter, Bristol, Birmingham, Aberdeen, and Liverpool, while three other Universities—Bath, Guelph in Canada, and Ulster—had made him a Doctor of Science. In addition he had been awarded a whole crop of medals, all of which he cherished save one. Iceland had for a long time held a special place in his heart both as the nesting ground of pinkfeet geese and as the scene of his wedding, and it had pleased him when its government had awarded him its highest honor, the Order of the Falcon. But Iceland's stance on whaling disillusioned and disgusted him. Its government had refused to endorse the moratorium on commercial whaling, and its fishing industry proposed to kill 120 fin and sei whales, both endangered, for "scientific purposes," and to sell half the meat to Japan. All his efforts to get the Icelandic government to change its mind proved unavailing, and the Order of the Falcon was returned.

In the spring of 1989 a holiday in the Virgin Islands went wrong. Peter was attacked by a virus, and his angina threatened to get out of hand. Richard Branson's helicopter picked up him and Philippa and took them to Puerto Rico, where they flew to Washington, D.C. and found a haven in the house of friends. The award of a medal at the zoo and a party at the British Embassy brought on more trouble; he contracted pneumonia in one lung, was taken to the hospital and convalesced with other friends before getting home at the end of May. This was the last of his almost countless travels.

It was not the last of his home-based activities. A new center, the eighth, was soon to be opened at Llanelli in South Wales, and building and landscaping operations based on his designs were under way. This center, financed by the Llanelli district council, was to be stocked entirely with eggs; no birds were to be sent there, thus, it was hoped, minimizing the risk of disease. At Castle Espie on Strangford lough, near Belfast, a wildfowl collection assembled by the Scotts' friends Paddie and Julie Mackie was to be leased to the Trust and managed by it as a ninth center. Ambitious plans for a wildfowl and wildlife reserve covering 110 acres in the London Borough of Richmond were on the drawing board; laid out on the site of a number of out-of-date reservoirs and their surrounding open land and named Barn Elms, the project was to be funded entirely by the Thames Water Company. It was designed in consultation with the Wildfowl Trust, which was to manage it. Peter had visited the site, studied the layout and was enormously excited by the project, which would, if all the plans were realized, become one of the most important urban nature reserves in the world.

For some years a shift had been taking place in the direction of the Trust's objectives. Put briefly, it was a shift from protecting birds themselves to protecting their habitat. If the wetlands went, the birds went too. Wildfowl cannot adapt to life without marshes, and water. Drainage and reclamation were proceeding at an ever accelerating pace; since the Trust had started water-meadows, bogs, marshes and peatland had vanished, ponds had been drained, rivers were shrinking, the croak of the frog was heard no longer, or only seldom, in the land. The conservationists' urgent task was now to save as many wetlands as possible. Should the Wildfowl Trust therefore become the Wetlands Trust to reflect its change of direction? Some thought it should, but Peter demurred; to him, birds were the heart of the matter; after some discussion, a compromise was reached and the name changed to The Wildfowl & Wetlands Trust. (In 1986, the year of its silver jubilee, World Wildlife Fund had also changed its name, in this case to World Wide Fund for Nature.) The Wetlands Trust's change of name was formally announced at a gathering in the Natural History Museum presided over by Prince Sadruddin Aga Khan; but halfway through the ceremony, Peter became ill and was taken to the Harley Street Clinic. He could still make light of adversity. "These recent illnesses I've had," he wrote, "would I think have been described by Mike Bratby as 'the beating of the wings.' I must say I miss Mike more than most. We should have laughed a lot at all these shenanigans."

It has been said that Peter belonged to a peculiarly British breed, the cultured tough: Gavin Maxwell, Peter Townsend, Patrick Leigh-Fermor were quoted as other examples. Tough he certainly was. As to culture, English intellectuals have tended to look toward the ivory tower for their cultural figures and, with some exceptions, few scientists have been welcomed in. Peter knew that he was not an egghead. But to suggest that culture is confined to those who make their homes in ivory towers would be a blinkered point of view. Ever since the earliest humans painted pictures of the animals they hunted on the walls of caves, nature has inspired the artist, in music and literature as well as in the graphic

arts. If an understanding and appreciation of nature is part of the body of knowledge and tradition and belief that makes up the sum of a culture, Peter was
certainly a cultured as well as a civilized man. "There was much of the poet in
him," Sir John Hackett has written, "in the true sense of the Greek origins of the
word, a doer, a creator, a maker, rather than in the later specialised sense of a
writer in verse."

James Barrie was his godfather, and Peter was called after the boy who
never grew up. Peter Scott did grow up, but in his character an element of
boyishness remained. It showed up in an enthusiasm that never staled. "Over-
enthusiasm is one of my most tedious social short-comings," he wrote to Sir
John Harvey-Jones, who became president of the Trust's Council in 1988. His
enthusiasm could be tedious when he tried too hard to pass it on to others, but
it underlay his brilliance as a naturalist and, in moderation, his charm as a man.
He never lost the child's wonder at the intricate beauty of a feather, a spider's
web, a chameleon's eye.

In his youth his mother and stepfather had moved, it was said, in a "golden
circle," and those who dwelt within it took success for granted; you would be
sure of climbing to the top of whichever tree you fancied, provided that your
aim was honorable and that you tried hard. Those brought up within that circle
were endowed with a self-confidence which might seem sublime, but there were
dangers: what if you fell short of expectations, what if you did not succeed? So,
through cracks in the crust of confidence, weevils of self-doubt would wriggle
in. While Peter did not allow the weevils to torment him, they were never far
away. Perhaps partly for this reason, he concentrated in his youth on the things
he knew he was good at and enjoyed, his sailing and wildfowling, with painting
as the sheet anchor of his life.

The war years were a turning point. On the one hand, they steeled his
self-confidence, since as a naval officer he succeeded and survived; on the other
hand, the failure of his first marriage chastened him, and experience of war at
sea measured the length of human achievement against the might of the elements and nature's changeless laws. He emerged a stronger, a wiser, and a hum-
bler man. "I always thought you a spoiled child of fortune and unbearably conceited" wrote Robert Hichens's widow. "The moment I met you again last winter [1947] 1 knew you were different." Then he found his vocation and his
mate; and the compulsion to succeed, implanted in childhood, took a new and
outward-looking turn. He had matured at last into the man of substance and
vision, the public figure that his mother had steadfastly believed he would become but did not live to see.

One of the qualities he discovered in himself during the war was that of
leadership. He found that he had the touch needed to make people follow him,
trust him, obey. Lord Wavell, in three lectures delivered at Trinity College in
1939, addressed himself to the question of what makes a good general; and

probably the same criteria apply to leaders in peacetime as to generals in war. The first quality he defined as robustness. When a new rifle was tested, it was buried for a few days in mud to see how it performed when it was extricated. A good general needs to survive and to keep his head in the mud of uncertainty, false information, sudden crises, logistic failures. The second attribute was courage, both physical and moral. Next, he must have "character" which, in Wavell's words, "simply means that he knows what he wants and has the courage and determination to get it." Then the good general must have an understanding of human nature; a spirit of adventure; an element of luck; and an instinct for the practical, the art of the possible. Above all, the root of the matter, he must have the will to win. "That is the first and true function of the leader, never to think the battle or the cause lost." All these qualities were Peter's. Above all, he had the will to win. Roger Tory Peterson called him "a mover and a shaker," able to organize and get things going because he was so direct.

In old age, he had the look of a benign and tolerant elder statesman bespectacled, baldish, friendly, with a humorous expression. He was standing beside Dr. David Bellamy at a prize-giving ceremony for children when a small boy pointed to him, and asked Dr. Bellamy, "Is he your father?" "No," was the reply, "but he's the father of conservation." Sir David Attenborough said that he was conservation's patron saint.

If posterity remembers him, that is what he will be remembered for: spreading the word of conservation when that word was scarcely known and the science of ecology in its infancy. He was a prophet and a pioneer, not only in delivering awful warnings but in trying to arrest and turn the tide of events that was leading, as he believed, to degradation of the planet and the impoverishment of mankind. The threatened species listed in his Red Data books were like the canaries that coal miners used to take down the pits to test the level of carbon dioxide: warnings of threats to the planet's health and to the safety of its inhabitants.

"Whether you like it or not," Spike Milligan wrote when congratulating Peter on his honors, "you have joined the Olympians." Many of the writers of letters of condolence addressed to his widow called him, quite simply, "a great man." Was this a true judgement? The answer depends on how greatness is measured, and there is no accepted rule. He inspired a lot of people with his ideas and his example, he made them think, he gave pleasure with his paintings and writings, he was foremost in directing the thoughts of a generation toward a way in which mankind could live in harmony and balance with nature at a time when, if he continued on his present course, mankind would ultimately be destroyed. His was a religious cause with a secular god. Possibly the misty vision of the Earth Mother and her acolyte the Green Man could be glimpsed beyond a screen of television masts and computers, but that is a speculation beyond the reach of this biography. Only time will tell whether his and other people's warnings will be heeded or whether, like the voice of the Boojum in his favorite poem, they will prove to be "only a weary and wandering sigh ... only a breeze that went by."

On August 18, with Dafila and her two children, he walked around the grounds at Slimbridge for the last time. It was a pleasant place in which to stroll on a fine morning; paths wound among trees and shrubs whose foliage was reflected in lakes set among reeds and willows, with islands for birds to rest and nest on, and here and there a small waterfall tumbling over rocks. Birds from every corner of the globe dived and waded, flapped and preened, every species in mutual toler-ance of each other; true, there were individual quarrels and, in spring, mass rapes by mallards; but shovelers did not dispute their territory with teal, scaup (having no alternative) unite to drive off wigeon, and a lasting peace existed between them all and man, the ancient enemy. In the minds of the captive birds, fear had been cast out, to be replaced by trust and sociability; they bustled round human feet, pecked at human ankles, and fed out of human hands. It was all as its founder had wished it to be.

On this last perambulation perhaps Peter paused to watch pale pink Chilean flamingos standing ankle-deep in water, their graceful serpentine necks curved to allow their bills to filter algae from the water. Flamingos gave him special pleasure, not only for their beauty and their strangeness—those match stick legs, the single egg laid on a miniature castle, a seventy-year lifespan or more—but because, the Trust's staff, with great patience, had overcome the birds' reluctance to breed in captivity. Four of the world's six species had raised their young here. Only the lessers, despite attempts by means of mirrors to fool them into thinking that the flock was larger than it actually was, had refused to lay even a single egg. Perhaps Peter gave them a reproachful look as he passed by.

Continuing on his way, he would pass a hide designed especially for the disabled; then the tall Acrow tower overlooking the Dumbles where great win-ter flocks of wild geese came to forage; the grove of oaks where his mother's famous statue, "Here am I, send me," now stands; the tropical house where he could pause among the lush vegetation to listen to a gurgling waterfall and watch hummingbirds no larger than moths quivering round food containers concealed among palm fronds and bell-shaped scarlet flowers: all these he saw with eyes as keen as ever to notice a new family of spotted tree ducks, a free-winged snow goose flying over, the latch of a gate that needed attention. Then back by Tommy's Loop to remind him of his former curator and old friend, to the reception hall crowded with children rubbing brasses, drawing ducks, clam-bering in and out of mock nests, gazing at wall displays, or scrambling into the cinema to watch a nature film.

If his energy did not flag he might continue past the shop and restau-rant, whose patrons could watch the scarlet Caribbean flamingos from the windows, past the Berkeley New Decoy which had played its part in attracting him to Slimbridge; then would come a walk along a path concealed by high banks and thick vegetation to reach the Holden tower, to be rewarded by a view over ponds and fields toward the seawall on the one hand and, on the other, across the Rushy Pen, with Falcon's tower rearing its crest above the trees. It was all his own inspiration, realized with the help of many willing hands and enthusiastic colleagues; but he was as determined as ever to suppress temptations luring him into the trap of self-satisfaction. How, he asked himself, had he come to be so famous? Pure chance,

> and the accident that I should have been around, earning a good living at painting, and having time to be involved in the world conservation scene, and perhaps having a certain talent for taking the chair at meetings ... How could I possibly have deserved a CBE, a knighthood, a CH and an FRS? How lucky can you be when you don't deserve it—and quite certainly I don't. I know my limitations only too well. The only sure thing is the love of my children and my wonderful Phil. Was anyone ever so blessed? I have now to grow old gracefully and not gripe about my neckache and arthritic hip. I have to take a back seat and avoid back seat driving, and come to terms with my evaporating memory, and not to be upset when decisions are taken by others who no longer think it worth consulting me. These things are simply part of the passage of time. And life is still good.

It was good when he sat in the garden with roses in bloom, neat rows of vegetables beyond, the dog at his feet, and music playing from the studio. Music had always been important to him, associated sometimes with the music of his geese: the cry of pinkfeet evoked a Beethoven symphony, the call of other wild geese brought to his mind the Sanctus in Bach's mass in B minor. His taste was for the great composers, masters of harmony and order, rather than for works of the more experimental and discordant moderns. In later years he became obsessed by Mahler.

His walk round the grounds with his daughter and grandchildren was the subject of the last entry in his diaries, signed off with a perfect little drawing of a edbreasted goose. Preparations were by then well advanced for celebrations to mark his eightieth birthday on September 14. It was not to be. The next heart attack was final, and he died in the hospital in Bristol on August 29, 1989. Fortune did not desert him at the end; his family were with him, and there was to be no lingering on a stage on which the curtain had fallen and the audience gone. His epitaph had been written for him a century and a half before by William Savage Landor:

Nature I loved, and after Nature, Art;
I warmed both hands before the fire of life;
It sinks, and I am ready to depart.

His ashes were scattered on the Dumbles, where the music of the wild geese he had loved so well would soon be heard again.

A Picture of Geese
When the moon is clear and full in the sky,
And the wild geese come in from the sand,
And the tide whispers up and the curlews cry—
Then I think that I understand.

Is it only for worms that the curlews call
"Cur-lee" as they go to feed?
But how can I understand at all
If worms are all they need?

Is it only potatoes on cold black earth
That the geese are looking for;
Or for grass at the edge of a northern firth
Where the sea comes in with a roar?

But it's life to a man who can understand
And it shall be life to me;
And then, when the geese come in from the sand,
Through me all men shall see.

ENDNOTE:

[1] In November 1986 two scientists from York University came to Slimbridge to analyse and put on computer Peter's fish records. He was delighted, and believed that his identifications might turn out to be 'one of the most extensive biogeographical records of any fish group of veterbrate animals.' His fish counts are now being used in a worldwide study of the distribution of coral fish.

Select Bibliography

Anderson, Verily, *The Last of the Eccentrics*, Hodder, 1972

Anonymous, *The Frontier of a Barony; The New Grounds at Slimbridge*, 1948

Barnes, James N., *Let's Save Antarctica,* Greenhouse, 1982

Barnett, Corelli, *Engage the Enemy More Closely*, Hodder, 1991

Begbie, Eric (ed.), *The New Wildfowler*, Stanley Paul, 1979

Beken of Cowes, *The America's Cup*, Collins Harvill, 1990

Bolton, David, *Race Against Time*, Methuen, 1990

Brock, M. & E., *H. H. Asquith: Letters to Venetia Stanley*, O.U.P., 1982

Brown, Leslie, *The Mystery of the Flamingos*, 1959

Bryant, Arthur, *The Turn of the Tide*

Chatwin, Bruce, *In Patagonia*, Cape, 1977

Churchill, Winston, *The Second World War*, 5 vols., Cassell, 1948–52

Cook, Tony and Pilcher, R. E. M., *The History of Borough Fen Decoy*, Ely, 1982

De Roy Moore, Tiu, *Galápagos: Islands Lost in Time*, Allen & Unwin, 1980

Dinsdale, Tim, *Loch Ness Monster*, Routledge, 1976

Dunbar, Janet, *J. M. Barrie*, Collins, 1970

Farr, Diana, *Gilbert Cannan*, Chatto, 1978

Fitter, Richard, *The Penitent Butchers*, Fauna Preservation Society, 1978

Fox, Uffa, *Joys of Life*, Newnes, 1966

Fraser, David, *Alanbrooke*, Collins, 1982

Grigg, John, *Nancy Astor*, Sidgwick & Jackson, 1980

Haig-Thomas, David, *Tracks in the Snow*, Hodder, 1939

Harvey-Jones, Sir John, *Making it Happen*, Collins, 1988

Heald, Tim, *A Portrait of Prince Philip*, Hodder, 1991

Hickman, John, *The Enchanted Islands*, Nelson, 1985

Humphries, John, *Hunter's Fen*, David & Charles, 1986

Huxley, Elspeth, *Scott of the Antarctic*, Weidenfeld, 1977

Huxley, Julian, *Memories II*, Allen & Unwin

Huxley, Juliette, *Wild Lives of Africa*, Collins, 1963

IUCN, *A Strategy for Antarctic Conservation*, IUCN, Gland
James, Lawrence, *The Golden Warrior*, Weidenfeld & Nicolson, 1990
Johnson, Peter, *The Encyclopedia of Yachting*, Kindersley, London, 1988
Kear, Janet and Duplaix-Hall, Nicole, *Flamingos*, Poyser, 1975
Kear, Janet, *Man and Wildfowl*, Poyser, 1980
Kear, Janet & Berger, A. J., *The Hawaiian Goose*, T. & A. D. Poyser, 1980
Kennet, Kathleen, *Homage*
Kennet, Lord, *Portrait of an Artist*
Knutsford, Viscount, *In Black and White*, Arnold, 1926
Lever, Christopher, *Naturalized Animals of the British Isles*, 1977
Lorenz, Konrad, *King Solomon's Ring*, Methuen, 1952
Luard, Nicholas, *The Wildlife Parks of Africa*, Michael Joseph, 1985
Melville, Herman, *Moby Dick*, Random House, 1930
Mountford, Guy, *Back from the Brink*, Hutchinson, 1978
Newman, L. H., *Nature Parliament*, Dent, 1952
Owen, Wills & Salmon, *Wildfowl in Great Britain*, 2nd ed., C.U.P., 1963
Parsons, Christopher, *True to Nature*, 1982
Penrose, Barrie and Freeman, Simon, *Conspiracy of Silence*, Grafton, 1986
Roskill, Capt. S. W., *The War at Sea: 1939–1945*, vols. I & II, HMSO, 1954 &
        1957
Scott, Peter, *Morning Flight*, Country Life, 1935
—*Wild Chorus*, Country Life, 1938
—*The Battle of the Narrow Seas*, Country Life, 1945
—*Portrait Drawings*, 1949
—*Key to the Wildfowl of the World*, Severn Wildfowl Trust, 1950
—*Wild Geese and Eskimos*, Country Life, 1951
—*Geography, Birds & Mammals of Perry River*, Arctic Institute of N. America,1956
—*Coloured Key to the Wildfowl of the World*, Wildfowl Trust, 1957
—*Faraway Look I*, Cassell, 1960
—*Faraway Look II*, Cassell, 1960
—*The Eye of the Wind*, Hodder, 1961
—*Waterfowl*, Berkshire Printing Co., 1963
—*Observations of Wildlife*, Phaidon, 1980
—*Travel Diaries of a Naturalist*, 3 vols., Collins Harvill, 1983–87
Scott, Peter and Boyd, H., *Wildfowl of the British Isles*, Country Life, 1957
Scott, Peter and Fisher, J., *1,000 Geese*, Collins, 1953
Scott, Peter and Scott, Philippa, *Animals in Africa*, Cassell, 1962
—*The Swans Fly In*, Wildfowl Trust, 1983
Scott, Philippa, *Lucky Me*, Kenilworth Press, 1990
Shackleton, Keith, *Tidelines*
Sitwell, Nigel, *Happy the Man*, Sphere Books, 1967
Stein, Gertrude, *The Autobiography of Alice B. Toklas*, Literary Guild, N.Y.

Van Camden Heilner, *Duck Shooting*, Hutchinson, 1951
Vincent, Jack, *Web of Experience*, PP South Africa, 1989
WWF, *The Launching of a New Ark*, Collins, 1965
Wavell, Sir Archibald, *Generals and Generalship*, Times, 1941
Wells, H. G., *Sanderson of Oundle*, Chatto and Windus, 1924
Whyte, Constance, *More than a Legend*, Hamish Hamilton, 1957
Wilkinson, Norman, *A Brush with Life*, Seeley Service, 1969
Willock, Colin, *Kenzie, the Wild Goose Man*, Deutsch, 1962
—*The World of Survival*, Deutsch, 1978
Witchell, Nicholas, *The Loch Ness Story*, Corgi, 1989
Young, E. Hilton, *A Bird in the Bush*, Country Life, 1936

In addition to his published works, Peter Scott illustrated, in whole or in part, some seventy-eight books and booklets.

Index